Britain and Nigeria: Exploitation or Development?

Edited by Toyin Falola

Zed Books Ltd.
London and New Jersey

Britain and Nigeria: Exploitation or Development? was first published by Zed Books Ltd., 57 Caledonian Road, London N1 9BU, UK, and 171 First Avenue, Atlantic Highlands, New Jersey 07716, USA, in 1987.

Cover designed by Ian Hawkins.
Printed in the United Kingdom by The Bath Press, Avon.

British Library Cataloguing in Publication Data

Britain and Nigeria: exploitation or development?
  1. Imperialism—History
2. Nigeria—Economic conditions—To 1960 3. Great Britain—Foreign relations
I. Falola, Toyin
330.9669′03   HC1055

ISBN 0-86232-303-7
ISBN 0-86232-304-5 Pbk

To:

Yusufu Bala Usman
and
Bade Onimode

Contents

List of Contributors   vi

1. **Introduction: Colonialism and Exploitation**
   J. Ihonvbere and Toyin Falola   1
   Neo-Classical Explanations of Colonial Expansion   4
   Marx and the Historical Mission of Colonialism   8
   Colonialism, Exploitation and Underdevelopment   19
   Conclusions   24

2. **Patterns of Pre-colonial Exploitation** *L.I. Izuakor*   32
   Introduction   32
   The Coastal Frontier, c. 1472-1830   38
   The Hinterland Frontier, 1830-1900   41
   Modalities of Exploitation   44
   Nigerian Reaction   50
   Conclusion   52

3. **Quest for Further Exploitation: British Colonial Occupation of Nigeria** *L.I. Izuakor*   55
   Introduction   55
   Interpretations of Modern Imperialism   56
   British Colonialism in Nigeria   59
   Conclusion   64

4. **The Infrastructure of Exploitation: Transport, Monetary Changes, Banking etc.** *S.A. Olanrewaju*   66
   Introduction   66
   The Transport Infrastructure   66
   Monetary Changes   71
   Banking   74
   Administration   76
   Conclusion   78

5. **Production for the Metropolis: Agriculture and Forest Products** *J.O. Ahazuem and Toyin Falola*   80
   Peasants and Agriculture   81
   Agricultural Production for Export   82
   Conclusion   87

6. **Production for the Metropolis: the Extractive Industries**
  A.G. Adebayo and Toyin Falola   91
  Pre-colonial Mining in Nigeria   92
  Colonial Mining and the Capitalist Takeover of the Mining
    Industry in Nigeria   92
  Who Controls the Companies?   99
  Labour Exploitation in the Extractive Industries   101
  Production and Profits   108
  Conclusion   111

7. **Industrialisation as Tokenism** *A.A. Lawal*   114

8. **Trading with the Metropolis: an Unequal Exchange**
  O.N. Njoku   124
  Introduction   124
  The Farmer   125
  The Nigerian Middleman   130
  Wage Labour   135
  The Colonial Government   136
  Conclusion   138

9. **Exploitation of Labour: Waged and Forced** *D.C. Obadike*   142
  Introduction   142
  Prelude to British Exploitation of Nigerian Labour: the
    Colonial Armed Forces in Nigeria, 1862-1918   143
  Brtitish Exploitation of Nigerian Labour: the Recruitment of
    Carriers   147
  British Exploitation of Nigerian Labour: Road and Railway
    Line Construction   151
  British Exploitation of Nigerian Labour: Working in the
    Minefields   157
  Conclusion   159

10. **Contributions to War Efforts** *O.N. Njoku*   164
  Introduction   164
  Affirmation of Loyalty   165
  From Words to Action   169
  Fruits of Sacrifice   174
  Men and Agricultural Export Supplies   181

11. **Sharing Profits with Subjects: the Colonial Fiscal Policy**
  A.A. Lawal   186

12. **The Illusion of Economic Development:** *J. Ihonvbere and
  Toyin Falola*   200
  Introduction   200
  The Development Controversy   201
  Early Foundations of Neo-Colonialist Capitalist
    Underdevelopment   205

Conclusion   217

13. The Transition to Neo-Colonialism *S.O. Osoba*   223
    Economic and Fiscal Measures   224
    Political Measures   235
    Creating the Nucleus of a Nigerian Diplomatic Corps   242

    Index   249

List of Contributors

S.O. Osoba teaches history at the University of Ife, Nigeria. He is a well-known Marxist, and co-editor of *Topics On Nigerian Social and Economic History*. He is currently working on income distribution in Nigeria.

O.N. Njoku teaches history at the University of Nigeria, Nsukka, but is currently in the Department of History, Dalhousie University, Halifax, Canada. He has done extensive work on Nigeria's foreign trade and the impact of the World Wars on Nigeria.

A.A. Lawal teaches history at the University of Lagos, Nigeria. His Ph.D. thesis on the colonial fiscal policy in Nigeria will soon be published.

S.A. Olanrewaju teaches economics at the University of Ife, Nigeria. He has recently co-edited *Nigerian Transport Systems*.

D.C. Obadike is a history teacher at the University of Jos, Nigeria. He specialises in Nigerian economic history and has written numerous articles in books and journals.

A.G. Adebayo works on revenue allocation and the Nigerian petroleum industry. He is the co-author of *A Summary of West African History* and *A History of West Africa*.

L.I. Izuakor trained at the University of Michigan, USA, where he obtained his Ph.D. He is interested in the 19th century history of Nigeria.

J. Ihonvbere currently teaches international relations at the University of Ife, Nigeria. He is the author of *The Nigerian Petroleum Industry: An Annotated Bibliography* and the co-author of *Towards A Political Economy of Nigeria*.

Toyin Falola, the editor of this volume, teaches history at the University of Ife, Nigeria. He has written and co-authored seven other books, including (with Julius Ihonvbere) *The Rise and Fall of Nigeria's Second Republic 1979-1984*. In addition, he has co-edited five books on Nigerian History. He is currently associate editor of the *Lusophone Areas Studies Journal*, and editor of *ODU: A Journal of West African Studies*.

1. Introduction: Colonialism and Exploitation

J. Ihonvbere and Toyin Falola

> English capital has come in and built the railways and
> constructed the harbours and cleared the channels; it has
> also introduced new cultures and improved old ones — it
> has built roads and towns and established markets; it has
> introduced banks and a convenient currency; it has
> exploited minerals. More than this, English government
> has brought peace and security and abolished slavery.
> The result is an enormous expansion of trade, in which the
> natives performed their part and reaped their reward.
> Alan Mcphee, *The Economic Revolution In British West
> Africa*. (London, Routledge and Sons, 1926, p.104)

> Under colonial rule any economic benefits that may have
> accrued to the African resulted from accident not design,
> by-products of the primitive economic system the colonial
> powers instituted to carry from Africa its raw materials for
> processing in the factories of Europe, in exchange for a
> strictly limited range of European manufactures. The
> principal beneficiaries were the stockholders of the
> companies importing and processing the raw materials,
> and those that produced the goods exported to Africa in
> exchange: assorted cloths, tobacco, alcohol and rice, and
> of course the materials for the development of the transport
> system that could facilitate the economic regime.
> M. Crowder, *West Africa Under Colonial Rule*, (London,
> Hutchinson, 1981 edition) p.274.

There are two major perspectives on colonialism: exploitation and underdevelopment. On the one hand, there are writers who contend that colonialism
did not entail exploitation. They point to the fact that colonies such as
Nigeria before contact with British colonialists were static, unproductive,
characterised by inter-ethnic wars, insecurity and a total lack of capabilities
to accumulate, innovate or invest. To this body of writers, it was the need
to spread civilisation and the benefits of the industrial revolution and to
break down the barriers to surplus generation and backwardness that
prompted Britain to move into areas that became its colonies in Asia, Latin

America, Africa and the Caribbean.

With varying degrees of sophistication, this position has been rationalised by providing data and statistics of how colonialism expanded the purchasing power of 'poor natives' and the local markets, how the colonial state constructed schools, hospitals, roads, offices, stopped inter-ethnic conflicts and other 'social vices' such as human sacrifices and the killing of twins. The introduction of christianity, a new currency and a new language – and the subjugation of processes of state and class formation and the consequent incorporation of the power-elite into the world capitalist system – are presented as evidences of development and contribution to the upliftment of barbaric and backward societies to progress. These static societies became imbued with vigour with

> the appearance of European trading firms, missionaries sowing new ideas and bringing education, and lately an externally imposed government . . . Most significant of all was the offering by traders of rewards for the sale of particular crops which were in demand abroad – principally palm oil and palm kernels, and later cocoa, rubber and groundnuts.[1]

Thus, until the 'appearance of European trading firms', Helleiner contends, there was no culture, education, commerce, craft or any serious effort at agricultural progress in Nigeria. These became possible with the aid of missionaries and an 'imposed government' as well as the 'rewards' offered for the labour and effort of Nigerian producers.

Against the largely Eurocentric, circular, parochial and misleading interpretation above, there are writers who identify the dynamics, developments and institutions in pre-colonial Nigeria (to restrict the argument to the context of this book) and employ their findings to contrast developments in the colonial period. Such efforts have also contributed significantly to the study of post-colonial Nigeria, particularly in terms of explaining the relationship between colonial legacies and post-colonial developmental patterns. In their studies they note that colonialism completely subjugated traditional patterns of state and class formation, introduced alien institutions and initiated very extensive programmes which facilitated exploitation and the extraction of surpluses from the colonies in order to aid the development of the centre. As Aimé Césaire argues, colonialism was accompanied by forced proletarianisation and mystification, brutality, cruelty, sadism, conflict, forced labour, theft, compulsory crops, mistrust, arrogance, brainless elite and degraded masses. He goes on, colonialism meant:

> societies drained of their essence, cultures trampled underfoot, institutions undermined, lands confiscated, religions smashed, magnificent artistic creations destroyed, extraordinary *possibilities* wiped out . . . natural economies that have been disrupted . . . food crops destroyed, malnutrition permanently introduced, agricultural development oriented solely toward the benefit of metropolitan countries . . . the looting of products, the looting of raw materials . . .[2]

Césaire is obviously not too harsh on the colonialists given the contemporary consequences of the colonial experience – poverty, class contradictions, institutional decay, unstable state structures, low accumulative capacity, undeveloped social classes, co-existence of modes of production, illiteracy, in fact all the features of underdeveloped and peripheralised social formations in the international division of labour. Any serious desire to study the historical experiences of colonised societies must therefore, refuse to take the classical perspectives seriously given its misleading approach to the understanding of socio-economic and political realities in precolonial societies, the impact of colonialism and how this impact laid the basis for post-colonial developments and contradictions.

More often than not, the objective conditions in pre-colonial Africa is the bone of contention between writers on the impact of colonialism in the continent. Even in the body of literature which tends to underrate the developments of this period, facts and data have been presented which demonstrate the 'diversity and complexity of economic activities and of social relations of production, in sharp contrast with the assumptions of many economists of simple, traditional, subsistence economies'.[3] The colonial Commissioner to the Interior of Yorubaland in 1890 wrote on precolonial manufacturing:

> each compound has several of its members busily engaged in spinning, dyeing and weaving. I have indeed calculated, from personal observations and enquiries, that 25 per cent of the population are engaged in the preparation of yarn, dyes and cloth during the greater portion of their hours of labour. In addition to this every farm has its patch of cotton and many people are engaged from time to time in picking and cleaning the fibre, while others make it their business at certain times of the year to grow and collect dye plants . . .[4]

Long distance trade within Africa and Nigeria in particular was very active in precolonial times. In fact, with the decline of the major empires, the trans-Saharan trade routes shifted to Kano, Zaria and Katsina in the 19th century thus stimulating trade and accumulation. The proto-bourgeoisie which the British administration was to incorporate in the northern emirates emerged in this period. J. E. Flint, writing on manufacturing in this period, has noted that

> women engaged in the manufacture of their household pots, baskets and clothing as part of their normal household duties. Other crafts had become more specialized, especially the metal working industries. Blacksmiths were specialists . . . some towns became centres where blacksmiths had congregated in cooperative guilds numbering several dozen craftsmen.[5]

This development also took place in the societies in southern Nigeria. As Sheila Smith notes,

> production for exchange, and the division of labour, had advanced to

the point where a substantial body of artisans existed, organised into craft guilds, and concentrated in major towns. Although the separation of agriculture and industry was far from complete, with many house-holds producing and processing a wide range of agricultural and *non-agricultural goods*, local and long distance trade were well developed, and many commodity currencies were in use, such as cowrie shells, brass rods and manillas, as well as slaves.[6]

The numerous inter-ethnic wars were part of the process of state formation and political development. The Ekiti-Parapo Wars, Egba-Dahomey wars, the conquests of Oba Ewuare of Benin or the Ibadan wars were not different from the numerous wars in Europe before the emergence of the modern state system.

The point in this brief discussion of the precolonial period is not aimed at glorifying the social relations of production and accumulation prevalent in precolonial Nigeria. Obviously, there were efforts by factions and fractions of dominant elites to impose hegemony on less established forces. Exploitation and appropriation of surpluses took place often rationalised in ethnic, caste, sex and even religious terms. The main point, however, is to demonstrate that precolonial 'Nigeria' was not static and that conditions for accumulation, exploitation, state and class formation, etc., existed. Myopic positions, such as was expressed by Marcello Caetano that the

> blacks in Africa must be directed and moulded by Europeans but they are indispensable as assistants to the latter . . . The Africans by themselves did not know how to develop the territories they inhabited for millenia, they did not account for a single useful invention nor any usable technical discovery, no conquest that counts in the evolution of humanity, nothing that can compare to the accomplishments in the areas of culture and technology by Europeans or even by Asia,[7]

cannot be taken seriously. Even if such positions were valid, one can still evaluate colonial contributions to these societies by looking at specific achievements and foundations laid for postcolonial development. This is what other chapters in this collection seek to do. The remainder of this contribution would seek to look at: 1) neo-classical theoretical rationalisations for colonial expansion; 2) the arguments of Marx, Engels and Lenin on the historical mission of colonialism and other forms of imperialist expansion; and 3) the practical exposition of the linkage between colonialism, exploitation and underdevelopment in the works of writers such as Fanon, Rodney and Césaire.

Neo-Classical Explanations of Colonial Expansion

An attempt to examine explanations based on myths and ego such as the search for 'the barbarians', the need to 'spread the glory of God' or Western Civilisation and so on, would be puerile. True, some participants in the colonial endeavour had truly humanistic or religious inclinations, though they had to operate within a system which had other economic, social and political intentions.

D. K. Fieldhouse, in criticising Marxian explanations of colonial expansion and exploitation, argues that rather than being economic, colonialism was the precipitate of Europe's 'political impulses' and military rivalries and that the missionaries, explorers and adventurers who had put pressure on European nations to search for colonies had no economic interests. The economic interests of the merchants were merely incidental.[8] R. Robinson and J. Gallagher have, in line with Fieldhouse, argued that colonialism can hardly be held or regarded as an exploitative mission embarked upon by the nations of Europe. On the contrary, they contend, it was the outcome of the search for national honour, diplomatic competition and struggles arising from the balance of power in Europe.[9] Finally, along these lines, L. H. Gann and P. Duignan, in a study which deliberately over-looked all the means by which the colonies were exploited and under-developed, argued that the colonies were a burden which cost the mother countries a lot of money. To both authors, the colonial venture was one which drained the metropole of resources and manpower.[10] Taken together, these perspectives are rather simplistic and escapist. Not only do they demonstrate a lack of understanding of the dynamic factors and forces which prompted colonialist expansion but also of developments within colonised societies. Thus, they neglected the origins and nature of the colonial state, the subjugation and incorporation of proto-bourgeois elements, the nurturing of a dependent state and social class as well as the numerous institutions and structures which facilitated the re-orientation of colonised formations and the extraction of surpluses.

Efforts to transcend these escapist interpretations have attempted to focus on the economic dimension of colonialism. However, rather than deny the forces that compelled colonial expansion, this perspective attempts to highlight the contributions (stimulations) which the colonial experience made to precolonial societies. These arguments hinge upon the fact that colonialism did not exploit its colonies, rather it 'opened up' the hitherto closed and static formations through the expansion of agriculture and trade (particularly international trade), the construction of transport and other communication facilities, the introduction of foreign produced consumer goods and luxury items and the provision of amenities and inducements which made the peasant work harder. Most of the advocates of this perspective draw heavily on the work of Hla Myint in applying Adam Smith's notion that external trade serves as a 'vent for surplus production' in economies with limited domestic markets, thus promoting production for export.[11] Explaining the fundamentals of the vent-for-surplus theory, R.E. Caves wrote that it

> depicts the effects of trade on growth as involving the exploitation of resources lacking in that place and at that time, any alternative uses of significant economic value. The existence of these 'surplus' resources

reflects the state of economic organisation in general and not a failure of the market mechanism in a narrow sense. The pace of growth and the pattern of international trade associated with the absorption of such resources gives these models their distinctive stamp.[12]

Myint in turn identifies the two major resources which were not put to any 'significant economic' use prior to contact with colonialism as land and labour which was under-employed in the production process. Assuming that production methods did not change over time in precolonial societies and that large-scale immigration did not take place, Myint concludes that 'there must have been considerable amount of under-employed or surplus labour' in peasant families, and 'there was abundant waste land waiting to be cultivated, but labour remained underemployed because there was a lack of effective demand for its potential increase in output'.[13] Thus, given the fact that peasant families possessed equal potential and 'produced' similar goods and services, there was little room for exchange or trade. All that colonialism (often referred to as international trade by Myint) did was to

> create 'effective demand' by linking up the world market demand for the type of things which the peasant could produce with the surplus productive capacity the peasant had locked up in the subsistence economy.[14]

To support the validity of this perspective, Myint points to the steady growth in the export of commodities from the colonies since the 'opening up' through contact with colonialism. Moreover, infrastructural development in the colonies, the introduction of law and order, the encouragement the colonial state gave to expatriate import-export businesses and the introduction of institutions which promoted surplus extraction were all part of the process of 'drawing an increasing volume of hitherto unused or surplus resources into export production'.[15]

The entry of merchant firms into the colonial import-export activity with the full protection and support of the colonial state is seen by Myint as advantageous to the peasant producers who were often offered an 'inducement to increase export production by selling them imported goods'. In fact, through the importation of inferior and cheaply produced goods from Europe and the forceful transfer of tastes, Myint concludes that by 'stimulating new wants among the peasants, the expansion of imports was a major dynamic force facilitating the expansion of exports'.[16] Thus, by selling wines, used clothes, perfumes and other commodities to the peasants, the colonial state did not need taxation, forced labour, state plantations, monetary inducements, etc., to encourage or force peasants to produce particular cash crops. Finally, Myint and the vent-for-surplus theorists conclude that since the effort put into production for export by the peasant was drawn from the 'reserve' of hitherto unutilised or underutilised labour and land, 'international trade', or to put it blankly, colonial imperialism, had only helped such societies to expand production and exchange and thus the march to progress. Like Myint, they often conclude that 'for the most part . . . indigenous peoples of the underdeveloped countries took to export production on a voluntary basis and enjoyed a clear gain by being able to satisfy their developing wants for the new imported commodities'.[17]

This approach has formed the analytical basis for several case studies of export growth and development in underdeveloped regions, particularly in Western Africa.[18] Helleiner, who has produced a very detailed account of agricultural and economic development in pre- and postcolonial Nigeria, makes the ridiculous observation, in spite of available information, that:

> Beyond offering peasant farmers a vent for their potential surplus production the foreigner did next to nothing to alter the technological backwardness of the economy. Since production functions were left largely untouched, he cannot be accused of introducing an export bias to the economy. All that he did was to dangle sufficiently attractive prices before the producers' noses to persuade them to convert potential into actual surpluses by increasing their inputs.[19]

In support of this contention, Helleiner argues that 'output increased because the terms at which leisure could be traded for material goods altered'. These material goods included cloth, weapons and salt, more of which 'could be obtained for their products than ever before'.[20]

Taken together, the vent-for-surplus theorists are perhaps correct in identifying the 'rational' responses of peasant producers to price incentives. But their complete neglect of the social and political relations of production and power which determine and condition such responses creates a big gap in any attempt to employ the theory in defence of colonial exploitation. There appears to be a deliberate desire to neglect or overlook the military, economic and social as well as political organisation of precolonial formations. For instance to what extent can one speak of 'unused labour' or 'under-utilised labour' in precolonial societies, even if we admit that land was surplus? The amount of time spent on specific agricultural tasks varied by season and even on a daily basis, market periods were equally seasonal in order to allow long-distance traders enough time to arrive among other reasons, while several people were often involved in more than one occupation. A cash crop producer could also be an artisan or a food crop producer. The theory, therefore, neglects the role and processes of capital formation in the growth of precolonial society. In addition, the vent-for-surplus analysis attempts to demonstrate the constancy of the output of non-traded food and of manufactures, only by assertion while it ignores aspects of labour reallocation.[21] The emphasis on 'voluntarism' is not tenable since

> the imposition of taxes payable in the colonial currency was a means of forcing Africans to produce commodities for which European demand existed, hence constraining the ability to 'choose'.[22]

If the purpose of the theorists was to provide an argument that would exonerate the colonialists from criticisms such as the introduction of export bias through administrative and political compulsions and manipulations, exploitation and mal-development, then its starting-point of conceiving such precolonial formations as a

> simple, subsistence society, isolated from international trade in which the inhabitants have much leisure time, simple tastes, and consume little apart from food [is not only a] fantasy [but] an 'idle savage' mythology which has no basis in reality.[23]

Such propositions as the vent-for-surplus theory neglect the numerous wars, the trans-Saharan trade, the bronze-casting and ironworks, the various empires, even the slave trade with Europe and relations with the metropolis in the period of 'informal empire'. It is therefore difficult to accept this perspective as a basis on which to study precolonial or colonial Nigeria. Whatever form of 'development' took place in the colonial period was very indirect or

> took place in sectors limited almost exclusively to production for export, the import trade, and related collection and distribution services. These sectors did not directly affect the bulk of the population, . . . what modern economic growth did occur . . . was directed to filling overseas market needs and providing markets for European manufactured goods. It took place within a framework which viewed metropolitan, not colonial interests as dominant.[24]

Marx and the Historical Mission of Colonialism

Unlike the vent-for-surplus theory, the views of Marx, Engels and Lenin did not deny that colonialism exploited the colonies or that the activities of the metropolis were capable of distorting and peripheralising the colonies. However, there are significant areas of difference, particularly in terms of emphasis in the works of Marx and Lenin. Though Marx did not discuss Africa or Nigeria, his discussion of Asiatic society or mode of production provides the closest correlation to the Nigerian reality. Given his understanding of what he termed Asiatic society, he drew the conclusion, not unlike the vent-for-surplus theorists, that autonomous development was virtually impossible within such static and backward societies. Therefore, according to Marx, such formations required an external stimulus or push to break loose from the shackles in which they were encased. This was to be the historical mission of colonialism in India, China and other colonies. With the advent of colonialism, the forces of production would be modernised and revolutionised, the formations would be integrated into a dynamic capitalist system and conditions for the emergence of viable capitalism would be established.

Perhaps the point should be made that though Marx might have been Eurocentric or ignorant of the dynamics within these so-called Asiatic formations prior to contact with colonialism, his thinking was influenced by the logic of his idea that a socialist revolution *must* inevitably be borne out of the contradictions of capitalist society. Thus, given the backwardness of the forces and factors of production in pre-capitalist formations, the intrusion of advanced forces and institutions of capitalism from the metropolis is, at least, likely to speed up the process towards capitalist development and popular revolution. But had Marx over-estimated the so-called historical mission of colonialism? Was he, in his eagerness to have his antagonistic social classes within the capitalist mode of production, forced to adopt a simplistic, Eurocentric, even apologetic, posture (at least at the beginning)? And, could it be that his lack of information about the nature of accumulation, power relations, agriculture, etc., in precolonial societies influenced his views? Finally, given his clear understanding of the nature of the capitalist class and state as well as factors which prompt imperialist expansion, how come that Marx, if even initially, was so optimistic about a so-called historical role of colonial expansion, domination and exploitation?

There is no doubt that as far as Marx was concerned, Asiatic society was stagnant and backward. Thus, even though British colonialism was bound to exploit such a society, it was still capable of creating a 'world after its own image'. In the *Communist Manifesto* Marx and Engels had written that in the impending struggle in Europe for the establishment of a socialist society, the two antagonistic forces confronting one another are the proletariat and the bourgeoisie. Thus, the only way in which these backward formations can be expected to become part of this inevitable historical movement is for the forces holding them back to be eliminated:

> England has broken down the entire framework of Indian society, without any symptoms of reconstructing it yet appearing. This loss of the old world . . . separates Hindustan . . . from all ancient traditions and from the whole of its past history.[25]

This had been possible because it was a situation where a dynamic capitalist mode of production and accumulation confronted a stagnant, traditional and almost natural 'mode of production'. To Marx, therefore, what colonialism was doing in India as well as other areas which approximated Asiatic formations was laying the 'material foundations of Western society in Asia':

> England has to fulfil a double mission in India. One destructive, the other regenerating – the annihilation of old Asiatic Society, and the laying of the material foundations of Western Society in Asia.[26]

There was nothing good in Asiatic society, so it had to be 'annihilated'. Other non-Western invaders of Asia had, for instance, according to Marx, been 'Hindocised', but the British were of course 'superior'. The British destroyed Hindu civilization by 'breaking up the native communities, by uprooting the native industry and by levelling all that was great and elevated in the native society'.[27] Though destruction and exploitation fill the pages of British rule in India (as well as in Nigeria), the process of regeneration was evident in 1853 to Marx.[28]

Some of the signs of regeneration included the introduction of electric telegraph, a new army which was to be the '*sine qua non* of Indian self-emancipation', the free press 'introduced for the first time into Asiatic society', education 'under English superintendence', the emergence of a 'fresh class . . . endowed with the requirements for government and imbued with European science', regular and rapid communication with Europe and finally, freedom from the 'prime law of stagnation'. As we have noted earlier in this chapter, the perception that most of these developments were novel is misleading and in fact historically inaccurate. While it is true that these developments took place in all colonies, in more 'modern' forms, the reasons behind their introduction, the uses to which they were put by the colonial state, their quality and the extent to which they were available for popular use were completely misunderstood by Marx. Even the vent-for-surplus theorists agree that the introduction of transportation, communication, 'law and order' and even administration were all part of the process of encouraging the expansion of production for export. The new army was introduced not for the emancipation of the colonies, but to act as an appendage of the state, help with the discipline and pacification of recalcitrant villages, chiefs and workers as well as protect the 'name and glory of the Queen', and the new class that was introduced was to be groomed to facilitate the extractive and exploitative activities of the merchant firms and made to have a stake in the unequal relations of production and accumulation implanted in the colonial period. Invariably, this class was to capture political (but not economic) power and maintain a neocolonial relationship with the metropolis. Education was not introduced in order to promote progress, the understanding of society and the development of the human intellect. Rather, in all colonies, the emphasis was on the production of interpreters, messengers, clerks, cooks and errand boys. As Césaire puts it:

> Security? Culture? The rule of law? In the meantime, I look around and wherever there are colonizers and colonized face to face, I see force, brutality, and in a parody of education, the hasty manufacture of a few subordinate functionaries, 'boys', artisans, office clerks, and interpreters necessary for the smooth operation of business.[29]

Therefore, the point must be made that British colonialism, in its process of 'developing' its colonies or in the process of breaking and incorporating precolonial relations and forces of production, introduced institutions, amenities, and relations which consolidated its domination and promoted extraction of economic surpluses. The destruction of precolonial formations and relations of power must therefore be seen as only a necessary pre-requisite for effective domination, incorporation and exploitation.

On further reflection on the nature of colonialism, Marx was forced in 1881 to criticise certain actions of European colonialism as vandalistic and barbaric. Even then, his underlying assumption about the ability of colonialism to generate a new era in backward societies by breaking the 'near total stability' and inability of self-reproduction through an almost natural law, remained constant. For instance, he maintained that

> English interference having placed the spinner in Lancashire and the
> weaver in Bengal, or sweeping away both Hindoo spinner and weaver,
> dissolved these small semi-barbarian, semi-civilized communities, by
> blowing up their economical basis, and thus produced the greatest,
> and to speak the truth, the only *social* revolution ever heard of in
> Asia.[30]

More specifically, Marx observed:

> England, it is true, in causing a social revolution in Hindostan, was
> actuated only by the vilest interests, and was stupid in her manner of
> enforcing them. But that is not the question. The question is, can
> mankind fulfil its destiny without a fundamental revolution in the
> social state of Asia? If not, whatever may have been the crimes of
> England *she was the unconscious tool of history in bringing about
> that revolution.*[31]

This largely apologetic position neglects the truth that England was a very
conscious tool in bringing about a revolution which distorted and relegated
these formations to the periphery of the world capitalist system through
unbridled exploitation and failure to introduce viable institutions. As Eric
Hobsbawm, Paul Baran and Maurice Dobb have very well demonstrated in
their studies, these societies were in several respects not inferior to England.
In fact, Hobsbawm provides evidence to demonstrate the superiority of
Indian textile industry to that of the British until the latter physically
destroyed it in order to generate an Indian market for British textiles.[32]

There are two important points made by Marx which captured correctly,
the possible consequences of British exploitation of its colonies. First he
notes that:

> All the English bourgeoisie may be forced to do will neither emancipate
> nor materially meet the social condition of the masses of the people,
> depending not only on the development of the productive powers, but
> on their appropriation by the people. *But what they will not fail to do
> is to lay the material premises for both, has the bourgeoisie ever done
> more?* Has it ever effected a progress without dragging individuals and
> peoples through blood and dirt . . .

Secondly, Marx, in line with the futurist notion which does not appear to
follow from the initial optimism concerning colonialism, declared that:

> The devastating effects of English industry when contemplated with
> regard to India, a country as vast as Europe, and containing 150 millions
> of acres, are palpable and confounding. But we must not forget that
> they are only organic results of the whole system of production as it is
> now constituted. That production rests on the supreme rule of capital.
> The centralisation of capital is essential to the existence of capital as
> an independent power. The destructive influence of that centralisation
> upon the markets of the world does reveal, in the most gigantic

dimensions, the inherent organic laws of political economy now at work in every civilised town. *The bourgeois period of history has to create the material basis of the new world* – on the one hand the universal intercourse, on the other hand the development of the productive powers of man and the transformation of material production into a scientific domination of natural agencies.[33]

Perhaps the problem with Marx's fundamental position – that colonialism had a 'progressive' historical mission – was that while he was willing to accept the fact that Europe was able to revolutionise its productive powers 'autonomously', he found it difficult to accept the possibility of so-called Asiatic societies, through internal dynamics of production, power and exchange to also revolutionise their forces and relations of production. But a clear understanding of the factors which prompted colonial expansion – beyond adventurism, search for Prester John, political rivalries in Europe, etc. – would reveal that colonialism right from its inception had an exploitative goal. The mechanisms with which this was executed further militated against the revolutionising of productive forces. In fact, given the goal of colonialism, it was not necessary to revolutionise the productive capacities of colonised formations. Thus, the primary goals of colonial expansion were domination and exploitation, and it was flexible enough as an exploitative epoch in the history of capitalism to create and introduce conditions which would promote exploitation while at the same time it oppressed or destroyed those that were likely to challenge it. This flexibility was determined by the level of resistance the colonial agents met with, the extent and level of socio-political organisation, the quality and quantity of resources involved and the level of development of productive forces.

Marx's obvious Eurocentrism and over-enthusiasm prevented him from emphasising the point that given the *nature* of the colonising countries as well as the agents employed in the process and the goals they pursued, it would be antithetical for colonialism to create competitors rather than markets and plantations. In fact, Marx continued to emphasise the superiority of Western culture and science, as if precolonial formations lacked culture and science. On China, to take an example on which he wrote, while he was against the avarice behind the opium war, his position on the 'positive' consequences of capitalist penetration was similar to that on India:

> Complete isolation was the prime condition of the preservation of old China. That isolation having come to a violent end by the medium of England, dissolution must follow as surely as that of a mummy carefully preserved in a hermetically sealed coffin, whenever it is brought into contact with the open air.[34]

Thus, in spite of his reservations, in China opium would be one of the commodities that was bound to contribute to the destruction of the 'sleeping' or stagnant Chinese society. Hence he wrote that whatever the social causes, and whatever religious, dynastic or national shape they may assume, that have brought about the chronic rebellions subsisting in China for about ten years past, and now gathered together in one formidable revolution, the occasion of this outbreak has unquestionably been afforded by the English cannon forcing upon China that soporific drug called opium.[35]

A similar position was adopted by Engels in the case of Algeria following colonisation by France. Engels described the event as 'an important and fortunate event for the progress of civilisation'.[36]

Marx and Engels ignored the simple fact that if colonial exploitation required the arrest of what Césaire calls 'extraordinary possibilities' and the destruction of dynamic sectors of precolonial formations in order to institute metropolitan hegemony, its forces would ultimately be concentrated on the maintenance of that hegemony rather than the promotion of 'regeneration'. Umberto Melotti has noted in an interesting work on *Marx and the Third World* that

> some people have even accused Marx and Engels of blinkered ethnocentricity, accusing them of taking an uncritically favourable view of European colonial expansion. Others even in the Marxist camp, have held that, initially at least, they failed to see the progressive nature of national liberation movements.

B. Sutchiffe blames Marx for believing that 'capitalism would industrialize the world' and for failing to spell out the full consequences of capitalist penetration in the case of India. M. B. Brown argues that Marx's idea that the railway was 'truly the forerunner of modern industry' in India was wrong because 'this was almost precisely what did not happen, at least for a hundred years'. On the contrary, he notes that what took place was the de-industrialisation process forced by 'the distorting effect of the international division of labour'. In his own criticism of Marx and Engels, Samir Amin contends that

> the distinctive problems of transition to peripheral capitalism largely escaped Marx's notice, and this accounts for his mistaken notion about the future development of the 'colonial problem' ... [The] pattern of transition to peripheral capitalism is, in fact, fundamentally different from that of transition to central capitalism.

R. Palme Dutt adds another criticism when he notes that 'the victory of foreign capitalism in India differed from the victory of capitalism in Europe, in that the destructive process was not accompanied by any corresponding growth of new forces' as Marx had expected. Finally, Paul Baran argues that

> accelerating with irresistible energy the maturing of *some* of the basic prerequisites for the development of a capitalistic system, the intrusion of Western capitalism in the now underdeveloped countries blocked with equal force the ripening of others.[37]

These criticisms are not off the mark, even if not exhaustive. It is important to note, however, that Marx and Engels wrote with Europe as their background and their prime concern was with the immediate and remote factors that would promote the revolutionary process in Europe and European Russia. Their limited knowledge of colonialism in practice mediated their theoretical formulations, even though it is difficult not to fault their inability to relate unbridled exploitation to distortion and underdevelopment. Engels, writing to Kautsky in 1882, was very optimistic that the socialist revolution would take place first in Europe and North America, and 'semi-civilized countries' would 'of themselves follow in their wake; economic needs, if anything, will see to that'.[38] But to him, these 'semi-civilized' countries, first had to become capitalist like Europe and colonialism was going to be the tool.

These theorists (Marx and Engels) placed considerable faith in the ability of British investors and entrepreneurs, through their activities in the colonies, to ensure the creation not only of a capitalist class, but also of a consumer population and the antagonistic social classes that would facilitate the socialist revolution. This expectation contradicts the reality. Geoffrey Kay for instance notes:

> For a period the East India Company arrogated political power to itself and acted as the state. The result was not the relatively slow transformation of the economic structure on the basis of which a revolutionary reconstruction of the social and political order could eventually take place; but a sharp rupture in the process of historical development. In the Americas and Australia whole civilisations were wiped out; West Africa was reduced to a slave market and no society escaped without being turned into a corrupt parody of its former self. The degree of social incoherence that arose would have made the establishment of industrial capitalism impossible even if this had been historically practical. What it did allow, in fact what it made essential, was external colonial domination, either direct or indirect, and in this way gave a spurious basis to the hypocritical claims of the colonising powers that they brought civilisation and order to a world of barbarism and chaos.[39]

The later revisions that Marx and Engels were to make on their positions relating to colonialism, exploitation and (under)development are equally not very convincing, though these were made in view of the glaring destructive consequences of colonial exploitation and the rising tempo of nationalist movements in colonised territories. The owners of capital lived in England and they invested in India, Nigeria and other colonies with the primary goal of making profit and maintaining capitalist hegemony over the periphery. Where accumulation and exploitation could take place by capitalising on existing political and social systems, we had so-called indirect rule and made limited restructurings. Where there were massive resistance and favourable climatic conditions, we had direct rule or settler colonialism. In fact, in its exploitative mission, colonial capitalism had a way of adapting to existing social relations of production in the process of incorporation.

Capitalism in the colonies did not need to revolutionise the forces of production in order to further exploitation. Neo-classical theorists would agree that cash crops can be obtained in three ways: 1) forced labour on colonial plantations, 2) forced labour on settler plantations and 3) legal and price 'inducements' to encourage expanded peasant production of specific cash crops. The introduction of taxation, colonial currencies and so on would only be aspects of the total process of surplus extraction. Taste transfer, minimal wage employment and the introduction of currency as well as propaganda in the area of education and culture would create the required market for the excess of goods produced in metropolitan industries, thus completing the exploitative cycle. As the hegemonic power, the transformative initiative lay in the control of the capitalist and this initiative was conditioned by his needs. The racialist aspects of colonialism also appeared to have been lost to Marx and Engels who constantly referred to the colonies as 'barbaric', 'semi-civilized' and 'backward'. Though racial discrimination was often more pronounced in areas where settler colonialism existed and was more often than not a rationalisation for the perpetuation of colonialist domination and exploitation, most of the colonial officers sincerely believed in the racial inferiority of the colonised. Hence the strenuous efforts to completely de-humanise the colonised, thus creating psychological and social excuses for not involving the 'savages' in the dynamic process of structural transformation and capital accumulation. On the contrary, the 'barbarians' were made to produce crops for the metropolis, service the colonial machine as soldiers, court clerks, interpreters and so on and help in the process of incorporation into world capitalism and the transfer of surpluses to the centre.

In *Capital*, Marx attempted to reverse his ethnocentric position of colonial expansion and exploitation:

> To what extent (merchant capital) brings about a dissolution of the old mode of production depends on its solidity and internal structure. And whither this process of dissolution will lead, in other words, what mode of production will replace the old, does not depend on commerce but on the character of the old mode of production itself. . . . The obstacles presented by the internal solidity and organisation of pre-capitalistic, national modes of production to the corrosive influence of commerce are strikingly illustrated in the intercourse of the English with India and China.[40]

This revision is an improvement. The 'obstacles' largely become suppressed under direct colonisation and intensified exploitation particularly in periods of crisis in the metropolis. However, it does provide some insights into the possibility of the co-existence of modes of production, though as we have argued, the failure to break down the pre-capitalist modes in colonised formations completely was largely deliberate. The multi-layered nature of the international capitalist system born out of centuries of subjugation, incorporation and exploitation was not completely lost on Marx. He notes

15

that a

> new international division of labour, a division suited to the require-
> ments of the chief centres of modern industry springs up and converts
> one part of the globe into a chiefly agricultural field of production for
> supplying the other part of which remains a chiefly industrial field.[41]

Writing on British colonialism in Ireland, Marx's concern was how the
revolution in Ireland would serve as a pre-condition for the revolution in
England. Thus it was not the revolutionary possibilities within the colonies
per se but their significance for the prospects of the revolution in the
metropolis that was crucial to Marx. It is insufficient to emphasise the
historical role of colonialism and capitalism. As we have seen in contemporary
times, even with the maintenance of neo-colonial relationships with the
periphery, capitalism has not been performing this so-called historic mission.
If anything, the institutions and social relations which were employed in the
distortion and exploitation of the periphery have been deepened and
expanded. Colonialism was supposed to create social classes that would
continue to revolutionise the forces of production. This process was supposed
to generate social contradictions that were in turn to lead to the overthrow
of the capitalist system along with colonialism or after a bourgeois-nationalist
phase. According to Marx, the bourgeoisie that was to be created

> . . . by the rapid improvement of all instruments of production, by the
> immensely facilitated means of communication, draws all, even the most
> barbarian nations, into civilisation. The cheap prices of its commodities
> are the artillery with which it batters down all Chinese walls, with
> which it forces the barbarian's intensely obstinate hatred of foreigners
> to capitulate. It compels all nations, on pain of extinction, to adopt
> the bourgeois mode of production, it compels them to introduce what
> it calls civilisation into their midst i.e. to become bourgeois themselves.
> In one word, *it creates a world after its own image.*[42]

Unfortunately, this did not happen. The English bourgeoisie did not create
anything after its own image. Rather it created a dependent social class, an
economy orientated to meet its own needs, a culture distorted and an
international system in which the metropolis would be dominant. True, the
colonies were incorporated into a world capitalist system. But they were to
serve as markets, dumping grounds for outmoded goods and sources of raw
materials. And this was possible because the forces of production were not
completely revolutionised and where some changes took place, these were
half-hearted and very limited, thus stultifying the emergence of the expected
historical benefits. As Colin Leys has argued, Marx

> left a lot of loose ends, apparent inconsistencies and unanswered
> problems, and although he anticipated much that is now an essential
> part of underdevelopment theory — for instance the growth of mono-
> poly capitalism — the world has not stood still. . . . Underdevelopment

theory is thus partly a correction and partly an expansion of Marx's interpretation of history, an expansion of his method and central ideas to a problem which in a world scale, was still in its embryo at his death: the failure of the countries of Asia, Africa and Latin America to follow a path of autonomous capitalist developments, leading to their regeneration.[43]

There are other works within the Marxist stream which contribute to the correction of Marx and Engels' perspectives on colonialism. Essentially, this body of literature begin by explaining the dynamics and contradictions of capitalist development and accumulation in the metropolis. The factors which compelled the advanced capitalist countries to seek colonies are partly explained thus:

> Overproduction in the sense of an excessive manufacturing plant and surplus capital which could not find sound investments within the country, forced Great Britain, Germany, Holland and France to place larger and larger portions of their economic resources outside the area of their present political domain, and then to stimulate a policy of political expansion so as to take in the new areas.[44]

Thus, according to Hobson, it was the contradiction of internal industrial expansion that created the need for colonies. The only way to ensure the success of the venture was through domination and incorporation. If there were no colonies, capital accumulation and domestic rates of interest would be severely affected. In an argument which underscores the fact that colonialism never set out to develop the colonies but to exploit and incorporate them, Paul Sweezy and Leo Huberman have noted that

> there is no doubt that Marx was fully aware of the causal relationship between the development of capitalism in Europe and the development of the underdevelopment in the rest of the world. He had the basic elements of a theory of capitalism as a global system and the pity is that his followers did not see this in good time and understand the importance of extending and developing his ideas. If they had, they surely could not have believed that the colonies and dependencies of the capitalist empires were in a state of 'feudalism' or that crippled and dependent economies could produce other than a crippled and dependent bourgeoisie.[45]

Lenin made it quite clear in his works that colonial expansion, domination and exploitation represented the highest attempt by imperialist states to further their search for wealth, markets, areas for new investments and political control. While it is often one or more of these factors that prompted the need for colonies, the underlying cause was the contradictions that emerged from the crystallisation of class forces, the development of production relations and the full concentration of monopolies and the consequent need for new outlets for investments and exploitation. To Lenin therefore, colonialism cannot be divorced from exploitation, given the objective factors which necessitated colonial expansion, the practice of

17

colonialism and the consequences this practice had on the colonised peoples and territories. He notes for instance that

> the export of capital influences and greatly accelerates the development of capitalism in those countries to which it is exported. While, therefore, the export of capital may tend to a certain extent to arrest development in the capital-exporting countries, it can only do so by expanding and deepening the further development of capitalism throughout the world.[46]

It is, however, important to add that right from the beginning, Lenin never under-estimated the main reason for colonial expansion: exploitation — and the possible consequences of such exploitation: underdevelopment. The need to create a linkage between the metropolitan and colonial (or periphery's) market and introduce institutions and structures which reinforce this metropolis-periphery (or dominant-dominated) relationship are integral parts of colonialist policies:

> Monopolist capitalist associations, cartels, syndicates and trusts first divided the home market among themselves and obtained more or less complete possession of the industry of their own country. But under capitalism the home market is inevitably bound up with the foreign market. As the export of capital increased, and as the foreign and colonial connections and 'spheres of influence' of the big monopolist associations expanded, things 'naturally' gravitated towards the formation of international cartels.[47]

Perhaps another factor which enables Lenin's formulations to capture the concrete conditions of colonial formations was that he did not see these societies as 'static'. He believed that colonial exploitation, be it in the form of political domination or the extraction of economic surpluses, inevitably generates its own contradictions and crisis.

Finally, while one cannot quarrel with the position of Marx in terms of colonialism's historical mission, it is obvious that this 'mission' must be located within the dynamics of capitalist development in the metropolis and the objective conditions which necessitated the export of capital, the search for sources of raw materials, areas to dump surplus populations and outmoded technology as well as win political advantages over other imperialist forces. Nonetheless, these goals cannot be achieved in the colonised societies unless hitherto existing structures, institutions and processes are subjugated, distorted and incorporated in order to further colonial hegemony and exploitation within an unequal world capitalist system.

So far, we have examined mainly the works of Marx, Engels and Lenin who wrote with a purely European background. It is essential to examine also the contributions of others who more or less witnessed or experienced colonial domination and exploitation, and even the process of the transition to neocolonial dependence.

Colonialism, Exploitation and Underdevelopment

In the works of Kwame Nkrumah, Aguibou Yansane, Walter Rodney and Aimé Césaire (to mention just a few), colonialism had no positive intent towards the colony right from the beginning. It was a mission undertaken with the sole purpose of extending and consolidating the interests of the metropolis at the expense of the colonies. In fact, colonialism is another term for exploitation or underdevelopment. To this group of authors, given the nature of the metropolitan state and bourgeoisie and the internal contradictions and class struggles which precipitated the need for colonies, there was no way in which colonialism could have been a mission undertaken for the sole purpose of promoting growth and development in the colony. As Çesaire has argued, to know what colonialism is, it is perhaps more rewarding to know what it is not:

> . . . neither evangelization, nor a philanthropic enterprise, nor a desire to push back the frontiers of ignorance, disease and tyranny, nor a project undertaken for the greater glory of God, nor an attempt to extend the rule of law. To admit once and for all, without flinching at the consequences that the decisive actors here are the adventurer and the pirate, the wholesale grocer and the ship owner, the gold digger and the merchant, appetite and force, and behind them, the baleful projected shadow of a form of civilization which, at a certain point in its history, finds itself obliged, for internal reasons, to extend to a world scale the competition of its antagonistic economies.[48]

Césaire concludes his definition of colonialism in terms of the forces which prompted it, its practice and its consequences by noting that 'between *colonization* and *civilization* there is an infinite distance'.[49] This description provides a strong background to the observation by Fola Soremekun on Angola at independence after almost a century of Portuguese colonialism, that the country

> inherited a chaotic economy, remnant of a capitalist system. The banks had been looted almost to emptiness − diamond mines had been robbed − The workers were enraged and bitter by the history of past oppression. There was virtually no food to eat.[50]

Patrick Manning has suggested in an interesting work how colonialism could be evaluated in order to determine whether it was exploitative or beneficial to the colonised and the colonies. While the general ideological thrust of his work appears to attempt to whip up support for colonial policies, as Toyin Falola rightly notes, 'no theory can obscure the fact that colonialism and exploitation can never be divorced from one another'.[51] According to Manning, a colonial government should be judged on the basis of equality in trade, transfer of technology, local investments, taxation and government services. Where these factors operate in favour of the colonies, the efforts of the metropolis must be praised and regarded as positive and vice versa.[52] If these parameters are employed in the evaluation of colonial policies, it would become obvious that the metropolis had one goal — to exploit. Given the domination of political and trading institutions, the power unilaterally to fix prices and determine which crops to produce, the skewed allocation of amenities and distorted pattern of investments, the underdevelopment of indigenous entrepreneurs, the imposition of numerous forms of taxes to facilitate the collection of funds to run the colonial bureaucracy as well as to compel the indigenes to engage in activities through which they could earn money — mainly cash crop production — and finally, the establishment of unviable political and administrative institutions, colonial policies were hardly aimed at ensuring development. In fact, a cursory look at the international division of labour today would reveal that these former colonies in Africa in particular are effectively peripheralised within the world capitalist system. For one thing this demonstrates that colonialism's historical mission had distorting and stultifying effects on the forces of production in the colonial period. On the other hand, it also shows that the factors and forces which had continued to contribute to the reproduction of these distortions and contradictions in the postcolonial period were introduced in the colonial period in such a way that only a fundamental restructuring of the total pattern of production, exchange and appropriation can rectify extant situations. Geoffrey Kay, in reference to the exploitative mission of colonialism, notes that rather than lay a foundation for the development of capitalist relations and forces of production, 'capital created underdevelopment not because it exploited the underdeveloped world but because it did not exploit it enough'.[53] This succinct observation, often overlooked in the analysis of colonialism, relates to the existence of unviable, uninstitutionalised and contradictory structures, relations and modes of production. Though these facilitated the reproduction of colonial relations, they are incapable of performing similar roles in postcolonial periods without the compulsion and violence and metropolitan support which the colonial state had enjoyed:

> The history of underdevelopment proper, as opposed to its prehistory opened in the middle of the nineteenth century when industrial capital completed the subordination of merchant capital in Britain. At this time Britain was not only the leading industrial country but also the major imperial power with colonies and spheres of influence in North and South America, the Mediterranean and South East Europe, Africa and Asia. Development in Britain therefore had powerful repercussions throughout the whole world.[54]

If *development* involves structural changes, it also involves capital accumulation by the *indigenous* population. There is no way in which we can regard the capital accumulated by the colonial state on behalf of the metropolitan bourgeoisie as having been undertaken to aid the growth and development of colonised societies and social forces. For this argument to be tenable i.e. that colonialism aided development in the colony, such 'development' must be seen to have involved increases (in) productivity, equalisation in the distribution of the social product and the emergence of *indigenous institutions* whose relations with the outside world and particularly with the developed centres of the international economy, are characterised by equality rather than by dependence or subordination.[55]

Colonial expansion and domination did not involve any of these features, rather it ensured the disarticulation of the economy and the underdevelopment of indigenous institutions and social classes. This situation of underdevelopment and exploitation in the colonial (even neocolonial) period, does not preclude increases in the production export crops, GNP, conspicuous consumption, changes in taste and leisure periods and the accumulation of money capital by a few indigenous elements. But accumulation by major factions and fractions of the bourgeoisie becomes dependent on the accumulative activities and needs of the metropolis. As Aguibou Yansane has rightly noted,

> the lever of the colonial machinery of control was located in the metropolitan country. . . . Through force and coercion and decrees, the colonial administration maintained law and order. Using African forced labour, the colonizers opened new roads, built railroads, bridges, hospitals and schools and thereby incorporated (sometimes marginally) the colonized people into the mercantile and commercial activities of the colonial enterprises and banks . . . the value of the colonies was mainly as a source of cheap, private production of raw materials and minerals.[56]

Yansane, in a review of the theory of colonisation and decolonisation, concludes that following incorporation by metropolitan capital under the supervision of the colonial and metropolitan states, political, economic and social institutions were established to continue European domination, to subordinate the African people and to strengthen their attachment to the expanding European capitalist economic and trading activities from the fifteenth century to the present. Therefore the explanation of the African's poverty has to take into account the nature of their association with Europeans and their relation to the process of production.[57]

This perspective which agrees with those of Fanon, Rodney and Césaire differs from that of Marx because its explanation of the 'historical' mission of colonialism takes its roots from development within metropolitan capitalism, goes through the experiences of the colonised and projects these into the postcolonial epoch. Commenting on class formation, Césaire explains the comprador and largely unproductive nature of the African bourgeoisie thus: 'in a parody of education, the hasty manufacture of a few thousand subordinate functionaries "boys", artisans, office clerks and interpreters necessary'[58] for the promotion of exploitation and the programmed transition to neo-colonial dependence This point is crucial given the fact that these 'functionaries' did not emerge organically through their productive or accumulative activities in relation to other non-bourgeois forces. Their emergence as agents, shareholders, bureaucrats, marketing board licensed agents and so on, was dependent on the goodwill and conditioning of the colonial state, thus the roots of their dependence were laid in this period.

In the Preface to *The Wretched of the Earth*, Jean-Paul Sartre observed that:

> The European elite undertook to manufacture a native elite. They picked out promising adolescents, they branded them, as with a red hot iron, with the principles of Western culture they stuffed their mouths with high sounding phrases, grand glutinous works that stuck to the teeth. After a short stay in the mother country they were sent home, white washed.[59]

If capitalist development, as we have pointed out earlier on, requires a national bourgeoisie rather than a comprador or dependent one i.e. it requires a bourgeois class which accumulates internally through the extensive utilisation of its organisation and access to the state to exploit internal forces of production and invests its surpluses in production rather than in leisure, commerce and distribution, it is easy to evaluate the colonial contribution to the emergence of this class. Such a capitalist class did not exist in Africa or Nigeria prior to colonialism. Marx had expected colonialism to create a bourgeois class. However, Frantz Fanon has argued that after political independence, the underdeveloped indigenous forces found themselves in a dilemma because:

> This native bourgeoisie will realise, with its mouth watering, that it lacks something essential to a bourgeoisie: Money. The bourgeoisie of an underdeveloped country is a bourgeoisie in spirit only. It is not its economic strength, nor the dynamism of its leaders, nor the breadth of its ideas that ensures its peculiar quality of bourgeoisie. . . . It is the position it holds in the new national administration which will give it strength and serenity. If the government gives it enough time and opportunity, this bourgeoisie will manage to put away enough money to stiffen its domination. But it will always reveal itself as incapable of giving birth to an authentic bourgeois society with all the economic and industrial consequences which this entails.[60]

Kwame Nkrumah, who had to work within colonial restraints and later preside over a neocolonial country, put the mission of colonialism very bluntly when he noted that '[b]eneath the "humanitarian" and "appeasement" shibboleths of colonial governments, a proper scrutiny leads one to discover nothing but deception, hypocrisy, oppression and exploitation',[61] and specifically on Britain, he notes that in

> an attempt to reconcile the inherent contradictions within her capitalistic economy, she has two courses only left to keep her home population from starvation; either her population must be dispersed in the colonial territories, or she must guarantee subsistence to them by *exploitation of the colonies*.[62]

The extent of the underdevelopment of the indigenous power-elite in the colonial period is underscored by the observation that at independence it

was corrupt, weak, alienated from non-bourgeois forces and had 'practically
no economic power, and in any case it is in no way commensurate with the
bourgeoisie of the mother country which it hopes to replace'.[63] This native
bourgeoisie 'is not engaged in production, nor in invention, nor building, nor
labour, it is completely canalized into activities of the intermediary type'.[64]

While it is true that given the frequent crises experienced within the
metropolis, the alignment and re-alignment of class forces in the periphery
following independence and the strategic importance of some peripheral
areas to the centre, there have been struggles to strengthen not only the
political power of the dominant forces but also their accumulative base,
these have been postcolonial developments. Except in societies where national
liberation was combined with the struggle for a socialist society, the
structures and contradictions implanted in the colonial period have
continued to militate against sectoral linkages, industrialisation, cultural
revival, technological take off and political stability.

In an empirical study of the African experience, Walter Rodney concluded
that 'colonialism had only one hand — it was a one-armed bandit'[65] and that
'hardly anything was done that could remotely be termed a service to the
African people'[66] in the colonial period:

> There can be little dispute over the credibility of the data which are
> available to amply demonstrate that colonialism for the most part aimed
> at developing the metropoles and only allowed certain crumbs to the
> colonies as incidental by-products of exploitation . . . colonialism was
> hardly any better than the fascism against which Britain was fighting . . .
> Europeans were in the colonial game, because it was damned profitable,
> and that was that.[67]

Without mentioning Marx, Rodney vehemently disputes the idea that
colonialism introduced 'the dynamic features of capitalism such as private
property in land, private ownership of the other means of production and
money relations'[68], by making a distinction between *capitalist elements* and
capitalism as a total system. He argues instead that:

> colonialism introduced some elements of capitalism into Africa . . .
> However, colonialism did not transform Africa into a capitalist society
> comparable to the metropoles. Had it done that, one might have
> complained of the brutalities and inequalities of capitalism, but it could
> not have then been said that colonialism failed to advance Africa along
> that path of human historical development . . . *Colonialism did not
> create a capital owning and factory-owning class among Africans or
> even inside Africa, nor did it create an urbanised proletariat of any
> significance* (particularly outside South Africa). In other words,
> capitalism in the form of colonialism failed to perform in Africa the
> tasks it had performed in Europe in changing social relations and
> liberating the forces of production.[69]

This criticism exposes the ideological and political goals of the colonial state
in the process of distorting the colony so as to lay the foundation for neo-

colonial dependence and continued exploitation. In the process of creating 'development' in the colony, therefore, the direct and indirect actions of the colonial state not only ensured that the colonies were converted into 'non-manufacturing dependencies' but also ensured that they were prevented 'from acquiring the knowledge of modern means and techniques for developing their own industries'.[70] Indicators of this distortion and exploitation other than economic balkanisation and concentration on the production of a few cash crops solely for export include a heavy dependence on foreign inputs and technology, the perception of Western consumerist culture as superior and a guaranteed dominant role for foreign capital. Perhaps, a most important consequence of the colonial experience beyond the nature of dominant classes is the nature of the neocolonial state. The weakness and instability of this state is a direct precipitate of the ruthless exploitation and disarticulation of the social formation in the colonial period, the alien and unviable institutions — armed forces and bureaucracy — introduced and the fact that significant sections of the population were left outside the hegemony of the state. These forces have continued to challenge the control and power of the state thus rendering the latter inherently incapable of supporting the emergence of a dynamic capitalist class.

Colonialism, by arresting the natural processes of state and class formation, half-heartedly 'revolutionising' production factors, forcibly and prematurely bringing together peoples of varying cultures, laid the foundation for political instability, social strife and poverty in the colonies:

> colonialism blocked the further evolution of national solidarity, because it destroyed the particular Asian and African states which were principal agents for achieving the liquidation of fragmented loyalties . . . What came to be called tribalism at the beginning of the new epoch of political independence . . . was itself a product of the way people were brought together under colonialism so as to be exploited.[71]

The logic of capitalist expansion and accumulation which prompted various stages of imperialist domination did not include the need to generate external social forces capable of competing effectively in so-called free trade, but in fact to destroy such forces and establish conditions likely to facilitate exploitation.

Conclusions

The other chapters in this book deal with the specifics of colonial domination, distortion and exploitation of Nigeria. Nonetheless, it is important to high-light here a few ways in which the foregoing conceptual discussion of colonialism and exploitation explains the Nigerian reality.

The traditional argument that precolonial Nigeria was a mixed-capitalist economy, one based on communalism but with strong adherence to the principles of private property is, more often than not, an attempt to rationalise the contradictions and exploitations of postcolonial peripheral capitalist Nigeria.[72] Not only is it difficult to determine the specific origin of the so-called 'traditional Nigerian society', but this argument completely ignores the fact that the state of socio-economic and political arrangements met by the British imperialists were precipitates of the development of productive forces, the dynamics of state formation and some accumulation through local and long-distance trade. The exploitation and accumulation of this period were often rationalised in cultural, religious and even political terms. In fact, the period of 'informal empire' which predated the imposition of formal colonialism in the 19th century contributed significantly to stimulating the productive capacity and accumulative process within the social formation. The emergence of a proto-bourgeoisie in the north which had accumulated capital and 'status' through the long-distance trans-Saharan trade and in the south through the coastal trade in slaves and other raw goods, was directly stimulated in the period of 'informal empire'. This state of social development was to be incorporated into the exploitative and incorporative mission of British colonialism in Nigeria.

Perhaps more important is the fact that arguments which attempt to trace contemporary peripheral capitalist relations in Nigeria to the precolonial society, either neglect the exploitative and distorting effects of British colonialism or interpret these as positive contributions to the emancipation from traditional rulers, poverty, civil wars and so on. Nonetheless, the point must be made that even if we can identify a wide gulf between the level of development in Britain in the 19th century as compared to Nigeria, the Nigerian reality reflected an *undeveloped* pre-capitalist state of affairs with 'extraordinary possibilities' for the development and expansion of productive and accumulative capacities. The direct *underdevelopment* and peripheralisation of the Nigerian formation were precipitates of British colonial exploitation of the country and the programmed transition to neocolonial dependence.

The pre-direct colonial domination of Nigeria witnessed the introduction of forces and factors which destabilised Nigerian development and drained it of its most productive and healthy manpower through the slave trade. The period also witnessed the institutionalisation of unequal relations of exchange and the orientation of the local producers to meet the need of the European market through so-called legitimate trade. The slave trade was a direct transfer of potential economic surplus from Nigeria to Britain and its colonies. The British state and bourgeoisie thus exploited Nigeria by creating internal conditions of instability and depopulation which were later to make direct colonisation easy, at the same time promoting accumulation in the metropolis and plantation colonies through the use of free slave labour. The appropriation of the slave's labour and person meant the appropriation of generations of descendants of slaves even if it was to be rationalised in more subtle forms after the abolition of the slave trade. The depopulation, instability and destruction of lives and property in Nigeria during the slave raids directly disrupted production relations, stunted domestic labour forces and distorted the natural pattern of state and class formation.

Following the industrial revolution which had replaced men with machines, the increasing militancy and struggles of the slaves, minor revolts by religious and other fractions of the British bourgeoisie, the slave trade was 'abolished', but carefully replaced with a 'legitimate' (but very unequal) trade in agricultural and other goods which were to meet the needs of British industries and bourgeois elements. The primary objectives for imposing direct colonial rule following the post-1885 scramble for Africa included the need to win strategic advantages over other imperialist nations. Underlying these 'strategic' advantages however is the need to obtain a cheap and constant supply of raw materials, to satisfy British industries and secure a market for the products of the expanding British industries, outlets for investments in areas that would further the supply of raw materials and finally, the opportunity to provide employment for idle British labour.[73] The unequal trade in rubber, cotton, palm-oil, hides and skins, timber, groundnuts, palm-kernel, tin, coal and even petroleum witnessed the underpayment of local producers, the under-development of indigenous entrepreneurs to the advantage of British investors, the provision of amenities to facilitate extraction and transportation and emphasis and investments in sectors which were of interest to the British bourgeoisie. These actions were then rationalised in terms of Nigeria's comparative advantage in the production of raw materials without any effort to explain the principal beneficiary of the exchange or the pattern of distribution of costs and benefits. While the local market was converted into a dumping-ground, education and state propaganda were employed to create the necessary tastes in order to ensure constant profits for British capitalists. The circulation of the new currency was ensured through the imposition of all sorts of taxes which were to be paid in the local currency which in turn could only be acquired through the sale of cash crops or government employment:

> The mechanisms of colonialism in Nigeria centred around the colonial state and economy. They included military conquest and political coercion through British monopoly of the colonial state apparatus, the manipulation of this political power for unequal trade, capital import, cultural penetration through christianity and colonial education, as well as the dissemination of the British 'illusion of the colonial epoch'.[74]

The colonial state managed the Nigerian economy to the advantage (immediate and long-term) of the metropolis, through a variety of direct and indirect means:

> The colonial state and economy were manned largely by the British. This constituted employment opportunities for the British labour force. Political and cultural domination, like the imposition of English language, dress, education, religion and law, were not goals in themselves but means of integrating Nigeria into Britain to facilitate exploitation.[75]

In colonial Nigeria, all monetary transactions were controlled and manipulated in the interest of the metropolis by the West African Currency Board which operated under the tutelage of the Bank of England. Commercial banking, import-export trade and internal business activities were completely dominated by British enterprises such as the United African Company (UAC), John Holt and G.B. Ollivant. The surpluses accumulated by all these concerns, firms and institutions were regularly transferred to Britain to subsidise the accumulative activities of the British bourgeoisie. The pattern of state subsidy, protection and discrimination enjoyed in Nigeria by British investors, not only discouraged local investors but also ensured the dependence of the Nigerian economy on initiatives and developments in the metropolis. The excessive emphasis placed on the production of cash crops, the failure to encourage viable capitalist agriculture and the failure to encourage sectoral linkages, for instance, between industry and agriculture contributed to the disarticulation and underdevelopment of the Nigerian economy. The agricultural sector in particular

> lost any internal stimulus for development. Indeed, the naked exposure of the country's agriculture to the vagaries of the imperialist market may well be one of the most permanent damages of British colonialism to Nigerian development. It has ensured the stagnation, or even degeneration, of Nigerian agriculture to this day.[76]

Since one of the principal goals of British colonisation of Nigeria was to protect the market for the exclusive sale of British goods, the development of industrial capacity would have been antithetical. Colonial policies, in furtherance of the metropolis's exploitative goals, discouraged investments in sectors with significant backwash effects capable of stimulating medium or small local efforts or the spread of investments into sectors which would make the creation of sectoral linkages inevitable. The lack of regard for spatial effects of industrial location distorted the spatial system and the biased policies of locating amenities in the few urban centres ensured that these worked in the interest of British capitalists. The educational system itself contributed to the alienation of the Nigerian through severe miseducation and diseducation thus consolidating the subservient mentality and outlook to the world; the genesis of the unproductive comprador bourgeoisie was thus laid. Thus, by 1921, 40 per cent of those who were educated in southern Nigeria, like the colonial agents, lived in thirteen urban centres with less than 2 per cent of the total population. The colonial state however ensured that this educated class of Nigerians was effectively barred from any meaningful participation in the politics and economy of the country. The domination of the financial sector by British finance capital and the poverty of the local bourgeoisie ensured that credit went only to foreign investors. Barclays Bank and the Bank of British West Africa (now Standard Bank) were the giants in this sector and by 1959, a year before political independence, foreign banks controlled about 70 per cent of total savings in the country. The rate of industrial development was so poor that at independence, manufacturing and processing accounted for only 3.6 per cent of Gross Domestic Product.

And this meagre figure was under full foreign control:

> . . . the loss of local control over the new production process marked
> the beginning of the loss of self-reliance by the Nigerian economy.
> This loss was exacerbated and reinforced by the external orientation
> of the colonial economy. In sharp contrast to their pre-colonial
> production of goods and services for their own use, Nigerian
> participants in the colonial economy produced excessively for the
> world market.[77]

Finally, it is not disputable that British colonialism in Nigeria led to the
establishment of schools, hospitals, bureaucracy, an armed force, roads, a
new language, religion and culture, amongst other things. However, given the
destructive and exploitative goals to which these were put by the colonial
state with the active support of the British bourgeoisie, at best these
developments can be described as either unintended or simply to facilitate
the penetration of the hinterland, the management of contradictions and the
furtherance of exploitation and incorporation. Most of the developments
were introduced with the interests of the metropolis in mind. The limited
industrial efforts, distorted spatial system, alienating education system,
distorted and outward-oriented agricultural system, the establishment of an
unstable peripheral state and contradictions arising from cultural domination,
all furthered Nigeria's peripheralisation and unequal incorporation into an
exploitative world capitalist system. Thus, whether in Nigeria or in any part
of the colonised Third World, colonialism cannot be divorced from
domination, exploitation and unequal incorporation.[78]

References

1. Gerald K. Helleiner, *Peasant Agriculture, Government and Economic
Growth in Nigeria* (Homewood, Ill: R.D. Irwin, 1966), p.3.
2. Aimé Césaire, *Discourse on Colonialism* (New York and London:
Monthly Review Press, 1972), pp.21-22.
3. Sheila Smith, 'Colonialism in Economic Theory: The Experience of
Nigeria', *Journal of Development Studies*, 15, 2, January 1979, p.40.
4. Cited in ibid., pp.40-41.
5. J.E. Flint, 'Economic Change in West Africa in the Nineteenth Century"
in J.F.A. Ajayi and M. Crowder (eds), *History of West Africa, Vol. II*
(London: Longman, 1974), p.387.
6. Smith, op. cit., p.41.
7. M. Caetano, *Os Nativos na Economia Africana* (Limitada Coimbra
Editora, 1954), p.16.
8. See D.K. Fieldhouse, 'Imperialism: A Historiographical Revision',
Economic History Review (2nd Series), 14, 2, 1961.
9. See R. Robinson and J. Gallagher, *Africa and the Victorians: The
Official Mind of Imperialism* (London: Macmillan, 1965).
10. See L.H. Gann and P. Duignan, *Burden of Empire* (New York: Praeger,

1967).

11. See Hla Myint 'The "Classical Theory" of International Trade and the Underdeveloped Countries', *Economic Journal*, 68, June 1958. See also the collection in R.E. Caves and H.G. Johnson (eds), *Readings in International Economics* (Homewood, Ill: R. D. Irwin, 1968); and G.K. Helleiner, op. cit.

12. R.E. Caves, 'Vent for Surplus Models of Trade and Growth' in R.E. Caves and H.G. Johnson (eds), op. cit., p.96.

13. Hla Myint, *The Economies of the Developing Countries* (London: Hutchinson, 1967), p.42.

14. Ibid., p.43.

15. Hla Myint, *Economic Theory and the Underdeveloped Countries* (London: Oxford University Press, 1971), p.129.

16. See Myint, *The Economies of the Developing Countries*, op. cit., pp.40-44.

17. Myint, *Economic Theory*, op. cit., p.142.

18. See R. Szereszewski, *Structural Changes in the Economy of Ghana, 1891-1911* (London, 1965); G.K. Helleiner, *Peasant Agriculture*, op. cit. and 'Typology in Development Theory: The Land Surplus Economy', *Food Research Institute Studies* 6, 2, 1966 and R. Szereszewski and C.M. Elliott, 'Agriculture and Economic Development in Africa: Theory and Experience 1880-1914', in E.L. Jones and S.J. Woolf (eds), *Agrarian Change and Economic Development* (London, 1969).

19. Helleiner, op. cit., p.12.

20. Ibid.

21. Sheila Smith, op. cit., p.54.

22. Ibid., p.55.

23. Ibid.

24. Reginald Green and Ann Seidman, *Unity or Poverty? The Economics of Pan Africanism* (Baltimore: Penguin Books, 1968), pp.31-32.

25. Karl Marx, 'The British Rule in India' in Robert C. Tucker (ed), *The Marx-Engels Reader* (New York: W.W. Norton and Co., 1978), pp.654-655.

26. Karl Marx, 'The Future Results of British Rule in India', in ibid. p.659.

27. Ibid.

28. Ibid., p.660.

29. Aimé Césaire, op. cit., p.21.

30. Marx, 'British Rule in India', op. cit., p.657.

31. Ibid., p.658 (emphasis added).

32. See Paul Baran, *The Political Economy of Growth* (New York: Monthly Review Press, 1957), Maurice Dobb, *Studies in the Development of Capitalism* (London: Routeledge and Sons, 1963 Rev. ed.) and Eric Hobsbawm, *Industry and Empire* (London: Penguin,

33. Marx "Future Results . . .", op. cit., pp. 663-664 (emphasis added).

34. Karl Marx, 'Revolution in China and in Europe' in Umberto Melotti, *Marx and the Third World* (London: Macmillan, 1977), p.117.

35. Ibid.

36. Cited in ibid.

37. See S.B. Sutcliffe, 'Imperialism and Industrialisation in the Third World' in R. Owen and B. Sutcliffe (eds), *Studies in the Theories of Imperialism* (London, 1972), p.180-181; M.B. Brown, 'A Critique of Marxist Theories of Imperialism' in ibid., p.47; Samir Amin, *Accumulation on a World Scale* (New York and London: Monthly Review Press, 1974), pp.39 and 390; Palme Dutt

in his collection *India Today* (Calcutta, 1970), p.87, and Paul Baran, *The Political Economy of Growth*, op. cit., p.143.

38. Cited in Colin Leys, *Underdevelopment in Kenya: The Political Economy of Neocolonialism* (Beverley Hills and Los Angeles: University of California Press, 1975), p.1.

39. Geoffrey Kay, *Development and Underdevelopment: A Marxist Analysis* (London: Macmillan, 1975), pp.98-99. See also his *The Political Economy of Colonialism in Ghana* (London: Cambridge University Press, 1972).

40. Karl Marx, *Capital*, Volume III (Moscow: Progress Publishers, 1966), pp.232-233.

41. Karl Marx, *Capital*, Volume I (Moscow: Progress Publishers, 1978), p.425.

42. Karl Marx, cited in Melotti, op. cit., p.121 (emphasis added).

43. Colin Leys, op. cit., p.7.

44. J.A. Hobson, *Imperialism: A Study* (London: Allen and Unwin, 1939), p.18.

45. Leo Huberman and Paul Sweezy, *Socialism in Cuba* (New York: Monthly Review Press, 1969), p.8.

46. V.I. Lenin, *Imperialism, the Highest Stage of Capitalism* (Moscow: Progress Publishers, 1978), p.62.

47. Ibid., p.64.

48. Césaire, op. cit., pp.10-11.

49. Ibid., p.11.

50. F. Soremekun, 'Angola's Foreign Policy', Seminar Paper, History Department, University of Ife, Ile-Ife, Nigeria, 1981/82 Session, p.14.

51. Toyin Falola, 'Colonialism and Exploitation: The Case of Portugal in Africa', *Lusophone Areas Studies Journal*, 1, 1, January 1983, p.60.

52. See Patrick Manning, 'Analysing the Costs and Benefits of Colonialism', *African Economic History Review*, 1, 2, Fall 1974, pp.15-22.

53. Geoffrey Kay, *Development and Underdevelopment*, op. cit., p.x.

54. Ibid., p.105.

55. E.A. Brett, *Colonialism and Underdevelopment in East Africa* (London: Heinemann Press, 1974), p.18.

56. Aguibon Yansane. 'Decolonization, Dependency and Development in Africa: The Theory Revisited' in A.Y. Yansane (ed), *Decolonization and Dependency – Problems of Development in African Societies* (Westport: Greenwood Press, 1980), p.8.

57. Ibid., p.9.

58. Césaire, op. cit. p.

59. Jean-Paul Sartre, 'Preface' to Frantz Fanon, *The Wretched of the Earth* (New York: Grove Press, 1978), p.7.

60. Frantz Fanon, op. cit. (Penguin 1967 Edition), pp.143-144.

61. Kwame Nkrumah, *Towards Colonial Freedom: Africa in the Struggle Against World Imperialism* (London: Panaf, 1979), p.xvi.

62. Ibid., p.xvii.

63. Frantz Fanon, op. cit., pp.149-150.

64. Ibid.

65. Walter Rodney, *How Europe Underdeveloped Africa* (Washington D.C.: Howard University Press, 1974), p.205.

66. Ibid.

67. Ibid., p.213.

68. Ibid., p.215.

69. Ibid., pp.215-16 (emphasis added). Rodney also argues that 'it is fairly obvious that capitalists do not set out to create other capitalists, who would be rivals. On the contrary, the tendency of capitalism in Europe from the beginning was one of competition, elimination, and monopoly. Therefore, when the stage was reached, the metropolitan capitalists had no intention of allowing rivals to arise in the dependencies. However, in spite of what the metropoles wanted, some local capitalist did emerge in Asia and Latin America. *Africa is a significant exception in the sense that compared with other colonized peoples, far fewer Africans had access even to the middle ranges of the bourgeoisie'* (p.216 emphasis added).

70. Kwame Nkrumah, op. cit., p.10.

71. Walter Rodney, op. cit., pp.228-229.

72. See for instance Nnamdi Azikiwe, 'Re-Orientation of Nigerian Ideologies', *Weekly Star*, 2, January 1977, pp.12-13.

73. For detailed discussions see W. Smith, *Slaves and Palm Oil, Economic Transition and Politics on the Western Slave Coast, 1870-94* (Chicago: Chicago University Press, 1968); K.O. Dike, *Trade and Politics in the Niger Delta, 1830-85* (Oxford: Clarendon Press, 1956); Michael Crowder, *The Story of Nigeria* (London: Allen and Unwin, 1962); and Walter Rodney, *West Africa and the Atlantic Slave Trade* (Nairobi: East African Publishing House, 1967).

74. Bade Onimode, 'Imperialism and Nigerian Development' in O. Nnoli, *Path to Nigerian Development* (Dakar: Codesria, 1981), p.81.

75. Ibid.

76. Ibid., pp.82-83.

77. O. Nnoli, 'A Short History of Nigerian Underdevelopment' in *Path to Nigerian Development*, op. cit., p.105.

78. See the Collection in R.C. Edwards et al (eds), *The Capitalist System* (Engelwood Cliffs: N.J. Prentice-Hall, 1972); O. Nnoli (ed), *Path to Nigerian Development*, op. cit.; Issa G. Shivji, *Class Struggles in Tanzania* (Dar es Salaam: Tanzania Publishing House, 1976); Amilcar Cabral, *The Struggle in Guinea* (Cambridge, Mass: Africa Research Group Reprint, n.d.); R.O. Ekundare, *An Economic History of Nigeria* (London: Methuen and Co, 1973), and A. Chinwezu, *The West and the Rest of Us: White Predators, Black Slavers, and the African Elite* (New York: Random House, 1975).

2. Patterns of Pre-colonial Exploitation

L. I. Izuakor

Introduction

For the sake of convenience of handling, we divide the study into two broad phases, namely, the 'coastal frontier' phase (c.1472–1830) and the 'hinterland frontier' phase (1830–1900).

The first phase was characterised mainly by the slave trade in which the coastal area formed the meeting point between the European slave dealers and their Nigerian counterparts. During the period the sailing ships remained the basic mode of transportation between Europe and Nigeria on the one hand and between Europe and America on the other.

The hinterland frontier phase witnessed the introduction of the steamship in Nigerian waters. This facilitated British penetration into the hinterland. During the period palm produce, not slaves, formed the major item of export trade. British trading firms started the process of establishing trading stations in the hinterland. This is not to suggest that the coastal areas became irrelevant to Anglo-Nigerian trade because of the push to the hinterland frontier. On the contrary, they maintained their pre-eminent position in the trade. This was facilitated by their convenient location on the seashore in an age when the absence of the railway and good roads made internal communication within the country extremely difficult.

British precolonial exploitation was the work of individual merchants, trading firms and chartered companies. The English ship captains and their crew, debased by the iniquitous traffic in human cargoes, were scarcely esteemed higher than degenerates even by their own countrymen. Despising them for their streak of cruelty and brutality, Alan Burns referred to them as 'ruffians of the worst kind'.[1] Agreeing with him, Arthur Norton Cook described their conduct as 'frequently outrageous'.[2] An eyewitness revealed that one Capt. Williams of the *Little Pearl* routinely 'amused himself by making the black Portuguese cook swallow live cockroaches . . .'[3]

It must be observed, however, that the supercargoes could ill-afford to despise or antagonise the indigenous middlemen in the Euro-Nigerian trade. Frequently, the chiefs, who had arrogated to themselves the role of middlemen, were greeted by the ship captains with a gun salute.

The European merchants did not outclass their Nigerian counterparts in astuteness, for, having discovered the cunning propensity of the European traders to the coast, the latter resorted to the same sharp practices introduced by the European traders. Describing the game of hide-and-seek played by the parties in which the Nigerian middlemen appeared to be winning in the 1860s, W.W. Reade notes that in Bonny

> . . . the black traders [were] now almost too much for the white ones in these matters of low cunning which enter so largely into the commerce . . .[4]

But neither side would stretch their 'dirty tricks' too far for fear of ruining their lucrative business.

The early precolonial economic exploitation of Nigeria was concentrated on the coastal areas of the country. The reasons for this are not far to seek. Firstly, by the middle of the fifteenth century, when the Portuguese made a debut on the Nigerian coast, the hinterland was to them *terra incognita* and remained largely so until the first half of the nineteenth century when Richard and John Lander succeeded in tracing the course of the Niger and revealed to the British merchants the opportunities for trade in the hinterland. Thereafter emphasis was placed on the exploitation of the resources of the hinterland.

Secondly, the ocean-sailing vessels used by the English traders were not adapted for use in the labyrinthine creeks and rivulets in the hinterland. They could, however, manage to penetrate a short distance from the coast. Thus, the English traders were content to anchor their vessels in the coastal harbours, and the direct exploitation of the hinterland awaited the improvement of the steam engine.

Thirdly, any tantalising expectation of penetrating into the hinterland was nullified, among other reasons, by the prevailing notion amongst the Europeans that the hinterland was a 'white man's grave', for even along the coast the 'noxious vapours', presumably issuing from the marshes, were believed to cause sickness and death among the Europeans.

Finally, the coastal middlemen, who stood to lose their brokerage if the Europeans penetrated into the hinterland to buy commodities at their source of supply, understandably blocked attempts by the Europeans to by-pass them. Nonetheless, they cooperated with the European traders and supplied them with the commodities they demanded, especially slaves. In 1699, for instance, an eyewitness account notes that in Bonny:

> As soon as the blacks could see our ship off at sea, they immediately went up the river to buy slaves. . .[5]

Perhaps what the excited European narrator did not understand was that the apparent haste of the middlemen was a tactical move to prevent the merchants from venturing into the hinterland from where they could threaten their position and influence. By the middle of the nineteenth century, the middlemen were still suspicious of the intentions of the Europeans. As one One Okekuno, an Egba chief told Richard Burton, all Europeans were 'liars and rascals'.[6] In order to protect their authority and influence against foreign encroachment, the middlemen were prepared to obstruct European penetration into the hinterland. In all, there would appear to be little or no compulsive incentive for the English traders to venture beyond the coastlands. In the nineteenth century, however, the British humanitarian, missionary, philanthropic and commercial organisations decided to venture inland, smashing the then real and imagined obstacles in their way.

Although the coastal areas remained the centre of British commercial exploitation during the period, the commodities sold to the merchants were produced in the hinterland. As S.J.S. Cookey has pointed out, 'the Delta people . . . had little to offer the European vessels that visited the area.'[7]

Most of the slaves were sent down to the coast from Igboland and Yoruba-land in the hinterland. Some were brought down from Igalaland through the River Niger. In fact, before the dominance of the slave trade, the peoples of the Niger delta had long been engaged in long-distance trade with the hinterland. The Atlantic slave trade merely intensified the process. The coast, therefore, served mainly as the entrepôt for siphoning abroad the resources of the hinterland and for the distribution of European merchandise.

Initially, the European traders bought ivory, pepper, palm-oil and dye. Later, the dearth of labour in the silver mines, tobacco, cotton and sugar plantations in the New World changed the character of the trade. Human cargoes replaced forest products as the mainstay of the trans-Atlantic trade. During the nineteenth century, however, sylvan products once again became the mainstay of the Anglo-Nigerian trade.

It remains for us, at this juncture, to define the operative word 'exploitation', which has both benevolent and baneful connotations. Contextually, it is used to refer to the British exploitation of the human and material resources of Nigeria for selfish ends. This precluded any deliberate effort to harness these resources for the economic improvement of the country; rather, it involved the spiriting away of these resources to foreign lands, especially Britain, for the enhancement of that country's economic performance. Thus, while millions of the indigenous people were carted away to produce wealth for their enslavers, the Nigerian peoples received in exchange perishable consumer goods, some of which impaired local production and craftsmanship.

Origins

The Portuguese pioneered a daring maritime contact with the coast of West Africa in the fifteenth century. However, it was the British, more than the Portuguese, who for more than four centuries, fully exploited this new relationship. Equipped with what then was superior maritime technology, supported by the crown, and anxious to break the stifling monopoly by the Arab middlemen over the European commerce with the Orient, the Portuguese sent out explorers in the 1440s in search of a new sea route to the East.

It was during one of the voyages of exploration that a Portuguese sailor named Ruy de Sequeira arrived in Benin in 1472. Thirteen years later, another Portuguese, John Affonso d'Aveiro sailed to the Benin river where he purchased some pepper, blue cloths and ivory which he took back to Lisbon. Oba Ozolua of Benin, who 'showed readiness to permit [trade]'[8] with the Europeans, allowed the Portuguese to establish a factory at the port of Ughoton (Gwato). Thus was established a long period of regular maritime contact between Europe and parts of what later came to be known as Nigeria.

The Portuguese claim to a monopoly of trade and dominion in the eastern hemisphere was given a legal status by a treaty signed on 7 June 1494 at Tordesillas, demarcating Portuguese and Spanish spheres of control. The dividing line ran north and south 370 leagues to the west of the Cape Verde Islands. The lands to the west of the line were given to Spain and those to the east to Portugal. The Papal Bull (as the treaty was called) notwithstanding, interlopers from other nations, notably France and England, who regarded Portuguese monopoly as a fiction, engaged in privateering in the Bights of Benin and Biafra where Portugal was supposed to be in control. The King of Portugal protested to King Edward VI of England, but the protests were ignored by the English interlopers. However, in 1556, Queen Mary issued an order banning her subjects from interfering in the Guinea, Benin and Mina areas. Very little attempt was made to enforce the ban. Consequently, in 1561, the Portuguese dispatched an official to England to protest against the English 'illegal' trade to the Guinea. The occasion for this round of protests was the rumour that English merchants were 'rigging and preparing their ships . . .'[9] for a commercial venture to Guinea. The Portuguese knew they were up against the wall in the matter of restricting English activities to the Guinea, for Queen Elizabeth's only action was to instruct that any expeditions to Guinea be reported in advance to the Lord High Admiral.

In 1553, a group of English merchants challenged Portuguese claim to monopoly on the coast of Guinea.[10] That year they sent out two ships, the *Primrose* and the *Lion*, to the Benin river, under the command of Capt. Thomas Wyndham. As if to complete their effrontery, the English merchants secured the services of a Portuguese ship captain, Antonio Anes Pinteado, to pilot the ships to the Benin river. Pinteado, described as 'wise, discreet and sober', took a grave risk, for sometimes the interlopers ran a gauntlet against Portuguese cruisers. However, the interlopers were encouraged by the fact that the long West African coastline of undefended creeks and rivers could hardly be policed effectively by the Portuguese. At any event, the irresistible lure of expected profits from a successful venture buoyed the resolve of Pinteado and his sponsors.

Viewed from the commercial perspective, Wyndham's venture was a huge success, for within thirty days they had collected 80 tons of pepper and some quantity of gold and ivory.[11] But from the standpoint of humanism, the huge profits less than compensated for the high mortality rate of the crews. Out of 140 men who set out for Benin only 40 returned to Plymouth. Pinteado, Wyndham and 98 others died of sickness, probably malaria. That notwithstanding, Wyndham's mission inaugurated four centuries of British economic exploitation of Nigeria.

The Wyndham commercial venture so excited English merchants that the following year another fleet was fitted and sent to the Guinea under the command of John Lok. The adventurers set out in three ships, namely, the *Trinity, John Evangelist*, and the *Bartholomew*. The venture was a distinct success. By a stroke of luck only twenty-four members of the crew were reported dead, and the sponsors coolly garnered a staggering 1,000% profit[12] from the sale of gold, ivory and 'certaine blacke slaves where of some were tall and strong men. . . '.[13]

It is not clear why there appears to have been a decrease in the English activity on the coast between 1554 and 1588, in which year Queen Elizabeth granted a patent to merchants of London and Devonshire for trade on the northern Guinea coast for ten years. However, it could be cautiously surmised that the burgeoning slave trade and greater Portuguese surveillance accounted for the seeming hiatus. John Lok reported to his sponsors that four 'great' Spanish ships, including one of 700 tons, were laying ambush on the coast. Furthermore, the Spanish silver and gold mines in the New World were in dire need of cheap labour to extract the precious metals. At the instigation of Bartolome de Las Casas, bishop of Chiapa in Mexico, Spain sought African labour to work the mines. The slave trade was certainly more profitable than the trade in forest products. Consequently, in 1562, Sir John Hawkins secured the backing of a syndicate of London merchants for a commercial venture to West Africa. In the vicinity of present-day Sierra Leone, he seized roughly 400 Africans 'partly by force and partly by other means'. An eyewitness account illustrates the savagery of Hawkins and his fellow slavers:

> In this island [Sherbro?] we stayed certain daies, going every day on shore to take the Inhabitants, with burning and spoiling their townes. . .[14]

The captured Africans were carted away to Haiti where they yielded a handsome profit. It is a measure of Hawkins' success that he returned to Guinea in 1564 and 1567. Soon, English merchants concentrated on the slave trade, especially as the English commercialisation of parts of the West Indies had intensified the demand for slaves. As the slaves could be obtained with greater facility in the region of Upper Guinea, there was no incentive for the English merchants to step on Portuguese toes by hacking their way into the Kingdom of Benin.

Although the slave trade exerted a greater pull on the European merchants in general than did pepper or ivory, James Welsh, an English merchant captain, sailed up the Benin river in 1588. There he bought pepper, ivory, palm oil and blue cloth. He made such a handsome profit from the venture that he returned to Benin two years later and took back to England 589 sacks of pepper, 150 elephant tusks, and 32 barrels of palm oil.[15]

At this point it is worth mentioning that Welsh's visit to the Benin river coincided with the defeat of the apparently invincible Spanish Armada by the

English navy. Encouraged by the spectacular feat of the English seamen, and imbued with a feeling of naval superiority over the most powerful sea power of the age, English merchants began to engage more forcefully in the slave trade. Indeed, by the middle of the seventeenth century, English slaving activities had been organised on a more solid and regular basis. The Portuguese could no longer pretend to be in control of the trade along the coast of Guinea as they had lost out to the more aggressive Dutch competitors. In 1638, for instance, the Dutch captured the strategic commercial centre of Sao Jorge da Mina. In 1642 Axim also fell to them.

On their part, the English slavers received royal support which boosted their activities. In 1564, when John Hawkins returned to the coast of Guinea, four of the nine vessels involved in the slaving voyage belonged to Queen Elizabeth. For their protection, the vessels were fitted with bronze cannon as well as corslets, cuirasses, pikes, bows and arrows — all from the Tower of London. The sailors were alleged to have been engaged by 'order and permission of the queen'.[16]

Apart from direct involvement in the slave trade, the crown granted royal charters to joint-stock companies for the purpose of trading in designated areas. Thus, in 1618, James I granted a charter to the Company of Adventurers of London trading into Parts of Africa. Again, in 1631, Charles I granted the right to another group of English merchants trading to 'Guinea, Binney [Benin] and Angola'. Later, in 1663, an English company, formed in 1660, was granted a royal charter as The Company of Royal Adventurers of England Trading to Africa. The Royal Company was authorised to supply 3,000 slaves annually to the English possessions in the West Indies. In their petition for a charter, the directors of the company argued succinctly that slave labour was indispensable to the West Indian plantation economy. According to them,

> ... the trade of Africa is so necessary to England that the very being of the Plantations depends upon the supply of negro servants . . .[17]

Among the 213 shareholders of the company were the King himself, the Duke of York, Lord Ashley, and the Earl of Bath.

As Portuguese influence declined on the coast of Guinea, that of the Dutch and the English waxed. The Dutch, having freed themselves from the excruciating Spanish control and subordination, and imbued with the Calvinist philosophy of the 'elect' of God, gave expression to their liberation in aggressive commercial and maritime competition with the rest of Europe. As a consequence, there developed a fierce competition between the Dutch and English merchants for the control of the Guinea trade. In time, the Dutch were forced to abandon their commercial interests on the Guinea coast, leaving the English in effective control. Although the English chartered companies enjoyed monopoly rights over the coastal trade, interlopers, as always, nibbled at the profitable slave trade.

The participation of English merchants in the coastal slave trade was strengthened by the treaty of Utrecht (1713) which terminated the War of Spanish Succession (1700-1713). Exhausted by the protracted war, Spain

conceded to England, through the *Asiento*, the right to supply 4,800 slaves
annually to the Spanish colonies in America. The insistence of the English
on the *Asiento*, which had nothing to do with the royal succession in Spain,
underscores the overwhelming importance of the slave trade in the trans-
Atlantic commerce. English trading companies, individual merchants, and
chartered companies swarmed the Niger delta area in quest of human cargoes.
There they set up factories and established regular contact with the indigenous
middlemen for the supply of slaves and victuals, and for the distribution of
European goods. As the demand for slaves increased tremendously, the
demand for forest products declined correspondingly.

The Coastal Frontier, c.1472–1830

When the Portuguese first established commercial contact with the Kingdom
of Benin, they expected to harvest a rich mine of gold in the region. But they
found instead of gold some pepper and ivory, though not in such quantities
as they later found in India. As late as 1672, the Royal African Company
still hoped to discover the 'Golden Mines' supposedly existing on the Guinea
coast. In the end, the expectation remained as elusive as ever.

However, by 1562, when Sir John Hawkins appeared on the Guinea coast,
interest had shifted to the slave trade. From that time onwards English
merchants trading to the Nigerian coast paid more attention to the slave trade
and less to trade in other forest products as a result of the insatiable demand
for cheap labour in the Americas. European criminals, political offenders,
convicts and indentured labourers transported across the Atlantic to the New
World were incapable of working effectively the tobacco and sugar plantations.
Quite often, exhausted by tropical diseases for which they had minimal
resistance, they sickened and died. Some Native Americans who were captured
and forced to work the land by the plantation owners made good their escape
where the terrain was familiar to them.

Meanwhile, the search for cheap labour continued. The answer was found
in the forcible transportation of Africans to the New World. The unfortunate
Africans, who were marooned in a foreign land, could not escape to their
homeland and were forced to toil in the plantations accumulating wealth for
the plantation owners.

For the English slave traders the triangular trade was tedious and hazardous.
Yet the profits accruing from a successful venture more than compensated
for the privations of the supercargoes and the ship's crew.

Organising the Slave Trade

Unlike the Portuguese, the English slave merchants did not consider it
necessary to build fortresses on the delta coast; rather, they transacted their
business with the coastal middlemen aboard their ships. Usually, the middle-
men-cum-chiefs were invited by the English supercargoes to their ships for
the purpose of 'breaking trade' and receiving custom duty known as 'comey'.[18]

The chiefs were received with fanfare and due ceremony which included, among other things, a royal gun salute and an invitation to sumptuous dinner. Thereafter the chiefs' officials and other notables were free to do business with the supercargoes.

Indeed, the supercargoes went out of their way to win and retain the friendship of the coastal chiefs. One means by which this was achieved was through giving presents to the chiefs and higher officials. In 1703, for example, an assortment of presents given to the king of Bonny included a hat, a fire-lock, and nine bunches of beads.[19] Besides the presents, the supercargoes habitually gave out goods on 'trust' or credit to the chiefs and their principals in order to facilitate their trade with the hinterland and to keep their friend-ship afloat.

In exchange for the European merchanise the middlemen supplied the supercargoes with victuals, notably, yams, water, wood, rice, fowls and vegetables; the major trade goods being slaves, ivory and palm produce. After 1830, palm-oil became the dominant Nigerian export as the demand for slaves declined. But in the seventeenth and eighteenth centuries, slaves remained the premier Nigerian export. In 1771 alone, 63 English ships shipped 23,301 Nigerians from the Bight of Benin to the West Indies. It is estimated that of the 74,000 slaves shipped annually to the Americas, the English merchants were responsible for 38,000 of them. Out of this number 14,000 came from Bonny and New Calabar.[20]

The vast majority of the slaves supplied to the supercargoes came, not from the coast, but from the hinterland, mainly Igboland and Yorubaland. There they were obtained in a variety of ways. One such method, which would also appear to be the major source of supply, was through kidnapping. Writing in 1789, Olaudah Equiano, tells us that he was a kidnap victim.[21] It may never be known how many people were captured in that way. But the fact that tall watchtowers were erected at strategic points in Igbo villages and children huddled there for safety when the adults were away from home, is indicative of the pervasive nature of organised kidnap parties for the procurement of slaves.

Of course, it should not be understood that the watchtowers were built solely for the protection of children against kidnappers: they were also vantage positions for scanning the horizon for signs of any enemy movements.

Perhaps more people were enslaved through kidnapping than has been imagined. The practice whereby itinerant traders travelled in large troupes comprising 80-120 men would seem to suggest that they sought to pre-empt kidnappers, even though women and children were the main targets of kidnappers. It is not being suggested that the *raison d'etre* of the large troupes was the fear of kidnappers, for, among other things, companionship afforded by the troupes, protection of the traders against bandits and wild animals are factors which cannot be easily glossed over.

Most of the kidnap victims and other captives were sold either in the open slave markets such as the Agbagwu market in Ozuakoli or were disposed of surreptitiously in the private compounds of the slave dealers.

The latter practice was intensified after the slave trade had been illegalised by an act of the British parliament. As A.E. Afigbo has noted, the selling of slaves in parts of Igboland was 'a secret and often nocturnal [transaction] in which the victim was hurried out of his familiar environment under cover of darkness.'[22] The slaves were ultimately taken down to the coastal frontier and thence to the American plantations. A few of them were shipped to Europe where they served as domestic slaves.

The ingenious Aro people, who were known to the coastal and hinterland traders as purveyors of slaves, established settlements in non-Aro villages in Igboland largely to keep a tight rein on the hinterland trade. In addition, and for the same reason, they deviously combined the oracular functions of their revered and feared deity, *Ibini Ukpabi*,[23] with their commercial enterprise. In short, the deity was commercialised. It became a source of slave supply. Some of the victims of *Ibini Ukpabi*, supposedly 'eaten' by it, were actually whisked off to the coast through the Cross River and eventually sold as slaves.

Whenever the Aro considered it advantageous, they entered into a symbiotic arrangement with Abam and Ada warriors who fought wars in which neither side had any direct stake. As widely travelled and privileged *umu Chukwu* (God's children), the Aro negotiated with one or more warring communities to secure for them the services of mercenaries. The mercenaries were apparently too willing to oblige, for one of the conditions of manhood in their respective communities was a demonstration of prowess in battles, the proof of which was human heads brought back home from the field of battle. Having attained their goal, the Abam and Ada warriors turned over some of the victims of the inter-group wars to their mentors, the Aro, who in turn sold them as slaves.

As in Igboland, so it was in Yorubaland. Slaves who were sold to the English traders in Lagos and Badagry were generally kidnap victims, war captives, delinquents and criminals. During the nineteenth century, the incessant Yoruba civil wars became a veritable source of slaves.

During the period under review, the coastal frontier served the British very well as an artery for the economic exploitation of the hinterland. The coastal middlemen prospered economically and politically, for with their newly acquired wealth, they were enabled to consolidate their political position.

It is true that the coastal states prospered commercially, but this was not accompanied by real economic development. It suited the British to sell only consumer goods, some of which competed with local products such as textiles and salt, but not advanced technology which would improve local production. Indeed, some farsighted coastal chiefs long wrestled with this problem and made unsuccessful moves to acquire the technology necessary for real economic development. In 1842, for example, King Eyamba of Calabar wanted from the British merchants 'something for make work and trade . . . some seed for cotton and coffee . . . and some man [to] come teach way for do it'.[24] It is undeniable that the acquisition of advanced technology by Nigerians would certainly undermine British ambition in the country because it would revolutionise production techniques and challenge the very basis for British commercial exploitation. It is not surprising, therefore, that such aspirations were discouraged.

What was worse for the country, it was the cream of the population — the able-bodied capable of economic activity — that were uprooted from their socio-economic milieu. The decrepit, the infirm and the very old were left to manage as best they could. Thus, when 'indirect' influence gave way to 'effective' occupation it was relatively easy for scores of British soldiers armed with Maxim guns to overcome Nigerian polities.

The Hinterland Frontier, 1830–1900

It is possible to discern two dinstinct changes in the British pattern of exploitation of Nigeria during the period 1830-1900. The first was the shift from the slave — to 'legitimate' trade. This was facilitated greatly by the suppression of the slave trade and slavery throughout the British empire. The second change concerned the gradual shift of the 'frontier of opportunity' from the coast to the hinterland. The successful penetration of the hinterland by the British was facilitated by the invention of the steamship and by the use of quinine as an antidote to malaria fever. As aptly summed up by Dorothy Wellesley, Sir George Goldie's biographer, 'access to the interior of Africa was not known to Europe till the steam engine was ready to exploit it'.[25]

In 1807, an Act of the British parliament prohibited the slave trade to British nationals. In 1833, another Act went further to abolish slavery throughout the British empire. It would seem ironical that the British, who were the greatest slave traders on the Nigerian coast, were the leading exponents of its abolition. Rationalising the apparent contradiction, Reginald Coupland contends that the abolitionists were motivated by altruism to spearhead the campaign.[26] The assertion has been questioned by some scholars[27] who have suggested that economic rather than humanitarian factors screwed the coffin of slavery and the slave trade. True, it is doubtful that the appeal of the humanitarians to the British sense of morality would have moved the commercial class but for the economic imperatives resulting from, among other factors, the overproduction of sugar in the West Indies by means of slave labour, and the recognition that slave labour was antagonistic to industrial capitalism. In other words, the abolitionists succeeded because, to perceptive minds, having outlived its usefulness, slave labour had committed economic suicide. By 1805, for instance, only 2 per cent of British export tonnage was employed in the slave trade,[28] as the shippers made more profit from transporting sugar and cotton than slaves. In all, the humanitarians were able to win the support of those whose business interests would be served best, not by the slave trade, but by 'legitimate' trade.

British economic interests dictated that an alternative to the slave trade must be found. The industrial revolution, which brought about the use of machines and a rapid growth and expansion of industries, accelerated the demand for a wide range of tropical products, notably, cotton, palm-oil and groundnuts — all of which could not be produced in the West Indies. In addition, the mass-produced goods had to be sold. Africa had the potential for a large market. Hence, the industrialists were not averse to illegalising the slave trade.

In their search for 'legitimate' trade in Nigeria, the British merchants gradually gave up the slave trade in favour of trade in palm produce and other primary products. It must be emphasised that the merchants never completely abandoned palm-oil during the heyday of the slave trade. As David Northrup has pointed out, there was no incompatibility of the slave and palm-oil trades.[29] Indeed, during the mid-1790s, the export of palm-oil from the Bight of Biafra to Britain averaged 150 tons annually.[30] This is understandable because in spite of the pre-eminence of the slave trade the new machines of industrial Britain needed to be lubricated and, in the absence of petroleum products, palm-oil came in handily as a lubricant, and palm-trees grew luxuriantly in Nigeria. But even in the 1830s, when the slave trade had long been proscribed, as soon as a slave trader arrived in the Bight of Biafra, we are told, the trade in palm-oil took the back stage until the slave merchant had been supplied.[31]

Unlike the slaves who were self-transporting, bulky palm-oil needed to be conveyed from the source to the river ports and thence to the seaport. Although the Cross River and the Niger offered a reliable means of internal communication, the hinterland traders were scarcely equipped to handle effectively the transportation of palm produce which had to be conveyed by means of head porterage from the inland source to the river depot. In order to facilitate the flow of palm produce and by-pass the coastal middlemen, British merchants more than ever before sought to locate trading stations in the hinterland.

When the British firms eventually penetrated into the hinterland, they erected permanent trading stations, including 'cask houses' for the storage of palm-oil. Usually, the stations were located on a 'beach' for access to the river. Moreover, unlike what obtained during the slave trade, resident British personnel were stationed in the trading posts. In 1862, for example, there were roughly 278 Europeans in New Calabar, 278 in Bonny, and 300 in Old Calabar.[32]

Changes which were taking place in the eastern delta were also occuring slowly in the Lagos area. In 1842, a British naval officer with the British Anti-slaving Squadron at Bonny and Calabar reported gleefully that in the Bight of Biafra the slave trade had been 'done up these three years; it is not carried on at all'.[33] This was due partly to the activities of the British Squadron and partly to the orderly transition from the slave trade to 'legitimate' trade. However, internal slavery continued in spite of its abolition.

In contrast to the Niger delta now intensely engaged in the palm-oil trade, Lagos was reported to be actively involved in the slave trade as late as 1859.[34]

Table 2.1:
Selected Exports From Lagos, 1857.

Commodity	Quantity Exported
Palm Oil	4,942 tons
Native Cloths	50,000 tons
Ivory	24,118 lbs.
Cotton	114,848 lbs.

Source: P.A. Talbot, *The Peoples of Southern Nigeria*, vol. 1 (London: Frank Cass, 1926), p.109.

By the beginning of the second half of the nineteenth century the Lagos area was beginning to adjust to the new commercial order. The Niger delta embraced the changes with greater assiduity. Whereas in 1857 Lagos exported about 5,000 tons of palm-oil, the River Bonny area alone exported more than double the volume of exports from the Bight of Benin as a whole.[35] The reason would not seem to lie solely in the existence of more palm trees in the hinterland of the Bight of Biafra: perhaps it had to do also with the persistence of the slave trade in Lagos and Badagry and the pervasive Yoruba civil wars.

A major development in the British pattern of exploitation during this period was the opening up of another frontier of opportunity — the hinterland frontier — to British merchants. After 1797, when Mungo Park unsuccessfully made the last attempt to trace the course of the Niger, several other expeditioners were despatched to unravel what to the British was the 'mystery of the Niger'. After John and Richard Lander had solved the riddle in 1830, vigorous attempts were made to put their achievement to practical use. The seemingly limitless opportunities for trade with the hinterland revealed by the Landers aroused the interest of English mercantile firms, causing emphasis to be placed on the exploitation of the resources of the hinterland. The British government, with the support of the merchant firms, sent out several expeditions to the Niger in 1832, 1841, 1854 and 1857, the moving spirit of the ventures being Macgregor Laird, a Liverpool merchant whose primary aim was

> . . . to establish a Commercial Intercourse with Central Africa via the Niger, [and] open new fields of enterprise to the Mercantile world. . .[36]

Laird was anxious to establish trading stations in the hinterland to be serviced by regular steamers. It was hoped that, unlike the vulnerable sailing ships, the wonder steamers would be in a position to 'prevent the Delta tribes from stopping the passage of [British merchants] above them. . . .'[37] The ambition of the firms was realised to a very great extent, for in spite of sporadic attacks on the steamers by the riverain communities on the Niger, by 1869, the British merchants had succeeded in establishing a toehold in the upper part of the Niger and on the Benue, too, although exploitation on a regular basis started in 1874 when the West African Company succeeded in buying ivory at Bomasha on the Benue.

Modalities of Exploitation

Abortive Permanent Settlement

The first most ambitious attempt by the British to exploit the resources of the hinterland directly rather than through the coastal middlemen was made in 1841, involving the establishment of a permanent British settlement at Lokoja. The expedition was a large one, comprising three steamers. In the expedition were, among others, four commissioners to negotiate treaties, and scientists to investigate the vegetation, soil, animals and climate. There were also commercial agents and agents of the Agricultural Society. A model cotton plantation was planned. The settlement, it was hoped, would stimulate the demand for British goods which would be exchanged for local produce.

The settlement actually made a start but high mortality among the settlers (48 died within two months) caused the venture to be abandoned. Thus, malaria, which had given Nigeria the unenviable reputation among the Europeans of being a 'white man's grave', saved the country the painful experience of Southern Rhodesia (now Zimbabwe), Angola, Algeria and South Africa, among others, where European settlement, with its obvious implications for the indigenous people, was foisted on the African population.

Trading Companies

The systematic exploitation of Nigeria was the work of trading firms. A Manchester firm, the West African Company, was among the earliest British firms to establish a trading post in the hinterland. It opened a station at Lokoja in 1865, under the supervision of William McCoskry (better known to Lagosians as Apongbon). In 1876, two companies, the Central African Company (London), and Messrs Alexander Miller Brothers and Co. (Glasgow), commenced commercial activities on the Benue. To these must be added James Pinnock and Co. (Liverpool) which had been operating in the Niger delta and its valley.

In addition, several little known companies had begun to follow the 'frontier of opportunity' into the hinterland.

In general, the companies established trading stations all along the banks of the Niger and Benue. They engaged in competition and rivalry for the control of the trade. This moved Consul Hopkins to observe in 1878 that

> It is almost impossible to describe the constant bickerings between these rival factories . . . In one instance as many as five companies established trading posts in one town on the Niger.[38]

Before too long the activities of the companies would be streamlined through the sagacity of an individual merchant. Meanwhile, posts were established at Akassa, Abo, Ndoni, Osomari, Onitsha, Lokoja, Egga and other riverain communities.

The British government actively encouraged the commercial firms in their exploitation of the country. In 1872, the Foreign Office transferred the consulate from Fernando Po to Calabar in response to the widening frontier of exploitation which the location of the consulate offshore was ill-suited to handle.

Although the trading firms moved into the hinterland rather late, their business turnover there was quite impressive, giving hope for higher expectations in the future. In 1878, the value of exports through the Niger to Britain was estimated to be £309,200.[39] The value is spectacular when it is remembered that seven years earlier, the total exports from the hinterland were valued at £55,000. More importantly, new crops from the savanna belt were added to the palm produce and ivory, indicating the widening orbit of the hinterland frontier.

The numerous trading firms both in the hinterland and along the coast competed aggressively with one another for a greater share of the trade. Nonetheless, they made enough profits to be able to stay in business. But Sir George Taubman Goldie, an astute businessman and empire-builder, who preferred monopoly to free trade, amalgamated the competing firms (1879) under the name of the United African Company.[40] In 1882, its name was changed to the National African Company. With increased capital[41] and personnel, the company was enabled to enlarge and extend British exploitation on the Niger and Benue by refurbishing the existing facilities in the old trading posts and establishing new ones, too. The Company rapidly bought out the two French firms in the area, namely, Compagnie du Sénégal et de la Côte Occidentale d'Afrique, and the Compagnie Française de l'Afrique Équatoriale. Whereupon the road was clear for a complete British monopoly in the hinterland. Goldie got what he wanted, and within a short period of time he set up hundreds of trading stations and bullied the local rulers into signing spurious treaties which granted the National African Company monopoly rights over trade. With the gunboats at the ready to enforce the terms of the various treaties and cow the uncooperative local rulers into submission, Goldie soon established a commercial fief. In 1886, the company was granted a royal charter and its name was changed to the Royal Niger Company. Charged with administrative functions also, Goldie controlled not only a commercial empire but a political one too.

A look at the powers of the Royal Niger Company will show the comprehensiveness of its rights to exploit the resources of Nigeria. It was empowered to act as 'merchants, carriers, or in any other capacity'. Its powers further included the right to

> purchase, or otherwise acquire, open and work mines, forests, quarries, fisheries, and manufactories; and to stock, cultivate and improve any of the lands of the Company, erect buildings thereon, and sell the produce thereof.[42]

The Company was further authorised to exercise sovereign rights over the polities acquired through treaties. Thus, British exploitation of Nigeria through private companies received the blessing of the Foreign Office.

Goldie applied himself to his responsibilities zealously and very soon he enlarged the domain of the company to include Yola, Adamawa, Borgu, Sokoto and Gwandu. By 1892, Goldie had signed some 360 treaties with local chiefs which the Foreign Office ratified. It is a measure of Goldie's success that Nigeria as a whole was saved for formal British colonialism in spite of German and French designs on parts of the country.

Consular Authority

A consequence of the steady rise in the growth of British enterprise on the coast was the corresponding increase in the number of British firms and individual merchants involved in the Anglo-Nigerian trade. As should be expected, misunderstanding between the supercargoes and the middlemen was not uncommon. In 1844, for instance, a scuffle occurred between the supercargoes and Bonny traders. King Pepple intervened, seized the British captains and refused to release them until they dismantled their guns. It is not without good reason that the supercargoes were called 'oil ruffians', for, among other acts of lawlessness committed by them, they frequently resorted to hijacking of palm-oil, an act known as 'chopping oil'. Such acts of lawlessness which sometimes occasioned violence did not conduce to political stability and security. In their one-sided version, the supercargoes made it appear to the Foreign Office as if their commercial interests were in perpetual danger. Thus, in 1849, the Foreign Office, convinced of the compelling need to regulate Anglo-Nigerian trade and protect the interests of the supercargoes, appointed John Beecroft as the first British Consul to the Bight of Benin and Biafra — a position he held until 1854.

The British consuls, backed by the dreadful gunboats, intervened in local politics to the detriment of the local rulers. As far back as 1837, Rear-Admiral Patrick Campbell had instructed Commander Robert Craigie to 'cause all proper countenance and protection' to be given to British merchants, by 'sending one of the small cruisers into the River occasionally for that purpose'.[43] And the British Consuls never hesitated to call in the warships to back up the claims of British merchants. In 1847, for instance, Consul Beecroft sent a warship to Calabar to assert British claims over the city.

Consul Beecroft personified the arrogance of British Consuls in the Bights of Benin and Biafra. He imposed fines on the coastal chiefs, overawed them by the bombardment of their domain, deposed and installed chiefs as he saw fit. In all these, he was overbearing and high-handed. In 1854, he deposed King Pepple of Bonny for daring to protect his legitimate interests. Pepple who was offended by the unwillingness of the British merchants and government to honour the 1848 treaty duly negotiated and signed by him and Her Britannic Majesty, took steps to obtain redress. He suspended all trade with British merchants and decreed that in future Bonny traders would take 'trusts' only through him. By adopting these measures, Pepple temporarily dealt a devastating blow to British commerce in Bonny.

It is possible to discern two motives behind Pepple's order prohibiting his subjects from receiving 'trusts' from the supercargoes. The first motive, one may surmise, was aimed at the British government. It was to constrain the government to ratify the 1848 treaty. The Foreign Office accepted responsibility for the delay which was explained away as due to 'accidental circumstances'. But the obdurate Consul Beecroft would brook no appeasement. He was determined to deal with Pepple. The second motive, which was more abiding, would seem to be an attempt by Pepple to rationalise the 'trust' system, for both the supercargoes and the coastal middlemen had begun to abuse its use. During the nineteenth century, there was a widespread practice among the 'trust' receivers either to vanish with the goods given to them on credit or to supply much later than expected the goods for which the 'trust' had been given. What was more, the competing agents of trading firms gave out goods on 'trust' indiscriminately which is why a middleman could receive a 'double trust', that is, from different agents.

Pepple was concerned that the abuse of the 'trust' adversely affected trade and security. While attempting to recover the debts owed them, unscrupulous agents resorted to the law of the jungle by 'chopping oil', that is, seizing any oil being transported in canoes. This act of piracy and lawlessness occasioned chaos and insecurity. Pepple's attempt to regularise the system through centralisation and coordination was held against him as an act of monopoly and highhandedness.

Pepple's actions were clearly inconvenient to the British merchants who called on the willing consul to intervene and protect their investment. Consequently, Pepple was deposed and exiled. His deposition, which suited the British merchants, resulted, not from his inability to maintain law and order, but from his head-on collision with British commercial interests.

The British were determined to deal ruthlessly with any ruler who stood in their way in matters of widening the commercial frontier into the hinterland. In Itsekiriland the British Consul intervened to remove what was considered to be an impediment to British commerce in the person of Nana Olomu, 'Governor of the River'. The responsibilities of the Governor included the supervision of the commercial establishments of the ruler, the *Olu*, and the collection of 'comey' from the European vessels. In 1884, Nana was constitutionally appointed Governor in succession to his father, Olomu. His appointment was recognised by the British Consul who was personally present at the election.

Nana soon elevated the position of the Governor as a result of his remarkable business acumen. As a powerful, and successful, trader-prince, his business practices (including unilateral trade stoppages) proved irritating to the British traders who alleged that Nana barred their entry to the hinterland markets, forbade free trade and, while pretending to be loyal to the British government, was actually doing everything to undermine it.[44] The accusation against Nana was frivolous and unfounded yet he was deposed and deported in 1894. The crucial point is that the consul, prompted by howls of protests from the supercargoes, decided to remove what the merchants viewed as a thorn in their flesh. This high-handed action of the Consul, calculated to appease the merchants, is a further testimony of the conscious endeavour to 'extend the range of British manufactures, and open new fields of trade'[45] — an aspiration which would brook no opposition.

One more interventionist tradition of the British consuls will suffice to illustrate the arrogant manner in which the consuls summarily dealt with powerful coastal chiefs: the deposition of King Jaja, the founder of Opobo (Opobu) town. Jaja was in firm control of the trade between Opobo and the hinterland. He resisted repeated attempts by the supercargoes to deal directly with his Igbo and Ibibio suppliers of palm-oil. Indeed, Jaja's right to exclusive control of the hinterland markets was recognised by the British government. A clause in the 1873 treaty between Jaja and Her Britannic Majesty's Government prohibited any British vessel from proceeding inland beyond the beach opposite Hippopotamus Creek.[46] The supercargoes resented Jaja's tight rein on the hinterland trade and flooded the Foreign Office with orchestrated complaints against him, their ultimate aim being Jaja's destruction.

Indeed, Consul Johnston, a willing ally of the commercial interests, lamented that

> . . . their [European] trade is stopped by the machination of one of the most grasping, unscrupulous, and overbearing of mushroom kings [Jaja] who ever attempted to throttle the growing commerce of white men with the interior.[47]

Thus convinced, Johnston sought to remove the obstacle in the way of British merchants and commerce. This found expression in the deposition and banishment of Jaja to the West Indies after a dubious trial at Accra.

It is not surprising that Jaja was removed arbitrarily, for the Foreign Office had avowed that

> Where there is money to be made our Merchants will be certain to intrude themselves . . . if they establish a lucrative trade [duty] compels us to protect them.[48]

The surprise, however, is that it took the Foreign Office so long to acquiesce in Jaja's removal; the reason being that it revelled in indecision on the question of a positive 'forward policy' in Nigeria. The British were prepared to maintain 'indirect influence' in Nigeria through the agency of the merchants. At the proper time and setting the flag would then follow the trade to consolidate the merchants' *fait accompli*. Thus, Jaja was removed in order for the merchants to play their role as the 'pathfinders of British influence'.

The Missionary Factor

It may be easy to summarise the aim of the Christian missionaries in Nigeria as the winning of converts. Even in this simplistic sense, their activities would have far-reaching consequences on the peoples of Nigeria, especially as the process of christianisation necessarily involved the propagation of the virtues of the three Cs — Christianity, Civilization and Commerce. It was T.F. Buxton who in 1839 enunciated missionary aspirations in a moving verse:

> Let missionaries and schoolmasters, the plough and the spade, go together, and agriculture will flourish; the avenues to legitimate commerce will be opened . . .[49]

One implication of Buxton's philosophy is that missionaries would pave the way for more extensive British exploitation of the resources of Nigeria. He considered proselytisation and commerce to be complementary – together they formed the kernel of civilisation. Buxton believed that the abolition of the slave trade created a vacuum which must be filled by Christianity and 'legitimate' trade. In effect, Buxton challenged British merchants and commercial interests to invest in Nigeria. By so doing, they would reap economic benefits while at the same time lessening the 'white man's burden' in the country.

Another implication of Buxton's treatise was that British exploitation, which had been centuries-old, would have to wear a cloak of respectability: it had to change from the traffic in human beings to 'legitimate' commerce. All the same, it was the same British people who had to determine what was 'legitimate' and what was not, what to sell to the indigenous people and what to buy from them. And they chose to sell to them those commodities that would enhance the British economy while inhibiting the diversification and improvement of the Nigerian economy.

In practical terms the missionaries did, in places where they arrived before the merchants, promote the patronage of British goods by Nigerian peoples. Where certain types of British goods were already in demand, the missionaries stimulated the demand for a wider range of British goods. Where they established schools and churches, there arose the demand for books, pencils, pens, bricks, sacramental wines, clothes and the like. In this way, they broke new ground for British commerce and exploitation.

Some of the activities and reports of the pioneer missionaries had far-reaching political implications for the British Foreign Office. They sent back home reports critical of the ability of the local rulers to maintain peace, law and order in their areas of suzerainty. They argued, as Buxton had done earlier, that commerce could not thrive in an atmosphere of political insecurity. Therefore they called on the British government to take over political control of the polities in order to promote peace and security, which were essential for commercial prosperity. Hope Waddell of the Scottish Presbyterian Mission in Calabar called for a warship to stake out British claim to Calabar vis-a-vis the French designs on the region. The Rev. Thomas B. Freeman called attention to the commercial possibilities of Abeokuta. Thereafter Consul Beecroft visited the town. In 1846, Thomas Hutton, Agent-General of Thomas Hutton and Co., also visited Abeokuta to assess its commercial potential.

In all these, the call for the protection of British citizens and property – be they missionaries or commercial agents – kept recurring in the various reports sent home by the pioneer missionaries. England, which owed much of her economic prosperity to commerce, could ill-afford to abandon her commercial class together with the vanguard of her 'civilising mission' — the missionaries — to the vagaries of local politics.

Missionaries often found themselves very much obliged by trading firms. It was Rev. Henry Venn, C.M.S. honorary secretary (1841-1872), who invited the Manchester Chamber of Commerce to invest in cotton growing and processing in Abeokuta. One may also mention that in 1847, Thomas Hutton donated money to the missionary efforts at Abeokuta. The missionaries and the merchants might not have been the best of friends, nonetheless, they were fellow Europeans carrying their 'white man's burden' in a foreign land, even if differently. Thus, even when the missionaries frowned at some of the methods and behaviour of the 'oil ruffians', they were hedged about in their reaction by circumspection. Thus, to a lesser degree, the missionaries were implicated in the British selfish exploitation of Nigeria.

Nigerian Reaction

The response of the indigenous people of Nigeria to British exploitation varied from place to place. Generally, however, it oscillated between cooperation and hostility, depending on the disposition of the local rulers and their subjects on the one hand and the comportment of the British nationals on the other. Where the ruler benefited from the commercial relationship with the British company agents the climate was auspicious for mutual co-operation, but where the authority of the ruler appeared to be threatened the latter tended to adopt a hostile attitude.

Initially, though, the indigenous people received the British company agents and traders with a large dose of suspicion. This helps to explain why the Lander brothers were seized in 1830 by the Obi of Aboh. Rather than keep their promise to King Boy of Brass they absconded, thereby creating the impression among the indigenous people that the British were perfidious. Against this background of mistrust, it becomes intelligible to us why in 1879 the agent of the West African Company at Bomasha was assassinated by the Tiv, compelling the company to evacuate the Benue valley temporarily.

But if the Bomasha incident is indicative of the hostile attitude of the indigenes to British exploitation, the relationship between King Masaba of Bida and the British agents was predicated on mutual cooperation. Dr. W.B. Baikie, a member of the 1857 expedition up the Niger, established the first government post at Lokoja. During his stay at Lokoja he wisely maintained friendly relations with Masaba, and could count on his loyalty. In appreciation of his loyalty, the British periodically showered Masaba with presents and actually named a trading steamer *King Masaba*. An official of the Foreign Office, who visited Lokoja was 'struck by the evident loyalty and reverence with which [Masaba] treated any matter relating to Her Majesty . . .'[50] Masaba's personal 'loyalty' notwithstanding, the government station was not spared sporadic harassment from Masaba's subjects, which contributed to its evacuation in 1869. One might like to suggest that Masaba's apparent 'loyalty' stemmed, not so much from any special love for the British, as from his ambition to acquire firearms.

Further down the Niger local reaction to British exploitation was marked by outright hostility, occasioning violence. The people of Onitsha, for instance, resenting alien intrusion and exploitation, attacked and pillaged the factory belonging to the United African Company. Nevertheless, having assessed the commercial possibilities of the hinterland frontier, the British merchants colluded with the Consul to impose themselves on the local people. Thus, in 1879, a gunboat, *H.M.S. Pioneer*, was despatched to Onitsha to teach the people a sharp lesson. After three days of shelling the town, 270 soldiers (blue-jackets and Hausa police) attacked the town and left a smouldering rubble behind them as they proceeded upstream. Later, Aboh, Idah, Aguleri, Obosi and Asaba, among other towns, attracted similar visitations. This did not prevent the towns of Osomari, Oko and Atani from attacking the visible signs of alien meddlesomeness, the trading posts in their midst.

The remark of a missionary in 1879 clearly illustrates what would seem to be the prevailing attitude of the lower Niger area to British exploitation during the period. Writing about the relationship between David McIntosh, the chief agent of the United African Company, and the indigenes of the lower Niger area, the missionary observed:

> He [McIntosh] is at war with the people of Atani . . . because they did not like to trade with him . . . The violence on the river [Niger] is awful — and where it will end I do not know.[51]

The way the clashes ended is not far to seek; less than two decades later the British government established 'formal influence' over Nigeria and ushered in colonialism.

West of the Niger the same attitude of mistrust and suspicion of British motives prevailed. The impression had been created that generally the British merchants and company agents were unreliable. In 1851, Consul Beecroft authorised the bombardment of Lagos on the ground that the Oba, Kosoko, was an active slave dealer. Meanwhile, the British government strove to extirpate the slave trade. Kosoko was deposed and Akitoye, 'who was quite willing to make himself an instrument of British policy', was installed the Oba. The British crusade against the slave trade was the occasion for the removal of Kosoko. The real cause of it was the conviction of the British that Kosoko was 'trying by every means in his power to annoy and damage the British'[52] mercantile interests — a situation to which the British Consul was largely unreconciled. Although Kosoko had been humiliated, his shadow continued to haunt the 'king makers', the British consular authority.

In 1897, the kingdom of Benin, which was one of the earliest places to be visited by the Europeans, gave a violent expression to its cumulative resentment against British intrusion and exploitation. That year, Acting Consul-General Phillips defied the Oba and proceeded to Benin regardless of the

Oba's instruction to the contrary. He did not live to tell his tale, for he and a large portion of his entourage were dispatched by the Oba's soldiers. When the British counter-attacked they came face-to-face with a thicket of resistance.

Conclusion

The British precolonial exploitation of Nigeria was achieved mainly through trade. At first, the British merchants and the Nigerian middlemen treated one another on the basis of equality. Later, however, the appointment of British Consuls to regulate the Anglo-Nigerian trade tilted the balance in favour of the supercargoes, for the Consuls, backed by warships, succeeded in bull-dozing their way. They arrogated to themselves the right to make and unmake local rulers, interpret commercial treaties, and obtain redress for the trumped up grievances of the supercargoes.

The Nigerian rulers did not succumb meekly to the dictates of the over-bearing Consuls. They resisted, though unsuccessfully, alien imposition and interference through diplomacy and violence.

The Anglo-Nigerian trading relationship was one-sided in the sense that the merchandise imported into the country consisted of either worthless luxuries or cheap manufactures, most of which discouraged Nigerian crafts and improvements on production techniques. Worse for the country, while the goods exported, especially millions of human labour, contributed to the rise of the industrial revolution in England, Nigeria was impoverished. When the industrial revolution got underway, the primary products from Nigeria helped to sustain it. When the British could proudly point at the then prosperous towns of Liverpool and Manchester as a symbol of their gains from their exploitation of Nigeria, what the Nigerian middlemen could possibly show for over four centuries of commercial transactions with Britain would be depopulation, worthless trinkets and ornaments, guns and gun-powder, and technological underdevelopment.

The merchants apart, Christian missionaries played a part in the exploita-tion of Nigeria. The Buxtonian philosophy of 'civilisation' by means of the Bible and the plough encouraged the British mercantile interests, industrialists and capitalists to invest in the country. True, the missionaries were not only interested in proselytisation; they were not averse to uninterrupted British commercial preponderance in the country. As the 'pathfinders of British influence' in parts of Nigeria where they preceded the traders, the missionaries assiduously collected information on the human and material resources on the spot and sent back reports to a receptive audience in England. Where necessary, as in Calabar, the missionaries beckoned to the warships to protect British interests. If the missionaries laid the groundwork for British exploitation in parts of Nigeria during the precolonial period, the benefits were reaped during the next phase of Nigerian history — the colonial period.

References

1. Sir Alan Burns, *History of Nigeria*, 7th edn. (London: Allen and Unwin, 1969), p.109.
2. Arthur Norton Cook, *British Enterprise in Nigeria* (London: Frank Cass, 1964), p.56.
3. Daniel P. Mannix, *Black Cargoes* (New York: Viking, 1962), p.144.
4. W.W. Reade, *Savage Africa*, cited in Thomas Hodgkin, *Nigerian Perspectives: An Anthology* (London: OUP, 1960), p.282.
5. J. Barbot, *Description of the Coasts of North and South Guinea* (London: Churchill, 1732), p.458.
6. Cited in A.H.M. Kirk-Greene, 'Expansion on the Benue, 1830–1900', *Journal of Historical Society of Nigeria*, 1, 3, 1958, p.215.
7. S.J.S. Cookey, *King Jaja of the Niger Delta: His Life and Times, 1821–1891* (New York: Nok, 1974), p.18.
8. A.F.C. Ryder, *Benin and the Europeans, 1485-1897* (London: Longmans, 1969), pp.30-31.
9. Elizabeth Donnan, *Documents Illustrative of the History of the Slave Trade to America*, Vol. 1, 1441-1700 (New York: Octagon, 1969), p.12.
10. Foreigners (excluding the French and English) contracted (*Asiento*) with Spain to supply slaves to Spanish American colonies. The slaves were obtained from West Africa, the Portuguese area of control.
11. Burns, op. cit., p.68.
12. Cook, op. cit., p.21.
13. Donnan, op. cit., p.9.
14. Ibid., p.48.
15. Burns, p.69.
16. Donnan, p.63.
17. Ibid., p.164.
18. In 1792, for instance, Capt. Crow paid a comey of £400 at Bonny. See G.I. Jones, *The Trading States of the Oil Rivers* (London: OUP, 1963), p.95.
19. Barbot, op. cit., p.559.
20. Cited in Burns, op. cit., p.73.
21. Paul Edwards (ed), *Equiano's Travels* (London: Heinemann, 1967), p.16.
22. A.E. Afigbo, 'Trade and Trade Routes in the Nineteenth Century Nsukka', *Journal of the Historical Society of Nigeria*, 8, 1, 1973, pp.77-9.
23. The influence of Ibini Ukpabi extended to non-Igbo speaking areas, including the Niger Delta, Idah, Idoma, Cross River and, of course, throughout most parts of Igboland.
24. Cited in Elizabeth Isichei, *The Ibo and the Europeans* (London: Faber and Faber, 1973), p.54.
25. D.V. Wellesley, *Sir George Goldie, Founder of Nigeria* (London: Macmillan, 1934), p.10.
26. Reginald Coupland, *The British Anti-Slavery Movement* (London: OUP, 1933).
27. See, for instance, Eric Williams, *Slavery and Capitalism* (London: Deutsch, 1964).
28. Adu Boahen, *Topics in West African History* (London: Longman, 1964), p.117.

29. David Northrup, 'The Compatibility of the Slave and Palm Oil Trades in the Bight of Biafra', *Journal of African History*, 12, 3(1976), pp.353-364.

30. Ibid., p.358.

31. Macgregor Laird and R.A.K. Oldfield, *Narrative of an Expedition into the Interior of Africa* (London: Bentley, 1837), pp.11, 358.

32. G.I. Jones, op. cit., p.74.

33. Cited in Burns, op. cit., p.108.

34. Robert S. Smith, *The Lagos Consulate, 1851-1861* (Lagos: Macmillan, 1978), p.2.

35. P.A. Talbot, *The Peoples of Southern Nigeria*, Vol. 1 (London: Frank Cass, 1926), p.61.

36. Cited in A.H.M. Kirk-Greene, op. cit., p.217.

37. Ibid., p.221.

38. Cited in K.O. Dike, *Trade and Politics in the Niger Delta, 1830-1885* (London: OUP, 1972), p.209.

39. Ibid., p.205. The exports included ivory, shea butter, beniseed and groundnuts.

40. The companies were the West African Company, Central African Company, Miller Brothers and Co., and James Pinnock.

41. The company's capital was increased from £125,000 to £1,000,000.

42. Cited in Arthur Norton Cook, op. cit., p.89.

43. C.W. Newbury, *British Policy Towards West Africa: Select Documents, 1786-1874* (Oxford: OUP, 1965), p.377.

44. Obaro Ikime, *Merchant Prince of the Niger Delta* (London: Heinemann, 1968), p.94.

45. C.W. Newbury, op. cit., p.384.

46. Reproduced in K.O. Dike, op. cit., Appendix C.

47. Cited in J.C. Anene, *Southern Nigeria in Transition, 1885-1906* (London: Cambridge University Press, 1966), p.83.

48. Cited in Isichei, op. cit., p.110.

49. T.F. Buxton, *The African Slave Trade and its Remedy* (London: Frank Cass, 1967), p.511.

50. For details, see K.O. Dike, op. cit., p.206.

51. Cited in Isichei, op. cit., p.109.

52. Burns, op. cit., p.117.

3. Quest for Further Exploitation: British Colonial Occupation of Nigeria

L. I. Izuakor

Introduction

The establishment of the Protectorate of Northern Nigeria on 1 January 1900 was the culmination of British 'creeping colonialism' which began in 1861 with the occupation of Lagos. Before 1880, the British Foreign Office was content to leave the exploitation of Nigerian resources in the competent hands of private enterprise. The reason was simple. Britain was superbly confident of her commercial, naval and industrial superiority vis-a-vis the rest of Europe. Essentially, this awareness formed the basis of the mid-Victorian policy of advance by commercial enterprise. As the 'workshop of the world', and, confident of her industrial, commercial and naval superiority, Britain was content to maintain 'informal influence' around the globe. As yet there was no cause to interfere with the free play of market forces, especially as it was obvious that 'by great superiority of general commerce and the carrying trade everywhere [the British] have acquired an immense political influence in . . . the world'.[1] Thus as far as the British were concerned, 'free trade and private enterprise had guaranteed progress and profits'.[2]

In the 1880s, however, the late Victorians were not as self-confident of their industrial paramountcy as the mid-Victorians had been some thirty years before. Among other reasons, the depression of the 1880s and the stiff competition from continental Europe and America had shaken the confidence of the once ebulliently optimistic British populace. Britain was steadily losing her premier place in industrial and commercial advancement. Consequently, profits shrank, expectations trembled and the 'national arrogance perhaps grew less candid',[3] causing the commercial groups to grope desperately for a means of deliverance from the encircling gloom.

The official mind which usually extolled the principle and practice of *laissez-faire* in economic matters found itself between the horns of a dilemma. Was there any way out of the problem? Would the proponents of 'informal Empire' suddenly retrench this principle and embrace 'formal colonialism'?

To many a perceptive mind, the new problem needed an entirely new approach. Lord Salisbury, who visualised the necessity for economic imperialism with its handmaid — political intervention — warned:

> If we mean to hold our own against the efforts of the civilised powers
> of the world to strangle our commerce by their prohibitive finance
> we must be prepared to take the requisite measures to open new
> markets for ourselves . . . and must not be afraid if that effort, which
> is vital to our industries, should bring with it new responsibilities of
> empire and government.[4]

Here Salisbury, the Foreign Secretary, was courting the ire of the anti-
imperialists while placating the jingoists. But there was no doubt in the
mind of Salisbury, the so-called 'reluctant imperialist', that new markets in
the 'half-civilised or uncivilised nations' would 'smooth the path of British
enterprise and . . . facilitate the application of British capital'.[5] To Salisbury,
the returns on commercial investment would perhaps justify the cost of
political involvement. To be sure, Salisbury's voice was not a lone one.
He was supported by the Chambers of Commerce and the British press.
Be that as it may, would the parsimonious British policy-makers endorse a
policy of further colonial encumbrances?

It is the burden of this study to demonstrate that British colonialism in
Nigeria, contrary to the strategic argument, resulted from the simple logic of
economic and commercial imperatives. True, there had been no calculated
policy to conquer and administer Nigeria until the economic necessities of
the 1880s conspired with the European ambitions in Africa to force Britain
into resorting to physical protection in local mercantile difficulties in
Nigeria.

It will be necessary at this stage to consider some of the major theories
of modern imperialism as a background against which the argument in this
study will, hopefully, become intelligible.

Interpretations of Modern Imperialism

Economic Interpretation

In his book, *Imperialism: A Study*,[6] published in 1902, J.A. Hobson, whose
thesis would seem to have been influenced by his first-hand experience of
the Anglo-Boer War (1899–1902), posits that underconsumption, maldistribu-
tion of wealth, and oversaving were responsible for the rise of imperialism.
Put differently, Hobson argues that industrial nations tended to produce
surplus goods which the local public could not consume. At the same time,
the capitalists who had accumulated huge profits (oversaving) sought for
investment markets overseas, preferably under the flag. In this way, a small
group of powerful industrialists managed to father imperialism.

A major criticism against Hobson's thesis is that he apparently failed to
analyse the long-standing phenomenon of imperialism. He based his analysis
on the empirical contemporary events. We do know that the trans-Atlantic
slave trade was induced, not by industrialists in search of new markets for
their surplus goods, but by the sheer economic necessity of exploiting the
resources of the New World. Thus, as far as Nigeria is concerned, British

imperialism which started about the sixteenth century cannot be explained in terms of the underconsumptionist theory.

For V.I. Lenin,[7] the determinant of modern imperialism is capitalism. Unlike Hobson though, Lenin rested his thesis on finance capitalism. According to him, imperialism is the end-result of finance capitalism. In search of investment markets overseas, financiers who had formed monopolies, cartels and trusts. influenced politicians to impose political control over weaker societies. Such control was desirable as a means of ensuring security of investment and highest returns in the less competitive colonial markets. The struggle for markets, Lenin argued, would necessarily result in fierce competition among the industrial nations. In the course of this rivalry capitalism itself would be overthrown by the imperial wars it had unleashed.

One may like to note the circumstances surrounding Lenin's thesis. He was worried that the working class, rather than team up and free themselves from the clutches of capitalism, would join hands with their capitalist oppressors in defence of capitalism during the First World War. Against this background one suspects that Lenin's thesis was intended to serve as propaganda material, among other things. Be that as it may, the circumstances surrounding the emergence of his thesis should not destroy the essence of his erudite argument.

However, practical experience has flawed Lenin's thesis. Statistics show that between 1870 and 1911, Britain invested much more in the technologically advanced nations than in the so-called primitive societies. During the period British investments in the USA stood at £688 million; Canada, £372 million; Australia, £380 million; and the whole of West Africa, £29 million. In 1900 alone, British trade with industrial nations stood at £711 million as against the figure of £237 million for her trade with the empire.[8]

In spite of the above statistics which have punctured Lenin's interpretation of imperialism, his thesis has a tantalisingly minute relevance in the rise of British colonialism in Nigeria. This relevance, which must be interpreted with caution, concerns only the economic factor as a motive for imperialism. The British trading firms in Nigeria were impelled by the profit motive to invest in the country. Supporting the economic underpinning of British political control in Nigeria, the *Pall Mall Gazette* proudly editorialised in 1899:

> Nor have we gone to the equatorial regions from religious or humanitarian motives. . . . Still less have we sought out the African in order to endow him with the vices of western civilization . . . the dominating force which has taken us to Equatorial Africa is the desire for trade.[9]

Yet it has been claimed by Robinson and Gallagher that commercially Africa was worthless; its only value being strategic — for the defence of India.

Psychological Interpretation

Joseph Schumpeter has postulated that the determinants of modern imperialism are rooted in human psychology. In his book[10] published in

1919, Schumpeter argued that contrary to the Hobson-Lenin thesis, capitalism is a benign, reformable institution and that it is antithetical to imperialism. Imperialism, he posited, is motivated by non-pecuniary 'objectless' disposition on the part of a state to unlimited forcible expansion. That is to say, imperialism is atavistic. The imperialists engage in expansionist wars for the sake of expanding and not for any targeted national goal. It then follows that imperialism is a hang-over from man's primitive past, especially as its vital force is the Freudian *id*.

One would have great difficulty trying to convince others that Schumpeter's thesis fits the Nigerian experience. In any event, it is doubtful that statesmen and rulers in the past engaged in warring simply as a pastime. War is a serious business and its causes, remote and immediate, must have a more abiding relevance to national or group interest than buffoonery.

Political Interpretation

Ronald Robinson and John Gallagher[11] view the motive for British imperialism in Africa in terms of strategy — the need to secure the Suez Canal for the defence of the economically more worthwhile British Raj in India. The occasion for British colonialism in Africa, they argue, was the internal crisis in the continent. This crisis dragged them into Africa and the deepening crises there kept them in bondage.

It is true that in 1882 the British dabbled into Egypt's internal politics and from there they struggled to prevent the French from gaining control of the headwaters of the Nile, hence the British incursion into the Sudan. It is also true that whoever controlled the Suez Canal was in a position to control the gateway to India. This fact underscored British interest in Egypt.

But what is not so clear is the relationship between the British struggle for the control of Nigeria and the strategic importance of Egypt. If, in the calculation of the British politicians, Africa was just a 'gigantic footnote to the great Indian Empire' does it follow that Nigeria was a footnote to Egypt?

But more importantly, Robinson and Gallagher failed to explain why Britain colonised India in the first instance. Certainly, the British occupation of India was not a freakish, atavistic venture; the decision was consciously made in an age when retrenchment was the watchword of the British policy-makers. The Portuguese who painstakingly persevered in the quest for a sea-route to India had an eye on the fabulously profitable trade with the East in which the Muslim middlemen had for centuries taken the lion's share. Earlier, during the Middle Ages Marco Polo's sojourn in Asia and his subsequent revelation in his memoirs of Oriental wealth suggested to Westerners that 'there was in the East wealth such as Europe had never dreamed of, and held. . . .'[12]

The Portuguese made such handsome profits from their trade in pepper, cinnamon and other spices, silk, precious stones and luxury goods that the appetite of the rest of Europe was keenly whetted. As a consequence, there developed a stiff rivalry among European nations for the control of the trade. In the end Britain edged out the other European competitors in India and controlled the country politically.

In the final analysis, British imperialism in India was stimulated by economic considerations arising from the actuality or the potentiality of economic gains in that country. As in India, so it was in Nigeria, where the prime mover of British imperialism was rooted in economic imperatives.

It is dangerous, however, to depend unduly on a mono-causal explanation of historical events. Historical events are complex and often so interwoven that only a multi-dimensional interpretation can bring out the deeper intricacies of a single event such as the British occupation of Nigeria. However, one can assert without a grave risk of contradiction that other factors which influenced British imperialism in Nigeria revolve around economic self-interest which was the linchpin of that episode in Nigerian history.

British Colonialism in Nigeria

In the fifteenth century, the Portuguese pioneered a daring maritime contact with West Africa. They were motivated primarily by the need to circumvent the monopoly of the Muslim middlemen over the overland European commerce with the Orient. As yet the Portuguese were not out for wars of conquest for the sake of expanding.

It was the lucrative Portuguese monopoly of the trade in sylvan products (later dominated by the slave trade) with West Africa which attracted the British merchants to the coast of West Africa. And, up to 1870, the prevailing politico-economic conditions in both Europe and West Africa ensured the effectiveness of the British policy of 'indirect influence'.

However, as these politico-economic conditions began to change after 1870 it became necessary to review the *modus operandi*. The Berlin West Africa conference (1884–85) reinforced the need for this review by resolving that those European Powers with claims to African territories show proof of their 'effective occupation'. British merchants had staked out claims to parts of Nigeria and the economic difficulties they were encountering there forced them to call for government intervention. In this way, what started as a benign commercial relationship between the coastal traders and European merchants culminated in the British occupation of Nigeria. This underscores our argument that economic factors were the prime movers of British political intervention in Nigeria in the 1880s.

Of course, the establishment of commercial contact on a regular basis between a technologically advanced society and an underdeveloped one carried the risk of political intervention by the former. Although, initially the British exerted only an 'informal influence' in Nigeria, the fact that their commercial interests might be threatened by insecurity (actual or imagined) implied that physical force might be employed in defence of these vital interests. And even if political control was not the objective of that intervention, the temptation to exert that control was a real possibility.

The appointment in 1849 of John Beecroft as the first British Consul to the Bights of Benin and Biafra reinforces the argument that British commercial interests on the coast had to be protected. The Consul's main task was to regulate trade in the Bights of Benin and Biafra. In addition to that, he was interested in opening up the hinterland to British commerce. Consul Beecroft and his successors never hesitated to use the British Navy to assert the rights of British traders. In the process some coastal rulers were forcibly dethroned and exiled simply because the supercargoes ('oil ruffians') managed to convince the Consuls that their commercial interests were being seriously threatened due to the inability of the coastal rulers to maintain law and order in their areas of authority. Thus, it will be difficult to explain the role of the Consuls in local politics without placing emphasis on British economic self-interest.

When the slave trade had outlived its usefulness, British industrialists and capitalists shifted their interest to 'legitimate' trade in forest products. But the African slave dealers, who were led into the iniquitous traffic in human cargoes by their foreign collaborators, were flabbergasted by the *volte-face* of the European slave-dealers. Some were unwilling to give up the slave trade. The British missionaries and philanthropists joined hands with politicians to decry the continued existence of slavery in Africa. The result was the dispatch of naval squadrons to the West African coastline to enforce the embargo on the slave trade. Thus, missionaries, industrialists, merchants and politicians became partners in furthering British economic interests in Nigeria. They succeeded in eliminating the slave trade and extending British commercial empire in the hinterland.

In a foreign environment and amidst alien people whose culture they hardly understood, the missionaries, feeling insecure and marooned, called on their home government for protection. Indeed, it was at the request of Rev. Thomas Birch Freeman and Thomas Hutton, a merchant with business establishments in Badagry, that soldiers were sent to Badagry to protect the mission and commercial posts. Again, in 1847, Hope Waddell of the Scottish Presbyterian Mission in Calabar, alerted Consul Beecroft on the French designs on Calabar. Then a British warship sailed into Calabar and planted the British flag. Thus, as A.G. Hopkins has correctly observed,

> The missionaries, too, acting on their traditional postulate about the relationship between commercial prosperity and the progress of Christianity in Africa, urged the metropolitan governments to adopt more positive policies.[13]

After 1830, thanks to the expedition of the Lander brothers, the British trading firms on the coastland of Nigeria began to push into the hinterland. Thus a formal extension of the British sphere of 'informal influence' unwittingly prepared the ground for formal colonialism as it broadened the arena for contact between an advanced industrial culture and a 'backward' one. This contact would inevitably lead to a clash, especially as the commercial agents in the hinterland and some missionaries were greeted by the hostility of the indigenous people whose lifestyles appeared threatened by aliens. In fact, in 1867, the Egba who had been 'wary of receiving missionaries lest it should lead to political results'[14] actually attacked and expelled Christians and their churches in Abeokuta.[15]

The endemic Yoruba wars of the nineteenth century, as well as the persistent slaving activities in parts of the hinterland hardly conduced to 'legitimate' trade. In 1854, for instance, the deposed Oba Kosoko of Lagos was recognised by Consul Benjamin Campbell as the ruler of Palma and Lekke, largely because of his promise to encourage 'legitimate' commerce in the area. Again, the Aro Expedition (1901–1902) was undertaken largely to smash the assumed citadel of the slave trade in order to pave the way for the extension of 'legitimate' trade in the hinterland. Thus, 'where "trade" faltered', observed Alan Ryder, 'the "flag" stepped forward in defence of economic paramountcy'.[16]

In places the violent reaction of the indigenous people against the oppressive rule of the Royal Niger Company was construed by the British officials as a deliberate attempt to undermine British economic self-interest. Thus, the Akassa War (1895) was scorned as a raid on the company headquarters. Yet it attracted high-handed reprisals in defence of British trade which the Royal Niger Company had monopolised.

What was more, the local British officials were not averse to colonial expansion and control. It was they who, together with the traders and missionaries, influenced Palmerston to authorise the bombardment of Lagos (1851). Even when Oba Kosoko had been deposed and Akitoye enthroned by the British, the missionaries and traders complained that the more tractable Akitoye and his successors could not guarantee the safety of their property, and that the slave trade was still a veritable occupation – a situation which called for deeper British political involvement.

The local officials who were hampered by the parsimony of the home Treasury tended to support further extension of their area of authority as a means of collecting more revenue (mainly customs duties) from the outlying districts. In January 1863, for instance, Henry Freeman, governor of Lagos (1862–1865), arbitrarily annexed the port town of Badagry to the territory of Lagos and collected import duties on goods entering the town. Similarly, he sent troops to occupy Palma forcibly. This action enabled the collector of customs to collect import duties in the district.

The commercial agents contributed significantly to the rise of colonialism in Nigeria. They exerted pressure on the officials to impose *Pax Britannica* as a means of securing for them a conducive economic environment. When the incensed Onitsha inhabitants looted the United African Company's factory (1879), it was at the request of the Company's agents that the *H.M.S. Pioneer* was despatched to bombard the town.

Indeed, one might agree with A.G. Hopkins that

> the main reason why Britain decided to move into the interior was because the officials and politicians who were responsible for colonial policy gave way to commercial pressure groups and to the local

administration both of which favoured expansion in order to solve the economic problems which had . . . become acute in the 1880s.[17]

Gradually, therefore, the attempt to protect British economic imperialism in Nigeria made possible the abandonment of the Foreign Office policy of 'informal empire' in favour of colonial control. As Palmerston had accurately observed in 1860,

> It may be true in one sense that trade ought not to be enforced by cannon balls, but on the other hand trade cannot flourish without security, and that security may be unattainable without the exhibition of physical force.[18]

And, the energetic British traders in Nigeria did not find it too hard convincing the not altogether uninterested local administration that there existed in the hinterland justifiable grounds for the use of physical force. These grounds stemmed from, among other things, the 'difficulties of declining profits'.[19]

The 'declining profits' were the concomitant of the depression which occurred both in Europe and West Africa between 1885 and 1895. It undermined British commercial expansion into the hinterland of Nigeria. The British merchants were looking for a way out of their choking problems when they pressured the government to abandon its idealistic policy of 'informal empire' for a realistic 'forward policy'. And the British government had a stake in the prosperity of her patriotic merchants who, after all, were carrying the 'white man's burden' in Nigeria through commercial penetration.

The depression was real and the plight of the merchants serious. In 1851, for example, a ton of palm-oil which cost between £10 and £20 in Lagos fetched £40 in Liverpool. But by 1886, the price had dropped to £22 in Liverpool — representing a 45% fall in prices. This drop had far-reaching consequences when it is remembered that between 1880 and 1892, palm produce averaged 82.5% of all exports from Lagos.[20] Indeed, some firms were forced to close down. Whereas in 1880 twelve European firms were doing good business in Lagos, by 1892 only five of them managed to stay alive, some precariously.[21]

The toll of the depression on British commerce apart, other intractable forces impinged on free trade in the hinterland of the Nigerian coast. The British firms had to contend with the stranglehold of the African middlemen on the hinterland trade, more so when the bulk of the exports were produced in the hinterland. In the hinterland of Lagos, the Egba and the Ijebu held the key to the trade between Lagos on one hand and the hinterland on the other. Their energetic middlemen blockaded the trade by closing the trade routes whenever the political situation warranted such action. And this inconvenient closure of the trade routes was aggravated by the insecurity caused by the abiding Yoruba wars of the nineteenth century. Yet it was Egbaland which by 1892 was the leading source of palm produce that reached Lagos. When in 1891 the Ijebu closed the trade routes passing through their territory, neither the offer of an annual subvention of £500 nor the delegation led by governor Denton to Ijebu Ode could secure for the merchants access to the hinterland markets through Ijebuland. However, when Denton rattled the sabre in 1892, the Ijebu people were prepared to lift the blockade, if only temporarily.

But the Ijebu people were not alone in resorting to economic blockade; the Egba people also employed the same political weapon. Because the merchants could not break through this barrier the government was obliged to come to their rescue. Thus, the 'frantic requests of the Liverpool lobby for British intervention, dragged a reluctant British Government into the Yoruba hinterland'.

Further to the north-east of Lagos, the British merchants encountered the monopolistic practices of the powerful middlemen. As late as 1896, the Oba of Benin still controlled the trade in his kingdom through his agents. These agents have been described as

> the king's messengers; [who] look after the various trading centres. [They] levy blackmail broadcasts, (sic) any new articles coming into the country, [and] bar the sale to anyone but themselves.[22]

A similar situation existed in the eastern delta. There the British merchants were prevented from expanding into the hinterland by the jealous coastal middlemen. King Jaja of Opobo, for instance, forestalled all attempts by the British merchants to break his firm control over the trade between Opobo and its hinterland. In Itsekiriland Nana Olomu ('Governor of the River') successfully barred the British merchants from trading directly with the hinterland producers of palm oil. In both cases the merchants complained bitterly to the office of the Consul which deported Jaja (1887) and Nana (1894). Thereafter the merchants extended their trading frontier beyond the coastline.

What has emerged so far is that the local administration used physical force to smash local impediments to British commercial expansion, and this 'forward policy' was adopted because of the economic crisis of the 1880s. It is possible that most of the merchant groups had no clear idea of the extent of the resources available in the hinterland, yet the economic crisis left them with no better alternative than to seek relief in the markets beyond their pale of commercial enterprise. And the local officials, who pursued the policy of advance by commercial enterprise, had to range governmental might behind the mercantile pathfinders of British influence.

It must not be understood, however, that economic motives, acting in isolation, brought about British quest for further exploitation of Nigeria. Indeed other forces contributed to British colonisation of the country. In the face of the fierce French competition in West Africa, the British were compelled to jettison the principle of *laissez-faire* and make good their claim to that territory which later came to be known as Nigeria. The French were speedily extending their power eastwards from Senegal to Dahomey. Britain could not be expected to sit back and watch her interests compromised through default. From their base in Dahomey the French were trying to secure a foothold in Yorubaland. In fact, in 1887, they claimed to have obtained a treaty from the Alake of Abeokuta, permitting them to link

Porto Nova and Abeokuta by a railway line.

The famous 'race to Nikki' (1894) clearly illustrates the delicate steeple-chase between the French and the British in West Africa. However, where British commercial interests were minimal, they were prepared to compromise, but where these interests were most promising (as in the Lower Niger) the British were prepared to take the French head-on 'even', as Joseph Chamberlain put it, 'at the risk of war'.[23] Fortunately for Britain, Capt. (later Lord) Lugard pre-empted Capt. Decoeur's party in Nikki by a hair's breadth — five days. As Lugard had obtained a treaty from the ruler of Nikki the French were prepared to beat a retreat.

Initially, the British were content to exert their influence in Nigeria through the trading companies. Stressing this point in 1890, Salisbury reaffirmed that in the Niger region 'the interests of this country are the interests of the Royal Niger Company'[24], i.e. commercial interests. Indeed, when the Company was granted a royal charter in 1886 it was mandated to extend British authority to areas where it did not exist. In the process of extending British authority the Company indulged in filibustering which created new frontier problems that had to be solved through government involvement. In time the Company overstretched its resources at a crucial period when the European Powers were busy carving out 'spheres of influence' in Africa. Consequently, Joseph Chamberlain, the Colonial Secretary, introduced the 'imperial factor' in the extension of British authority. The charter of the Company was revoked on 1 January 1900, and the Colonial Office took over the administration of Nigeria. From that year a formal type of colonialism emerged in Nigeria.

Conclusion

All in all, one could reasonably argue that British intervention in Nigeria was a political act calculated to protect British mercantile interests. On the influence of economic interests, on government policy, A.M. Rose has aptly noted:

> There can be little doubt that the great bulk of business pressures on, and intervention in, government . . . are simply additional ways of making sales, increasing the profit margin [if] sales, obtaining raw materials at lower cost, or protecting markets. That is, they are purely 'economic', . . .[25]

It was as a result of these pressures that in 1849 the Foreign Office appointed the first consul to the Bight of Benin and Biafra, primarily to regulate the Anglo-Nigerian trade. This interventionist act turned out to be the prelude to a formal political imperialism. African rulers might put up gallant resistance according to their ability, but British technological superiority ensured that repeating rifles and the Maxim gun would reduce these resistances to a mere inconvenience, a tokenism.

References

1. B. Semmel, *The Rise of Free Trade Imperialism* (London: Cambridge University Press, 1970), p.8.

2. A.G. Hopkins, 'Economic Imperialism in West Africa: Lagos, 1880-1892', *Economic History Review*, 21, 3 (1968), p.585.

3. Ronald Robinson and John Gallagher with Alice Denny, *Africa and the Victorians* (New York: Doubleday, 1968), p.3.

4. *The Times*, 14 May 1895.

5. *Hansard*, 4th series, 36 (1895), pp.698-99.

6. J.A. Hobson, *Imperialism: A Study* (London: George Allen & Unwin, 1902).

7. V.I. Lenin, *Imperialism: the Highest Stage of Capitalism* (New York: International Publishers, 1935).

8. A.P. Thornton, *The Imperial Idea and Its Enemies* (New York: Doubleday, 1968), p.113.

9. Cited in G.N. Uzoigwe, *Britain and the Conquest of Africa: The Age of Salisbury* (Ann Arbor: University of Michigan Press, 1974), pp.27-28.

10. Joseph A. Schumpeter, *Imperialism and Social Class* (New York, 1951).

11. Robinson and Gallagher, op. cit.

12. Wallace K. Ferguson and G. Bruun, *A Survey of Western Civilization*, 3rd edn. (Boston: Houghton Mifflin, 1962), p.366.

13. A.G. Hopkins, *An Economic History of West Africa* (London: Longman, 1973), p.156.

14. Cited in Paul M. Mbaeyi, *British Military and Naval Forces in West African History, 1807-1874* (New York, Nok, 1978), p.137.

15. J.F.A. Ajayi, *Christian Missions in the Making of Nigeria, 1841-1891* (London: Longman, 1965), pp.201-2.

16. A.F.C. Ryder, *Benin and The Europeans, 1485-1897* (London: Longmans, 1969), p.260.

17. A.G. Hopkins, 'Economic Imperialism . . .', p.603.

18. Cited in Bernard Porter, *The Lion's Share: A Short History of British Imperialism 1850-1970* (New York: Longman, 1977), p.11.

19. Robinson and Gallagher, op. cit., p.11.

20. A.G. Hopkins, 'Economic Imperialism . . .', p.585.

21. Walter I. Ofonagoro, *Trade and Imperialism in Southern Nigeria, 1881-1929* (New York: Nok, 1979), p.12.

22. Cited in Ryder, op. cit., p.276.

23. Robinson and Gallagher, op. cit., p.505.

24. Cited in Porter, op. cit., p.166.

25. A.M. Rose, *The Power Structure* (New York: OUP, 1967), pp.101-2.

4. The Infrastructure of Exploitation: Transport, Monetary Changes, Banking, etc.

S. A. Olanrewaju

Introduction

The exploitation of Nigeria by the British was facilitated greatly by the process of 'opening up' Nigeria to British trade. The 'opening up' would not have been possible, but for the provision of essential infrastructural facilities such as railways, motorable roads and navigable rivers. The European commercial community preferred to wait on the coast until Britain created the conditions necessary for successful and profitable operation of European enterprises in the remote hinterland.

Trading with the local community was also facilitated by promoting a highly monetised economy and providing banking facilities. Britain also provided the type of administration that was concerned with regulating the conditions governing the interaction of the European commercial community with the local population in the former's favour. The establishment of the colonial administration was made possible by the conquest and occupation of the country. This was a major step taken by the British to open Nigeria to political domination and economic exploitation.

In this chapter, we examine how four types of infrastructure of exploitation, transport, monetary changes, banking, and administration, were used to promote British economic exploitation of Nigeria during the colonial period. Bourgeois writers often refer to the creation of social infrastructural facilities as a concrete step taken by the British colonial administration in Nigeria to bring about rapid economic development. The point that is often missed by such bourgeois scholars is that the provision of infrastructural facilities was a means to an end. The end itself was the economic exploitation of the colony. The machinery of the colonial government was used to create those infrastructural facilities considered essential to the successful and profitable operation of European enterprises in Nigeria.

The Transport Infrastructure

The history of transport development in Nigeria during the colonial period centred on the development of the inland waterways, railways, and roads. Air transport was relatively undeveloped during this period. Even today, air transportation in Nigeria is still largely limited to the high income bracket.

Inland Waterways

The establishment of European commercial concerns in the hinterland was the essence of British policy in Nigeria during the early part of this century. In the absence of railways and roads, the only way to pursue this policy initially was to make the existing waterways navigable. One traditional limitation of inland water transportation in Nigeria had been the seasonality of the rivers. Rivers and creeks leading from coastal trading depots to the inland markets were often silted up and blocked by snags.

Ofonagoro has observed that in the face of the limited navigability of the rivers, Britain's immediate concern was dredging of the rivers in southern Nigeria to render them navigable by river craft drawing at least five feet of water on a year-round basis, so as to open the river basins to direct exploitation by British traders.[1] In order to bring out enormous quantities of produce still hidden in the hinterland, efforts were made to render all the coastal creeks and rivers navigable for the launches, stern wheelers, lighters, and generally large rivercraft of the European traders.

The initiative for an improved communication system in Nigeria was actually taken by the European merchants. One important instrument used by the merchants was lobbying. Incessant pressure was applied on every administration installed in southern Nigeria between 1885 and 1914 to improve the navigability of the coastal rivers. As Ofonagoro has further indicated, records show that Governors and High Commissioners visiting Liverpool were certain to be dined and wined at the expense of the Chambers of Commerce to provide an avenue for discussing the need for clearing the creeks on the coasts and the building of railways and good roads.[2] This was to make it possible for the merchants to realise the expectation of substantial increases in the quantity of raw materials available for export from the forests of the hinterland.

The provision of an improved communication system was also essential for the British administrative officers in the course of their duty. With the establishment of the Northern Protectorate and the subsequent amalgamation of the Southern and the Northern Protectorates in 1914, the need to extend the British administration to the hinterland became urgent. The important role of a good communication system in the task of the British administrative officers at that time can therefore not be over-emphasised.

The coastal creeks and rivers of Lagos and Yorubaland had already been carefully explored, dredged, and mapped by the Lagos Government by the turn of the nineteenth century. By 1896, travel by larger rivercraft through the lagoon and creeks linking the Western Delta with Lagos was for the first time possible. Similarly, the exploration of the eastern waters resulted in the discovery of a region abounding with natural products and reached by water in two or three days. However, the influence of water transport was limited to the areas around river basins.

Railways

The European commercial community in Lagos and their counterparts in the Niger delta did not expand operations to the hinterland until the construction of the Railways. In fact, the initiative for the construction of the railways in Nigeria came from the European merchants, through constant pressures on the colonial administration. By the 1890s, such pressures for the construction of the railways into the hinterland had gathered momentum.

Railway construction started in 1898, with a line extending in a north-easterly direction from Lagos. This was a period when there were no roads except those within the townships. By 1901, the line had reached Ibadan, a distance of about 193 kilometres. In 1909, railway lines totalling 486 kilo-metres and extending to the banks of the River Niger at Jebba had been constructed.[3]

At this time, Sir Fredrick Lugard (later Lord Lugard) was the Governor of the Northern Protectorate. In order to provide a link between the north and his administrative headquarters at Zungeru, as well as with the ports of Forcados and Burutu, a railway terminal port was opened at Baro and the railway line of 561 kilometres in length was laid between Baro and Kano. By 1915, a bridge had been constructed on the River Niger at Jebba. This made it possible to extend the railway northwards to join the Baro–Kano line at Minna. Between 1912 and 1914, the Bauchi light railway (0.762 metre gauge) was constructed from Zaria to Bukuru to facilitate the evacuation of tin from Bauchi Plateau where tin-mining had already started.

While the western rail connections with the north from the sea had been well established by 1914, nothing was done about the eastern railway scheme, even though an eastern line was known to be essential to the future development of Nigeria. When Lugard was finally committed to the Baro-Kano line, the eastern scheme lost his support and was temporarily dropped.

Early in 1914, coal was discovered near Enugu. The need for the evacuation of coal from the Enugu line to the coast led to the revival of interest in the eastern railway project. Consequently, the Port Harcourt-Enugu railway project was started in 1914 and by 1916 the line had reached Enugu. The first world war interrupted construction until 1922 when the extension of the line beyond Enugu began, reaching the River Benue at Makurdi in 1924.

During the same period, construction also started south-eastwards from Kaduna junction. This line met the one constructed northwards from Makurdi at Kafanchan and the route was opened to the public in April 1927. This was followed by a line from Kafanchan to Bukuru and thence to Jos, opened also in 1927. This line made it possible to rail the tin obtained from the Plateau directly to Port Harcourt. The train ferry across the River Benue was replaced by a bridge in 1932.

With the completion in 1927 of the main railway lines which were to form the backbone of the railway system in Nigeria, consideration was then given to the provision of rail feeder-links. The Zaria-Gusau branch was opened in 1929. The line was later extended by 48 kilometres to Kaura Namoda and completed in October 1929. This branch line serves the groundnut and cotton producing areas of the former Zaria, Katsina and Sokoto provinces. Other branch lines include the Kano-Ringim-Nguru completed in October 1930; the Ifo-Idogo line completed in June, 1930; and finally the Borno extension completed in 1964. With the commissioning of the Borno extension, Nigeria had about 3,505 kilometres of single line railway track all of 1.0668 metre gauge, details of which are given in Table 4.1 below.

Table 4.1
The Nigerian Railway System Route Kilometres

(a)	*Main Line Section*	*Kilometres*
	Lagos/Apapa-Kano	1,126.51
	Apapa Local-Ebute Metta Junction	8.05
	Port Harcourt-Kaduna Junction	915.69
	Kafanchan-Jos	101.39
	Kuru-Maiduguri	641.51
		2,793.16
(b)	*Branch Line Section*	
	Minna-Baro	178.63
	Zaria-Kaura Namoda	220.47
	Ifo Junction-Idogo	43.46
	Kano-Nguru	230.13
	Elelenwa-Alesa Eleme oil Refinery	9.65
	Ogbaho-Nkalagu	14.48
	Enugu-Iva Valley	8.04
	Enugu-Obwetti	8.04
	Total (a) and (b)	*3,506.04*

Source: Nzegwu, T.I.O. (1973), 'Project Identification in the N.R.C.' (A paper presented at the workshop on the Transport Sector Planning for the Third National Development Plan held at the University of Ibadan, Faculty of Social Sciences), p.4.

Railway construction in Nigeria was not meant to serve the development needs of the country. Although the railways served a strategic purpose of penetrating into the interior to open up the hinterland, and had an indirect impact on agricultural production, mineral exploitation, industrial development and urbanisation, the motive and pattern of railway development were exploitative. As the above discussion shows, rail lines were constructed to link strategic mineral deposit regions and fertile agricultural lands with the coastal ports. For example tin-ore and coal deposits in Jos and Enugu respectively were instrumental to the extension of the rail lines to these areas. Also the large-scale production and exportation of groundnuts in the groundnut-producing centre of Kano became possible only when the railway had provided an economic means of transport to the sea. For example, groundnut production increased from about 2,032 metric tons in 1912 to 199,442 metric tons by 1929; by 1960 exports exceeded half a million metric tons a year.[4]

Also, the quality of the rail trucks support the viewpoint that railway construction was not meant to serve the development needs of Nigeria. Unlike the wide standard gauge system developed in Europe, the narrow gauge system was developed in Nigeria. Apart from being narrow, the tracks present a high ratio of curvature to route kilometres. This is because the tracks follow contour levels in order to minimise cutting, embanking and tunnelling. Consequently right from the time of construction, the Nigerian railway system was confronted with speed restraint. While railways in some developed countries have achieved a speed of 192 kilometres per hour, the average speed on the Nigerian railway system is about 32 kilometres per hour for passenger trains and about 19 kilometres per hour for goods train.[5] This low speed has greatly impeded the performance of the Nigerian railways and has limited their competitiveness with the road transport.

Road Transport

Before the advent of the British administration in Nigeria, the dominant mode of land transportation was by porters and draught animals over bush paths. The earliest efforts at road transport improvement were directed toward the widening of bush paths between settlements.

With the seat of the Northern Government established at Zungeru, Lugard planned to build a mule-road from Zungeru to Zaria, and then on to Sokoto, Katsina and Maiduguri. However, with the authorisation of the Baro-Kano railway line in 1907, the cart-road which was begun in 1904 was abandoned at Tegina, 32 kilometres north of Zungeru.[6] With the completion of the Baro-Kano railway in 1910, the government's attention was turned to the Zungeru-Zaria road which was eventually completed in 1914.[7] The chief motive for the construction of the mule-road was to reduce the strain thrown on the inland provinces in the provision of porters for the British officials.

In the south, where draught animals could not be used owing to the tsetse fly, the possibilities of motor transport served as an early stimulus to the building of roads. The first motorable road in Nigeria was built in 1906 from Ibadan to Oyo and it was linked to the railways by a railway-operated road transport service. This was followed by similar services from Osogbo to Ife, Ilesa, Ogbomoso, and from Ede to Iwo.[8] In the east, as early as 1903, a superintendent of roads was based in Calabar to begin the survey and construction of roads in the eastern provinces. By 1914, there were 3,200 kilometres of motorable roads in the country.[9]

The road, being an instrument of exploitation, was also not intended by the colonial administrators to serve the development needs of Nigeria, but rather their own economic interest. As earlier indicated, road construction in Nigeria was first and foremost aimed at serving the administrative needs of the British administrative officers in Nigeria. Secondly, like the railway, roads were aimed at promoting trade in the hinterland.

Initially roads were constructed to feed the railways. Even the Nigerian railways played a substantial role in early road development efforts in Nigeria. So, such roads served as a means of extending railway influence to places far removed from the railway lines. This enabled the European business community in Nigeria to expand its sphere of influence to places which hitherto could not be reached by either water or the railways.

By 1960 when Nigeria attained independence about 46,173 kilometres of road length had been constructed. Table 4.2 shows the classification of the road length by region and by type of surfacing. The structure of road development identified in Table 4.2 also supports the thesis that the creation of transport infrastructural facilities by the colonial administration was not meant to serve the development needs of Nigeria. Out of a total road length of 46,173 kilometres, only 5,004 kilometres (or 10.84 per cent of the total) were tarred. Out of the total 5,004 kilometres of tarred roads, 126 kilometres (2.52 per cent) were constructed in Lagos federal capital. If bitumen surfacing is regarded as a measure of quality of roads, the statistics above tend to suggest that the bulk of the road length in Nigeria (about 89 per cent of total) constructed during the colonial period was of poor quality.

Table 4.2

Region	Total Road Length (kms)	Tarred Roads (kms)	Percentage of Tarred to Total Road length
West	12,147	2,144	17.65
East	14,026	1,060	7.58
North	20,000	1,800	9.00
Nigeria	46,173	5,004	10.84

Source: H. Robinson, et. al., *The Economic Coordination of Transport Development in Nigeria* (California: Stanford Research Institute, 1960), p.137.

Monetary Changes

A monetised economy is a necessary condition for meaningful trade in a country. In the absence of money, trading is done by bartering, that is by exchanging one commodity for another. Trade-by-barter is however cumbersome because it requires a double coincidence of wants. That is, you not only have to want what I have, but I also must want what you have.

As barter transactions grew, society formed the habit of assessing prices in terms of standard articles which gradually enjoyed preferential treatment and wide acceptance as medium of exchange. Long before the trade of Nigeria and its hinterland came to be dominated by the mercantile houses from Liverpool, Glasgow and London, the people possessed a well established currency system which consisted of brass rods, manillas, copper wires and cowries. Where guns were accepted as medium of exchange, as in the case of the Niger delta, they were usually valued in terms of manillas. Slaves were also used as units of account but not as a medium of exchange.[10]

Manillas were already in use in Benin as early as 1522, while brass rods were the currency of the Upper Cross River up to the Cameroons mountains. Both manillas and brass rods were very stable monetary media and were widely accepted by both the European and African traders, the general public, and initially by the colonial administration, as legal tender. The cowry was also widely used as a currency both in Yorubaland and Igboland.

To enhance the exploitation of colonial Nigeria by Britain, it was necessary for the latter to control the monetary system of the colony. The demonetisation of the local currencies was the first step in achieving this objective. Britain saw that it was to her economic advantage to assume that currency was non-existent in the colony before the advent of the British administration. British officials therefore spoke glibly of replacing 'barter' with coin. The local currencies were referred to as 'trade goods' rather than currencies and the British administration in Nigeria insisted that all payments should be made in British currency. The British currency was practically forced upon the people for they could not get goods without it.

In the delta, the local population resisted the imposition of the British currency. They were determined to accept nothing but the traditional currency. Even the local educated elite availed themselves of British money only when they made remittances to England.[11] So, early in the twentieth century, the British currency circulated within very narrow limits. The gold coins were never taken up country by the delta middlemen. Rather, they kept them in circulation in the vicinity of the government stations on the coast, where they were used in the payment of revenue.

Ofonagoro gave a number of reasons for the unrelenting resistance to the introduction of the British currency in the delta and its hinterland. The first is the low purchasing power of money in the area. Brass rods and the classes of manillas valued at 3d each constituted the highest denomination of local currencies. Historical evidence shows that Africans in the Niger Coast Protectorate could live very well on 3d per day early in the twentieth century. In fact, that was the Government's normal per diem allowance to its employees.[12] The point being made is that one could support life on less than one manilla or brass rod (the equivalent of 3d) a day. Thus, the common man had little or no use for those denominations of British coin, higher than 3d. The silver half-crown (2s. 6d) was thus a very large sum to contemporaries, not to talk of higher denominations of the British currency.

Secondly, the commercial middlemen of the delta coast controlled the flow of manillas into the hinterland markets. Demonetisation of this currency medium would therefore deprive them of a valuable asset, and they would have no control over the new currency which was to replace the manillas. Also, even a damaged manilla was still useful to the local population. Damaged manillas were usually broken up and used as substitutes for bullets. So the African population saw in the preservation of the manilla a guarantee of their continued ability to defend themselves in the event of an external attack.

To make the introduction of the British currency effective, official opinion was unanimous on two things. The first was the need to ban further importation of manillas, brass rods and other traditional currencies. The second was the withdrawal of existing traditional currencies already in circulation. The Colonial Office preferred an arrangement that would not involve any cost to the British Government. The British Government however warmly anticipated profits on the currency change.

The case of Lagos, where the British currency had been imposed since 1881, gave an indication of the anticipated profits. John Holt estimated that the British Mint made a profit of 33 per cent on the silver coinage of Lagos.[13] Another estimate by W.A. Mercer showed that on every £10,000 of silver coinage for West Africa, the Mint made a profit (excluding the cost of recoining any worn coin) of £5,581, which amounted to 56 per cent profit.[14] Until the creation of the West African Currency Board and the issuing of a distinctive local coinage by the colonial governments of British West Africa, these handsome profits were secured by the British Mint. In addition, the local consumer was expected to accept the full liability for the loss of his accumulated savings when the local currencies were replaced by the British currency.

As the area of acceptance of British currency broadened and the local currencies circulated within correspondingly narrower limits, the Nigerian economy was burdened with two currency systems, until the circulation of the local currencies was finally stopped by legislation. The compulsory withdrawal of the manilla from circulation was finally authorised by the Nigerian Legislative Council in 1948. In 'operation manilla', which lasted from October 1948 to April 1949, teams of Treasury functionaries invaded the countryside, collecting manillas and exchanging them for British money at an unattractive rate of a half-penny each. Thirty-two million manillas were recovered in this operation at a net cost of £248,000 to the Government. However, manillas continued to circulate in the villages well into the early 1950s.

The cowrie served as a subsidiary currency, catering for the small buying needs of the population. To drive the cowrie out of circulation, the British Government introduced British coins in the denominations of 1d, ½d and ¼d to replace cowries. To give the new subsidiary coinage a fighting chance of replacing cowries, it was thought necessary, as in the case of manillas and brass rods, to restrict the supply of the shell currency by prohibiting all further imports of this monetary medium. This was accomplished through the Importation of Cowries Prohibition Proclamation, No. 6 of 1904. The continued use of cowries as currency was thus barely tolerated and could be terminated by law at any time, at the High Commissioner's pleasure. Furthermore, the High Commissioner was empowered to make rules regulating, restricting or prohibiting the use of cowries as currency within the Southern Protectorate from time to time.

Paper money in the denominations of £1, 10s., 2s., and 1s., was also introduced as part of the colonial currency changes during the First World War. Initially, there was considerable local prejudice against this type of currency, but later it gradually became widely accepted. However, it survived in the £1 and 10s denominations only.

No doubt, the introduction of the British currency in Nigeria, was meant to complement the British trade in the colony in order to enhance the exploitation of Nigeria by the British imperialists. It gave Britain control over money supply in the colony. The monetary change was also deemed necessary to have a uniform and widely accepted currency system within the confines of the new Nigerian market – a system which enhanced British manipulation of the colonial monetary system to her economic advantage.

Banking

The first bank in Nigeria – the Bank of British West Africa – was established in 1894 with the objective of providing banking services for the British trading enterprises and the British colonial administrations already established on the west coast of Africa. It was also initially the opinion of the Crown Agents in Nigeria that the introduction of banking facilities would greatly assist in the extension of the use of British currency in the country.

The Bank of British West Africa was owned by Alfred Jones, a shipping magnate whose shipping lines had monopolised the shipping trade of British West Africa. Also, from its inception in 1894, the Bank of British West Africa enjoyed the patronage of the Government of Lagos and the monopoly of all banking business in that colony. To prevent the monopoly of the banking business in the whole of southern Nigeria by the shipping magnate, the European commercial community on the delta coast was very apprehensive of the extension of banking privileges to the Bank of British West Africa over the Niger Coast Protectorate.

The European commercial community in southern Nigeria was determined to prevent this by all means at their disposal. Consequently in 1900, the directors of the three most important firms on the delta coast: the Niger Company, the African Association Ltd., and Messrs Miller, Brother and Co. Ltd., established the Anglo-African Bank and put in a strong bid for the banking business of the Government of Southern Nigeria.[15] The Colonial Office was however fully aware of the objectives of its founders, especially as regards their intention of using it to stop the Bank of British West Africa from entering the Oil Rivers. It was also obvious to all the parties concerned that the colonial economy in 1900 was not ripe for two banks. Sir Ralph Moor, the Crown Agent in Old Calabar, urged the Colonial Office to encourage the two competing monopolies – the merchants and the shipping companies – to merge their banking operations.[16] In fact under the circumstance then existing in Southern Nigeria there was no real local demand for a bank, not to talk of two competing banks.

After twelve years of futile struggle, the firms and the shipping companies took Moor's advice and merged their competing banks in 1912. The taking over of the Anglo-African Bank helped to entrench the position of the Bank of British West Africa in Southern Nigeria, and its monopoly in the banking field continued unchallenged until 1926, when Barclays Bank was established. These two British Banks dominated banking operations in Nigeria up to the early 1930s.

The expatriate banks were predominantly concerned with meeting the needs of the expatriate enterprises and the Government. They did nothing to develop local entrepreneurship since they provided few or no loans and advances to the local people. Most borrowers acceptable to the banks were expatriates. The African traders (both large and small) experienced great difficulty in obtaining financial assistance due to lack of confidence by the banks in their creditworthiness. Since the expatriate banks did nothing to promote local entrepreneurship and mainly promoted the interests of the imperialists, the introduction of banking facilities in Nigeria is, in our opinion, essentially another infrastructure of exploitation of the colonial economy.

In the late 1920s and the early 1930s efforts were made by some Nigerians to break through this duopolistic hold of the credit of the economy by the two British banks. Two of the earliest pioneers were businessmen from the Gold Coast (now Ghana), Samuel Duncan and W. Tete Ansah. The latter in conjunction with some leading Nigerians (Candido da Rocha, A.A. Oshodi, P.A. Williams, and D.A. Taylor) acquired the Industrial and Commercial Bank which had been established as an overseas bank in London in 1914 by Lord Lyredon. The bank however failed during the great depression. In 1930 it went into compulsory liquidation.

The second African banking venture was the Mercantile Bank Ltd., founded in 1931 by three Nigerian Directors, Dr. A. Maja, Mr T.A. Doherty, and Mr H.A. Subair. The bank suffered the fate of its predecessor and went into voluntary liquidation in 1936. During its short career, the bank experienced great difficulty in attracting either deposits or capital from the public.

The third African banking venture, the National Bank of Nigeria, was incorporated in Lagos in 1933. It was with the incorporation of the National Bank of Nigeria that the history of African banking effectively began. By the early 1950s, the National Bank of Nigeria had become acceptable to the Nigerian financial and trading community.

In the post-second world war period, more indigenous banks were established in Nigeria. The Agbonmagbe Bank (now Wema Bank) was established in 1945, the Nigerian Farmers and Commercial Bank in 1947, the African Continental Bank Ltd. in 1948, and the Pan Nigerian Bank in 1951. These and other banks were attracted into the banking field by both the general boom of the post-war economic condition, and the evident success of the National Bank of Nigeria.

By the early 1950s, the development of mushroom banks caused the colonial administration to enact legislation to regulate the banking system in Nigeria. The Banking Ordinance of 1952, prescribed the minimum paid-up capital of £12,500 required before the financial secretary could issue a banking licence to a proposed banker. The paid-up capital for banks with headquarters outside Nigeria should not be less than £100,000. Banks were also expected to maintain an adequate degree of liquidity. The banks must have a reserved Fund representing 20 per cent of their profits. Other provisions of the ordinance were that the banking business should be conducted only by a company and that no bank could loan more than £300 to one of its directors without due security.

This new law was a great setback to the development of the indigenous banking system in Nigeria. The provisions of minimum paid-up capital, adequate liquidity and reserve fund, could not be met by most mushroom banks. Hence, the 1950s witnessed the failure of many indigenous banks, notable among which was the Nigerian Farmers' Bank. However, a few banking institutions survived this very difficult period. They included the National Bank of Nigeria, Agbonmagbe Bank, Merchant Bank, and the African Continental Bank.

Steps were taken to strengthen the indigenous banks, when Nigerians assumed power in the regions in 1957. The monopoly of Government banking business by the British banks was halted. The African Continental Bank became the depository of the public funds for the old Eastern Region, and the National Bank for the old Western Region. Viewed within the context of the decolonisation of the banking system, this action was a great landmark and most desirable. It was also a remarkable decision necessary for the development of the indigenous banking system.

The establishment of the Central Bank of Nigeria appears to be the last step taken during the colonial period to enhance banking services in Nigeria. The establishment of the Central Bank of Nigeria marked the end of the old colonial monetary system in which the West African pound was tied to British sterling. It also made possible the replacement of the old West African currency system by a new Nigerian currency system.

The instrument establishing the Central Bank of Nigeria listed as its principal objectives: the issue of legal tender currency, the maintenance of external reserves to safeguard the international value of the currency, the promotion of monetary stability and a sound financial structure, and service as banker and financial adviser to the Federal Government. The Central Bank is also the banker to bankers and lender of last resort, and the supreme controller of the credit capacity of the banking system.

Administration

In the words of R.O. Ekundare, 'the British government's efforts to establish good and orderly government in Nigeria in order to make it easier to exploit the country's natural resources took precedence over other economic considerations'.[17] Without direct administration over Nigeria, it would have been impossible for Britain to introduce such changes as 'improved' transportation, money and banking facilities, which have been used to advantage by the British imperialists to further their own economic interest.

The first direct British political interference in Nigeria came in 1851, with the British military action against Lagos, under the false impression of an effort to force King Kosoko of Lagos to abandon the slave trade.

By 1900 British influence in Nigeria had greatly expanded. The British took over the administration of the northern territories of Nigeria in 1900 and proclaimed the area the Protectorate of Northern Nigeria. At the same time, the protectorate of Southern Nigeria was created to replace the Niger Coast Protectorate. In 1906, the Colony and Protectorate of Lagos became part of the new Protectorate of Southern Nigeria.

As Britain expanded its influence in Nigeria, it strove towards achieving a unified type of administration. Finally in 1914, the Northern and Southern Protectorates were amalgamated to form Nigeria. The unification was considered desirable and expedient in order to centralise the administrative control of the country, and hence facilitate 'better' utilisation of resources. The pertinent question here is, better utilisation of resources in whose interest? Undoubtedly, it was in the economic interest of the imperialists.

To gain better grip of the country, the colonial administrators introduced the so-called system of indirect rule administration. The essence of this system of government was ruling the country through its own natural leaders. This entailed the use of existing machinery and an endeavour to improve it. Basic to this system of government was the need to find an effective channel of communication between the government and the masses of the people. During the colonial regime, the natural rulers served as such effective channel. The Oba, Emir, Obi, etc. were integrated into the process of rule and they had their own duties to perform, with an acknowledged status and responsibilities.

The system of indirect rule could be regarded as a child of expediency — an emergency device. It was not motivated as such by the desire to give Nigerians a say in the government. Rather, it was necessitated by a number of factors, namely: the paucity of British administrative staff; inadequate funds; and lack of knowledge of, and familiarity with, the local conditions, customs and traditions of Nigerians. Lord Lugard recognised that ruling through the people's recognised leaders would be cheaper and more efficient and was unlikely to anger the masses and lead to a breakdown of law and order which might occur in the event of direct rule. These reasons for indirect rule are purely exploitative. The system was meant to serve British political and economic interests.

The system of indirect rule was highly successful in Northern Nigeria, partially successful in Western Nigeria, but a failure in Eastern Nigeria. In Northern Nigeria, there was already in existence the basic machinery needed for administration and taxation. There were also many administrative officials such as the Waziri (Chief minister); the Alkali (Chief Justice), Dogari (Chief of Police or Emir's Body Guard); Maaji (Emir's Treasurer); Madaki (War

Minister); and Dandokai (Police men) to mention just a few of them.[18] The method of collecting taxes such as the cattle taxes had also been evolved and there were Native Treasuries in their rudimentary forms. These existing native institutions with their officials were adopted by Lord Lugard, with a minor modification namely, that the Residents were to supervise and guide the Emirs. Also, the tradition of submission to centralised authorities also facilitated the system of indirect rule in Northern Nigeria.

In Western Nigeria, the Oba, unlike the Emir, had no absolute authority over his subjects. There was a multitude of associations including those of palace women, the Ogboni, and the traditional chiefs all of whom wielded indirect influence on the natural ruler. For example, if a King became too oppressive, his subjects would advise him to commit suicide and he had no option but to yield to their advice. Power and authority were dispersed not concentrated in one person or institution. It was against the custom of the people for the Yoruba Oba to appear in public except on special occasions. He also rarely travelled outside his kingdom. As a result it was difficult to make him an effective executive head of a Native Administration as a Northern Emir was.

In Eastern Nigeria, the British administrators could not find hereditary, traditional rulers as in the North and West. So, they had to create Warrant Chiefs who did not enjoy the support and confidence of the people. This was why the system of indirect rule of government ran into problems in the East.

Conclusion

The provision of infrastructural facilities in Nigeria by the Colonial administration was not meant to serve the development needs of the country, but rather it was aimed at serving the economic interests of the British imperialists. The provision of transport facilities — navigable waterways, railways and roads — helped to open up the hinterland to the economic exploitation of the imperialists. Such transport facilities were constructed to link strategic mineral deposits and fertile agricultural lands with the seaports to facilitate exports of the minerals and products to the so-called mother country.

Similarly, monetary changes and the provision of banking facilities in the colony were meant to facilitate British trade with the African population. They also ensured the direct control of the money supply of the colony by Britain. Britain gained tremendously from such financial arrangements, while the local population suffered untold losses.

Finally, the provision of infrastructural facilities could not have been possible but for the direct administration of the country by Britain. The imperialists were interested in the type of administration which was cheap to operate, but which ensured maximum benefits to the metropolis.

References

1. W.I. Ofonagoro, *Trade and Imperialism in Southern Nigeria 1881-1929* (London: NOK Publishers International, 1979), p.191.

2. Ibid., p.192.

3. S.A. Olanrewaju, *The Economics of Rail Transport in Nigeria: A study in Transport Cost Analysis* (Unpublished M.Sc. Thesis, University of Ibadan, 1974), p.44.

4. H. Robinson, et. al., *The Economic Coordination of Transport Development in Nigeria,* (Menho Park: Stanford Research Institute, 1961), p.37.

5. S.A. Olanrewaju, 'Administration of the Nigerian Railway Corporation', *The Nigerian Journal of Public Affairs*, VI, 1 (1976), p.50.

6. S.O. Onakomaiya, *Highway Development in Nigeria: A Review of Policies and Programmes, 1900-1980*, NISER, Monograph Series No 5, 1977, p.1.

7. A. Akinfemoa, *A Specialist List of Records on the subject Roads and Bridges from the Government Secretariat Record Group*, National Archives, Headquarters, Ibadan, 1965.

8. G. Walker, *Nigerian Transport in 1950: An example of an underdeveloped Tropical Territory*, (London: Colonial Office, 1955) cited in Onakomaiya, op. cit., p.3.

9. Onakomaiya, op. cit., p.3.

10. Ofonagoro, op. cit., p.250.

11. CO/520/4, Committee on the Currency of the West African Colonies, Revision of Minutes of Evidence, November 17, 1899, Q 653; cited in Ofonagoro, op. cit., p.251.

12. Ofonagoro, op. cit., p.255.

13. Holt Papers, Box 19, File 4, John Holt to Thomas Welsh, November 6, 1891 (London).

14. CO/520/4, Minutes, W.A. Mercer to R.L. Antrobus, March 23, 1900. PRO, London.

15. Ofonagoro, op. cit., pp.376-377.

16. Ibid., p.377.

17. R.O. Ekundare, *An Economic History of Nigeria, 1860-1960* (London: Methuen & Co, 1973), p.12. We do not, however, share the view that government was 'good and orderly'.

18. S.A. Oladosu, *Kaduna Essays in Local Government* (Monograph, 1981, published by author), p.5.

5. Production for the Metropolis: Agriculture and Forest Products

J. O. Ahazuem and Toyin Falola

Introduction

Agriculture was the mainstay of the Nigerian colonial economy. It employed over four-fifths of the population and contributed over 60 percent of the national income.[1] Agricultural production in colonial Nigeria divides vaguely into domestic and export both of which were in the hands of small farmers each cultivating about 1.2 to 2.4 hectares of land. The former usually involved the production of food crops and such other items as kolanuts, palm-oil, livestock, etc., for both subsistence and internal trade.[2] Export production, the dominant sector of the economy, laid emphasis on the production of export or cash crops for the external market.

Agricultural exports were perhaps the most important aspect of the British programme of exploitation. Nigeria became the world's largest exporter of groundnuts and palm produce and the second largest exporter of cocoa. These three crops provided about 70 percent of the value of Nigerian exports. Cotton, rubber and timber were also integrated into the capitalist economy. Two factors brought about this transformation of the economy: a) the urge, by Britain, to secure and control important raw materials, principally agricultural and forest products native to Nigeria, which were needed by British industries; and b) the desire to establish new markets for the finished products of these industries.

To transform Nigeria into an effective market for British industrial goods, Britain modified the precolonial economic structure from a family mode of production to a colonial capitalist mode of production. A new economic relationship dominantly based on money emerged. This was achieved partly through persuasion, coercion, taxation and the creation of new wants. British administrators devoted their time to persuading Nigerian peasants to produce crops for the European market. Consequently, new crops such as cocoa and groundnuts were introduced into the agricultural system while the ancient oil-palm industry on which 'legitimate' trade had been anchored[3] was given a new lease of life. Furthermore, by parading cheap and mass-produced goods of European industries in all corners of the country, European as well as African traders succeeded in creating new wants hitherto unknown in the indigenous system. The desire to meet these new wants and to acquire some

80

surplus wealth for future consumption encouraged the peasant farmer to work harder on cash crops. As land and labour were generally available, the colonial administration benefited from these inputs, and built infrastructure to enable the evacuation of goods, and also took to active policing in order to check resistance and rebellions which could disrupt their economic programme.

Peasants and Agriculture

The Nigerian peasants were turned into producers of raw materials for the benefit of Lebanese traders and European exporters. Most became poor farmers or labourers working for the privileged emergent bourgeois farmers or absentee landlords. Colonialism also gave rise to the use of labourers on a large scale. Many of these labourers were employed in mines and others in plantations owned by rich Nigerian farmers. Generally, labourers were poorly paid and over-worked.

The income which these peasants received was so low that no appreciable changes were made in their standard of living. Large-scale cocoa farmers escaped from poverty; but labourers and small-scale farmers did not. Because of the low prices which cotton, groundnuts and palm products attracted, the peasants engaged in their cultivation were impoverished and produced only the quantities in return for cash in order to pay their taxes, buy foodstuffs and a few luxuries. In other words, production was mostly geared to buying necessary goods and paying taxes. The peasants living in areas where cash crops did not thrive well were forced, partly because of the need to pay tax, to migrate to cash crop-producing areas where they worked as labourers. To confound the peasants' problem, foreign traders deliberately gave out monetary loans or sold on credit in order to turn them into debtors. Debtors, of course, must repay their loans; and for them to do this, they had to increase production. Thus, indebtedness was used as a weapon to raise production.

A number of other measures impoverished the peasants. First, the colonial government did little or nothing to encourage subsistence or low-value export crops. They also did not improve agricultural techniques. Hence, the peasants did not learn much from the so-called European advanced techniques of agriculture. Rather than help the peasants, the British encouraged them to over-exploit their land with the consequence that land in many areas became unproductive.

Secondly, the colonial government encouraged the importation of goods which could be locally produced in order to divert the attention of the peasants to export crops.

It should, however, be pointed out that the colonial economy created a few rich farmers. These were those who benefited from the large-scale cultivation of cocoa and coffee in south-western Nigeria. Bourgeois cocoa and coffee planters made money from the relatively high prices (i.e. compared to other crops) which both crops attracted, and were also able to acquire more land to expand their farms at the expense of the poor farmers.

The successful attempts at forcing the peasants to produce for European markets had many consequences on the Nigerian economy. In the first place, it upset the indigenous economy: it led to

> disequilibrium, for instance shortages in the supply of traditional crops, changes in land use creating changes in land tenure, the ending of some old farming methods, unsatisfied demand for new farming skills, displacement of people and shifts in population, the uneven development of different regions, the dependence of the economy on a few export crops, and associated with all these, profoundly unbalanced economic growth.[4]

Secondly, the colonial agricultural measures 'changed the distribution of productive effort into those commodities which are to the benefit'[5] of Europe. Thirdly, colonial agricultural measures

> increase[d] the supply of the commodities which are more profitable to the capitalist. The increase in the supply of such commodities may pose threats of starvation to simple commodity producers (e.g. in the event of a shift from food crop to cash crop production) and reinforce his marginalisation (e.g. as the new techniques he is forced to adopt lead him into dependence and debt).[6]

Fourthly,

> these measures often entail[ed] an increase in the rate of exploitation, in the sense that they compell[ed] the peasant producer to put in more labour-time and costly inputs, which increase the profit of the capitalist while yielding to the peasant producer a return possibly much less than his increased input.[7]

Finally,

> they effectively devalue[d] the peasants labour-time by channelling his productive effort into areas, techniques and commodities which render him less competitive with the capitalist.[8]

Agricultural Production for Export

The colonial government took exceptional interest in the cultivation of palm-oil, palm-kernel, groundnut, cocoa, cotton and rubber, all of which became the key crops. Four main factors were responsible for the successful large-scale cultivation of these products. The first was that the colonial government adopted persuasive and coercive measures to secure the cooperation, willingly or unwillingly, of the peasants. The colonial government accepted the view expressed by the Liverpool Chamber of Commerce in June 1917 that:

All the energies of the native peoples should be directed towards the production of raw materials, and should be encouraged to produce greater variety and greater quantities of the produce of their country.[9]

The second was the favourable nature of the Nigerian environment for these crops. Economic factors such as the creation of new job opportunities, the building of infrastructure, notably roads and railways, and the prices which the crops attracted were the third reason. Finally, Nigeria had been a predominantly agrarian society before the imposition of colonial rule, and only some of the crops were new to them.

Oil-Palm Produce

The oil-palm (*Elaeis guineensis*) is indigenous to the forest belt of Nigeria. The oil-palm occurs with particular abundance in the eastern region, stretching from Calabar to the banks of the Niger and also in the forest areas of Western Nigeria. It extends for a distance of about 450 miles from the sea and covers a total area of about 70,000 square miles.[10] For centuries, the oil-palm has been used domestically for a variety of purposes such as supplying materials for food, shelter, medicine, fuel and illumination.

Oil-palm products were among the earliest Nigerian commodities to enter the European market. But it was not until the 19th century, when the so-called 'legitimate' trade was inaugurated, that palm-oil became a major European import. This enhanced demand for oil-palm products was necessitated by the needs of the industrial revolution which required lubricating oils for the purpose of keeping the wheels of industry turning. Palm-oil was a basic ingredient in the manufacture of tin-plate, soap, margarine, cooking fats, candles and lubricating greases. In the same manner palm-kernel oil was used in the manufacture of soap, margarine, candle and pharmaceutical products, while the residual kernel cake was a valuable livestock feed. Between 1900 and 1960, export of palm-oil rose over fourfold while that of kernels rose from over 85,000 tons in 1900 to more than 400,000 tons by 1960, an increase of about fivefold (see Table 5.1). Palm produce exports also rose in value from about £1.5 million in 1900 to over £40 million in 1960. At the beginning of the century, the value of palm produce accounted for about 81.5 percent of the total value of all domestic exports, but with time this ascendancy was challenged by other domestic exports like cocoa and groundnuts. Nonetheless, after 1940 the share of the two oil-palm products in the total value of domestic exports averaged 25 percent annually.

The marketing of palm-oil and kernel was done through agents licensed by the various Regional Produce Marketing Boards which controlled the export of palm produce in each region. Each licensed buying agent, mostly expatriate firms such as John Holt, Miller Brothers, G.B. Ollivant, United Africa Company, etc., had a number of middlemen who received cash advances in return for produce. These middlemen ranged from the wayside agents to the itinerant buyers who moved about on bicycles from house to house and from one village market to another in search of oil and kernel to buy. The sight of the latter, each carrying a basket containing as many as six kerosene tins of oil or a sack of kernel, was a common occurrence along the bush tracks and major roads in the country. The oil purchased by the licensed buying agents was delivered in large drums to bulk plants at the coastal cities (e.g. Opobo and Port Harcourt).

Cocoa

Cocoa, a South American crop found in the forest of the Amazon Basin, was introduced into Nigeria from Fernando Po. Tradition asserts that it reached Nigeria about 1874 through the help of one Squiss Bamego who established a cocoa plantation in Bonny. It was from here that knowledge of the cultivation of cocoa spread inland. Attempts at plantation production at Onitsha and Abushi by the Royal Niger Company in the 1880s proved unsuccessful. And, as in the Gold Coast (Ghana), the industry was developed entirely by indigenous farmers. The Nigerian cocoa belt covers a total area of over 10,000 square miles. At least, a tenth of this area (i.e. 1,000 sq. miles) was under intensive cocoa culture. The principal cocoa-producing areas in Nigeria were Ibadan and Ife-Ilesha Division of Oyo province and in parts of Ondo, Abeokuta and Ijebu provinces all in the old Western Region. Collectively they accounted for 95% of cocoa production in Nigeria with the other 5% coming from the south-eastern and mid-western parts.

The first export of cocoa was made in 1895 when 21 tons were shipped. In 1900 exports rose to 202 tons valued at £9,000 increasing to 17,155 tons in 1920 valued at £1.23 million, indicating an increase of over 84% in production and 137% in revenue respectively. By 1960 cocoa exports had reached 154,176 tons valued at nearly £37 million (see Table 5.1). Nigeria became the third world producer after Ghana and Brazil.

The consumers of Nigerian cocoa were mainly the United Kingdom, the United States of America and the Netherlands. The crop was hardly used locally.

Cocoa, like oil-palm produce, was marketed through licensed buying agents appointed by the Cocoa Marketing Boards. The Marketing Boards, established after the Second World War, have been vehemently criticised for their 'exploitative' role as 'tax-gatherers' for the governments.[11] Ake sees them as 'an instrument of robbery' since they were used to force African producers to accept prices well below the world commodity prices.[12] These criticisms stem from the fact that much of the huge surpluses accumulated by the Boards was used for other purposes than price stabilisation thereby denying the peasant producers of their entitlements.

Groundnuts

The Nigerian groundnut belt lies almost wholly within the Kano region where the crop was formerly grown for subsistence. The cultivation of groundnuts as an export commodity developed considerably during the colonial period. Two technical factors made this possible: firstly the perfecting of the hydrogenation process which made possible the large-scale utilisation of the oil in the food industries, namely margarine. Secondly, the extension of rail transport from Lagos to Kano in 1912 which decisively linked this area with the world trade network. With these, groundnut cultivation was transformed into one of the leading agricultural industries in the country. Between 1911 and 1937 an estimated one million acres of land came under the crop. In 1900, 599 tons of groundnut valued at only £4,000 were exported. By 1920 it had reached 45,409 tons worth £1.12 million, increasing to 396,904 tons worth over £23 million by 1955 in which year Nigeria became the world's largest producer of the crop.[13] Table 5.1 gives a clearer picture of the annual volume and value of groundnut exports from Nigeria.

The greatest centres of groundnut production in order of precedence were Kano, Katsina, Sokoto and Borno. For example, during the 1958-9 and 1959-60 seasons, Kano alone accounted for 51 and 46% of the total groundnuts purchased. But when put together the four provinces accounted for 91 and 85% respectively of all groundnut purchases during the same period. Groundnuts, like cocoa and oil palm produce, constituted a major source of revenue. For instance between 1949 and 1960, both the Groundnut Marketing Board and the Northern Regional Marketing Board provided the government in the form of loans and grants the sum of nearly £14 million for agricultural and industrial programmes.[14] Furthermore it has been estimated that over 60 percent of the peasant population of Northern Nigeria was directly dependent on the groundnut industry.[15]

Cotton
The main cotton belt of Nigeria is located in the western part of Kano region where it overlaps with the groundnut belt, Katsina Province being by far the largest producer in the country. Outside Katsina the cotton belt extends north-westward into Sokoto Province and south-eastward into Zaria Province.[16]

The growing of cotton for European markets began in the first decade of the 20th century, even though Nigerian farmers had for several centuries undertaken the cultivation of cotton for local consumption.[17] Like groundnut, the production of cotton did not attain any significance until the railway reached Kano in 1911-12. The introduction of the 'Allen' cotton from Uganda in 1912 resulted in better-yielding varieties in the Samaru 26C and Samaru 26J which constituted the basis of the cotton industry in Northern Nigeria. The rapid spread of these new varieties was made possible by the strict intervention of the Agricultural Department in the activities of peasant farmers. Table 5.2 indicates the growth trend in both the volume and value of cotton exports for the years shown.

Rubber
In the early years of its development the Nigerian rubber industry relied on the tapping of indigenous rubber-bearing plants, namely the *Funtumia elastica* and the vines, *Landolphia* and *Clitandra* which grew wild in the forests. In 1895 the value of rubber exports from this source was £2,371,892, but due to reckless tapping and the consequent depletion of the resources the value

of rubber export dropped to a mere £131,000 in 1900. For the next ten years a number of communal farms of *Funtumia* were established in the Benin area and by 1910, about 700 villages had cultivated more than one and a quarter million trees.[18] The Para rubber tree (*Hevea brasiliensis*), upon which the world natural rubber industry is based, was introduced in 1913, and *Hevea* gradually replaced *Funtumia* as a source of rubber. The rubber industry was dominated by peasant farmers who operated on a very small scale, their farms varying from one to 25 acres. They depended essentially on family labour, although those with larger estates generally employed tappers on either wage basis or as share tappers whose remuneration depended on the proceeds of the day's job.

Table 5.2 shows the volume and value of rubber exports in Nigeria. Most of the rubber produced in Nigeria was exported to Britain, the United States of America, West Germany and the Netherlands.

Forest Products for Export

For centuries, the people of Nigeria had lived in and upon the forest. As an important economic resource, it provided them with shelter, food, meat, fuel, medicine, wood, etc. According to a World Bank report[19] published in 1955, Nigeria has about 14,500 square miles of high forests out of which 2,000 square miles[20] contain exploitable timber of commercial value. The most important timber reserves are located in Ijebu, Ondo and Benin Provinces of Western and Midwestern Nigeria respectively. Collectively they accounted for virtually the entire log output, for 70 percent of the sawn timber and 80 percent of the total value of timber produced.[21] The industry was facilitated in these parts by the relative abundance of species, a network of rivers, creeks and roads for floating and carrying the harvested logs. Since the timber industry is both labour and capital intensive, exploitation of timber was dominated by expatriate firms like the United Africa Company (UAC).

Table 5.3A and 5.3B indicate the nature, volume and value of timber export of Nigeria. As Egboh's study has shown,[22] timber exports from Nigeria up to the 1940s consisted primarily of the export of mahogany and secondary timber with a bit of ebony. After the Second World War, the export of sawn timber added a new dimension to the timber trade especially with the introduction of a number of saw mill companies in the country.

The economic importance of the timber industry to the colonial administration could be seen in the fact that, prior to the Second World War, timber exports represented less than one percent of the total exports and by 1955 it had risen to 3.5% of Nigeria's total exports and was valued at £4.6 million. By 1960 it had risen further to about £7 million with Midwestern Nigeria accounting for about 50% of the total amount and of the exported timber. Most of Nigeria's export timber found its way to Europe particularly to Britain where, for instance, mahogany was used for a multiplicity of purposes such as the manufacture of aircraft propellers during the war, furniture, ornamental construction work, panelling, ship building, etc.

Conclusion

The most crucial part of the British economic policy was the exploitation of Nigeria's agricultural and forest products. Agriculture was promoted in the interest of the European countries which needed the raw materials to feed their industries. The peasants were encouraged or coerced to produce cash crops to the detriment of food crops with the sad result that the money which they earned from the cash crops was lost in buying expensive food crops. The precolonial effort of the Nigerian farmer to balance the production of food and cash crops in a way favourable to his needs was no longer possible or advisable because the farmer had to find money (and this was possible by concentrating on cash crops) to pay tax or buy European imported goods.

Table 5.1
Principal Exports from Nigeria, 1900–1960

	Cocoa (Long		Palm Kernels (Long		Palm Oil (Long		Peanuts (Long	
Year	tons)	£000	tons)	£000	tons)	£000	tons)	£000
1900	202	9	85,624	834	45,508	681	599	4
1905	470	17	108,822	1,090	50,562	858	790	7
1910	2,932	101	172,907	2,451	76,851	1,742	995	9
1915	9,105	314	153,319	1,693	72,994	1,462	8,910	72
1920	17,155	1,238	207,010	5,718	84,856	4,677	45,409	1,120
1925	44,705	1,484	272,925	4,937	128,113	4,166	127,226	2,394
1930	52,331	1,756	260,022	3,679	135,801	3,250	146,371	2,196
1935	88,143	1,584	312,746	2,245	142,628	1,656	183,993	2,093
1940	89,737	1,583	235,521	1,500	132,723	1,099	169,480	1,476
1945	77,004	2,150	292,588	3,496	114,199	1,894	176,242	2,696
1950	99,949	18,984	415,906	16,694	173,010	12,072	311,221	15,237
1955	88,413	26,187	433,234	19,196	182,143	13,151	396,904	23,134
1960	154,176	36,772	418,176	26,062	183,360	13,982	332,916	22,878

Source: *Nigeria Trade Reports*, in Carl K. Eicher and Carl Liedholm (eds), *Growth & Development of the Nigerian Economy* (Michigan, 1970), p.11. Lagos, Government Printer.

Table 5.2
Exports of Cotton and Rubber, 1905–1960

	Cotton				*Rubber*	
	Volume	*Value*			*Volume*	*Value*
Year	*tons*	*£000*		*Year*	*tons*	*in £*
1905–9	1,383	–		1906	1,533	307,076
1915–19	2,112	–		1907	1,270	244,988
1920–4	3,940	–		1910	1,176	311,691
1925–9	6,038	–		1915	248	38,112
1930–4	4,594	–		1920	498	57,044
1935–9	8,332	–		1925	950	108,234
1940–4	9,913	–		1930	2,177	150,326
1946	6,612	536		1935	2,059	61,572
1948	4,635	476		1940	2,903	264,451
1949	9,984	1,448				*Value £000*
1950	12,623	2,975		1946	11,448	1,404
1953	17,707	5,518		1948	8,019	719
1955	33,174	9,380		1949	6,858	591
1958	33,705	7,845		1950	13,652	2,834
1959	36,884	7,301		1953	21,260	3,287
1960	26,974	6,207		1955	30,380	5,577
				1958	41,206	7,627
				1959	53,370	11,608
				1960	52,229	14,239

Sources: Cotton: Ekundare, *An Economic History of Nigeria 1860–1960*.
pp.170 and 285; Rubber: E.O. Egboh, *British Forestry Policy in
Nigeria 1897–1940* (University of Birmingham Ph.D. thesis, 1975),
pp.398–9 and E. Ekundare, op. cit., p.285.

Table 5.3A
Export of Timber Products from Nigeria, 1900–1940

					Secondary	
	Mahogany	*Value*	*Ebony*	*Value*	*Timber*	*Value*
Year	*(cu.ft.)*	*(£)*	*(tons)*	*(£)*	*(tons)*	*(£)*
1899	7,680	34,737	NA	–	Mainly Iroko	–
1900	13,250	58,374	NA	–	Obeche,	–
1905	173,791	11,919	NA	–	Mansonia	–
1910	15,198	60,191	50.15	116	etc.	–
1915	7,751	54,172	11	51	–	15
1918	9,016	68,480	–	–	–	186
1920	9,776	139,726	–	119	–	–
1925	2,033,720	307,257	45	381	655	4,998
1927	1,637,494	294,672	6	44	726	4,781

1929	1,872,999	242,952	485	589	7,343	51,728
1930	171,933	110,057	73	476	12,838	84,797
1931	157,753	76,353	–	181	–	51,591
1932	625,076	62,136	33	130	14,608	44,294
1933	736,298	58,444	11	118	19,398	44,578
1934	1,016,119	85,448	470	1,793	32,744	95,891
1935	1,028,349	85,552	444	1,882	2,855*	13,571
1936	215,158	46,775	188	655	954,036*	66,920
1938	634,491	53,225	–	–	884,381*	53,191
1939	135,226	9,439	–	–	817,514*	46,880
1940	387,397	46,397	–	–	106,611*	66,397

*cu.ft.

Source: E.O. Egboh, *British Forestry Policy in Nigeria*, op. cit., pp.378–88.

Table 5.3B
Export of Timber of Wood Products

Year	Logs cu.ft.	Value £000	Sawn Timber	Value £000	Plywood Veneer £000	Total Value
1934/38	NA	146	NA	19	NA	165,000
1939/43	1,213	86	476	101	–	187,000
1944/48	2,395	321	696	162	77	560,000
1949/53	9,958	2,705	837	408	442	3,555,000
1951	16,845	5,078	956	478	441	5,997,000
1952	7,706	2,153	949	507	523	3,183,000
1953	11,821	3,223	1,137	627	541	4,391,000
1955	–	–	–	–	–	4,600,000*
1960	–	–	–	–	–	7,000,000**

Sources: International Bank for Reconstruction and Development (IBRD)
Technical Report II; *The Economic Development of Nigeria*
(Baltimore: Johns Hopkins University Press, 1955), p.323.
*Buchanan, op. cit., p.174.
**Udo, op. cit., p.42.

References

1. Federal Government Development Programme 1962–68, Sessional Paper, No. 1, 1962, p.7.

2. For further details on the internal food trade, see H.A. Oluwasanmi, *Agriculture and the Nigerian Economic Development* (Oxford, 1966), Chapter 7 and E.O. Adejumobi, 'An Analysis of the Movement of Urban Food Prices in Nigeria 1954–65', *Niser Report Series*, No. 73, 1970, (Ibadan: Oxford University Press).

3. For details, see K.O. Dike, *Trade & Politics in the Niger Delta 1830–1885* (Oxford: OUP, 1966), Chapter 6.

4. C. Ake, *A Political Economy of Africa* (London: Longman, 1981), p.45.

5. Ibid., p.62.

6. Ibid., p.63.

7. Ibid.

8. Ibid.

9. C.O. 583/62 No. 3283, African Trade Section of the Liverpool Chamber of Commerce to Under Secretary, June 26 1917. PRO, London.

10. U.A.C. *Statistical & Economic Review*, No.7 March 1949, p.2.

11. H.W. Ord and I. Livingstone, *An Introduction to West African Economics* (Ibadan: Heinemann, 1976), p.162.

12. Ake, op. cit., p.70.

13. For details, see C.K. Eicher and C. Liedholm (eds), *Growth and Development of the Nigerian Economy* (East Lansing: Michigan State University Press, 1970), pp.30–51.

14. Oluwasanmi, op. cit., p.133.

15. Ibid., p.134.

16. R.K. Udo, *Geographical Regions of Nigeria* (Ibadan: Heinemann, 1970), pp.186–187.

17. In fact, until 1925 when interest shifted from cotton to cocoa growing because of its better returns, the south, particularly Yorubaland, was an important producer of the crop accounting for about one quarter of the country's total cotton export. See K.M. Buchanan and J.C. Pugh, *Land and People in Nigeria* (London: University of London Press, 1969), p.143.

18. E.O. Egboh, *British Forestry Policy in Nigeria: A Study in Colonial Exploitation of Forest Products 1897–1940* (unpublished Ph.D. Thesis, Birmingham University, 1975), pp.321–356.

19. IBRD, *The Economic Development of Nigeria* (Baltimore: Johns Hopkins University Press, 1955), p.318.

20. This would appear to be a gross under-estimate as recent sources indicate that the Midwest alone has over 2,000 sq. miles of forest. Information Department, *Midwestern Nigeria at a Glance* (Benin City, 1971), p.44.

21. Buchanan, op. cit., p.174.

22. Egboh, op. cit., p.20.

6. Production for the Metropolis: the Extractive Industries

A. G. Adebayo and Toyin Falola

Exploitation, as it will be applied in this chapter, has two meanings. First, it is taken as working or developing mines, water, hydro-carbon and other natural resources of a country. Second, it is considered to mean the use of these resources selfishly and for one's own profit. In short, exploitation in a colonial situation, as has already been defined in Chapter 1, consists in the production of goods and in using the proceeds from that produce to either develop the economy of the metropolis through direct investment in the processing and associated industries or to further develop the infrastructure of production, including machinery, transport and communications, health and other social services so that in the end the cost of producing the raw materials would be lowered.

Colonial economic policy in Nigeria, nay, in Africa, was based on this principle of exploitation. It envisaged the production of primary goods in the colonies and the exportation of such goods directly to the metropolis. Nevertheless, most of the earlier accounts of European colonial economic policy tend to conceive 'primary goods' in narrow terms, often using it to describe mainly agricultural goods. Michael Crowder, for instance, identified the cardinal principles of colonial economic policy in West Africa as the production and exportation of 'cash crops', consumption and importation of European manufactured goods, and trade between the colonies and the metropolis, thus leaving out of his definition the production and exportation of mineral products in the colonies.[1] In this chapter, it is one of our major concerns to show that British colonial exploitation of Nigerian minerals was as integral to the metropolis's overall economic policy as the production of agricultural raw materials.

We look first at the mining situation during the precolonial period. This section is immediately followed by the discussion of the capitalist take-over of the extractive industries and the large-scale exploitation of mineral resources in Nigeria. The ownership and control of the industries, the supply and exploitation of labour, and other inputs in the industry like transport and water supply are also discussed.

Pre-colonial Mining in Nigeria

Mining had been carried on in Nigeria even before the introduction of colonial rule.[2] The minerals then extracted were those which had immediate functional implications for the different Nigerian communities. For instance, mining and processing of gold became necessary because of its ornamental uses; while such minerals as iron and tin were produced and processed into weapons of war and implements for agricultural and household uses. Nigeria is blessed with large deposits of a variety of minerals,[3] and with the men and the knowledge to extract them from the soil and process them for various users. Precolonial Nigerian communities knew of the occurrence of, and adequately produced, such minerals as iron, tin, and gold.

Mining at this period had a number of features. First, production was based on household units, though there were large numbers of people who gave their labour for wages or as slaves. Even these did not function outside the context of the household (*gida* in Hausa, or *ebi* in Yoruba). The wage labourers were generally paid in kind. Production in precolonial Nigeria was localised, or at best regionalised. Tin straws produced in the Plateau region remained essentially in the savannah region; iron ore produced in Yorubaland hardly left the area. There was therefore no integration into the world market and this probably accounts for the low quantity of its production. Though capital existed in the mining and extractive industries at this time, capitalism had not developed, especially if capitalism is taken to mean a mode of production dependent on the systematic alienation of labour from subsistence agriculture and causing dissolution of social relations. Finally, the miners and other manufacturers formed guilds which protected the members, regulated the standards of production, controlled the methods of production and output, regulated prices and made rules on modes of admitting new members. These guilds were particularly more developed among the Yoruba, Hausa, Tiv, Nupe and Benin peoples. S.F. Nadel has written about the control which Nupe rulers had on the guilds and the number of such guilds among smiths, iron workers, carvers, etc. In the third place, exclusive reliance was placed by the miners on the minerals found in their area; that is, no attempt was made to learn about the extraction and processing of minerals that were not locally available.

Colonial Mining and the Capitalist Take-over of the Mining Industry in Nigeria

Unlike agriculture, the production of minerals did not receive adequate encouragement from the colonial government. Only a few minerals were therefore worked effectively during the colonial period in Nigeria. But those that received the attention of the British government faced concerted and serious exploitation. There are many reasons why the British government did not encourage mining of strategic minerals during the period. The first was that, like any shrewd imperialist, the British did not want to develop the mineral, and therefore the industrial and technological base of the colonies. Secondly, the officials did not want to risk taxpayers' money in risky adventures especially as it was not easy to determine the eventual cost price of the minerals. Moreover, it was considered less risky to involve foreign firms in the prospecting for and mining of minerals than to go into the business themselves. That was why, except for the coal that was mined by the Railway Department of the government, the extractive industries in Nigeria were left exclusively to the firms which then paid taxes to the government. The government's Geological Survey Department, however, rendered exploration services to the firms.

Tin

Colonial mining in Nigeria started with tin trading by the Royal Niger Company (RNC) at the close of the 19th century.[4] At this time, the Company was purchasing tin at one shilling a pound, amounting to £100 per ton of Ririwai tin. This price was considered unsatisfactory and the Company believed that to encourage large-scale production, production conditions had to change. Earlier, in its treaties signed with the local rulers in the Plateau and other parts of northern Nigeria, the RNC had inserted clauses to force the rulers to surrender their mineral rights or exclusive trade rights in minerals to the Company. In 1888, for instance, such a treaty was signed with the *emir* of Bauchi who gave up all mineral rights in return for a payment of £100 in salt.

It is essential at this stage to comment briefly on the treaties as a means to the establishment not only of colonial rule but also of mineral exploitation of Nigeria by the British. Though the treaties were dubious, and their authenticity highly doubtful, they had nevertheless become the basis upon which West Africa was partitioned and the tool with which the government took over the control of anything that was underground in Nigeria. In fact, the British authorities were ready to accept the treaties at their face value and determined how to compensate the Niger Company whose exclusive rights were being transferred. Thus was signed away, in most communities in Nigeria, and without any consciousness of it and its implications, all rights to land and minerals to the extent that when concessions were applied for later in the 20th century, it was the British that determined how large and for how many years the rights could be given. When the charter of the RNC was revoked, the Niger Company (as it then became) demanded compensation for its mineral rights in Northern Nigeria which would amount to 50% of the revenues accruing to government from mineral exploitation and for 99 years.[5]

Nevertheless, it was in the opening years of the 20th century that colonial tin-mining received enthusiasm. Through reports by British captains and colonial agents, as well as the Niger Company agents involved in the conquest of northern Nigeria, there started a mad rush for concessions in the tin-producing regions of Bauchi and Jos between 1902 and 1908. William Wallace, the Acting Commissioner for the British Government who undertook the conquest of Bauchi, found deposits of tin at Ririwai, obtained samples of this tin in 1902, and quickly applied for a concession in the name of his friend, Sargent. Another man, named George Macdonald, organised some business friends to contribute £20,000 and equipped an expedition with the aim of having a 5,000 square mile prospecting licence in the Bauchi highlands. By 1903, the Niger Company had started taking a stranglehold on the tin industry by despatching its engineer, George R. Nicolaus, an experienced miner fresh from Australia, to Nigeria to prospect for tin in the Plateau. He was soon followed by H.W. Laws, a graduate from the Royal School of Mines, who entered into Tilde with 600 carriers and 25 Yoruba troops. When the troops left, Laws armed his own men with hatchets and probed the south of Naraguta for tin. By 1905, Laws had established a smelter and a sawmill at Jos for processing tin. Rickard, Wallace's brother-in-law, was 'persuaded' in 1906 to sell his prospecting rights in the Bukuru area to the Niger Company. The Company was therefore accumulating concessions. Nevertheless, the Company was a trading one, and lacked the capital with which to mine. As such, its Board decided to sell all the concessions already acquired in the tin mines to new producers. All along the colonial government being established by Lugard paid little attention to mining except as an umpire regulating prospecting licences and their acquisition. When the Company decided to throw its concessions into the open, the government did not see anything wrong in it.

The first company to move in was Champion (Nigeria) Tin Fields under the Chairmanship of Segar R. Bastard. This company had had losses in Ghana gold mines, and in its own interest it sent a mining engineer, C.G. Lush, to Nigeria in 1909 who came to Jos and returned to Britain with the report that the Jos Plateau was rich in food and water, enjoyed an excellent climate for Europeans, and was probably the richest tinfield in the world.[6] Other 'visitors' came to Nigeria to ascertain the authenticity of Lush's claim. They included Walter Wethered whose father had a substantial interest in Cornish mines, and Balfour who came in the interest of Consolidated Gold Fields of South Africa. In 1910, the first prospecting licence was issued by government to Lucky Chance, an offshoot of the Niger Company. This was followed by other companies and agents representing several companies at once. By 1911, there had been about 200 of them, and it is recorded that Nigeria's tin stocks in London in that year had received about £3 million.[7]

The information upon which these investments were based was very shaky indeed; and according to the *Economist,*

> (there had never) been a boom based on such slender data, and buoyed up by more enthusiasm over mere prospects and rosy forecasts.[8]

It was reported that stock exchange regulations were so lax at the time that shares were advertised for sale even when a prospectus, a prospecting licence, and a mining lease had not been issued. In fact, one company, the Juga Mining and Water Power Company, was recorded as being floated in 1910 for £275,000 without any land title.[9] Why then was there this mad rush to prospect for and mine tin in Nigeria by these companies?

Some of the answers to this question could be found in the demand for tin at this time. Britain was a tin-producing and using country. She exported her tin products even to West Africa during the slave trade era. But by the close of the 19th century, significant developments had taken place in Britain and the United States of America which made the demand for tin far outstrip the production in Britain and Malaya. Additional avenues for tin importation were then sought. From the 1870s British capitalists began developing tinfields in Australia while the imperial expansion in Malaya brought more tin (Malaya was the richest known tin deposit in the world). Half of the tin used between 1891 and 1900 came from Malaya, while other sources of tin were found in the Netherlands East Indies, Bolivia and the Andes.[10] Tin itself was largely used by the steel mills because tinplate consists of 99 per cent steel. But during most of the 19th century, the German and American tin industries were competing favourably with the British. It was then essential that new British-controlled tin resources under the flag and at competitive prices be found. When reports of tin occurrence in Nigeria, and under the flag, came to Britain at the close of the 19th century, the mad rush started.

Even though the rush was unorganised, it seems that all those who partook in it gained even as early as 1914. According to a table provided by Bill Freund, the leading early tin-producing companies made profits which when calculated as a percentage of their share capital realised by 1914 was at least 12%. The Ropp Tin even made profit of 170% of its share capital. The Naraguta Company which produced 1,972 tons by April 1914 made 122.8% of its £175,000 share capital as profits.

At this early stage, some of the features that were to dominate the Nigerian tin industry in the coming years were being firmly established. They include the fact that production was not done by the companies as such. They organised the men, those individual, indigenous producers, and concentrated their efforts on prospecting for areas where tin deposit was heaviest. Secondly, the Niger Company continued to dominate the mine-fields. It served the mining companies as transporter, purveyor of all supplies, cash advancer and financier.[11] Control over transport was decisive and the Niger Company transported the tin over the whole distance, from Jos to Liverpool, raising and lowering its prices to fit the needs of the moment. Thirdly, smelting was not done in Nigeria. Laws had smelted tin in Jos and Tilden Pulani; but in 1909 the Niger Company decided to stop smelting operations and ship only the cassiterite (the tin ore). The attempt made by Wethered in 1911 to establish a commercial smelter failed, the Niger Company again frustrating his efforts. It seems that the British smelters were keen on having the Nigerian tin ore to 'sweeten' less pure ores imported from Bolivia.[12] The implications of these features will be discussed in their appropriate places.

The principal changes introduced by the companies in tin production can be summarised as follows:

a) the violent conquest of the Jos Plateau to prevent the indigenes from interfering in the mining and transportation of tin;

b) the complete dismantling of the Nigerian indigenous tin industry;

c) the creation of a large force of labourers who would be prepared to sell their labour for mining capital;

d) the provision through inducement, of an extensive market in foodstuffs, to feed this work-force;

e) the cooperation, even collusion, to keep labour cheap so that Nigerian tin would favourably compete in the world market with tin from other lands, and so that a low common wage rate in the Protectorate of Northern Nigeria would be established;

f) the construction of a railway with the advantages of transporting tin at increased speed from Jos to the Coast;

g) the establishment of legislation dispossessing the local people of their land and water rights so that capitalists could then take over with ease.[13]

Other Minerals

As with tin, so it was in other minerals to which the British became attracted in Nigeria. Coal was discovered at about the same time as companies were taking over tin production in Jos. The discovery was made in 1909 at Udi near Enugu. Exploitation for coal did not start until 1915, and the colonial government did not export the mineral until the 1930s.[14] But coal exploitation and use in Nigeria had implications beyond its exploitation. This lies in its property as a source of energy. In fact, exploration for coal was induced by the railway which was in need of coal for the train engines. The bulk of the coal produced was therefore utilised by the Nigerian Railway which in fact organised its production. Some other private companies also brought from this Department. Nigerian coal was useful not only as a source of energy but also as a raw material for the production of tar and synthetic fertiliser. However, it was found that the Nigerian deposit has a poor coking quality and therefore could not compete with industrial coal from other parts of the world. This probably explains why it was not exported until the 1930s.

In spite of its poor quality, however, the history of colonial exploitation of Nigeria will not be complete without a study of the colliery, an important arm of colonial administration in Nigeria. Because coal was produced in no other place in West Africa apart from Nigeria, Nigeria became the source of supply of the energy source on the West African coastline, the countries of which could no longer import coal from abroad because of the war.

The history of the exploitation of coal began with the discovery of the mineral in 1909 as a result of the pioneering efforts of officers of the Mineral Survey of Southern Nigeria. Its mining was inaugurated by the Railway Department in 1915; and until 1950 the administration of the colliery was undertaken by the Department (though in 1937 a separate Colliery Department was established). In 1950, responsibility for the mines was taken over by a Management Board and this immediately led to the formation of the Nigerian Coal Corporation through a colonial Ordinance.[15] It is therefore evident that throughout the colonial period, the colliery was a government venture. One then wishes to ask the question why the colonial government became so interested in coal as to enter directly into its mining.

One of the reasons for this was the need by the railway for coal, in Nigeria as well as in other British West African colonies especially the Gold Coast (Ghana). The Nigerian Railway consumed a monthly average of 33,000 tons of coal between 1937 and 1945; and as an agent of the Nigerian Coal Corporation it disposed of some 17,000 tons of coal monthly to other users including the Electricity Corporation of Nigeria (ECN), the Marine Department and other commercial houses. Coal was exported to Ghana and Sierra Leone; between 1930 and 1937, Nigeria exported an annual average of 34,687 tons to Ghana. In 1954, it was recorded that government obtained two orders each for 10,000 tons of coal for the Ghana Railways.[16]

The foregoing facts show that the development of the Nigerian coal industry and the railway were intertwined. With the opening of the first colliery at Udi, the port of Port Harcourt and the railway linking it with Enugu were constructed. To facilitate the transportation of coal to key areas of its use in Nigeria, the Eastern Railway was extended to Jos and Kaduna Junctions in the 1920s. From another perspective, one also sees this linkage of coal with the railway. In 1955, diesel engines were introduced to the railway and this sharply brought down the demand for coal. By 1959, this had declined so dramatically that coal mining operations soon became uneconomical.[17]

A 1954 account of the colliery shows that there were three mines at Enugu. They were Obwetti with a daily output of about 12,000 tons; Iva with 750 tons per day; and Hayes which produced 250 tons per day. A ropeway of about 4 kilometres ran from Hayes to Obwetti mines. This ropeway carried the mine output from Hayes to Obwetti by means of buckets travelling down steel ropes. This took care of the long haul by road.

The importance of the discovery of coal to the people of Eastern Nigeria was thus threefold. It hastened the extension of the railway from Port Harcourt to Enugu. It opened job opportunities to many people in the area and exposed them to wage employment. It brought some socio-economic changes to Eastern Nigeria.

These benefits derived by the people fell far short of the inhumanities to which the workers at the colliery were exposed. In fact it seems doubtful that we can say that the colliery opened job opportunities for the people in as much as those who secured these jobs were highly exploited. These factors of exploitation of labour will be discussed appropriately later.

Another mineral that became exploited by the colonial regime in Nigeria was columbite. This mineral was for a long time an untapped by-product of tin until it was sought for by manufacturers of gas turbines and jet engines and for welding chromium nickel and steel. This began during the Second World War. The government took advantage of the high demand for the mineral then to become the largest exporter of the commodity, thus producing about 85% of total world supply. The extraction of the mineral is similar to that of tin, i.e. the washing of the ore to remove the earth impurities. Nevertheless, trade in columbite, and therefore its tapping, declined due to poor market prices especially due to the reduction in the use of columbite in the production of aircraft engines by the United States, the largest consumer of the commodity.[18]

One final mineral in Nigeria, and one whose exploitation was not pushed with the same vigour, was petroleum. Petroleum exploration in the country was started by a German company, Nigerian Bitumen Corporation, which drilled 14 wells around Lagos in 1908.[19] It reported a prospect for oil in Nigeria and had the hope of extending the scope of its activities. But the First World War came, and as a German company, it faded away with the war. It was however the Company's hope and success that gave birth to a renewed interest started in 1937 by Shell d'Arcy Petroleum Development Company of Nigeria, an affiliate of the mineral oil companies Shell Petroleum Company and British Petroleum Company. This Company acquired the first mineral oil concession from the colonial government in 1938 and negotiated an oil exploration licence for the entire mainland of Nigeria, about 357,000 square miles.[20] Geological and geophysical probing in the following years were interrupted by World War II, though by 1946 it had been found that the areas showing oil-yielding structures were in southern Nigeria. In 1951 therefore, Shell-BP limited their oil exploration licence to about 58,000 square miles of southern Nigeria. In 1955 and 1957, these areas were further delimited to about 40,000 square miles. The following year, 1958, the Company struck oil in commercial quantities in Oloibiri in the Delta area. Production that year was 6,000 barrels per day (bpd).[21]

Shell-BP Petroleum Development Company of Nigeria, as Shell d'Arcy became called in 1956, was most favoured by the colonial government perhaps because of its taking the pioneer risk, and perhaps because the company was partly British. It reserved for itself all the areas known to be potentially rich in oil deposits. For instance, no other company was allowed into Nigeria to break Shell-BP's monopoly of oil prospecting licence until 1955 when Mobil Exploration (Nig.) Ltd., an affiliate of the American Socony-Mobil Oil Company, was granted an exploration licence. Even then, this did not cover the areas known by Shell-BP to be oil-rich but was limited to the north-western part of the country which had been abandoned by Shell-BP. It was no wonder then that in March 1961 when all those licences obtained by Mobil, including that covering 4,000 square miles of the Western Region, were due for renewal, the company returned them to the government because their geological and geophysical investigations reveal no promising results.[22]

At independence, Shell-BP was using as oil-mining leases only a third of its area under prospecting licence. It thus became possible for other companies to share in the promising oil exploitation of southern Nigeria. These developments lie beyond the time-scope of this study.

Unlike the other minerals whose production saw marked decline after independence, petroleum exploitation and marketing continued to develop after 1960, and it became the decisive source of Nigeria's revenues. The reasons for this have internal as well as international sources. Internally, oil brought quicker money than other minerals, even products, of Nigeria. Internationally, petroleum as a major and cheap source of energy started to witness a rise in prices, a greater demand, and attracted a more steady income for the producers after 1960 when the Organisation of Petroleum Exporting Countries (OPEC) was formed.[23] Throughout the whole period of its exploitation by the colonial government, next to nothing was done to regulate the activities of the companies, not to talk of controlling them.[24] There were those people who thought that the colonial administration in Nigeria did not know the extent of the occurrence of petroleum in Nigeria; else, they would not have granted the country its independence in 1960 without violence. This is not so. The British knew how potentially oil-rich Nigeria is and how much oil she had to import from Nigeria in later years. What she knew, which people who opined that belief did not know, was the fact that the activities of the companies would not be interferred with and that she stood to gain by the unequal relationship between Nigeria as a producer and the company as the owners of the oil-mining technology. What Britain however did not foresee was the development of an oil cartel as OPEC that could attempt to control prices of oil and lay production ceilings which would affect Western oil interests and make prices substantially rise.

The foregoing has introduced us to the entrance of foreign capital into the Nigerian extractive industries, foreign capital in the form of direct government involvement as in the colliery, and company operation as in petroleum and tin. At this stage, it is pertinent to discuss thematic issues of control of the industries, the quantity of each mineral produced, the prices charged for them and for whose benefit the profits were used, and such other avenues of exploitation as the cruelty in the use of labour and the erection of infrastructure of exploitation such as transport and communications facilities and health services.

Who Controls the Companies?

This question is of central concern to the whole problem of exploitation, especially in a colonial setting. We have established that the extractive industries in Nigeria were owned partly by the colonial government and partly by the companies. It seems therefore that these two owners separately and collectively controlled the activities of the companies in the industries. That the Nigerian people ever had any say in the administration of the companies, or even of the colonial government, was out of the question. Even nationalist activities then did not harp on the ills inherent in the extractive industries. The only group of Nigerians involved in the agitation were the labourers in the mines whose pay was quite low indeed. But it even seems here that agitation was limited to a form of passive resistance which involved running away from the mines when working conditions were poorest and coming back when they were better.

Individual prospectors at first entered the extractive industry in Nigeria before the era of operation by large firms when the deposit value of the mineral had been ascertained. Tin-mining in Nigeria exhibits this model of company takeover of what hitherto had been restricted to a few prospectors, indigenous or foreign. When the operation of small firms became inadequate, especially since they were involved in competition with each other, an amalgam of all the companies involved in tin in Nigeria was made. This was in 1939, an event that led to the creation of the Amalgamated Tin Mines of Nigeria Ltd. Nevertheless, it seemed that the small firms had certain advantages. Firstly, the minerals that were involved could be worked on a small scale with less massive financial resources. For instance, for many years the companies did not really produce the tin, they merely appropriated the produce of individual, small tributors. Secondly, small firms could transport their lighter equipment from the coast into the hinterland while it was impossible, until the joining of the northern with western and eastern railways, to carry heavy equipment needed by larger firms.

Associated with the question 'who controls the companies?' is the further question 'how was the control established?' Answers to these questions revolve around the physical conquest of the area around which the mines were located. This is, of course, an aspect of the general conquest and pacification of Nigeria by the British. In cases where the conquest preceded discovery, as was the case of petroleum and coal in southern Nigeria, it was easy to establish control, yet the indigenous population still had to be 'enticed' to work in the coal mines. However, tin produced a unique example of a physical, military campaign not only to make the tin-producing regions free of hostile 'natives' but also to make the indigenous tributors work in the mines.

At first, such independent prospectors as Laws and William Wallace met little challenge from the people. But as many more entered the tin region, and as they began moving into areas under the control of independent Birom, the story changed. Birom communities resented intruders and in April 1904, Jos and Gyel drove out the Niger Company employees and prospecting was temporarily halted. Lugard then saw the necessity of an expedition into the north-west. Gyel was put to the torch and an estimated 100 people were killed and injured.[25] Ganawurri was attacked while Nafam, Zigam and the Mwahavul were all 'pacified'. Despite this, resistance continued in the Plateau. In 1905, a convoy supplying the mines was attacked by the Rukuba. In 1906, however, Captain Howard became Resident of Bauchi. In a special tribute-gathering visit he made to the Plateau, Howard's forces destroyed Hoss, killing 25 and stealing all cattle; 34 people were killed at Fier; and in the Mwahavul country 98 men were killed.[26] During a tour of Tangale-Waja area, hundreds of men were murdered, villages destroyed and cattle stolen. From 1907 therefore, the tin-mining zones were relatively secure, though confrontation continued. For instance, S.W. Campbell, a veteran mining engineer in Ririwain Kano who was notorious for his high-handedness, was killed by the people, his body divided into parts and sent to various villages in the community. In May 1912 the government launched the Mada Patrol which wreaked a bitter revenge, destroying villages and killing an officially admitted figure of 142 people. In fact, the patrol refused to negotiate until all parts of Campbell, excepting a foot and a shinbone which were reported burnt, had been returned.[27] Punitive expeditions were carried into the Plateau until 1929 when peace was said to have been established.

The various communities were therefore dispossessed in two ways: their control over minerals and land were taken away. Lugard advocated the payment to the indigenous miners of a compensation of up to £50 per annum by the companies. But these were never heeded and no one could be said to have received this compensation.[28] As for the land, the communities where tin was found almost automatically lost all rights to their land. According to the first minerals proclamation for the territory, passed in 1902, miners (foreign prospectors) had the right to work any land they chose, subject to government licensing and leasing, even land considered to be sacred by the local religious cults. The miners could use water, wood except rubber and palm-oil, that was found growing on the land.[29]

The government made things easier for the companies by granting exclusive prospecting licences (EPLs) covering up to 20 square miles and mining leases (TMLs) covering 99 years, and over 5 square miles. The owner of an EPL was allowed to apply for a TML and the lease holder had the exclusive right to export tin out of Nigeria.[30] In 1909, a commission was established by government to revise the mining legislation which made it quite clear that the payment of compensation by the companies to the people whose land was taken was obligatory. But Governor Hesketh Bell made it plain that the local farmers had ten times the land they needed, thus implying compensation was not necessary.

Labour Exploitation in the Extractive Industries

According to Bill Freund, writing on labour and tin,

> Capital, in the form of commoditised goods obtaining value from the appropriation of labour, existed in Northern Nigeria for centuries before the beginning of colonial rule. Capitalism, as a mode of production making labour power a commodity, only really developed in the 20th century.[31]

This observation holds for other industrial and extractive ventures in other parts of Nigeria. Capitalism became established in Nigeria with the proletarianisation of people, forcing the ordinary people into selling their labour power to obtain the basic necessities of life. Rarely in any other sector of the Nigerian economy were people forced, even against their will, to sell their labour power as in the coal and tin mines.

It has been said that the earliest group of wage-earners in Nigeria were the workers in the mines. Quite so; but as we shall see presently, the wages were exploitative and low.

The kind of labour required in the Nigerian extractive industries was, for a long time, unskilled. Until machinery was introduced much later in the century, all that was needed was the skill the traditional tributors had before the arrival of the Europeans. Generally, the people who supplied the labour needed on the mines (coal and tin) did so because of two major things: dispossession and need for money. Dispossession had come through the seizure, as in the tin mines, of the land and mineral rights of the people by the companies and government. Those among the traditional miners who had nothing else to do invariably turned into labourers for the companies. The need for money derived from the quick monetarisation of the economy first through the introduction of cash crops and simultaneously through the taxation system. Tax especially drove the other categories of workers, who were not related to the production of minerals, into the mines. They came in large numbers to the Enugu coal mines in order to get money, raw cash, to pay tax.

The first category of labourers who were not so skilled in mining came from the villages and communities around the mines. These were most likely to be those dispossessed through acquisition of their land for mining purposes. Other groups, however, came from communities farther from the mines. A breakdown of the tin mine-workers provided by Bill Freund aptly shows this composition.[32] (See Table 6.1). This category of workers was regarded as the 'floating population' because most of them came in mainly to receive employment and then returned. This is especially true of the Hausa people at the tin mines. They were originally farmers and they came in the dry season only to go back at the beginning of the next planting season (when the first rains fell). The slave population also provided labour on the mines. They had run away from their masters and taken employment in the mines with the hope that as soon as they had enough money they would go back home to pay their manumission.[33] Laws especially made use of these slaves as early in the history of colonial tin mining as 1902.

How was this work force organised in the mines for production? This is a question whose answers border on exploitation. For the purpose of clarity, our discussion will be centred mostly on the tin mines, though we shall also refer to the coal mines when questions of inhumanity to man in the mines are discussed. At first the companies operating in the Nigerian tin industry coerced the government to organise a labour supply that would be based on recruitment on the model of the Rhodesian mines. The government was asked to force the Plateau population to work for the mines; and one recommendation from Langstow Cock, the Government Inspector of Mines in 1918, was that an estimated population of 40,000 male adults be made to work on the mines.[34] The government did not really agree with this recommendation. But it would appear that it did nothing when people were being conscripted. The organisation of these conscripts for production was however harsh and inhuman. This experiment was unsuccessful not only because the people resisted but also because it was costly for the companies because of desertions. Of the 2,167 labourers recruited from Bauchi, 885 deserted.[35]

From the 1920s onwards, 'voluntary' labour was favoured; and this kind was more complex to organise especially since the workers came of their own free will and could decide to leave whenever they were unjustly treated. For this voluntary labour, 'headmen' were used. These headmen picked their gangs which could number from ten to 40 men, most often men of the same origin as themselves. *Tin International* carried a report in 1942 where the successful headman was described as:

> one who commands respect and obedience from his gang and who looks after his labourers' welfare, lending them money when they require extra for some purchase or indulgence. The headman of course receives his interest on such loans. Although the labourer can leave the gang and move off elsewhere whenever he so desires, a good headman will keep his labourers together for long periods.[36]

Labour organisation under the headman system fell into two categories: tributing and contracting. The tributer was a seller of tin ore and had to sell to the licencee of the property on which he was working. Generally, the company that gave him the licence also provided him with the tools and housing. The tributer then organised his own gang of labourers. In real terms, the tributer was a piece-worker, because he conducted his affairs with little hindrance or supervision from the whites. The colonial officials did not like tributing because of this lack of supervision. The tributer often did the actual prospecting, discovering new tin deposits, and determined the spot where they would work with their licence. In general therefore, the tributer was more permanently wedded to tin-mining and earned more than contract labour. Tributing licences were introduced in 1921, though it often went on without licence and unknown to the government.

Contracting or task work consists of labourers organised and paid on the basis of the amount of tin produced or the yardage of earth moved. Contract labour offered lower wages and less autonomy for the worker. The companies owned the capital and directly controlled it. Task workers were the less skilled local migrants and they heavily out-numbered the tributers by a ratio of 7:5 according to the 1945 estimate. Among the contract labourers, the short-term workers were engaged in head-pans while the more stable and fairly skilled workers were engaged in pick-and-shovel stages. Task work needed a lot of supervision at guaranteed low pay as any extra effort on the part of the worker indicated extra leisure rather than cash. It then seems from the foregoing that tributing was more favourable to the skilled workers than contracting while the companies preferred contracting to piece-work involved in tributing.

Though tributing and contracting remained the dominant forms of labour organisation throughout the period, a good number of labourers were daily-paid workers. The 1945 estimate counted daily paid workers as constituting 16% of the total work force.[37] With the introduction of machinery to the mines, daily-paid workers began to grow in numbers: they were then engaged in tin washing in sluice-boxes and concentrating in jig plants. Mechanics, fitters, carpenters and clerical workers were all needed with the application of machinery and these were paid wages on a daily basis.

The miners were housed in camps and, by 1940, 200 such camps were counted on the Plateau. The camps were filthy and unhealthy, and a no-man's-land type of freedom prevailed. Mines managers were not good at maintaining authority, and the workers were free to come and leave as long as the tempo of mining was not decreased. Squatters were many who joined the miners in the camps and the companies and the NA police did nothing about them. A survey in 1945 of the Dorowa camp revealed 188 squatter households including 140 farmers, 13 cloth traders, 10 food traders, eight tailors, four Islamic teachers, three butchers and one lorry owner.[38]

Camp houses consisted of grass-thatched huts built close to each other. From the 1930s, they became cemented inside and outside. Each house was in theory suitable for a couple or a pair of workers. But in practice, they were overcrowded with between six and eight men sleeping in a hut. The cold condition of the Plateau itself made these houses unsuitable and the Birom people, one of the indigenous peoples of the mines region, chose to trek to the mines from their well-built, warm homes. Health conditions in the camps were bad. Venereal diseases and cerebro-spinal meningitis were easily spread

Table 6.1
Racial Distribution of Mine Labour, Jos Division, 1930

Hausa	6,498
Beriberi	1,906
Bagirmi	1,677
Fulani	1,097
Tera	648
Kerikeri	590
Shuwa Arab	424
Ibo	249
Yoruba	225
Babwe	221
Zaberma	154
Munshi	153
Bolewa	151
Nupe	95
Asabe (Ibo)	66
Barom	55
Other Northern Provinces	430
Other Southern Provinces	165
Native foreigners	16
Total	*14,817*

Source: Bill Freund, op. cit., Table p.85.

in the camps. Worse still, the companies assumed little responsibility for the workers' health.

The government tried to introduce pipe-borne water to the newer camps, but the old ones were generally neglected. It also forced the mines to begin spending money on incinerators, wells, slaughter slabs for the market, and concrete lined urinals. But in conditions of over-crowding these facilities were never enough. Diseases caused by exposure, poor diet and communicable illnesses took a heavy toll of the people's lives.[39] By the 1930s the biggest companies provided assistance in first aid and hospital care though they were under no government obligation to do so.

Organisation of labour for production also involved their pay. The mine workers were the earliest group of wage labourers in Nigeria; and they set the standard of low wages, almost free labour, which the colonial enterprise used in Nigeria. In the Nigerian tin industry, the wages were particularly low, and their fluctuations were also related to the world price of tin. The condition of the 1920–22 depressions particularly created a situation in which wages were reduced for the first time. During the rest of the 1920s when tin prices recovered handsomely, wages rose to an estimated weekly average of 5s. 6d in 1926 and 6s. 0d in 1927 in Plateau province. Bill Freund has stated that it is not easy to compare what the miners earned in the 1920s with what they had earned before the First World War. He says, for instance, that:

> Making an exact comparison presents several problems. We have only fragmentary evidence on hours of labour. In the mid-1920s, the wage was calculated for a 54-hour week of six nine-hour days, which probably represented little change from the past. However, the free food often supplementing the early wages appears to have been replaced in the 1920s by provision of subsidised food.[40]

Nevertheless, the comparison could be made with what the European labourers employed by the companies earned and what their counterparts who were blacks earned: the ratio was about 5:1.

From the end of 1928, wages began to fall with increasing rapidity; at the height of the Depression, miners earned only 2s. 6d or even less per week in 1932 to 1935.[41] This was quite low indeed; and according to one of Bill Freund's comparisons, the miner's average daily pay in 1935 could buy him only 3½ pounds of grain at 1½d a pound.[42] The miners were therefore earning barely enough to keep themselves alive; and worse still, the indigenous people of the Plateau had no other job to do as they had been dispossessed; and the tax collectors were on their heels, ready to take whatever they made in cash.

A similar pressure for employment in an industry that ensured a steady wage drove people to the coal-mines from far and near. The majority of the coal-miners came from nearby villages and were largely illiterates. But even though they were not literates, the Igbo local miners were as pugnacious as the Hausa tin miners were docile. Because of Igbo pugnacity, and because the colliery was being run by a government department, it became possible for wages in the coal mines to be higher than those at the tin mines. But even then, there were combined actions on the part of the miners to demonstrate their disagreement with the prevailing conditions through strikes. There were 'go-slow' strikes embarked upon in 1920 due to the unpopularity of paper money, in 1937 resulting from the restoration of the wage rate reduced during the Depression, and in 1949 caused by the introduction of explosives into the underground mines.

The organisation of labour and the condition of service of Enugu coal miners have been regarded as most favourable.[43] For instance, it is claimed that the 7,000 people employed at the mines were given annual leave with pay, provided with welfare shops and free cinema performances in their housing estates. It is also claimed that, unlike in England where coal-miners had to descend thousands of feet into the earth, the Enugu coal-miners worked in tunnels, five feet high, driven into the side of the hills. Thus, instead of crawling to his work and hewing coal while lying on his side, the Nigerian coal miner could get to his work without much discomfort; and as Nigerian coal-mines possessed no dangerous gas, the miners ran no risk of explosions and the accident rate in the Nigerian mines was the lowest in the world.

But, as Mr Afolabi Adenekan, Secretary-General of the Nigerian Trade Union Congress said in 1949, the government's labour policy in the mines was attractive on paper but left much to be desired in practice.[44] This much that was left constituted the cause of the strike of 1949 and the general riots that followed it. The strike is of central importance to this study, more so because of the revelations made at the inquiry set up to investigate the incidence.

On November 18, 1949, a most tragic incident occurred at the Enugu colliery when 19 miners were killed and 31 seriously injured. Before this date, the African miners had been on a 'go-slow' strike to enforce higher pay. Feelings ran high when the colliery management dismissed 250 miners and refused pay demands. Then followed the controversial removal of explosives from the mines to a central magazine for public safety by the police. It was reported that the police made three lifts without interference until they got to Iva Valley Mine where the police were attacked by a large crowd of miners, attempting to disarm the police and gain possession of the explosives store. It was also reported that the officer-in-charge of the police warned the miners without success; and when it seemed the policemen were going to be overwhelmed, they opened fire in self-defence. But people were not ready to accept this explanation, and at a time when nationalist feeling and consciousness were high and trade unionism at its nascent but effective stage, people demanded investigation and even took the law into their own hands. Riots took place in the major towns in eastern Nigeria, the report of which was summarised in *West Africa*. On November 22, a European was killed at Owerri, while yelling and fighting crowds ransacked the stores of G.B. Ollivant at Aba. In Port Harcourt, disturbances were so fierce that all white women and children were evacuated to the Government Rest House and put under guard. Tear-gas was used to disperse rioters at Onitsha while a curfew was imposed on Calabar. In Lagos, a mass rally was held in which people were supplied with cutlasses but asked not to use them yet. Mr Bode Thomas was said to have issued a release that

> There will be no further disorders. We cannot keep the people calm after what happened to the miners. The shooting has united the east and west as never before.[45]

Immediately after the incidents, an African-formed National Emergency Committee was quickly organised and this Committee swung into action, taking the miners' points of view and preparing a memorandum to be submitted to the Commission of Inquiry being set up by the Governor, Sir John Macpherson.[46]

Before the riots, it seemed that the condition of service at the coal-mines was deplorable indeed. The miners were paid between 3s 0d and 4s 0d daily for a 45-hour week. In addition, they received 4d a day underground allowance, 3d a day seniority pay, 5d a tub for easily hewn coal and 8½d for harder coal. The hewers earned 6s 6d on average a day. In 1949, the miners were demanding a 5s 10d daily pay which would bring their pay to about 8s 0d a day. By comparison, this was higher than what the companies paid the tin-miners. Moreover, the government argued that if this demand was granted, then Nigerian coal would become uncompetitive in West African markets because Nigerian coal and South African coal sold for about the same amount in Lagos and Accra respectively (i.e. 65s 0d a ton). It was also argued that the miners at the colliery had free housing, free medical services and free child welfare services; and that in spite of all these only a fifth of the normal coal output were turned over to the management.[47] Higher pay was, therefore, unjustifiable.

It however seemed that apart from wages other matters could easily bring disaffection between the miners and the colliery management. For instance, the Colliery's manager, Bracegirdle, admitted that he did not reply to a vital letter because it was 'temporarily lost in his office'. He also admitted that even after the miners had agreed to go back to work, he still dismissed 250 of them.[48] It then seemed correct to say that the government was subjecting the miners to what H.O. Davies called 'psychological atrocity'. Heads of government departments were intolerant of labour demands, and this was brought plainly out by Mr H.R. Honey's declaration that he resigned as labour officer a fortnight after arriving in Nigeria because of 'frustration' by other government officials:

> He wanted to explain the position to the miners but was not allowed to do so. He was told that this would be interpreted as a sign of weakness by the miners. This haughty attitude to the workers . . . is prevalent throughout the country and . . . has been the cause of much dissatisfaction in the past.[49]

It was pointed out at the Inquiry that officials were not always willing to see labour's point of view. According to Mr Afolabi Adenekan, there was not an occasion when government gave concession without pressure. Only the 'blue-eyed boys' – the non-unionists, were given promotion. Mr O. Mbadiwe, representing the National Emergency Committee, criticised what he described as the over-generous rates of European officers' salaries and asked that they be reduced.

These and some other acts of inhuman treatment were revealed by the miners or their representatives at the Inquiry; and this proves beyond all doubts that the oft publicised belief that the Enugu coal miners were not exploited by the Colliery Department was untrue.

Production and Profits

It is proper at this stage to see the quantity of minerals that were produced in Nigeria and the appropriation of the profits made. This eventually will lead us to the questions: who profited from the establishment of mining in Nigeria on a capitalist basis, why and in what form? It is essential to state that in answering these questions we might have to separate national Nigerian interests from the foreign investors' interests. Bourgeois development economists often argue that 'retained values' comprehend the economic impact of an industry on a specific geographical region. For instance, in 1929, engineer J.G. Foley estimated that Nigerian tin-mining generated a value of £2 million of which half was retained in Nigeria while 90% of the remaining half was retained in Great Britain.[50] This estimate does not take cognisance of the fact that of the amount retained in Nigeria, most went to wages; and such payments should have been calculated as part of the production cost. The Nigerian Chamber of Mines in 1930 also put it that the mines gave Africans 'the purchasing power to buy English cotton and other goods and to pay their taxes'. But according to Bill Freund,

> cash wages served primarily to valorise values in cash terms so as to squeeze free a surplus for the government and the trading firms.[51]

First, let us take the case of tin and see how labour power generated surplus was distributed. As shown in Table II, production on the tin mines changed with the market conditions and the international environment, especially the War and Depression.

On the eve of the First World War, the Niger Company was the king of the tinfields and it raised its capitalisation from £500,000 to £3 million. As the war progressed, this capitalisation began to produce effects. The price of imported necessities for the mines increased while that of tin also rose. In 1917, tin reached over £300 per ton in price. In 1918, the price rose substantially from £316 per ton in April to £337 per ton in October. In 1917, the declared profits of the Niger Company were £140,000 of which £40,000 came from mining; and in 1918, mining profits exceeded trading profits; and in 1919, the Company netted £80,000 profit from mining royalties and

Table 6.2
Nigerian tin production, 1915–1945 (in tons of ore)

1915	6.910	1926	10.595	1937	14,872
1916	8.187	1927	11,509	1938	12,382
1917	8,314	1928	13,041	1939	13,003
1918	8,434	1929	15,335	1940	14,843
1919	8,169	1930	11,902	1945	15,166
1920	7,382	1931	9,800		
1921	7,239	1932	6,000		
1922	7,319	1933	4,956		
1923	8,372	1934	6,897		
1924	8,857	1935	9,045		
1925	8,937	1936	13,432		

Source: Bill Freund, op. cit., pp.120, 122.

£43,000 from other mining profits.[52]

The Niger Company, however, left the economic scene and the vacuum it created in the mines was filled quickly by the competing firms and prices rose again. But in 1920 these firms collectively made a profit of £472,000 which is substantial but which when divided up amongst the 105 operators amounted to only £4,495 average. It then seems that the first decade of the capitalist venture in Nigeria ended with substantial profits to Niger Company, the big speculators from Europe, and a few firms. All these made haste to re-invest their profits not entirely in Nigeria but in the metropolis.[53]

Power needed by the heavy equipment which was introduced in the early 1920s was supplied by building a hydro-electric dam in Kwall. The Kwall project had been taken up and dropped by various companies when they discovered that government was not going to subsidise it. However, the Northern Nigeria (Bauchi) Company, headed by Sir Robert Hampson, persisted in the programme and received government subsidy. The project was at first estimated to cost the company £40,000. But when it was completed in 1924, it had taken £250,000.[54] The Kwall dam however had many advantages. It held water for the people for 9 months in the year and this held a firm grip on one aspect of the production itself. The Kurra Falls also had a potential hydro-electric power generation potential, and this was also done in 1925. This quickly expanded production.

The tin boom that followed in the 1930s brought in substantial profits for the companies (see Table 6.3). From 1932, the market conditions of tin began to brighten and, as a result of the restrictions, prices began to rise. Tin production from 1936 exceeded 10,000 tons of ore; and mining capital had taken advantage of the situation by giving lower wages to African miners, thus incurring low costs of production. One would have thought that with the boom and increase in prices wages would also rise. But this was not so, even the wages of the whites were cut. The end result was a higher profit accruing to the companies and it was reported that between 1929 and 1938 the

Table 6.3
Tin Boom, 1932-1938

Year	£ African Wages	Other costs of Production	Declared Profit	Profit as % of capital	Profit as % of costs
1931	139,000	636,000	9,800	0.2	1
1932	118,000	446,000	120,000	2	21
1933	98,000	231,000	283,000	5	86
1934	131,000	433,000	579,000	12	102
1935	147,000	560,000	778,000	16	110
1936	227,000	826,000	940,000	20	89
1937	329,000	1,026,000	1,249,000	27	92
1938	290,000	1,032,000	312,000	6	24

Source: Bill Freund, op. cit., p.124

average return to capital in the Nigerian tin mines was nearly 10 per cent per annum; and that the average percentage of profits compared to outlay costs was 57 per cent.[55]

The first significant shipping of columbite to the United States, the principal consumer of the product, was in 1936.[56] Columbite, which formerly had been discarded as worthless, along with tin mine tailings, was quickly recovered through an inexpensive and profitable business for those companies which had grounds in the areas where the deposit was rich.

On how the surplus was distributed, Bill Freund has this to say:

> Labour power received only £20 per ton; other costs amounted to £109. 10s. 0d (total cost of production amounting to £129. 10s. 0d). Some of these costs were really profits going to other capitalists from various servicing operations. Something over £20, a larger figure than in pre-war years, went to the state. More than £10 went to the United Africa Company as a result of the 1899 royalties deal. Of the £8 for European salaries, a small portion can be considered as labour payment but most belongs to the surplus as the portion paid out for labour supervision.[57]

A breakdown of the pay which the Africans received was very pathetic indeed. According to Bill Freund again

> . . . in a 54-hour week in 1927, the labourer worked 14½ hours for himself, 18½ hours for mining capital and 21 hours for the regime, for other capitalists and to defray the expenses of capital. In 1937, in a 50-hour week, he laboured in the same causes 4, 24 and 22 hours.[58]

The argument of development economists therefore that a percentage of the profits (or surplus) was retained in Nigeria seriously crumbles. It is obvious that both labour and land of Nigeria were exploited by the capitalists to produce for the metropolis.

Conclusion

Production of minerals for the metropolis is an integral aspect of colonial
economic policy. The way it was carried out in Nigeria especially smacks of
exploitation to the fullest of the land, water and human resources of the
colony. The British produced tin, columbite and petroleum directly for the
metropolis while coal was produced to service other arms of the imperial
policy, especially in providing the power with which the railway and other
machines and plants were generated. All the surpluses were predicated upon
the labour power of Nigerians some of whom were even martyred because
they dared to ask for more pay.

References

1. Michael Crowder, *Colonial West Africa: Collected Essays*, (London:
Frank Cass & Co. Ltd., 1978), p.244.

2. See Fell Godfrey, 'The mining industry in Nigeria' in *Journal of the
Royal African Society*, Vol. 38 (1938–39), pp.247-259; *Nigerian Handbook,
1931*, p.95; K. Buchanan and J. Pugh, *Land and People of Nigeria* (London:
University of London Press, 1962), p.179; and IBRD, *The Economic Development of Nigeria* (Baltimore: Johns Hopkins University Press, 1955), pp.54ff.

3. Geological Survey, Nigeria, *Mineral and Industry in Nigeria with notes
on the History of Geological Survey in Nigeria and the Cameroons* (Lagos:
Government Printer, 1975).

4. Bill Freund, *Capital and Labour in the Nigerian Tin Mines* (London:
Longmans, 1981).

5. Ibid.

6. A.F. Calvert, 'Tin in Nigeria', *Mining World*, Nov. 5 1910.

7. Rhodes House, Oxford (PH): MS. Africa, S85, Niger Company Papers,
Trigge to Scarbrough, July 10 1911, cited in Bill Freund, op. cit., p.37.

8. *Economist*, 22 June 1912.

9. RH:MS Africa S89, NC papers, Agent-General to Scarbrough, May 21
1910.

10. See Economic Intelligence Unit, *The London Metal Exchange* (London:
EU, 1958), p.8; William Fox, *Tin: The Working of a Commodity Agreement*
(London: Mining Journal Books Ltd., 1974), p.97; and Yip Yat Hoong,
Development of the Tin Mining Industry of Malaya (Kuala Lumpur: University
of Malaya Press, 1969), p.56.

11. Bill Freund, op. cit., table p.38.

12. Ibid., pp.39–40.

13. R. Howard Johnson, 'Birth of a Tinfield', *Mining Magazine*, Vol. XXXIII,
1, July 1925, p.15.

14. P. Bower, 'The Mining Industry', in Margery Perham (ed), *Mining,
Commerce and Finance in Nigeria* (London: Faber and Faber, 1948).

15. A.C.E. Armstrong, 'Coal mining in Nigeria', in *Commerce and Industry*
published in Lagos by the Ministry of Trade and Industry, 1955.

16. P. Bower, op. cit., pp.30–31.

17. A.C.E. Armstrong, op. cit.

18. See W.B. Morgan and J.C. Pugh, *West Africa* (London: Methuen & Co. Ltd., 1969); and *Nigerian Handbook* (London: HMSO, 1953).

19. See R.S. Pearson, *Petroleum and the Nigerian Economy*, (Stanford: Stanford University Press, 1970).

20. See L.H. Schatzl, *Petroleum in Nigeria* (Ibadan: published for Nigerian Institute of Social and Economic Research (NISER) by OUP, 1969), p.1.

21. Ibid., See also S.A. Madujibeya, 'Oil and Nigeria's economic development', *African Affairs*, No 300, July 1976.

22. *Annual Report of the Geological Survey Department for the year 1958/59*, (Lagos: Federal Government Printer, 1960).

23. See M. Abubakar Rimi, 'Oil and Nigeria's Diplomacy' M.A. Thesis, Sussex, University of Sussex, 1975.

24. Nigerian National Petroleum Corporation (NNPC), 'Petroleum in Nigeria — Development Role in Economic Development and Future Prospects', paper presented at Petroleum Products Marketing Conference, Warri, September, 1979.

25. See Tanya M. Baker, 'The Social Organisation of the Birom', Ph.D. Thesis, University of London, 1954, p.54.

26. PRO London: CO446/63, Wallace to Secretary of State, Colonies, March 26, 1907, cited in Freund, op. cit., p.45.

27. See *Mining Journal*, Vol. 98, August 17 1912, p.816; *African Mail*, June 12 1912; June 28 1912 and July 26 1912.

28. Freund, op. cit., p.48.

29. Ibid.

30. National Archives, Kaduna (NAK), SNP 9, 488/1923: The Minerals Proclamation of 1902, located in Royalties on Minerals and Mining Legislation similar to those obtained in Malaya as contained in G.C. Allen and Audrey G. Donnithorne, *Western Enterprise in Indonesia and Malaya: a study in economic development* (London: George Allen & Unwin, 1954), pp.154-155.

31. Freund, op. cit., p.73.

32. Ibid., p.85.

33. See C.K. Gonyok, 'Creation of labour for the tin mining industry in the Plateau, 1909–14 (or Proletarianisation?)', Ahmadu Bello University, Department of History Seminar paper, May 14 1977.

34. NAK: SNP 11N, 681m/1918, 'Increase of supply of labour for mining companies', Cock to Resident, June 8 1918.

35. NAK: Jos PROF 1/1, 201/1918, 'First Half-Yearly Report', Bauchi Province, 1918.

36. *Tin International*, July 1942.

37. NAK: KANOPROF; Minesfield Labour Advisory Board Report, November 1945.

38. KAK: Jos PROF 1, Mines Labour Camps: Declaration of Labour Health Areas, 1055/S.2, Memorandum, 1945.

39. Freund, op. cit., pp.97–98.

40. Ibid., p.82.

41. P. Bower, 'The Mining Industry', op. cit.

42. Freund, op. cit., p.82.

43. H.P. White and M.B. Cleave, *An Economic Geography of West Africa* (London: G. Bell & Sons Ltd., 1971), p.140.

44. 'At the Enugu Inquiry: Promotion for blue-eyed boys', *West Africa*,

31 December 1949, p.1232.

45. 'On the Spot: Full report of the disturbances', *West Africa*, 3 December 1949, p.1145.

46. Members of the Commission were Sir William Fitzgerald K.C. (Chairman), Mr R.W. Williams M.P., Mr Justice S.O. Quashie-Idun, Gold Coast Puisne Judge.

47. 'Riots, tear-gas and conscription at Enugu', *West Africa*, 26 November 1949, p.1119.

48. 'Labour Officer resigned through frustration', *West Africa*, 24 December 1949, p.1216.

49. Ibid.

50. Raymond F. Mikesell (ed), *Foreign Investment in the Petroleum and Mineral Industries* (Baltimore: Johns Hopkins University Press, 1971).

51. Freund, op. cit., p.110.

52. RH: MS. Africa, S.86, Niger Company papers, Trigge to Scarbrough, October 18 1917; October 7 1918; October 7 1919.

53. NAK: SNP 17/2, Kwall Falls Power Scheme, 12707, Vol. I, Report of Inspector of Mines, Treror Roberts, November 10 1925.

54. Freund, op. cit., p.113.

55. Freund, op. cit., p.125.

56. Edwin G. Charle, 'An appraisal of British Imperial policy with respect to the extraction of mineral resources in Nigeria', *Nigerian Economic and Social Studies*, VI, 1, March 1964.

57. Freund, op. cit., p.127.

58. Ibid.

7. Industrialisation as Tokenism

A. A. Lawal

One of the most vexed issues during the colonial period was the question of industrialisation. Right from the beginning, the British colonial attitude to the issue became an open secret notwithstanding the mounting pressures from the nationalist movements, foreign correspondents and some members of the commercial class in Lagos. To the British, industrialisation would defeat the principal objectives of colonialism and imperialism and it was better to preserve Nigeria as a large market for the progress of their trade.

This being so, various colonial policies were introduced and enforced not only to suppress local industries but to encourage increased consumption of British manufactures. Indeed, Nigerian consumers were discouraged from buying French, Japanese and German manufactures which successfully competed with British manufactures; hence the rising tide of smuggling activities across both the Dahomey-Nigeria and Cameroon-Nigeria borders.

The outbreak of the First World War and German atrocities induced the colonial government to introduce and enforce economic measures to regulate the sale and purchase of vegetable oils and supervise the distribution of manufactures. Indeed, the enforcement of the Defence of the Realm Act[1] discouraged the development of manufacturing enterprises in Nigeria right from 1918 onwards.

Hitherto however, such British companies as John Holt, Lever Brothers, Miller Brothers, Niger Company and others, had maintained a firm control and monopoly of the Nigerian market through their political influence in London and as a result of the favourable policies of the colonial government.

Administrative wisdom ought to have directed the colonial government to see the war-time scarcity of imports as an opportunity to use local resources for the manufacture of import substitutes, not only to encourage economic development in the realm of industrialisation but also to save a lot of money. It was rather ridiculous of the government to have encouraged the importation of meat when in fact over three million head of cattle and over six million sheep and goats were found in the various green pastures of Northern Nigeria.[2] Similarly, brick and tile making in properly constructed kilns should have saved the importation of much building material and improved the quality and permanency of houses.

War-time financial difficulties compelled the government to run shoe-string budgets and in the process it now became sensitive to the criticisms of the Lagos intelligentsia in regard to the utilisation of local raw material to manufacture import substitutes. Thus, sawmills were erected to provide adequate and cheap timber for furniture instead of importing it any longer. The carpentry workshop that was established in Lagos made furniture for all government houses, while the exploitation of the limestone deposits near Lokoja and Udi coal-field for making cement, saved the government from the prohibitive prices demanded by the importing firms.[3] Furthermore, the scarcity and high cost of iron sheets, which were much needed during the war, exposed the government to a lot of lamentable extravagance. To stem this anomaly therefore, roofing tiles were produced locally to save the government thousands of pounds.

These war-time experiments in rudimentary industrialisation showed that Nigeria possessed the necessary potential for rapid economic development. In fact, for thousands of years before the advent of Europeans with their 'civilising mission' the peoples of Nigeria had evolved their peculiar indigenous industry and developed unique and commendable skills in bronze-casting, ivory- and wood-carving, iron-working, basket-making, blacksmithing (manufacture of axe-heads, arrow-heads, hoe-heads, shackles, cutlasses, carved knives, war and ceremonial equipment); there were specialists in beadmaking and pottery (bowls, lamps, pots, plates) while wood carvers in the forest areas made naturalistic and geometric figures on door posts, staves of office or stools, and sold wooden trays, spoons, hair combs and dolls in the local markets.

Apart from the naturalistic forms of the Ife terracotta heads which symbolised the Nigerian cultural heritage, leather work and tanning stimulated the manufacture of sandals, skin-mats, bags, belts, sheaths and bellows to meet the need of other consumers. Of course, of great importance was the indigenous textile industry throughout Nigeria, in which vertical and horizontal treadle looms were used for the production of very thick and durable cotton cloths. The textile products were either made of plain white threads or multi-coloured threads for artistic effects or formation of geometric patterns. Local tailors and dyers depended mostly on the weavers just as farmers and hunters depended on the blacksmiths, etc.

The colonial masters were aware of all the above-mentioned essentials of industrialisation and even praised the qualities of some local manufactures. For example, their admiration for Kano cloths and Kano leather, famously known as 'Morocco leather', was an open secret. On the quality and value of Kano cloths, a British military officer remarked thus 'European manufactures cannot put on the market cotton stuffs approaching the quality and the wearing power of the Kano cloths at the same prices as it is charged for by the natives'.[4] He was convinced that because of its excellent design and durability, the hand-woven cloths would conveniently compete with imported textiles throughout West Africa and sell like hot cakes in the English summer markets. The impression of this observer was candidly buttressed by the revelation that many Europeans used Kano cloths for strong tropical suits, riding breeches and ladies' dresses in the 1920s.

Yet, instead of embarking on industrialisation at a slow pace, the colonial government remained unconcerned notwithstanding the mounting pressures for economic development. Even throughout the inter-war years (1920-1939) colonial industrial policy could be described as 'mercantile' because in effect, Nigeria remained an expanding market into which manufactures from the United Kingdom could be dumped at will. To justify this objective, measures introduced and enforced included trade restriction, regulation of customs by the use of the imperial preference and prohibition of trade, except under licence, with countries outside the sterling area.[5] In other words, a feature of the war-time measures still persisted in time of peace when all forms of hostilities had ended. Worse still, government regulations ensured the free passage of goods and free movement of European merchants but vigorously prohibited native manufacture in all facets of iron industry[6] to ensure regular importation of iron implements from the United Kingdom.

In their reaction to the clarion call for industrialisation, the colonial masters recommended the concept of natural evolution of industrial progress by which Nigeria should primarily be exporting raw materials in exchange for manufactured goods. Then later, she could improve her exports by better preparation with the objective of bringing them to the most finished state before export, thereby increasing their value, avoiding waste in preparation and utilizing by-products.[7] In this way the bulk to be exported would decrease in weight and could be cheaply transported by both sea and land.

But the establishment of factors of producing semi-manufactures is not synonymous with real and ideal industrial culture which ensures the much-needed advancement of material welfare, rapid transition from an agrarian to an industrial economy, establishment of local factories manned by well trained cheap labour to supply a great part of domestic needs and even compete successfully with the manufactures of other nations. Again an ideal industrial environment encourages the application of new methods and results of research and experiment in transport, and in labour-saving devices.

The British were ill-prepared to introduce ideal industrialisation because, according to their conviction, it was not part of their mission. They believed that they were destined to guide Africans along the path of progress while contemplating the time when Africans would, out of their own volition, manufacture for themselves instead of remaining dependent on European factories. They remarked:

> it is for the distant future to determine and we may safely leave posterity to deal with the problem, if and when it arises . . . Our present task is clear . . . we are shaping policies for the future . . . of the colonies in political, material and moral spheres.[8]

From the foregoing, the stand of the colonial government was very clear on the issue of industrialisation; henceforth it remained deaf to further pressures but forged ahead with the establishment of 'token' industries for the production of semi-manufactures and some consumer goods. Thus in some parts of southern Nigeria, mills were erected to crush palm kernels to secure a better quality oil and a large saving in freight charges. Similar mills were also used in the north for dealing with groundnuts to minimise transport charges by railway in the hinterland and by sea. Some ginneries easily separated the lint from the seed cotton while hydraulic presses were used for baling of cotton. And for the partial preparation of hides and skins, a few local tanneries helped in reducing their bulk and freight charges.[9] All in all, the introduction of these simple industrial processes aided by machinery, facilitated the production of better quality export crops with great reduction in labour and transport charges.

Apart from these establishments, the cement works functioned well and exported thousand tons of cement annually. A good number of sawmills and carpenter shops were fitted with sophisticated power-driven machinery in their exploitation of local timber for making shooks for oil, casks, doors, window frames and furniture, all of which were hitherto imported. Also, manufactured were twine, sacks, soap, candles and sugar to meet the demand of the local consumers. The salutary effect of all the initial industrial endeavours lay in the fact that the colonial government was able to conserve thousands of pounds which otherwise would have been expended on imports.

Yet Nigeria remained an exporter of cash crops as over 90% of her population were farmers still using the customary methods of farming and extracting vegetable oils — methods that were slow and wasteful in terms of time, labour and energy. Nevertheless, increased agricultural production and the annual increases in the figure of export crops did not result from drastic changes in, or better methods of production. In this regard, nature was just too generous to the local farmers.

Since the colonial masters declared openly that '. . . at the outset, European brains, capital and energy have not been, and never will be expended in developing the resources of Africa from motives of pure philanthropy',[10] Nigerians were content with the training received from them in letters, industry, politics and social development. For the British expected that under their rule, Nigeria would advance by the methods most consonant with her national genius.

This attitude led the colonial government to encourage learning of skills suitable only to the newly established cottage industries in the various schools, rather than proper industrial training essential for rapid economic development. Thus the pupils were trained in making furniture, office fittings, drills and tools, boots and book-binding. The rural industrial class consisted of artisans and mechanics employed in government and commercial workshops, especially those working with the railway, marine, public works and printing departments and handled power-driven machinery with skill. Because of their commendable aptitude over the years, they replaced Europeans in many departments without any supervision especially in the sections of highly technical work as acetylene welding and cutting, in pattern making from dimensional drawings and in the use of the lathe and modern machine tools.[11] However, this array of qualifications notwithstanding, their lamentable weakness was their inevitable poverty of sufficient general education to know the theoretical side of the work and reasons for the various mechanical processes.

So, up till the outbreak of the Second World War and thereafter, the pre-existing European mercantile houses like G.B. Ollivant, A.G. Leventis, Lever Brothers including such entrepreneurs as the Syrians, Egyptians and Lebanese were still in firm control of the Nigerian economy. With their ample capital and creditworthiness, they established branches of their departmental stores in various parts of the country. In the 1930s, the United African Company alone handled over 40% of Nigeria's export and import trade, and Nigerian businessmen were deprived of all opportunities to compete with them.[12]

Indeed, the Nigerian businessmen faced an insurmountable dilemma because they lacked goodwill with the banking houses which were owned by Europeans. They lacked creditworthiness and were not favoured by government economic restrictions either. The European firms often acted in concert to frustrate the Nigerian businessmen, yet several appeals for government's revision of the whole situation made no change. The Nigerian nationalists therefore adopted a policy of non-cooperation with the British. Their slogans 'Boycott', 'Back to the land', soon became popular to alert the general public and collectively enforce the policy of boycott of all European goods and dresses but not European books and cars, etc. The slogan was therefore instantly amended by Mazi Mbonu Ojike (a businessman) to read 'Boycott all the boycottables'.[13]

The economic measures enforced in the 1940s as a result of the war further dwarfed the industrial aspirations of Nigerians. There were restrictions on exports and imports, while several goods were under licence. In effect, Nigerian weavers were not permitted to export their handwoven clothes to Sierra Leone, the Gold Coast and Britain where they enjoyed a considerable demand.

But in an attempt to conserve foreign exchange, the colonial government embarked on sponsoring a number of mini-industrial projects to manufacture import substitutes to meet the needs of hundreds of British and American soldiers. Thus, through propaganda, demonstration plots, issue of seeds, guarantee of markets, offer of attractive prices, provision of transport and storage facilities by the government, the Department of Agriculture ran many farms to produce special foods for foreign soldiers while the Veterinary Department concentrated on canned meat, fruit juices and dairy products. In this way, public finance was appropriated to establish a cheese factory at Pankshin and dairies at Zaria, Sokoto, Kano, Ibadan and Lagos to supply milk.[14] The piggeries of the Department of Agriculture supplied meat for bacon production in 1942.

The Agege Garden also intensified its production of vegetables just as its counterparts accounted for hundreds of tons of potato and sugar in the north. Indeed, many bag, twine and rope industries that functioned during the war years earned the government a lot of money through the local sale of their products.[15] The foregoing confirmed that Nigeria had the necessary potentials for industrialisation but owing to the British conspiracy of neglect and their intent to reserve the Nigerian market for their manufactures, all the above-mentioned industrial projects were either withdrawn or overhauled at the disappearance of the foreign troops when the war ended.

The immediate effect of the war was the rural-urban migration of school leavers who looked for government jobs in the major towns. The nationalists who had not relented in their outcry for government assistance called for the establishment of industries to absorb thousands of unemployed people who roamed the streets. But as the government remained adamant, they concluded that only Nigerians would industrialise their economy themselves, hence the question 'Industrialisation before self-government'. In several public lectures and debates, the question was enthusiastically examined and a lot of arguments emanating from the various discussions were worthy of cogitation. Eventually, the nationalists resolved that Nigeria's stand should be on 'Self-government and Industrialisation'.[16]

It will be erroneous to interpret the introduction of a ten-year development plan (for the first time) under the United Kingdom Colonial Development and Welfare Act 1945[17] as a direct response of Britain to industrialise Nigeria. Instead, the plan was confined to a number of unrelated social welfare projects submitted by the various administrative departments and executed without any regard to specific needs, goals, targets and potentials of the various sectors of the colonial economy. So, one cannot call the endeavour a plan by modern standards. By 1954, about £14 million grant was given to Nigeria under the Welfare Acts, but £6.5 million was pumped into welfare schemes which turned out to be unrealistic, irrelevant, unproductive and generally out of tune with the post-war socio-economic changes.[18]

Fortunately, the Marketing Boards which were established after the war built ample reserves from their operations and promoted the development of industries making use of the raw materials produced in the areas. They even encouraged and financed industrial research in an attempt to rectify all the miserable anomalies of the doomed ten-year plan![19] More importantly, the rapid political and economic changes that occurred after the war culminated in the Macpherson Constitution of 1951 which provided for the establishment of strong regional governments and active involvement of Nigerians in their economic and political decisions. Henceforth, the British relaxed their control of Nigeria while Nigerians dominated regional administration. Each region now had and controlled a marketing board which served as the principal foundation of economic and financial development in Nigeria.

By 1954, the boards succeeded in coordinating their financial resources and well-defined programmes of economic development to quicken the tempo of industrial revolution. By the same year, evidence of this policy had begun to appear in several parts of Nigeria because the boards had expended £34 million on various projects and research, and yet kept surpluses totalling about £75 million.[20]

With the enforcement of the provisions of the 1954 Constitution, the federal and regional governments inaugurated five-year plans in 1955.

The Nigerian governments and the United Kingdom government jointly requested the International Bank for Reconstruction and Development to send a mission to Nigeria to assess her economic potentialities, study the available resources and make practical recommendations for future development.[21] The report of the Commission, eventually formed the basis for the regional five-year plans (1955–1960). Only the Western Region met its goals by 1960 and embarked on another five-year plan; nevertheless, the plans of other regions had to be extended to 1962.[22] The regional boards provided loans for industrial schemes which they formulated and even allied with foreign firms to launch new manufactures. The firms also gave members of the public ample opportunities to buy shares.

The establishment of the Federal Loans Board to give out loans for industrial projects designed by individuals or firms, also demonstrated the serious commitment of the central government to rapid economic development. Yet, a further step was taken between 1955 and 1958 with the practical enforcement of the Aid to Pioneer Industries Ordinance (1950) which led to the establishment of 30 new industries that were certified as 'pioneering'. The ordinance guaranteed tax relief to such industries in the first years of their existence.

In compliance with the recommendation of the International Bank for Reconstruction and Development, the National Economic Council was constituted in October 1955, as a forum for discussing national policies and the economic development plans of the regional governments. The body which had met several times, consisted of the prime minister, regional premiers and regional ministers concerned with economic development. Indeed the council succeeded in maintaining close cooperation between the regional governments over the years. In 1958, a Joint Planning Committee was established to advise the Council on matters referred to it and formulate central plans for economic improvements, thereby serving as a unifying factor in economic matters.[23]

One may at this juncture ask, 'What were the fruits of all these endeavours to ensure rapid industrialisation by 1958?' The first-ever 'Made-in-Nigeria' exhibition in February 1958 on the grounds of Lagos Racecourse, vividly convinced cynical observers that industrialisation had really begun in Nigeria.[24] The impressive assortment of manufactures on display soon became the talk of the town. About 123 exhibitors who came from various parts of the country displayed goods such as textiles, metal-working, building materials, food, drink, toilet material and printing material. In some sections there were the common dustbins, plastic products, carved tables from Awka, ceramics, mineral waters, beers, canned meat, canned jollof rice, a model of an oil-drilling plant, perfumes, outboard motor launches and prefabricated (motor) trailer bodies.

Although the foregoing has not highlighted the major role of the federal government vis-a-vis the performances of the regional governments in industrialisation efforts, it must be noted that at the federal level, no comparable organisation like the marketing board existed, but the Ministry of Economic Development, on behalf of the central government, performed functions similar to those carried out by the regional boards.

In 1959 the central government opened the Central Bank of Nigeria which since then has been controlling national monetary and fiscal policies in fostering the growth of a capital market. Under its auspices, securities and government stocks were sold and bought. In 1959 alone there was an over-subscription of £2½ million to the shares of the Federal Government of Nigeria Development Loan[25] — a testimony to the public consciousness in the sphere of public investments. The central government also channelled federal funds as equity investments into specific projects while its laws favoured the operations of capital-mobilising institutions, hence the establishment of Investment Company of Nigeria (ICON) in 1959[26] which granted medium- and long-term loans and purchased equity shares in Nigerian public and private companies. Its functions included underwriting and encouraging foreign investors to come to Nigeria.

Already the federal government had introduced a 'model industrial estate' in Lagos by November 1958. The 'estate' comprised a number of blocks, well furnished and equipped as workshops. Each of them was then let to an eligible small-scale industrialist or private businessman, based in Lagos, but who had no means of starting a business. The government ran the estate on a commercial basis but the regulations permitted the tenants, who made profits, to expand their workshops or build their own factories without depending on the government any longer.

By 1960, hundreds of factories had sprung up in the various towns throughout Nigeria. These factories further encouraged rapid urbanisation as a result of rural-urban migration of school leavers, a trend which still remains active today. Thus industrial centres were located in Lagos, Ikeja, Ibadan, Kano, Kaduna, Aba, Benin, Enugu and Port Harcourt, etc. The light industries which were commonplace included cigarette factories, breweries, textile mills (Kaduna), plywood factory (Sapele) and cotton ginneries in the north. The only heavy industries were coal mining in the east and two major cement works, one in the east and one in the west.

There is no doubt that tremendous changes occurred between 1950 and 1960 in the sphere of industrialisation because existing manufacturing establishments since 1950 had increased fivefold. Indeed, government investment outran revenue and this policy was facilitated by reliance on external resources which augmented the domestic product. For example, in 1950, Nigerian sterling reserves which stood at £263.1 million had by 1960 been overdrawn to £171.35 million. About £11 million loan was raised while £25 million was realised through Colonial Development and Welfare grants.[27]

The foregoing, no doubt, could convince an observer that Nigeria had travelled a long way in an attempt to ensure industrialisation of its economy. Then how do we draw the balance sheet? Can one really say that industrialisation was achieved up till independence? If the answer to this question is in the affirmative, then what type of industrialisation? One can only say that 'incipient' industrialisation maintained a fast pace because of the unrelenting efforts of the regional and federal governments.

By 1960, Nigeria was not yet an industrial society; instead, it remained an agricultural economy and most of its annual revenue derived from export crops. Its manufactures, which failed to satisfy local demand, were not exported either. Imports of consumer goods remained steady to supplement local substitutes. About 75% of the Nigerian population were still engaged in agriculture, which accounted for about 50% of total national product. There was no processing of export crops on a large scale yet, although Nigeria was in a rudimentary stage of mechanised agriculture.

By modern standards, one can regard the colonial industrialisation as 'tokenism'. In modern times, the objectives of serious-minded industrialisation policy and programmes must emphasise growth poles, linkage concept and sectoral allocation of funds in a national budget. For, according to the growth pole theory, the existence and localisation of certain growth poles and growth centres in a national economy can be developed through capital investment on certain criteria to ensure maximum multiplier effects on the economy. These growth poles and growth centres are tools for multi-sectoral development in a spatial setting.[28]

The phenomenon of forward and backward linkages automatically stimulates the diversion of productive inputs to other bigger projects which eventually can have a direct impact on the growth and the development of national wealth.[29] In other words, the linkage concept encourages accelerated progressive industrialisation within a short span, whereby the establishment of satellite industries would rely on master industries and both of them would enjoy some moderate comparative cost of production through mutual existence and understanding.

Forward linkage is the output sold out to other industries and used as input in productive activities. On the other hand, backward linkage is the output of other industries purchased and used as input in productive activities, hence the industrial interdependence and specialisation which stimulate maximised wealth and greatest addition to productivity. Thus far, it becomes unmistakably clear that in the colonial context all these features of modern and ideal industrialisation were lacking.

References

1. Akinjide Osuntokun, *Nigeria in the First World War*, (London: Longman, 1979), pp.50-51.

2. Ibid., p.2.

3. Ibid.

4. F.J.D. Lugard, *The Dual Mandate in British Tropical Africa*, (Reprinted, London: Frank Cass Ltd, 1965), p.445 fn.

5. *Nigeria Handbook 1932* (Lagos), p.249.

6. Wale Ademoyega, *The Federation of Nigeria from Earliest Times to Independence* (London: 1962), p.162.

7. Lugard, op. cit., p.509.

8. Ibid.

9. Lugard, op. cit., p.512.

10. Lugard, op. cit., p.617.

11. *West Africa*, 4 September 1920, p.421.

12. P.T. Bauer, *West African Trade* (London: Routledge and Kegan Paul, 1963), pp.56-67.

13. M. Ojike, *My Africa*, New Year Day, 1946 (published by author).

14. G.O. Olusanya, 'The Impact of the Second World War on Nigeria's Economy, An Explanatory Survey', *Oduma Magazine*, 2, 1, August 1974, pp.20-23.

15. Ibid.

16. Wale Ademoyega, op. cit., p.167.

17. An act by the same name was passed in 1940 and others in 1949, 1950 and 1955.

18. For more critical assessments of the plan, see O. Awolowo, *Path to Nigerian Freedom* (London: Faber and Faber, 1947), pp.19-20; A. Ojetunji, *Foundations of An African Economy — A study of Investment and Growth in Nigeria*, (New York, 1966), pp.150-188.

19. For details, see Carl K. Eicher and Carl Liedholm, (eds), *Growth and Development of the Nigerian Economy*, (East Lansing: Michigan University Press, 1970); the Nigerian Cocoa Marketing Board 1947; the Nigerian Groundnut Marketing Board 1949; the Nigerian Oil Palm Produce Marketing Board 1949 and the Nigerian Cotton Marketing Board 1949.

20. *Commonwealth Development and Its Financing, No 5, Nigeria*, (London: HMSO, 1963).

21. Wale Ademoyega, op. cit., p.170.

22. Paul O. Proehl, *Foreign Enterprise in Nigeria* (Ibadan: OUP, 1965), p.15.

23. Paul O. Proehl, op. cit., p.14.

24. Wale Ademoyega, op. cit., p.172, while declaring open the week-long exhibition, the Prime Minister, Alhaji Abubakar Tafa Balewa remarked enthusiastically, 'The industrialisation of Nigeria is not a matter for the future. It is here, it is started already'.

25. Wale Ademoyega, op. cit., p.173.

26. Minister of Finance Budget Finance 1964, Federal Ministry of Information, *The National Budget (1964)*, p.5.

27. Paul O. Proehl, op. cit., p.15.

28. T. Hermansen, and L.H. Klaasseu, et. al., United Nations Institute for Social Development Programme IV, Regional Development, UNRISD/70/c. 6, November 1970, pp.191-203.

29. Albert, O. Hirschman, *The Strategy of Economic Development* (New Haven: Yale University Press, 1958), pp.98-103.

8. Trading with the Metropolis: an Unequal Exchange

O. N. Njoku

Introduction

By the beginning of the 20th century, the Western European powers had virtually completed their self-appointed task of partitioning West Africa into colonies, although the exact boundaries of these colonies for some time continued to generate bad blood among the competing imperialists. It had by then become axiomatic to Britain that the Nigerian area was part of her booty from the partition exercise.

The motivating factors for the scramble for, and subsequent partition of, Africa by the imperial powers have remained an unresolved controversy. Nonetheless, the preponderance of economic calculations among the powers is a starting-point of honest debate. Lord Lugard, himself one of the foremost actors in that African tragedy, put his finger right on the spot when he declared that

> the partition of Africa was due primarily to the economic necessity of increasing the supplies of raw materials and food to meet the needs of industrialist Europe.[1]

Lugard should also have added that the colonies were, in addition, to serve as assured markets for the manufactures of the colonising powers. Throughout the British colonial regime in Nigeria, successive British political officers saw their primary assignment as ensuring maximum exploitation of the mineral and agricultural resources of the country and the canalisation of these to Britain. Nigeria was also treated as an assured market for British manufactures.

The transformation of Nigeria into a formal colony inaugurated a commercial regime distinctly characterised by inequality of exchange between the imperial power, Britain, and her Nigerian colony. It is not that the precolonial trade between the Nigerian peoples and the British had been equitable: in no way can the exchange of human beings for meretricious goods be considered equitable. But colonialism made possible capitalist penetration of the Nigerian economy and effected fundamental affinities between the metropolitan and the colonial economies. Trade between the metropolis and the colony promoted interdependence, but as Claude Ake has observed, this was 'an unequal inter-dependence'.[2] Nigeria was 'developed' in order to produce raw materials for Britain while importing manufactures and capital.

The net result of the situation for Nigeria was intense specialisation in a few raw materials, uneven development, lack of modern manufacturing industries and what D.K. Fieldhouse has appropriately referred to as 'metrocentrism'.[3]

In order for us to appreciate the foregoing contention, this chapter focuses on the role of the various interest groups involved in the trade with particular reference to what they did and their rewards. These groups included the Nigerian export farmers, the middlemen and wage-earners; and the foreign trading firms and the colonial government of Nigeria itself. It remains to caution, first that it is impossible to come out with a precise quantification of the inputs and returns of the groups involved. But a general trend can emerge which will, hopefully, provide a reasonable picture of the actual situation. Second, the colonial government of Nigeria's reward should be seen within the context of the rewards to British trading firms operating in Nigeria; both were two wings of the same brigade.

The Farmer

A distinguishing feature of the economy of colonial West Africa was the total absence of the white settlement characteristic of East and Southern Africa. One consequence of this was the near-absence of large-scale agricultural plantations of the European type. Agricultural production for export was consequently well in the firm control of indigenous farmers. Also agricultural produce were far and away the most important export of West Africa. The farmers who produced the export crops *ipso facto* occupied a very important place in the colonial economy. But, as we shall see presently, their rewards bore no relation to their exceedingly crucial inputs.

The colonialists – public officers and traders alike – were interested only in the export crops of Nigeria: palm oil and kernel, cocoa, groundnut, cotton and beniseed. And by the use of means legitimate and otherwise, they made the Nigerian export crop producers increase production to their possible maximum. Taxes and court fines, for instance, had to be paid in the colonial currency; which would normally be obtained by either selling produce to the European trading firms or by working for a wage for government or the firms.

Yet from a commercial point of view, colonial rule would appear to have dawned on Nigeria with an enormous promise of unending prosperity. Export products were in very high demand. Gradual improvement and extension of modern means of transportation steadily extended the frontiers of trade and opportunity into the hinterland from the coastal entrepots. The Nigerian producers on their side responded with corresponding alacrity and expectations. Their purchasing power increased seemingly without restraint. Opportunities to make wealth appeared limitless as European trading firms introduced an array of manufactures hitherto outside the reach of most consumers. A honeymoon was already developing between the European firms on the one hand and the producers and African middlemen on the other.

This honeymoon, however, turned out to be meteoric; and the first flush of rising expectations very quickly faded away. The problem revolved basically around the price factor. The prices of produce and imports, as Sylvia Leith-Ross aptly observes, were the hub around which the economic, and consequently much of the social wheel of the vast majority of Nigerians revolved.[4] The brutal fact was that the Nigerian export producer, like his counterparts in other sectors of the colonial economy never received a fair price for his exacting enterprise. A variety of factors, some providential, some artificial, were responsible for this. All of them boil down to what one may loosely refer to as the colonial situation.

The pricing policy of the European trading firms was anything but progressive. Their primary objective was to maximise profit even at the expense of the export crop producer. They did this basically by colluding to fix prices they paid for produce by arriving at market-sharing arrangements among themselves and by reducing to the barest minimum, if not completely eliminating, competition among themselves. In 1904–5, the Niger Company, the African Association, Alexander Miller Brothers and Co. and the Company of African Merchants reached a pooling agreement in respect of the trade in the Niger valley. The primary aim of the pool was 'restricting those outside firms from extending into other places'.[5] The Niger Co. again reached a similar agreement with John Holt and Co. in 1919 for the sole purpose of keeping down as low as possible the prices they paid for produce in eastern Nigeria. In this respect, a Niger Co. agent stationed at Oguta gleefully reported a few months after, 'we are pleased with what has been done in this regard'.[6]

The firms were able to achieve their selfish designs basically because of a striking peculiarity of the export-import trade not only of Nigeria in particular but of West Africa as a whole: the domination of the trade by a handful of European firms. At the beginning of the 20th century, there was, relatively speaking, some semblance at least of open commercial competition among the European firms operating in the Nigerian area. The Royal Niger Company which had at once been a trading firm and a government in the Niger valley had lost its royal charter in 1899. Although it still enjoyed commercial pre-eminence in this general area where it had also been in charge administratively, it could no longer use such a big stick as an armed force to keep other commercial rivals at bay. However, the passage of the years saw the systematic elimination of commercial competition in Nigeria, and the emergence of huge combines.

Fairly early in the colonial era, Allister Macmillan had cause to complain that it was easier to detail the goods the P.Z. and Co. did not deal in than those it did.[7] In 1919, Sir Hugh Clifford, Governor of Nigeria, complained bitterly about the major combines. In a despatch to the Secretary of State for the Colonies, Viscount Milner, he lamented that there were too many rings for the Nigerian producer, middleman and consumer to stand.[8]

1919 was, in fact, the year the African and Eastern Trade Corporation was formed to absorb, in the Gold Coast (Ghana), Messrs F. and A. Swanzy and the African Association; and, in Nigeria, Miller Brothers & Co, the African

Association, the Lagos Stores and African Traders Ltd. Meanwhile the Lever Brothers had swallowed up McIver and Co. and John Walkden and Co., and early in 1921 bought up the 'property, right and good will of the Niger Company' for £8½ million.[9]

Governor Clifford's lamentations came a decade before the emergence of a commercial octopus whose tentacles spread throughout the length and breadth of Nigeria with unparalleled thoroughness and comprehensiveness. The UAC, itself a wing of the Anglo-Dutch combine, Unilever, was a product of many decades of combinations dating back to the 19th century. The imposing stature of the UAC in the West African trade made babies of the combines about which Macmillan and Clifford had complained. By the end of the inter-war years, about two-thirds of West Africa's total export trade was controlled by seven firms, the most prominent of them being the UAC, John Holt and Co., and the SCOA and CFAO.[10] Even then the UAC controlled 40% of the whole. By then, too, 80% of Nigeria's external trade was reckoned to be in the hands of Lever Brothers.[11] By the beginning of World War II, it had long become, as Cyril Erhlich has observed, impossible to penetrate the ologopolistic barriers of these firms; barriers which were re-inforced by governmental controls.[12]

It was not that these firms just controlled the produce trade of West Africa, they also controlled the imports. The firms were integrated both vertically and horizontally. The UAC, for instance, had butter, soap, saw mill and singlet factories; cold storage plants, coastal boats, and a chain of retail shops dotted all over the major urban centres of Nigeria. It also had controlling interests in some shipping lines and an important voice in banks and financial institutions in Britain. Thus strategically positioned, the firms easily drove the Africans into what Walter Rodney refers to as 'the double squeeze'.[13] The firms could thus afford to ignore indigenous feelings and aspirations, and dictate prices of imports while at the same time foisting on the consumers whatever goods they chose to import.

One important result of all this was, as John Mars has shown, that the firms made profits far in excess of what might have been possible under greater competition.[14] In 1901–2, for instance, the African Association was reported by Acting Consul-General, Sir Ralph Moor, as being unwilling to venture into the hinterland in the wake of British 'opening up' of the interior of south-eastern Nigeria. Moor attributed this reluctance to the enormous profits the firm was making by merely sitting down at Calabar and waiting for indigenous middlemen to bring down produce from up-country.[15] In 1902, the firm made profits sufficient to encourage it to pay its shareholders 15% on ordinary shares, and 36% on founders' shares.[16]

Between 1901 and 1907 John Holt and Co. had its capital increased fivefold after penetrating the lower valley of the River Niger. Also, with the merger of the companies to form the African and Eastern Trade Corporation, the capital of the company exceeded £22 million, about threequarters of which was accounted for by business in West Africa. For the first two years of its existence, the Corporation paid income tax in the United Kingdom to the tune of £1,066,000. Dividends it paid on ordinary shares in 1919 stood at 32%. Thus, Ofonagoro concludes, imperialism in southern Nigeria was no case of importing excess capital and receiving raw materials in return. On the contrary, firms came to West African poorly financed, but soon made huge capital to enable them to expand in other parts of the world.[17]

Such profits were not restricted to periods of general economic prosperity. Despite the Great Depression of the late 1920s and 1930s, the UAC made a profit of £6,302,875 in 1934, and paid dividends of 15% on ordinary shares. On the whole, during the period September 1932 to 1938, its profit never averaged below 9%.[18] Yet this was a period of very severe economic depression.

For all their huge profits from their Nigerian trade, the firms put hardly anything in return, in the form of capital investments. True to capitalist ethics, they exacted maximum dividends for minimum input possible. Imperialism, Renate Zahar has aptly observed, does not introduce industrial capitalism, but mercantile capitalism.[19] Whatever developments the firms introduced were those they saw as absolutely inescapable pre-conditions for the successful achievement of their goal. Such efforts took place only in the areas of export production, leading to an enclave development which bore little or no relation with other non-export producing areas. The Nigerian economy thus developed incoherently, and was thus incapacitated from attaining autocentric growth.

Against the stranglehold foisted on them by the trading firms the Nigerian producers had no effective bargaining counter. These farmers numbered in their tens of thousands, operating in islands of production, and, therefore, were not in a position to present a united opposition against their oppressors. Their plight was not helped by the long chain of middlemen which, though performing a very useful role in external trade, were wont to exploit to their own selfish ends the ignorance and weakness of the farmers. These middlemen were made up of Africans and Levantines as well as European agents. Here and there, though, the farmers managed to find some vent for letting out their pent-up grievances.

The most dramatic and violent of such reactions was couched in the now well-orchestrated Aba women's protests of 1929 in eastern Nigeria. All too often, the political and cultural dimensions of the movement have been stressed. But it is now certain that economic grievances were a major catalyst of the movement. The Donald Kingdom Report on the disturbances clearly indicates this. The protests occurred during the Great Depression when the terms of trade went very drastically against the Nigerian export crop producer. At Umuahia and Aba, for example, the prices of a four-gallon tin of oil had slumped from 7s and 6s 10d, respectively, in December 1928 to 5s 10d and 5s 8d in December 1929.[20]

At the same time, the colonial government, intent on ensuring adequate revenue for itself, proceeded to effect high increases in the customs duties on a wide range of imports. For instance, the duty on tobacco rose from 1s 6d per pound (weight) during the Depression to 2s per lb and that on spirits from 1d to 2d per lb (weight).[21] This meant that the farmers were paying for imports at highly inflated prices at a time their produce were fetching less and less revenue. 'Unquestionably', notes the Donald Kingdom Report, 'they do regard it as a very real grievance that whilst they get less for what they sell, they should have to pay more for what they buy'.[22]

Worse still, the customs duties were so adjusted that the incidence of the increases fell squarely on the Nigerian consumers. For instance, in 1928, the 15% duties on imported foods which had been in operation was abolished. Since the European community were the primary consumers of these foods, the aim of the above measures was to ameliorate for them whatever hardship the depressed situation would have caused them.

Generally, however, the normal run of the reactions of the farmers and indigenous middlemen to their plight were trade boycotts or hold-ups by cocoa farmers, as in Ghana and western Nigeria in 1921 and 1937. But these hold-ups rarely had much effect basically because of the very weak or complete lack of financial resiliance by the farmers and African middlemen. The 1937 cocoa hold-up actually first took off in Ghana and spilled over into Nigeria. It all started as a result of cocoa-buying agreements reached by some firms in the two countries. This agreement, in sum, led to a drastic reduction in the price the cocoa farmers received in Ghana and Nigeria. The cocoa hold-up, however, made one significant achievement: it led to the setting up of the Nowell Commission by the British government. The Commission was to investigate the system of export trade in British West Africa. In its report, the Commission revealed a whole range of sharp practices adopted by the European firms, some of them dating back to the beginning of the century.[23]

It was not unusual for farmers unable to meet their financial obligations to mortgage their crops and eventually forfeit their farms to African middlemen, Levantine produce-buyers or European trading agents. This situation did occur among cocoa farmers in the western region of Nigeria.[24] These farmers, through a remarkable sense of enterprise and arduous labour, had succeeded without the aid either of the colonial government or of the expatriate trading firms, brought into being a flourishing cocoa industry. The plight of these farmers did not arise from normal price fluctuations for their produce but mainly from the evil machinations of the European trading pools.

So inequitable did many export farmers find the trading system that, whenever they could, they switched over from producing for export to producing for domestic consumption. In 1911, while both the colonial government and the British Cotton Growing Association were prompting cotton farmers in the Niger province of Northern Nigeria to produce more cotton, the people had already started to turn increasingly to yam cultivation.[25] Yam cultivation turned out to yield much greater returns to them. A similar turn-about was made by palm-oil producers in both the eastern and western regions of Nigeria. Exploiting the vast domestic market of Northern Nigeria, local produce traders began to rail palm oil to the north, where they made far greater profits than they did when they sold to the European firms. These local traders were able to offer higher prices to farmers for their produce. The competitive strength of domestic food traders reached its high water-mark during the World War II. They paid such higher prices for palm-oil that the trading firms were induced to complain officially that they could not even buy space in rail waggons to transport their own produce. In Calabar province oil-palm farmers abandoned palm-oil production and went into fishing and gari production.[26]

It is only fair to emphasise, as Fieldhouse has noted, that all African economies were subjected to the exigencies of world markets for primary produce and were buffeted by two major wars and a disastrous depression. Fieldhouse is also correct in his observation that there were too wide margins between the price the African farmer received for his produce and its f.o.b. price, as well as the prices he paid for imports and their c.i.f. prices. Fieldhouse, wrongly though, attributes the margins to handling costs.[27] The actual cause was the collusion among the giant firms to squeeze out as much as they could from their African counterparts. By the system of 'mark-up', prices of imports destined to West Africa were jacked up unreasonably high. And the emergence of the West Africa Shipping Conference ensured the success of this practice. This Conference eliminated almost all the shipping lines operating to West Africa, and was thus able to impose high tariffs on non-members.[28]

Nor was the situation remedied by the fact that the firms were able to foist shoddy goods on the consumers. These included inferior textiles, spiritous liquor, second-hand clothing, etc. Capital goods were conspicuous for their near absence. Some of the imports had the effect of eliminating traditional manufactures.

At the close of colonial rule the average Nigerian farmer remained indigent notwithstanding his arduous enterprise which had undeniably helped to build up the industrial capitalism of England. Unable to afford the expense, he would choose to die at home rather than go to a hospital to be faced with an impossible hospital bill. He could not educate his children nor live a modestly comfortable life. The structure of the colonial economy had no escape route for the indigenous people: its metrocentric base and 'consumerist orientations' made such an escape a dream impossible.

The Nigerian Middleman

In the British-Nigeria trade the Nigerian middlemen played a crucial role. However, neither the European firms nor yet the Nigerian farmers would seem to have appreciated, at least initially, that the functions of these middlemen were important to the colonial commercial regime. These two groups were wont to see the middlemen essentially as parasites on and a cog in the wheel of, the commercial progress of Nigeria. Late in the 19th century, the European trading firms were still oscillating in the coastal peripheries of

Nigeria. In their subsequent drive into the interior in the 20th century, the European firms had hoped to eliminate the services of the middlemen and so trade directly with the export crop producers. In this way, they hoped they would maximise their profits. But reality turned out in fact to be different. The tussle that ensued between the coastal middlemen and the European firms has been very well documented. Ultimately, the firms, aided by the colonial might, succeeded in pegging down the coastal middlemen. But as the firms gravitated into the hinterland, following the extension of transport and communication networks, a new breed of middlemen emerged whose services in the long run they found indispensable.

The Nigerian middlemen can be said to have performed three basic functions. They acted as frontiersmen in discovering and opening up new markets in the interior; they bulked produce and broke bulk in respect of imports. Gradual improvement and extension of modern means of transportation and communication meant a widening of trade frontiers from the coastal bases of the firms into the hinterland. Areas which had been outside of the trade nexus were being progressively brought into the web. As these frontiers of trade advanced so did some of the interior middlemen beat some kind of 'retreat' to scour for new markets still outside the trade nexus or just wavering on the verge of it. From a security point of view, it would not have been safe for the firms themselves to undertake such ventures, nor did they have the personnel to do so.

We have indicated earlier that the production of export crops in Nigeria was well in the hands of indigenous farmers. These farmers numbered in their tens of thousands and lived in scattered hamlets. They produced in small quantities and sold in even smaller quantities. It would, therefore, have been uneconomic for the expatriate firms, even if they had the personnel, to scour the remote areas to buy produce in very small quantities.

Nor were the operations of the middlemen limited to those remote areas where the European firms could not establish their 'beaches'. In the major urban areas where the trading firms invariably had their major depots, the firms still found the role of the urban middlemen indispensable in the chain of transmission of export produce. This class of middlemen, operating predominantly in the urban centres, complemented the functions of the rural middlemen. Their basic functions included sorting, blending, grading and bulking of produce in sufficiently sizeable quantities for sale to the European trading firms.

The UAC in its *Statistical and Economic Review* of 1949 testified to the critical role of the urban middlemen.[29] It noted that at Umuahia in eastern Nigeria, it was normal to see an indigenous middlemen operating in his produce buying shed just outside the precincts of the company's depots. The middleman bought palm-oil in 4-gallon kerosene tins, and by the use of a 'try-rod', tested the oil for quality and 'graded' it. He then poured the oil he had bought into 8-cwt. drums, according to grades. When a drum was filled, he sealed it and then just rolled it across into the company's depot for sale. In the case of palm kernel, the middleman bought the produce in small containers from traders from the interior. He then removed any shells or other extraneous particles still found on the kernels before pouring them into a sack. When a sack-load was obtained, he sewed it up and moved it to the company's depot for sale.

The trading firms, even contrary to their earlier expectations, found it very convenient and economical to allow the indigenous middleman to do the sorting, testing, grading and bulking of produce. These jobs would have cost them much more than the margins the middleman received for his input if they had employed their own paid personnel to do the jobs. On the part of the farmers, the rural middleman who scoured the remote markets buying produce from them saved them the problem of each having to take his own little produce to the trading firms' depots which invariably were located many kilometres away.[30]

The job of scouring the interior markets for produce was an arduous one. It meant that under the periodic market cycle characteristic of Nigeria domestic trade, the rural middlemen had to be perpetually on the move tramping from one market to another. Often they did this on foot, except for the very few 'affluent' ones who did so on bicycle. In some parts of Nigeria, notably the south, the rural roads were mostly footpaths and became very swampy during the rainy season, and some even turned into veritable water courses when it rained.

In the riverain areas of southern Nigeria the job was no less demanding. For instance, most communities on the River Niger and the other related rivers used the waterways as their chief means of transportation. Here casks of oil strung together in rafts had to be poled and guided through treacherous snags and other obstacles to navigation. The middlemen produce traders had to live for days or even weeks on the floating island of casks. At the shallow part of the rivers or where obstructions existed, the rafts had to be unmade and the casks rolled over the obstacle manually. The rafts were then re-made and the journey resumed. Depending on the number of obstacles encountered en route and the level of water, a journey from Oguta to Abonnema took from six days when the currents were high and swift to as much as a month during low currents.[31]

The middlemen's role often involved them in the sale of imports. Most middlemen operated a credit arrangement with one or the other of the trading firms. The UAC estimated that in the 1940s about a quarter of the value of trade in palm produce in southern Nigeria was financed through credit to African middlemen by expatriate trading firms.[32] The firms advanced imported goods to the middlemen in return for future delivery of produce. The goods the middlemen received at the shops of the trading firms were invariably in units larger than the average Nigerian would purchase. The middlemen, therefore, had to break the goods into very small units that were within the pecuniary capability of the consumers. Thus, for example, cigarettes and matches had to be broken into 'sticks' or 'fingers'; tobacco heads had to be cut into ¼d worth pieces; bars of soap were cut into several units. By making goods available in such small units, the middlemen stimulated the production efforts of the farmers who consumed the goods.

It should be appropriate at this point to pose the question: what were the returns to the middlemen for their very crucial contributions in promoting the import-export trade? We cannot say precisely whether or not the middlemen received a fair reward for their enterprise. We know only the prices at which they sold produce to the European firms but not the prices at which they bought same from the producers. Nevertheless, through oblique deductions a general pattern can emerge.

There is evidence that some middlemen and even women reaped rich harvests from their enterprise. Ome Okwei (1872-1943), the Merchant Queen of Ossomari, started trade in produce and imports with the Niger Company at the beginning of the 20th century with scarcely any substantial capital. When she died in 1943, she left a small fortune which included 24 houses in Onitsha and £5,000 in the bank.[33] Another successful Nigerian entrepreneur was Chief J.A. Obisesan who started business in 1914 in western Nigeria as a cocoa trader. He later went on to invest some of his capital in cocoa farms in which he employed paid labour. Then there was J.H. Doherty (1860-1928), who started trading on his own in 1891 with a meagre capital of £47. His was a success story almost unparalleled. Within the three years, 1899-1901, his average net receipts from sales amounted to nearly £500,000 per annum.[34]

The foregoing are the outstanding examples. They are often cited to indicate that Nigerian middlemen reaped fabulous rewards from their exterprise. In point of fact, however, these were exceptions. The Nigerian middlemen numbered in their thousands. The vast silent majority would seem to have ended up with no marked improvement in the condition of their lives. And like the farmers who produced the export crops, they would appear to have had little to show for all their productive endeavours.

The reasons for this derive basically from the same colonial circumstances under which they operated. The machinations of the trading firms which, we have seen above, adversely affected the conditions of the farmers also had negative consequences for the middlemen. In one respect, indeed, their plight might as well have been worse than that of the farmers. Their high degree of dependence on the trading firms for credit naturally played them into the clutches of the firms. To these firms they were obliged to sell their produce. The situation further narrowed down whatever chances of independent action they might otherwise have had. What is more, with frequent fluctuations in the prices of produce, the indebted middlemen often found that they had to give more produce to their creditors than they had earlier bargained for.

Those indigenous produce traders who tried to strike their own line of independent operation ran foul of the firms. The firms invariably responded by trying to stifle the genuine and legitimate aspirations and endeavours of such people. In 1918, a Niger Company agent made no secret of his annoyance that some Nigerian produce traders in eastern Nigeria had shipped their produce direct to Europe rather than sell to the trading firms. In a letter to his home office, he complained of 'native' dealers at New Calabar having shipped over 100 tons of produce to Europe in June, 1918. He was further agitated that other 'native' dealers operating at Port Harcourt and up the new rail line to Udi (Enugu) were also intending to ship their produce direct to Europe. The firms in collusion proceeded to allocate space in the ships in such a discriminatory manner that the indigenous exporters had no space assigned to them. This action had the effect the firms desired for as the same agent reported later, 'they are able to get very little way'.[35]

The middlemen's position was not helped by the cycle of economic depressions as well as the two major wars that occurred during the colonial period. There was a slump in the prices of primary produce in 1920-21. A more serious and prolonged one occurred in the late twenties and continued, with only a brief recovery in 1935-37, to the beginning of World War II. This depression was characterised by a dramatic collapse of prices of primary produce. It is true that these vicissitudes were global in context, but their effects were far more damaging to the Nigerian producers and middlemen than they were to the European trading interests. For one thing, the Nigerian middlemen, unlike the European trading firms, had very little, if any, market intelligence. They were unable consequently to have a forewarning of the approaching storms, and so were unable to brace themselves for the eventualities. They were caught unawares and least prepared. They invariably found themselves holding large stocks of old produce whose prices had tumbled down several times over.

For another thing, these middlemen lacked any capital reserve with which to keep afloat during the crisis periods. Nor was the situation abated by the inadequacy of the produce storage facilities these middlemen had. For these reasons, many middlemen produce traders, unable to keep afloat during those crisis periods, were liquidated.

The two great wars (1914-1919 and 1939-1945) also played their roles in confounding the difficulties of the Nigerian middlemen. During the first war, European markets for Nigerian exports were considerably narrowed down; the German market was completely closed down. Produce from Nigeria was more strictly canalised to Britain than ever before. The situation, as Michael Crowder observes, resulted in a dramatic fall in the prices of Nigerian exports.[36] Much harder times were yet to come with the Second World War. Official intervention in the produce trade of Nigeria, about which we shall hear more later, conferred on a handful of expatriate firms the sole right of buying produce for the British government. That action reduced the role of the indigenous middlemen in the export trade of Nigeria during that war to a very pale shadow of what it had previously been.

Of course, the problems of the Nigerian middlemen were shared to some extent by the small-scale European firms. Some of them were eliminated but the majority merged with stronger and bigger firms, and so survived. It is instructive in this respect that the combines, African and Eastern Trade Corporation and the UAC, emerged during the economic slumps of 1919-21 and 1928-35. Thus while the string of economic problems of colonial Nigeria had the general effect of weakening the positions of the Nigerian export producers and middlemen, it at the same time had the reverse effect of strengthening that of the major trading firms.

Wage Labour

It is proper at this point to indicate that the trading firms made use of the services of indigenous wage labour. This issue is mentioned here only briefly for the sake of coherence: it is discussed in some detail in another chapter. The firms needed the services of indigenous wage labour essentially for clerical jobs. These clerks became indispensable in the trading operations of the firms. They did the important job of keeping records of the sales and purchases of the firms. There were, of course, also paid labourers employed by the firms for the purpose, for example, of packing produce in the firms' depots and for head-loading same into lorries or waiting ships.

But although these wage-earners contributed immensely to build up the trade between Britain and Nigeria, the firms made next to no investment in men. Education was left almost entirely with Christian Missionary bodies. The aim of the missionary bodies themselves was not to produce highly educated Nigerians, and no attempts were made at all to give Nigerian workers mechanical and managerial education, except such as they managed unavoidably to acquire through on-the-job process. The greatest effort a company made on the question of giving Nigerians some higher education was when the UAC awarded a scholarship worth £300 to a Nigerian student.[37]

The wage prospects of the Nigerian worker in the employ of both government and the trading firms were unbelievably miserable. In 1943, the Leverhulme Commission was set up to look into the question of wages of workers. It came out with the depressing revelation that the wages of Nigerian workers were unpardonably low. Some received as low as 4d per day, while 1s 6d was considered equitable by a few firms.[38] This was at a time when war-time hyper-inflation was dealing a severe blow to the standard of living of the wage earners. On work-free days, workers had to farm to maintain subsistence existence.

What all this means is that the real earners in the British-Nigeria trade were the financiers, capitalists and industrialists in Britain. The Nigerian workers remained 'hewers of wood and fetchers of water'. The British firms made huge profits in their trade in Nigeria but hardly put in anything in return. This is what Walter Rodney refers to as 'exploitation without redress'.[39]

The agonies of the Nigerian workers did not always emanate only from a poor wage and their deplorable conditions of service. Occasionally they became the victims of the dishonesty and sharp practices of the European trading firms. Take for instance the case of the so-called Onitsha Industrial Ltd., which was registered as a company in June 1931 with one Mr Bowley, an Englishman, as a joint Managing Director. The Company 'took off' with a subscribed share capital of £1,675. This company apparently put out an enticing advertisement calling for labourers and artisans. Prospective employees had to pay refundable deposits ranging from £2 to £10. The total amount the company collected from such deposits came to £3,000. A further £5,548 was subscribed by indigenous share-holders.[40] The company turned out in the final analysis to be fake for it folded almost as fast as it sprang up. The Nigerian shareholders lost out; so did the employees who had made refundable deposits which turned out to be non-refundable. A series of long-drawn court litigations against the company followed; but all these came to nil. Mr John Murray Stuart-Young, an Englishman, was disgusted with the business oppression and duplicity from his countrymen. He made considerable efforts to protect the indigenes of Onitsha from excessive abuse. In doing so he fell foul of the trading firms. Through their ganging-up against him, he ended up a ruined man.[41]

The Colonial Government

The transformation of Nigeria into a formal colony of Britain meant that the metropolis could create the framework for economic activity, and thereby condition, or even determine, the direction of economic development. From an economic view point, this is the basic distinction between an informal colony and a formal one. The economic policy of the colonial regime in Nigeria ensured that the inequality of trade between the colony and the metropolis was upheld.

This economic policy may broadly be said to revolve around three basic themes: centre-periphery relationship between the colony and the metropolis, colonial self-sufficiency and laissez-faire. In context, 'centre-periphery' refers to that relationship between the centre (the metropolis) and the periphery (the colony) in which the interests of the former were accorded a place of central importance and those of the latter only a peripheral consideration in any economic calculations involving the two. The policy of self-sufficiency was pursued to ensure that the ruling power absolved itself from any financial responsibility to the colony. Nigeria, therefore, was expected to foot the bills of administration and socio-economic development from its own internally generated revenue. By the policy of laissez-faire, the colonial government claimed not to interfere with the normal working of economic or market forces. It rather saw, or claimed to see, itself as an impartial umpire whose sole function was to see that the rules of the game were obeyed.

The colonial government considered as one of its primary assignments the creation of an environment that would enable trade between Nigeria and Britain to flourish. To do this, two basic desiderata were considered imperative. First, the so-called Pax Britannica had to be imposed on the colonised. To this end, military conquest over, drastic visitations were meted out to communities that showed even the slightest symptoms of dissent. Second, the colonial government busied itself with the provision of modern means of transportation and communication. But, in strict compliance with the policy of self-sufficiency which had been enunciated in 1852 by Earl Grey, the developments were financed from the revenue of the colony.

In providing the transport and communication infrastructure the government was guided primarily by the consideration of ensuring easy evacuation of exports. Thus roads and railways were constructed to run vertically from the evacuation points at the coast to the areas of production in the hinterland. No attempts were made to extend modern transport infrastructure to non-export producing areas, no matter how otherwise richly endowed from the point of view of the domestic economy. Nor were any efforts made by government to develop the transport system in such a way as to stimulate domestic exchange. One result of government's action and inaction was the emergence of an enclave and dualistic economy; meaning that development in those favoured areas had little or no spread effect on the other areas. The economy that thus developed lacked coherence.

Government had claimed not to interfere with market forces, but to give them a free rein to determine the trend of exchange. Some commentators, such as Fieldhouse, think that, guided by that principle, the British administration 'evolved responsible attitudes and adopted the stance of umpire rather than protagonist'.[42] No statement can be further from the truth. The truth is that the so-called policy of laissez-faire was applied in a one-sided manner that placed British trading firms in a favourable position. First, laissez-faire in practice was hypocritical because it matched British firms and Nigerian traders in an unequal combat. In that mismatch, the colonial government, as Hopkins has aptly observed, saw its role as ensuring that the rules of the game were obeyed, not that they were changed.[43] But what was needed for a fair match was a change in the rules. In fact, it was in its unwillingness to check the excesses of the firms that the government had its greatest failure.

Second, laissez-faire was applied only in the trade between Nigerians and the British, and only when it suited the British. This policy was not extended to non-British firms. True, initially Britain, partly because of earlier agreements committing her to free trade, had a relatively liberal attitude in regard to free commerce. It was not long, however, in the colonial era in Nigeria, before her policy hardened in favour of protectionism. The process started in earnest on the eve of World War I, and reached its crescendo during the second. In 1917, the government imposed a total ban on the export of palm-oil from Nigeria except to the United Kingdom. The aim of the ban was to divert the export of the produce from Germany and the United States of America to Britain. This she succeeded in doing. Then between 1919 and 1922, she also imposed highly discriminatory duties on palm kernel and tin ore exported from Nigeria. The intention was again to canalise the trade in these exports to the United Kingdom.

When the Great Depression arrived in the late 1920s the colonial government tightened the noose on Nigeria. By now Britain had undeniably come to adopt a mercantilist and imperial interpretation of development in

Nigeria. Britain was now supplying more than 75 per cent of British West Africa's imports and was receiving more than 50 per cent of the exports.[44] In a very real sense, and in the true spirit of Joseph Chamberlain's doctrine of imperial estate, Nigeria had become a raw material supplier to, and an assured market for, British industries. In 1932, a severely stiffened quota system was slammed on cheap Japanese textile goods. The intention was to protect the anaemic and uncompetitive Lancashire textile industry which had been hit by the closure of a number of mills and the retrenchment of hundreds of the workers.

Then came World War II. The British introduced even more stringent measures. The war brought about severe shortages of raw materials to British industries, especially after Japan's seizure of the Far East. In 1939, the British Ministry of Food appropriated to itself the right of sole purchaser of primary products from British West Africa. This action was followed in 1942 by the setting up by the British of the West African Produce Control Board. The Board was charged with the responsibility of executing the decision of the Ministry of Food. The Board fixed prices at which farmers were paid for their produce. These prices were extremely meagre, especially against the background of the high demand for the produce, and war-time inflation. The pricing policy of the Board entailed very severe hardship on the producers.[45]

The cessation of hostilities in 1945 was not followed by a relaxation of the controls. Marketing Boards replaced the W.A.P.C.B., but their pricing policy remained identical with that of their predecessor. Under the guise of price stabilisation, farmers in Nigeria were compelled to receive roughly 66% of the value of their produce.[46] The Defence Regulations of 1939, which were made under the emergency imposed by the war, were dismantled. But they were replaced by the Exchange Control Ordinance of 1950. This Ordinance empowered the government to apply currency control and exchange restrictions to force dependencies to buy within Britain's own currency area and to surrender the bullion and foreign currency they earned to support the metropolitan currency.[47] The implications of all these measures are simple, and speak for themselves: Nigerians were forbidden by imperialist Britain to buy from the cheapest market and to sell to the highest bidder. After taking a hard look at the activities of Britain as well as France in Africa, Fieldhouse hands down an apt verdict: 'The case against Britain and France is that through their political and economic power, they took more out of Africa than they put in: that the *mise en valeur* was a cover for piracy'.

Conclusion

The dawn of the 20th century coincided with the establishment of direct British rule in Nigeria. The new regime created close affinities between the colonising country and the colonised in various fields, foremost among which was commerce. In that trade, Nigeria was treated as an outright inferior partner whose interests had no weight in the economic calculations of the imperial power. British-Nigeria trade was thus distinctly characterised by inequality of exchange. This situation was the direct outcome of the exploitative activities of the British firms operating in Nigeria, and the policy of the colonial government of Nigeria which lent support to the firms. Mercantilist influence persisted in the British-Nigeria trade even after its philosophical basis had ceased to be a dominant feature of British economic policy.

By 1960, the terminal year of colonial rule in Nigeria, sixty years or so of direct British rule had merely produced a veneer of social services, increased cash crop production and a small lopsided transport network designed to ensure the evacuation of produce from the hinterland. The vast majority of Nigerians had not witnessed any improvement in the conditions of their lives. They had not been exposed to anything near the basic benefits of Western education nor yet of modern medical services. Millions remained on their farms, smallholders, growing their crops by the same ancient methods, using the same crude tools their predecessors had used thousands of years earlier.

Apologists argue that colonial rule ushered in 'Pax Britannica' which reportedly replaced a state of anarchy and lawlessness of the interior. This weird claim has long been rebutted even by British writers. Macmillan, one such British writer, warned his countrymen, 'It is a facile boast that the boon of ordered government is our boast to Africa when they have had to foot the whole bill themselves'.[48]

References

1. F.D. Lugard, *The Dual Mandate in British Tropical Africa* (Edinburgh, 1922; Reprinted London: Frank Cass Ltd, 1965) p.613.

2. Claude Ake, *A Political Economy of Africa* (London: Oxford University Press, 1981), p.36.

3. D.K. Fieldhouse, 'The Economic Exploitation of Africa: Some British and French Comparisons' in P. Gifford and W.R. Louis (eds), *Britain and France in Africa* (New Haven: Longmans, 1971), p.641.

4. S. Leith-Ross, *African Women* (London, 1939, Revised ed., 1965), p.167.

5. Rhodes House, Oxford (RH), Mss. Afr. S. 96; Royal Niger Co., Miscellaneous papers, 1904-05, Vol. 12, p.4.

6. RH, Mss. Afr. S. 96; R.N.C., Misc. papers 1914-17, vol. 15.

7. A. Macmillan, *The Red Book of West Africa* (London, 1920, new imp. 1968), p.70.

8. CO 583/98: Clifford to C.O. 1921. PRO, London.

9. Ibid.

10. John Hatch, *Nigeria: A History* (London, 1971), pp.175-177.

11. Hatch, op. cit., p.360.

12. C. Ehrlich, 'Building and Caretaking: Economic Policy in British

Tropical Africa, 1890–1960', *Economic History Review*, 2nd Series, 4 (Nov. 1973), pp.649-66.

13. Walter Rodney, *How Europe Underdeveloped Africa* (Dar es Salaam: Tanzania Publishing House, 1972), p.172.

14. John Mars, 'Extra-territorial Enterprises', in M. Perham (ed.), *Mining, Commerce and Finance in Nigeria* (London, 1948), pp.70-87.

15. A.E. Afigbo, 'Trade and Politics on the Cross River, 1895–1905', *Transactions of the Historical Society of Ghana*, (1972), pp.22-49.

16. Afigbo, op. cit., p.45.

17. W.I. Ofonagoro, *Trade and Imperialism in Southern Nigeria: 1881–1929* (New York: NOK Publishers, 1979), pp.330, 343-344.

18. Michael Crowder, *West Africa Under Colonial Rule* (London: Hutchinsons, 1968), p.301.

19. R. Zahar, *Colonialism and Alienation* (Benin City, 1974), p.9.

20. Donald Kingdom, *Report of the Aba Commission of Inquiry*, (Lagos: Government Printer), p.102.

21. Kingdom, op. cit., p.103.

22. Kingdom, op. cit., p.104.

23. R.O. Ekundare, *An Economic History of Nigeria, 1860–1960* (London: Methuen, 1973), pp.199-200.

24. Ekundare, op. cit., p.206.

25. J.R. Mackie, Papers on Nigerian Agriculture, 1939–45; RH, Afr. S. 823 (1) (London).

26. Anne Martin, *The Oil Palm Economy of the Ibibio Farmer* (Ibadan, 1956), p.26.

27. Fieldhouse, op. cit., p.637.

28. J.F A. Ajayi & M. Crowder, 'West Africa, 1919–1939: the colonial situation', in J.F.A. Ajayi & M. Crowder (eds), *History of West Africa*, vol. II (London: Longman, 1974), p.529.

29. U.A.C., *Statistical and Economic Review*, No. 3 (March, 1949), pp.13-19

30. For the role of the African middlemen, see P.T. Bauer, *West African Trade* (London: Routledge and Kegan Paul, 1963), pp.32-34;

31. U.A.C., *Statistical and Economic Review*, No. 2 (Sept. 1948), p.18. See also Raymond G. Clough, *Oil River Trader* (London, 1972), p.5.

32. U.A.C., *S.E.R.* (1949), pp.20-25.

33. F. Ekejiuba, 'Omu Okwei, the Merchant Queen of Ossomari: a Biographical Sketch', *Journal of the Historical Society of Nigeria*, 3 (1967), pp.633-46.

34. For Obisesan and Doherty, see A.G. Hopkins, *An Economic History of West Africa* (London: Longmans, 1973), pp.240-41.

35. RH, Mss Afr. S. 99; misc. papers, 1914-17; vol. 15, p.4.

36. M. Crowder, 'West Africa and the 1914–18 War', *Bulletin de L'IFAN*, B. 30 (1968), pp.227-45.

37. J. Mars, op. cit., p.73.

38. Ibid.

39. Rodney, op. cit., p.164.

40. CO 583/182, File 1338; Onitsha Industrial Ltd., (1931).

41. Chinweizu, *The West and the Rest of Us* (London, 1978), pp.73-4.

42. Fieldhouse, op. cit., p.614.

43. Hopkins, op. cit., p.189.

44. Ibid., p.174.

45. G.O. Olusanya, *The Second World War and Politics in Nigeria* (Ibandan: Longmans, 1973), passim.

46. David E. Carney, *Government and Economy in British West Africa* (New Haven: Evans, 1961), p.108.

47. Ekundare, op. cit., p.328.

48. W.M. Macmillan, *Africa Emergent* (London, 1938), p.283.

9. Exploitation of Labour: Waged and Forced

D. C. Obadike

Introduction

The scramble for Africa and the establishment of colonial domination over the continent were designed primarily to enable the industrialised countries of Western Europe to make huge profits on investment.

The weapons at the disposal of the imperialist countries were enormous and when applied could assign specific roles to the dependent countries. Colonial estates could be transformed into areas of production of raw materials or converted into markets for finished goods. 'Black Africa's importance to the imperialists', points out A.T. Nzula, 'is by no means just a matter of raw materials' but also as consumer of European goods.[1]

Sometimes colonial government officials participated directly in the extraction of raw materials in the African colonies, a good example being coal mining in Nigeria, and sometimes they merely provided the basic infrastructural facilities while industrial and commercial agents from the metropolitan countries exploited the available mineral and agricultural resources. In some colonies native land was seized outright and shared out among white colonisers. In Nigeria the British imperialists did not take all the land: they had no need for all. They took only the best land (after thoroughly surveying the country) to make room for mines, roads, railway lines, harbours, Government Reserved Areas (G.R.A.) and military barracks. Even though land seizure in Nigeria cannot be compared with what took place in East and Southern Africa, the labour of Nigeria was equally brutally exploited by a process of naked forced labour, and by the payment of miserly wages to workers. The bulk of the labour used for the construction of infrastructures and for the production of raw materials was Nigerian labour. As in all black African countries, colonialism in Nigeria made it possible for new forms of slavery and social relations of production to be introduced as manifested in forced and wage labour.

Although colonial labour exploitation in Nigeria took some other forms, such as direct taxation which forced men to sell their labour power at any price in order to raise tax money, or by offering farmers very low prices for their produce, or by involving colonial subjects in all forms of unequal exchange, this chapter will concern itself specifically with British exploitation of Nigerian labour through the formulation and implementation of a colonial forced and wage labour policy.

Prelude to British Exploitation of Nigerian Labour: the Colonial Armed Forces in Nigeria, 1862–1918

One important weapon at the disposal of the imperialist countries was their ability to enlist the co-operation of weaker people to effect their own exploitation. The countries of Western Europe began their exploitation of West Africa by winning the co-operation of some indigenous people to pave the way for their own exploitation. Such indigenous collaborators have been described with such disguised names as 'trading partners', 'modernisers' or even 'noble savages'.

British exploitation of Nigerian labour in modern times actually commenced in 1862 when the British began to use the labour power of Nigerians to conquer and colonise Nigeria.[2] The genesis of this mode of exploitation dates back to the year when the Lagos Constabulary, otherwise known as 'Glover's Hausas' or 'The Forty Thieves', was established.[3] This force was raised by Captain J. Glover, R.N., the Administrator of Lagos and was used to prop up British influence and authority in Lagos.

Prior to the formation of this force, and for much of the nineteenth century, the British had tried two other sources of military recruitment for operations in West Africa. Initially troops of European origin were used to garrison sensitive positions on the West coast and, as S.C. Ukpabi has pointed out, these men were unsuitable and expensive. They recorded a high mortality rate and were never able to reconcile themselves to a tropical environment.[4]

To remedy the situation, men of the West India Regiment were tried. Although they were blacks and did not easily succumb with fever, they were equally unsuitable in many important aspects. In the first place, they were expensive to maintain since they were treated almost like European soldiers. Secondly, they were unfamiliar with bush fighting in the interior mainly because their training and equipment predisposed them to operations in coastal districts only. Thirdly, they were maintained by the British government which was generally reluctant to bear the financial cost of building an empire. The policy that soon emerged prescribed that each colony was to bear the cost of its own colonisation and exploitation; only profits were to be shipped to Britain. Finally, considering the fact that the British empire was expanding rapidly, and because of the large numbers of men that were required to advance and maintain British influence throughout West Africa, it was realised that neither European soldiers nor members of the West India Regiment could cope with the new assignment. These were the fundamental circumstances that constrained the British government to turn to West Africans for military operations in West Africa.

Already, it had been realised that West Africans were superior to Europeans and West Indians for military operations in West Africa. This realisation is borne out in a letter written in 1862 by Stanhope Freeman, Governor of the British possessions, resident in Sierra Leone, to the Duke of Newcastle. According to the Governor

> The expense of this establishment [of 600] is about one-fifth of what a similar number of regular troops would cost the Imperial Government, and the force [of Hausa Constabulary] is more efficient than the West Indian Regiment. One-fifth of the men are usually on the sick list in this place, while there is rarely more than one percent of the Hausa men ill; besides this, they require no commissariat, little or no transport, and nourish themselves on the products of the country, which are always to be had. Wearing no shoes, they do not get footsore on long marches, and the simplicity of their dress renders it both convenient and economical.[5]

These observations were taken note of and over time both British regular troops and men of the West India Regiment were replaced in British West Africa by men of West African origin.

In 1886 the Royal Niger Company was granted a Royal charter[6] partly in recognition of its services in the interior,[7] and partly because of Britain's clumsy and inconsistent attitude towards colonial expansion. In the same year the Company raised a constabulary force on the Lower Niger with the primary aim of extending British aggression and economic exploitation of Nigeria. The bulk of this force was made up of West Africans. Claude MacDonald reported that in 1889 this force comprised 5 English Officers, 2 Native Officers, 2 Sergeant Majors, 15 Sergeants, 16 Corporals and 308 Privates.[8] He further observed that five-eighths of the black soldiers was 'Fantees' (Modern Ghana), one-quarter Hausa and the rest Yoruba. According to MacDonald,

> The fighting qualities of these 3 people are . . . good, the Hausas are bold and plucky but in bush fighting are apt to get out of hand and think too much of loot . . . the Fantees are far steadier in the bush than the Hausas but lack individual pluck, they however fight well in a body.[9]

There were more Fante than Hausa and Yoruba in the Royal Niger Company forces because the initial practice was to recruit men in the Niger territories for service in the Gold Coast while men were recruited in the Gold Coast for service in the Niger territories. This policy was adopted because, as MacDonald explained, 'It had been thought that the Hausa would be unwilling to fight against the Mohamedans of the country. . . .'[10] Nevertheless, this assumption was soon proved wrong and the restriction was lifted. Writes MacDonald,

> [Mohamedans] have . . . been tried on more than one occasion in the punitive expeditions of the Royal Niger Company against Mohamedans on the Benue and have raised no objection, and considering that Mohamedans of India have frequently fought in India and in Egypt against their co-religionists, there seems to be no reason why the

Mohamedans of one part of Africa should not fight against those of another part.[11]

The Royal Niger Company used men of West African origin to conquer and consolidate British rule in Nigeria. Between 1886 and 1899 the forces of the Company fought over fifty battles in Nigeria and overwhelmed such scattered places as Patani and Akassa in the Delta, Keffi, and Wase on the Plateau, Ilorin and Bida in the north-west and Gloria, Ibo and Oguta in the south-east.[12]

Another British force raised in Nigeria during this period was the Niger Coast Protectorate Force (or Constabulary) under the command of Sir Ralph Moor. This force was very notorious on account of its brutality and was nicknamed also 'the forty thieves'.[13]

After the Berlin West African Conference of 1884-85 the British government became very much alarmed at French military drive and conquest of West Africa. By the 1890s it had become evident that the Constabulary forces of the Royal Niger Company were no longer capable of advancing British influences any further. Also, neither the Niger Coast Protectorate forces nor the Lagos 'Hausas' and the 2nd West India Regiment stationed in Lagos seemed capable of warding off the French menace. It was realised that if Britain should ever hope effectively to occupy any new territories in West Africa, or even contain French threats in those areas they (the British) already claimed, a powerful British army should be maintained in West Africa. Lord Lugard was consequently requested in 1897 by the Colonial Office to raise a West African Force of between 2,000 and 3,000 men for operations in West Africa.[14] This request was accepted and by the end of 1898 the West African Frontier Force had been formed.

The various detachments of the West African Frontier Force that were stationed in Nigeria were recruited locally. In reply to Lord Chamberlain's despatch regarding the formation of this force the Governor of Lagos, H. McCallum wrote:

> . . . If therefore, the new force is to be employed outside the confines of Yoruba I venture to submit that we should not depend on the Hausas entirely, but make up one battalion of Yorubas, who have a remarkable fine, smart appearance, and learn their drill rapidly. If you wire me authority to engage Yorubas to the number, say, of 700 to 1,000, I believe I could recruit them almost entirely from the Ibadan Warboys, who do not like an agricultural life after being so long engaged in warlike operations against the Ilorin.[15]

The initial strength of the West African Frontier Force was 2 Battalions consisting of 8 companies of 150 men under a Lieutenant-Colonel. The ratio of Europeans to Africans serving in this force was 1 to 14. More crucial than the racial composition of this force was the fact that the Europeans occupied the highest positions – commissioned and non-commissioned officers, medical officers, engineers, trainers, administrative officers (including Pay, Accounts and Transport)[16] while Nigerians were the fighting men. Many of these

Nigerians were killed or crippled during 'the little wars' that Britain fought in Nigeria during this great age of imperialism. Only on rare occasions were British officers hurt. Moreover, British officers were almost automatically promoted to higher ranks as soon as an expedition came to an end. In fact, many of the British officers looked forward to service in the tropics because it enabled them to climb to ranks they would never have reached in Europe. Besides this, service in the tropics enabled them to enjoy the luxury they would not have dreamt of back home.

What concerns us is the fact that the bulk of the fighting men of the West African Frontier Force stationed in Nigeria was recruited in Nigeria. This force enabled Britain to contain French threats and to consolidate British hold on Nigeria. As Ukpabi has pointed out, this innovation

> gave Chamberlain the lever he wanted in his dealing with the French. He came to rely less on European diplomacy and more on naked force, as personified by Lugard and the West African Frontier Force.[17]

Between 1898 and 1918 this force was used in constant 'punitive expeditions'. Also, the colonial government officials, the Emirs, the warrant chiefs and other agents of the government relied on it for support in their oppression of the people. As we shall see below, the West African Frontier Force backed the various Native Authorities in Northern Nigeria, enabling them to round up and hold down labour conscripts in mines and on construction sites. It also made the collection of taxes possible.

Another painful aspect of the colonial experience was that the Nigerians who served in the British armed forces were poorly paid. The Royal Niger Company paid its African soldiers the following wages[18]

Senior Native Officers	£3 17s 6d per month
Junior D.O.	£3. 0s 0d ” ”
Sergeant Major	£2 10s 0d ” ”
Sergeant	£2 0s 0d ” ”
Corporal	£1 15s 0d ” ”
Private	£1 10s 0d ” ”

As we have seen, almost all the members of this force were privates. Out of a total of 348 men, 308 were privates.

When the West African Frontier Force was formed the scales of pay for the Gold Coast and Lagos constabularies were adopted,[19] and after the amalgamation of the various forces into the Nigeria Regiments, this scale of pay was marginally raised but was kept in line with the deplorably low wages that prevailed in the country at this time. By 1900 wages were as follows[20]

"Kroo boys"	10s to £1 10s 0d per month
"Native Clerks"	£2 to £2 1s 0d per month
"Engineers"	£3 to £8 0s 0d ” ”
"Artificiers"	£3 to £12 0s 0d ” ”
"Tailors"	£2 10s to £5 6s ” ”
"Carpenters"	£2 10s to £4 0s 0d per month

Apart from their low wages, Nigerians who served in the colonial armed forces did all sorts of odd jobs. They built roads, served as porters and acted as domestic servants for their European Officers. Life was indeed very trying for men in the armed forces. Many who joined the army belonged to a class of Nigerians who had been partially or permanently displaced from ancestral lands, such as former slaves and fugitives. Writes Sir Charles Orr,

> A great number of slaves, many of whom had recently been captured in war, seized the opportunity to return to their country. Many deserted their masters and took service under the government, either as soldiers, police, transport carriers, or labourers in the Public Works Department.[21]

Others were restless men like the Yoruba 'war boys' (*omo ogun*) who, as we have seen, shunned an agricultural career after being so long engaged in the Yoruba Wars of the nineteenth century.

On the whole the formation of the various British armed forces in Nigeria had far-reaching social, political and economic consequences for the country. One of them, as Ukpabi has observed, was that Britain had, from the start, committed itself to the use of force in order to overcome African resistance on the West Coast and to establish British authority in this part of Africa.[22] Ukpabi further explains that having accepted this policy, the British government was prepared to advance the money necessary for the creation of such a force, even though the money spent in the conquest of any territory was charged to the account of the area so conquered and was recovered shortly after from that territory either by direct taxation, by confiscation of property or by the imposition of fines.[23] Furthermore, because Nigeria was conquered by force of arms, the British came to consider Nigerian wealth, body and soul, as belonging to the British Crown by right of conquest. Similarly, the forced labour laws that were passed during the early colonial period, the conscription of men into the British armed forces as occurred during the First and Second World Wars, the imposition of heavy taxation on povery-stricken rural communities, and the shooting and killing of protesting peasants and workers, were sanctioned because Britain acquired Nigeria by force of arms. Paradoxically, however, the initial conquest of Nigeria was made possible because Nigerians allowed themselves to be armed and instigated against fellow Nigerians. The foregoing discussion merely seeks to confirm the British exploited Nigerian labour to pave the way for further exploitation of Nigerian labour.

British Exploitation of Nigerian Labour: the Recruitment of Carriers

As early as 1895, Joseph Chamberlain, the Secretary of State for the Colonies, had recognised that many of the British colonies were in the condition of underdeveloped estates. He therefore advocated active co-operation between

Britain and the citizens of the British empire. Although what Chamberlain advocated was rather vague and narrow in its outlook, he can still be remembered as a 'progressive imperialist'. His 'constructive imperialism' did not embrace the stimulation of empire trade and resources alone, but also included some attempts at solving some of the social problems of the British empire as a whole.[24]

Unfortunately, however, Chamberlain's aspirations could not be realised mainly because the guiding principle of British colonialism had not changed. The British Treasury remained generally unprepared to provide the necessary funds for the development of the colonies. Secondly, because the British colonial agents in the colonies lacked the necessary vision for colonial development, they succeeded in entrenching oppression where Chamberlain advocated co-operation. Their economic perception dictated that the door was to be left wide open for the raw materials of the colonies to flow to Britain in exchange for manufactured goods.[25] All colonial subjects who entertained contrary views or those whose actions seemed to retard the pace of surplus evacuation to Britain, were summarily taught the harsh lesson of dependency. The punitive expeditions of the first two decades of the twentieth century were basically meant to drive this lesson home.

Thus, while the Colonial Office in London endeavoured to avoid all fiscal obligations to the colonies, it expected the colonial governments to balance their budgets. At the same time, private enterprise, which was too eager to make huge profits on capital investment, expected the colonial officials not only to provide the infrastructure of roads, railway lines, harbours and security, but also to guarantee labour drafts at deplorably low wages. In fact, the whole tragic situation has been summed up by A.G. Hopkins when he noted that

> Economic policy was limited both in its philosophy and in its techniques. Govermments were not envisaged to play a central and dynamic part in developing the estates they had acquired, and in any case, they had little of the necessary expertise at their disposal.[26]

These were, indeed the fundamental circumstances that gave rise to forced labour not only in colonial Nigeria but also in most parts of Africa. In fact, forced labour was a strong feature of twentieth century colonialism throughout Africa.[27]

To displace labour and recruit those they wanted, colonial agents resorted to very tough measures.[28] In Northern Nigeria for instance, they turned the emirs into a social support for the oppression of the people.[29] Most of the northern emirates had been smashed by the British at the end of the nineteenth century but were immediately re-organised to act as a powerful instrument for the recruitment of forced labour.[30] In south-eastern Nigeria[31] and in Benin Province[32] where no powerful institutions of chiefs existed, the British created warrant chiefs and vested them with false and pretentious powers. A.E. Afigbo has described warrant chiefs as certain natives who the British thought were traditional chiefs and were given certificates of recognition and authority called warrants . . . The warrant enabled each of these men to sit in the Native Court from time to time to judge cases. It also empowered him to assume within his community he represented executive and judicial powers which were novel both in degree and territorial scope.[33]

Viewed objectively, therefore, warrant chiefs were not chiefs but government officials garbed in chiefly regalia. In most parts of southern Nigeria they were used to round up labour for public works. The power vested in them to exploit the labour of their people was prescribed in Proclamation No. 15 of 1903 which compelled all able-bodied men and women to work with or without pay, in accordance with the directives of these chiefs.[34] Refusal to render one's services when a warrant chief demanded it was an offence punishable by fine or by imprisonment or by flogging. Flogging was legalised under another proclamation which allowed officials to administer as many as twenty-four strokes of the cane to any African sentenced to flogging.[35] A wide range of offences was punishable by flogging. A policeman who slept on duty was instantly sentenced to flogging, so also was anyone who failed to provide a District Officer with yams, fowls, eggs and water when these were demanded.

To understand the reason for the adoption of such an unprogressive colonial policy we must begin by mentioning that one of the greatest problems which the new British administration had to face was that of transportation. In the absence of wheeled vehicles both British officials and private investors would have to recruit copious amounts of labour in the form of carriers. 'The British occupation', observes Sir Charles Orr, 'entailed a great demand of labour, both on the part of Government and of the natives'.[36] Allan Mcphee equally observed that 'The two vital problems that European capital has had to face have been transport and labour'.[37] To take transportation, for instance, it has been estimated that a carrier could take a head-load of between 50 and 60 pounds at a time, or the equivalent of 11 gallons of palm-oil, that is, about 3 four-gallon bins full of oil.[38] A porter was expected to travel a distance of between 15 and 25 miles a day, sometimes through rough terrain, carrying such a heavy load on his head. Based on this computation, it would have taken about 37 men to transport a ton of produce in one day[39] or 32 days for one man to transport the same load over a distance of 180 miles.[40] To compare the relative efficiencies of human porterage with modern transportation, it has been reckoned that the same weight (one ton) in a lorry required two men for a journey four times the distance and that 1,000 times this load could be carried by rail ten times the distance, employing about six men.[41]

To move all the raw materials that the British wished to export from Nigeria, the entire population of the country would have served as carriers. Even if all adult men and women in Nigeria could have at once been converted into professional carriers, it would still have been impossible for them to move the available exports. For, as Bill Freund has warned, 'men could not be expected to work as porters solidly for the entire year'.[42] This is to say that porters were not machines. There is no doubt that the colonial administration and European industrial and commercial capital had a real labour problem as most equipment, including Europeans in their hammocks, had to be moved about by porters, and Nigeria was a large colony indeed.

More crucial than this was the fact that the colonial administration did not want only carriers; it also wanted builders, miners, farmers, soldiers and domestic servants. If the books of His Imperial Majesty's business had to be balanced and show a profit, labour had to be procured cheaply or better still, free. The decision to exploit the human power of Nigerians was therefore in keeping with the colonial labour policy whose supreme aspirations was to appropriate surplus.

During the first decades of the twentieth century Britain exploited the labour of Nigerians when colonial agents compelled peasant populations to serve as carriers. The wage of carriers at this time was fixed at between 6d and 9d a day. Sometimes this wage was paid but in most cases it was not paid at all. In the latter case, carriers were recruited under the Compulsory Labour Proclamations which authorised colonial government officials to recruit labour with or without pay.

The first colonial officials travelled about a great deal on foot especially in southern Nigeria where pack animals were scarce. When on an ordinary tour of his district or division, an official was accompanied by a large retinue of carriers and an armed escort. More than 30 carriers were normally required during such a tour but in case of a punitive expedition, hundreds of carriers were sometimes recruited to carry supplies, equipment and ammunition.

The practice was, however, to dismiss the entire carrier force when an official arrived at a town and to draw new supplies from there. Local chiefs were usually summoned and asked to supply a specified number of carriers. Sometimes a messenger travelled in advance to inform the chiefs that the white man was coming and that such and such a number of carriers must be made available. Where the chiefs of a particular town failed to supply the desired number of carriers the chiefs themselves were compelled to serve as carriers. Entire villages are known to have been burnt down or the chiefs flogged and fined for failing to provide enough carriers.

In 1902 the Divisional Commissioner at Asaba, Widenham Forsbery, who was travelling to Onitsha-Olona stopped over at Okpanam and summoned the chiefs of this town. The chiefs were asked to provide 30 carriers. The chiefs dispersed and soon arrived with only 12. The Divisional Commissioner warned that if the exact number of carriers demanded were not instantly provided, some of the chiefs would be made to serve as carriers instead. On hearing this, 'the younger chiefs bolted', and the British seized five elders of the town and marched them, loads on their heads, to Issele-Azagba.[43] The Divisional Commissioner later returned to Okpanam to impose heavy fines on the town for failing to provide 30 carriers when they were first ordered to do so.[44] Also, a chief in the Agbor district was once asked by a District Officer, O.C. Crewe-Read, to supply carriers for his journey and when, after an honest attempt, the chief expressed regret at his inability to supply the required number, the District Officer 'cooly struck a match, and set fire to the poor man's home . . .'[45] In 1910 carriers were forcibly seized from churches during divine worship at the western towns of Iseri and Imuku.[46] Earlier in 1909 it was reported that many people drowned in Ikom on the Cross River in their bid to escape being conscripted as carriers.[47]

Carriers were also extensively used in Northern Nigeria for the transportation of supplies and equipment. Sometimes porters were hired at the rate of 6d a day, but in many cases they were not paid at all. Sir Charles Orr had observed carriers on the march with heavy loads on their heads, and being obliged to travel long distances.[48] Before the completion of the Jos-Zaria light railway line, porters were used to transport tin from the Jos minefield to Loko and Baro on the Niger, a distance of 180 miles. Orr considered the wage rate of 6d a day for porters and other unskilled mine workers as 'a good wage to a native who has few expenses, and whose daily food costs him perhaps a third of this sum'.[49] Another British agent, Alvan Wilson, considered 7d a day for porters around Lagos as an 'affluence to a people who have been accustomed to earn by hard and uncongenial labour an average of less than 2½d a day'.[50]

British colonial agents and the commercial firms did not relax their demand for carriers until the railway lines and motor roads were completed. Until then, certain rural communities, especially those on the Jos Plateau, were subjected to untold hardships when they were compelled, not only to serve as carriers but also to supply labour to minefields, and road and railway line construction projects. As we shall see in due course, the large-scale diversion of labour away from the domestic sector of the economy contributed immensely to the unprecedented rural poverty and food shortages that occurred in many parts of colonial Nigeria.

British Exploitation of Nigerian Labour: Road and Railway Line Construction

As no large mineral deposits had yet been struck in southern Nigeria during the first decade of the twentieth century, British efforts were directed towards the construction of roads, railway lines, harbours, government rest houses and European quarters. Many communities in southern Nigeria were plundered and stripped of their farmlands to make room for government projects. There were occasions when a village had to send as many as 200 men, women and children at a time to work on the roads. In 1906, the District Commissioner of Agbor testified that it was common to find 2,000 'Natives' at work for considerable periods.[51] He also noted that pressure was put upon the chiefs to supply labour, and, as a young man of Owa told him, the youths often said, 'This is a bad work that our fathers make us do'.[52]

One other aspect of this exercise was that when summoned to construction sites, heads of families had to provide their own food as well as providing for the families they left behind. Sometimes men were compelled to journey up to 20 kilometres to construction sites where they were forced to remain for five or more days. At the end of each tour they would be sent away without pay.[53] Some communities, such as those in the Agbor district of western Igboland, were so harassed by colonial officials that the arrival of a white man in a town often caused the entire population to flee into the bush; and when eventually they protested against the regime, several hundred of their members were shot dead and nine men, who were described as ringleaders, were publicly hanged.[54] The true cause of this tragedy could have disappeared from the pages of history if certain anti-imperialist groups had not pressurised the British Government in London to inquire into the reports. Among them were E.C. Morel, a critic of British imperialism, and the Aborigines Protection Society. Commenting on the Agbor tragedy, the Secretary of the Aborigines Protection Society wrote to the British Government declaring that

> It is submitted that this employment of forced labour, lending itself to grave abuse in the hands of injudicious administrators, is in the nature of slavery, and, in common with other arrangements now adopted in Southern Nigeria, is in no way justified by the fact that it may be more than a perpetuation of uncivilised methods which it is the proposed aim of British rule to displace by more enlightened machinery of government.[55]

The Colonial Office responded to this criticism by writing to the Government of Southern Nigeria regretting to learn that some native chiefs had been flogged and that much unnecessary and even useless work was demanded provoking very great discontent against the administration. The Colonial Office went on to denounce the practice of flogging and finally asked if any alternative system of labour recruitment had been worked out.[56]

Colonial government officials in Nigeria admitted that forced labour was used in Southern Nigeria but explained that it was a substitute for tribute and taxes. They further stated that the system seemed 'to be the best under present circumstances'.[57] In a bid to pacify the anti-imperialist groups in Britain, the Colonial Office bullied the local administrators in Nigeria. In a letter written to the Governor of Southern Nigeria the Colonial Office pointed out the limitations of forced labour and flogging, showing the dangers to which their abuse by indiscreet officers might lead. Finally, it warned that steps should be taken to prevent the recurrence of similar actions.[58]

This 'warning' was never heeded, nor did the Colonial Office show the slightest determination to enforce it. Rather than abolish it, forced labour remained an integral part of British colonial policy in Southern Nigeria. It was invoked whenever the administration wished. Sometimes it was disguised but it was not abolished.

Forced labour and flogging were equally adopted as part of the colonial labour policy in Northern Nigeria. The Northern Nigerian Road Proclamation of 1903 was one of the earliest enactments legalising compulsory labour in the north. The British had realised from the start that if the agricultural and mineral products of Northern Nigeria had to be delivered cheaply to Britain, Northern Nigeria had to be provided with motor roads and railway lines. Thus, the first economic objectives of British industrial capital in this area were 'to divert the supply of cotton from the Nigerian hand-looms to the power-looms of Lancashire',[59] to transport the groundnuts of Kano cheaply to the coastal ports, and to expand the production of tin by reducing the transport cost from the Plateau tinfields to the sea-ports. Let us consider the question of tin.

The Royal Niger Company had begun to export tin from Northern Nigeria by the last decade of the nineteenth century but the quantity being exported was very small mainly on account of transport problem. Tin had to be carried a distance of over 200 miles along bush track to Loko from where it was sent down the Niger in the Niger Company's water craft. Unfortunately, observes Sir Charles Orr, 'carriers were exceedingly scarce and difficult to obtain'.[60] Sir Charles felt it was imperative from the start that some means of transport to the navigable rivers other than porterage must be provided.[61] To solve the transport problem, therefore, the extension of the railway line from Lagos to Kano, with a branch line to Baro and another to the Plateau tinfields was hastily planned.

Work began on the northern lines in 1907 and much of the labour used for their construction was forced. The emirs were put under great pressure to supply labour and by 1908 thousands of Nupe, Gwari and Koro labour recruits were sweating it out on the Baro extension alone.[62] Some of the labour conscripts were brought in under the disguised name of 'political labour', a system whereby men were forced to work under pressure from both indigenous chiefs and colonial officials. According to Michael Mason, 'this system was devised to assure low wages and the absence of any form of labour consciousness'.[63] Moreover, once a chief had sent a man to work on the railway line construction it became part of his communal obligation to complete his assignment. If he failed to keep pace with the work gang, he never returned to the village, and if he did, he was severely punished and sent back to the construction site. On the Baro-Kano line, workers were formed into gangs of 25 men each. Each gang worked for three or four weeks and was replaced with another gang from the same district. The result of this policy, points out Wale Oyemakinde, was that 'No chance was given for the development of a voluntary work force'.[64] Their constant replacement, further points out Oyemakinde, also robbed the men of the 'special opportunity of associating with people and ideas from outside their immediate locality'.[65] These devices were adopted to enable European investors to recruit cheap and involuntary labour. Such transient, unskilled labour force posed no problems to its European employers. No housing, medical or other facilities were provided for workers as each gang was soon to return to its home village. Besides, the authority of the emirs and political officer was enough to keep the workers during the short intervals that they were required to work on the line. Finally, although these men were paid nine pence a day, they were required to pay three pence as tax.[66]

Apart from 'political labour', other forms of involuntary labour were used for the construction of railway lines in Northern Nigeria. Reports of abuse of workers were rampant. Men were sometimes paid as little as 2s 1d per week, and European foremen and African recruiters were accused of exploiting and brutalising workers. The Right Reverend Bishop Tugwell stated that it was difficult to distinguish the deplorable conditions of labour in the north from slavery. In his petition to the High Commissioner, he charged that the men did not volunteer their services but were forced to render service, that although they were nominally paid six pence a day, they did not actually receive this amount, that the men worked for nine or ten hours a day under revolting conditions, that men were indiscriminately and cruelly beaten up by overseers, and that if a man ran away from the construction site and returned to his village, he was sent back by his overlord, usually, after a good beating.[67]

Most of these charges were denied but from an inquiry set up to look into them it was confirmed that labour was not voluntarily supplied 'in the sense of their being recruited in the open labour market' and that in some provinces men were paid 3d per week.[68]

Similar hardships were suffered by the communities living in all the districts through which railway lines passed. By 1909 the Baro-Kano line had been completed and in the same year the Lagos Extension had reached Zaria province. In 1911 this track entered Kano but this did not mark the end of railway line construction in northern Nigeria. In the same year another line was begun. This was the Bauchi railway line which was intended to link up Plateau tinfields with Zaria and Kano. By 1912–13 when this line was being completed, another was begun in the eastern provinces. Starting from Port Harcourt, this line passed through the coal-bearing districts around Enugu, thence to Tiv land and then to Jos. The same tale of woe, of compulsory labour, of beating, of deplation of population and agricultural production characterised this period of Nigerian labour history.

The first colonial roads in northern Nigeria were equally constructed with forced labour. The Idah-Nsukka motor road which was started in 1922, was constructed with forced labour; so also were the Lokoja-Ankpa-Otukpo road, and the Idah-Anyigba road. The District Heads (the *onu*), the road builders, and the surveyors were 'extremely cruel to defenceless civilians who toiled on the roads'.[69] P.E. Okwoli has summed up the sad story with the following expression, *'Ikpa Ka ce ki ma nu'gwa, itali ce Ugwa'*, meaning, 'The road work that had no reward, the whip was the reward'.[70]

Accounts of forced labour abound in oral testimonies in parts of northern Nigeria. A Mwahavul elder of the Jos Plateau testified that the first person who made them do the work was the first European colonial administrator whom they nick-named 'Dogon Lamba'.[71] These people were forced to work on government projects but for their labour they were not paid. On top of this they were severely beaten up. 'We did not know anything about road construction . . . the white-men provided the digger and we used our hoes in the construction'.[72] Sometimes they went to work with their wives and daughters who were made to carry sand with baskets.

There is no doubt that the various ethnic groups on the Plateau suffered great hardships when their labour was exploited by British colonial agents. The railway construction was called 'the work of Dawka'. Dawka, according to them, was a chief of Panyam who led his people to Jos for railway line construction.[73] It was a period of great national hardships for Panyam was 80 kilometres away from Jos, and the railway line they constructed did not pass anywhere near their district. The work was difficult for, according to them, when the railway line passed through the forest they had to cut down trees with their axes. The construction was endless for after building the railway line they were asked to construct motor roads.[74]

Road and railway line construction was vigorously pursued during the first three decades of this century. The purpose was to facilitate the evacuation of surplus to Europe, and to facilitate troop movements to areas of unrest within Nigeria. Roads and railway lines were not meant to provide transport facilities for the local people hence their absence in areas that had no meaningful mineral or agricultural surplus to export to Europe. This is particularly true of railway lines which were built with money borrowed in Britain. Railway lines in Nigeria were not a social amenity but a capital investment. By 1960 when Nigeria won her political independence there were still hundreds of settlements in the country that were not linked up with motorable roads or railway lines.

British Exploitation of Nigerian Labour: Working in the Minefields

Apart from the idea of having come to administer the colony of Nigeria, the British were strongly committed to seizing the mineral wealth of the country. That this was definitely their idea about Nigeria is confirmed by the utterances and activities of leading colonial agents. In 1911 Sir Walter Egerton advised that the Government of Southern Nigeria should seize 'all lignite areas in the Niger valley, of which the chief are Okpanam, Ibusa and Obompa on the right bank and Newi on the left bank'.[75] He pointed out that these areas fell well within the land over which the Niger Company obtained control by means of treaties with the 'native' chiefs and that therefore the Government already had the desired control.[76]

Supporting this view, Lord Lugard stated that mineral rights in the Eastern and Central Provinces 'may properly be regarded as vested in the Crown by right of conquest'.[77] Thus, under the new Minerals Ordinance which was enacted in 1913, the indigenous communities were deprived of any share of fees, rents or profits likely to be derived by mining activities on their land. They were also denied the right to object to prospecting licences or mining leases being granted over their land.[78] Another colonial agent defended the British Government's determination to rob Nigerians of their mineral wealth by stating that it was necessary to abolish these provisions for sharing fees,

rents and royalties with the people while it could be done without hardship,
He wondered how the Government which spent large sums in exploring the
country for minerals should take rents and royalties from Europeans and
share them among the Nigerians who had done nothing for which they were
entitled to be paid.[79] He added that 'the idea of mineral rights had probably
never entered the native mind, and if the proposal is carried through he will
only lose something which he didn't know that he had'.[80]

These are only to illustrate the fact that the British regarded the mineral
deposits of Nigeria as the property of the British Crown and people.[81]
Nevertheless, to seize mineral deposits was one thing, to extract them was
another. Certainly British industrial agents would have to employ vast
amounts of labour to work the deposits. The necessary labour could not easily
be secured partly because labour was in short supply and partly because the
concessionaires were not prepared to offer reasonable wages to Nigerians
who might be prepared to offer themselves for employment. It is simple
economics that if 100 men offered themselves for employment at 1/- per man
per day, at 2/- a day, perhaps, two hundred men would turn up. Rather
than think on these lines, some Europeans concluded that the natives of the
Protectorate were not fond of work, and that it was 'very difficult to get out
of them anything like the worth of the money paid'.[82] Thus rather than
offer fair wages the mining companies experimented with forced conscription
of labour.

It was only in 1884 or 1885 that William Wallace, an agent of the Royal
Niger Company became aware of the existence of the Plateau tin industry.[83]
From 1885 therefore, the physical conquest of the Nigerian Plateau had
become inevitable. This was not only because 'no colonial power can tolerate
the presence of a free people' but also because tin was becoming a much
sought-after commodity.[84] The colonial regime was under great pressure to
throw open the tinfields and to provide security in an area that was believed
to be charged with inter-tribal strife. Military operations in this area actually
began in 1898 when the forces of the Royal Niger Company captured Wase
and lasted till 1916 when the annual punitive expeditions could be said to
have stopped.

As each district was subdued so did the colonial administration allow
European concessionaires to move in with promises of cheap labour. By
1915 there were at least 68 non-Nigerian individuals and companies with a
total capital of £6,359,907 in the Nigerian tinfields.[85] Some of these
enterprises barely survived but many of them made large profits. Such profits,
points out Freund, resulted from their control of land, from their exclusive
right to export tin and through the exercise of force.[86]

Throughout the first two decades of the twentieth century, the mining
companies continued to press the government to legalise forced labour on
the Plateau. In 1918 the government took a positive policy towards this
direction and, acting in concert with the Native Authorities, began to assemble
labour conscripts on the Plateau. Labour recruits arrived from such distant
places as Sokoto, Bornu and Bauchi provinces. However, as this method

proved inadequate in gathering enough labour, the local leaders were ordered to supply labour on contract. Again, this device proved corrupt and inefficient. Eventually, the government decided to introduce heavier taxation which they hoped would drive men into the mining camps to earn tax money.[87]

British exploitation of labour in the north reached its peak during the Second World War mainly because vast amounts of labour were required to produce tin, to serve in the military, to expand groundnut production and to supply food to the mining districts which had been restrained from food production.[88]

For most of the war period, labour conscripts were forcibly brought from many parts of the north to the Plateau where they suffered untold hardships. According to Freund, men were so poorly paid that they could not buy enough for a minimum diet and could not pay for firewood to provide warmth. Some walked about in rags, others were afflicted with all sorts of diseases. Many died from cold and exposure. The lucky ones took to their heels.[89] Others, especially the Tiv, 'volunteered' for military service rather than be sent to the mines.[90]

These hardships notwithstanding, the Colonial Office in London continued to pressurise the colonial administration in Nigeria to step up tin production. Conscripts continued to be brought to the minefields. Flogging and beating were intensified and desertees were searched for by NA officials. Those caught were thoroughly flogged, fined, imprisoned and compelled to work for months in the minefields to raise both fines and tax money.

Nigerians in the Eastern Provinces were spared the naked brutality of forced labour in the Enugu coal mines but all the same, the British exploited their labour by offering low wages to miners. Mineral exploration in the Central and Eastern Provinces was begun in 1903 and by 1908 large deposits of lignite had been discovered at Ibusa, Okpanam, Obomkpa and Newi.[91] While the Imperial Institute tested the value of the mineral for fuel purposes, large deposits of coal were discovered at Enugu in 1909.[92]

The discovery of coal further stimulated interest in the construction of both the Port Harcourt harbour and a railway line to link up the harbour with the coal-bearing districts around Enugu. The railway line reached Enugu in 1915 and work began at the Udi Coal Mines in that year. Output grew from nothing in 1915 to 25,000 tons in 1916, and by 1945 it had hit the 68,000 mark.[93]

Before 1916 coal was imported from Europe for use by the various railways in West Africa. The working of the Nigerian coal was therefore a most welcome prospect for the Nigerian colonial administration. In the first place, it saved it the sum which would have been spent on imported coal. Secondly, Nigerian coal was sold to some African countries which went a long way towards augmenting the foreign earnings of Nigeria.

However, the Nigerians who worked in the coal mines were not adequately rewarded. In 1916 labourers were employed underground at the Enugu coalfields at the rate of 1/- per ton of coal extracted, while those who worked on the surface were paid at the rate of 6d a day.[94] Working underground was a risky exercise and men were known to have died while discharging their duties. As for the men who worked on the surface, 6d a day was hardly enough to keep them permanently on the job. The poor wages offered at the coal mines resulted into grave discontent and a rapid labour fluctuation. Men would pour into the minefields during the short dry season in search of jobs, but would disappear as soon as the planting season set in, thereby starving the colliery of labour for nine out of the twelve months of the year.

Rather than improve the labour conditions in the mines, the colonial administration institutionalised brutality. 'The colliery department', writes S.N. Nwabara, 'was about the largest labour employer in Iboland, but the employees were mainly paid daily — a position that was fraught with uncertainty and economic insecurity for the labourers'.[95] Before 1945, further points out Nwabara, the miners had begun to demand, with little success, improvements in their working conditions, wages and health amenities.[96] The administration failed to reason with the workers, and when they struck in 1949 many of their members were shot dead.[97]

Yoruba people were spared the more heinous forms of the labour exploitation of this period. In the first place, no large mineral deposits were discovered in western Nigeria and no important minerals were worked.

Secondly, the construction of Lagos harbour and the Western Railway line were begun soon after the Yoruba Wars of the nineteenth century were brought to an end. The result was that there was available a large 'floating' labour which 'voluntarily' offered itself for employment at any price. It is said that there was so much 'floating' labour in parts of Yorubaland that the 'neighbouring British Colonies' continued to 'look to Lagos for an additional supply of labourers for railway purposes, or as recruits for their defence or Police Force'.[98] In due course, however, the Lagos administration protested against this practice, especially after the neighbouring French colony of Dahomey requested for 1,000 labourers to take part in railway line construction there.[99]

Thirdly, cocoa cultivation spread so rapidly in some parts of Yorubaland that many men turned to the new crop rather than allow their labour to be unduly exploited by the British imperial, industrial and commercial agents. S.S. Berry has shown how some men from the Ondo district had come to work on road construction projects around Lagos but soon returned to their home towns to experiment with cocoa.[100] In any case, even those who turned to cocoa cultivation were soon to find out that there was no means of escaping from the realities of British imperialism. Their labour was equally exploited when the price which the British industrial houses offered them were far below the export prices of the crop. It was partly in an attempt to check this form of labour exploitation that political agitation in Western Nigeria took a very radical turn during the 1930s and 1940s. The coastal intelligentsia and the bourgeois nationalists succeeded in forming a strong political alliance with the inland farmers, traders and oppressed workers. They began to agitate, first, for higher prices of their export crops, and then, not just for a better place within the colonial band-wagon, but for a complete dismemberment of the British colonial regime. This aspect of the labour history of Nigeria is, however, outside the scope of this work.

Conclusion

Although the crude forms of New World slavery had been abolished in the nineteenth century, British imperialists introduced new forms of slavery into twentieth century Nigeria as manifested by forced labour and the payment of deplorably low wages. The decision to force men to render unpaid and inadequately remunerated services were part of British colonial labour policy which aimed at making colonialism a profitable business. All sectors of the British economy — private and public — derived huge profits from the working of the obnoxious colonial labour policy.

The entire exercise affected Nigerians negatively. Among other things, it assigned to them the inevitable dependency role which, in turn, elaborated the channels for further exploitation of the colony. It invariably resulted in the diversion of populations away from the rural areas to the artificially created mining and administrative centres of the country. Furthermore it made it possible for labour to be transferred from production for internal consumption to production for export with far-reaching socio-economic consequences. It hastened the process by which the Nigerian peasantry was proletarianised. Above all, it gave rise to unprecedented food shortages, rural poverty, urban misery, labour disaffection and class tension.

On the psychological level, Nigerians who were brought up in the bizarre atmosphere of the colonial forced labour system have remained disenchanted with all forms of wage labour. Some of them who have not forgotten the brutality and uncertainty that characterised service in the colonial economy still describe all forms of paid labour as 'the white man's work', hence *aikin bature* (Hausa) or *olu beke* (Igbo) or *ise ijoba* (Yoruba). In fact, the recent labour crisis in Nigeria, the poor disposition of Nigerians towards wage labour, and the general inefficiency of the Nigerian labourer when compared with his, say, Japanese or Chinese counterparts, can be traced back to the colonial period when Nigerian peasants 'from the bush' were hastily and harshly driven into a wage labour market.

This chapter has demonstrated how the British exploited Nigerian labour for the benefit of British commercial and industrial capital with painful repercussions for Nigerians.

It has also confirmed that the fundamental reason for owning a colony was to exploit, not only the colony's mineral and agricultural wealth, but also its labour resources.

References

1. A.T. Nzula, et al, *Forced Labour in Colonial Africa*, Edited and introduced by Robin Cohen (London: Zed Press, 1979), p.27.

2. Britain had exploited Nigerian labour through the agency of the Atlantic slave trade. The major cities of Britain were built upon Britain's ability to exploit the labour of Africans during the Atlantic trade period. Britain made the vital transition from feudalism to capitalism because of the wealth she accumulated from the Atlantic Slave trade. From 1862, however, Britain resorted to a new form of labour exploitation because the old-fashioned type of slavery had been proscribed.

3. A.H.M. Kirk-Greene, 'A Preliminary Note on New Sources for Nigerian Military History', *Journal of the Historical Society of Nigeria*, 3, 1, 1964, p.129.

4. S.C. Ukpabi, 'The Origins of the West African Frontier Force', *Journal of the Historical Society of Nigeria*, 3, 3, 1966, p.488.

5. Governor Stanhope Freeman to the Duke of Newcastle, 9 October 1862. Quoted in Kirk-Greene, op. cit., p.129.

6. J.E. Flint, *Sir George Goldie and the Making of Nigeria* (Oxford, 1960), p.82.

7. *The Church Missionary Intelligencer*, 1896, p.433.

8. FO84/2019, Military notes on the Countries of West Africa visited by Major MacDonald, July to November 1889.

9. Ibid.

10. Ibid.

11. Ibid.

12. Kirk-Greene, op. cit., pp.135-138.

13. Ukapbi, op. cit., p.491.

14. C.W. Newbury, *British Policy Towards West Africa, Select Documents, 1875-1914*, Vol. 2 (Oxford, 1971), pp.405-418.

15. CO879/61 No.545 Quoted in ibid., p.405.

16. This is based on the figures given in CO879/54, No.563, Lord Selborne: Memorandum, Military Forces in West Africa, 20 June, 1890 in Newbury, op. cit., p.409.

17. Ukpabi, op. cit., p.499.

18. FO84/2019. Military notes on the Countries of West Africa visited by Major MacDonald, July to November 1889.

19. CO579/54 no 563, Lord Selborne: Memorandum, Military Forces in West Africa, 20 June, 1898, in Newbury, op. cit., pp.409-411.

20. CO520/3. From the Annual Report for 1899-1900. Rates and Wages and Cost of Living in Southern Niger, 1900.

21. Sir Charles Orr, *The Making of Northern Nigeria* (London: Oxford University Press, 1965), p.203.

22. Ukpabi, op. cit., p.500.

23. Ibid.

24. S.B. Saul, 'The Economic Significance of "Constructive Imperialism" ', *Journal of Economic History*, XVII, 1, 1975, p.174-75.

25. D.C. Ohadike, 'The Second World War and the First Colonial Development Plan for Nigeria: 1946-55' (M.A. Dissertation, University of Birmingham, 1977), p.8.

26. A.G. Hopkins, *An Economic History of West Africa* (London: Longman,

1973), p.189.

27. See for instance Peter C.W. Gutkind, Robin Cohen and Jean Copans (eds), *African Labour History* (London, 1976). See also A.T. Nzula et al, op. cit.

28. Some of these measures included judicial enactments, forced abolition of domestic slavery, forced conscription of labour, military patrols, taxation and displacement of rural communities from ancestral lands. Claude MacDonald had argued that domestic slavery was prevalent throughout the Protectorate of Southern Nigeria and that it constituted the entire social life of the majority of the various tribes. He further argued that domestic slavery and other forms of service were not conducive to the development of the spirit of enterprise but tended to retard economic progress. He advocated that forced labour in the right direction would help to eradicate such social evils. He further argued that while tribute labour benefited only the slave owners, forced labour on public projects benefited the entire population (FO.O. 2/85, H.M.B.s Niger Coast Protectorate, Claude MacDonald to Foreign Office, 17 December 1895).

29. Nzula, et al, op. cit., p.41.

30. Ibid.

31. A.E. Afigbu, *The Warrant Chiefs* (London, 1972), p.6.

32. Phillip A. Igbafe, *Benin under British Administration, 1897–1938* (London, 1979), p.223.

33. Afigbo, op. cit., p.6.

34. For Proclamations 1899–1906 see CO588/1.

35. Ibid.

36. Orr, op. cit., p.202.

37. Allan McPhee, *The Economic Revolution in British West Africa* (New York, 1926), p.55.

38. Newbury, op. cit., p.446.

39. Bill Freund, *Capital and Labour in the Nigerian Tin Mines* (London: Routledge and Kegan Paul, 1981), p.58.

40. McPhee, op. cit., p.54.

41. Ibid.

42. Freund, op. cit., p.58.

43. CO520/18/7937 of 29 February, 1903, Widenham Fosbery to the High Commissioner.

44. Ibid.

45. *West Africa*, 14 August 1906. (extract).

46. T.N. Tamuno, *The Evolution of the Nigerian State* (Ibadan, 1972), p.319.

47. Ibid., p.320.

48. Orr, op. cit., pp.210-217.

49. Ibid., pp.210-211.

50. Newbury, op. cit., p.446.

51. CO520/37 of 22 November, 1906, J. Watt to Acting Provincial Commissioner, Central Province. 8 September 1906.

52. Ibid.

53. *West Africa*, 14 August 1906.

54. CO520/37 of October 11, 1906 – In the Supreme Court of Southern Nigeria. At the Assizes holden at Agbor from August to November, 1906.

55. CO520/39 of 19 September, 1906. The Aborigines Protection Society

to the Earl of Elgin, Secretary of State for the Colonies.

56. CO520/38 Confidential Despatch, Colonial Office to the Governor, Southern Nigeria, 29 December 1906.

57. CO520/46 of 31 May 1907, Walter Egerton to Colonial Office, 28 May 1907.

58. CO520/38 Confidential Despatch. Colonial Office to the Governor, Southern Nigeria, 29 December 1906.

59. McPhee, op. cit., p.49.

60. Orr, op. cit., p.210.

61. Ibid.

62. Michael Mason, 'Working on the Railway: Forced Labour in Northern Nigeria: 1907–1912' in Peter C.W. Gutkind, Robin Cohen and Jean Copans (eds), op. cit., pp.60-62.

63. Ibid., p.60.

64. Wale Oyemakinde, 'Railway Construction and Operation in Nigeria, 1895–1911: Labour Problems and Socio-Economic Impact', *Journal of the Historical Society of Nigeria*, VII, 2, 1974, p.316.

65. Ibid.

66. Ibid., p.318.

67. Mason, op. cit., p.65.

68. Ibid., p.66.

69. Nathaniel Audu Ameh, 'An Agrarian History of Ogugu-Igala in the Nineteenth and Twentieth-centuries' A Special Research Project, Department of History, University of Jos, 1981, p.59.

70. P.E. Okwoli, *A Short History of Igala* (Ilorin, 1973), p.99.

71. Charles Temple was nicknamed 'Dogon Lamba' in Northern Nigeria, probably on account of his military badges.

72. Daguo Bakatshak of Kopal Panyam in Elizabeth Isichei and Peter Yearwood (eds) *Jos Oral History and Literature Texts* (One Hermantan, 1981) Department of History, University of Jos, Jos, p.33.

73. Dakoram Dishuhar of Panyam, in ibid., p.63.

74. Ibid.,

75. CO520/101 Confidential Despatch of 7 March 1911, Walter Egerton to Lewis Harcourt, Colonial Office.

76. Ibid.

77. CO520/128 Confidential enclosure of 29 December, 1913. Lord Lugard to the Secretary of State for the Colonies, 11 December, 1913.

78. Minerals Ordinance of 1912 amended in 1913 as Minerals Ordinance, 1913. See CO520/128 Confidential 144642 of 29 December, 1913.

79. CO520/118 of 10 June, 1912. Draft Comment, signed, A.I.H. Colonial Office, 2 January, 1912.

80. Ibid.

81. In all the treaties purported to have been signed by African chiefs and British agents during the second half of the nineteenth century, the local chiefs were said to have promised British agents the sole right to mine or dispose of mining rights in any portion of their territories. Article III of a typical Royal Niger Company Treaty reads: 'We (the undersigned Kings of) . . . give to the Company and their assigns for ever, the sole right to mine in our territory'. See FO2/167 for Treaties of the Royal Niger Company. See also CO879/50, Confidential, Africa (West) No.539, Memorandum on the claims of Britain and France in the Basin of the Middle and Lower Niger.

82. CO520/3 Annual Report for Southern Nigeria, 1899–1900,

83. J.J. Grace, 'Tin Mining on the Plateau before 1920', in Elizabeth Isichei (ed) *Studies in The History of Plateau State, Nigeria* (London, 1982), p.181. See also McPhee, op. cit., p.56.

84. Elizabeth Isichei, 'Colonialism Resisted' in Isichei (ed), op. cit., p.209.

85. Arthur Norton Cook, *British Enterprise in Nigeria* (London, 1964), p.229.

86. Freund, op. cit., p.39.

87. Ibid., pp.74–75.

88. M.Y. Mangvwat, 'Colonial Economy and Class Formation in Plateau Province, 1902–1954'. Paper presented at the 27th Annual Congress of the Historical Society of Nigeria, Port Harcourt, 13-17 April 1982, pp.6-12. Mangvwat argues that the farmers of the Plateau Province were dispossessed of most of their farm lands by the colonial government and the mining companies. In addition to this, goes on Mangvwat, farming communities were turned into unskilled labourers on the minefields.

89. Freund, op. cit., p.139.

90. D.C. Dorward, 'An unknown Nigerian Export., Tiv benniseed production, 1900–1960'. *Journal of African History*, 16, 3, 1975, p.447.

91. CO520/101/6586 of 27 February, 1911. Enclosed in Confidential Despatch to Colonial Office by the Governor of Southern Nigeria, dated 30 January, 1911.

92. CO520/99 *Times* December 3, 1910 (extract). Lignite Deposit in Southern Nigeria. From a special correspondent, Onitsha, 21 November, 1910.

93. S.N. Nwabara, *Iboland, A Century of Contact with Britain, 1860-1960* (London, 1977), pp.217-18.

94. Ibid., p.219.

95. Ibid., p.221.

96. Ibid.

97. Ibid., p.222.

98. Newbury, op. cit., p.502.

99. Ibid., p.403.

100. S.S. Berry, 'Christianity and the Rise of Cocoa-Growing in Ibadan and Ondo', *Journal of the Historical Society of Nigeria*, IV, 3, 1969, pp. 439-451.

10. Contributions to War Efforts

O. N. Njoku

Introduction

Nigeria was most intensively exploited by Britain during the two World Wars. This is a fact which seems to be hardly appreciated by commentators on British colonial economic policy in Nigeria. The omission of this subject in standard Nigerian history books is a testimony to this. Yet Nigeria's contributions to Britain's war efforts, though hardly articulated in the texts, were invaluable. Existing literature has rather emphasised such issues as the impact of the wars on Nigerian political development, political integration and the like.[1]

Relatively, in the literature, scholars have paid more attention to the First World War than to the Second,[2] although information on even the First is very patchy and of uneven quality. In part because the Second World War has received less attention than the First, and in part because, on sober contemplation, one found that squeezing the subject of Nigeria's contributions in the two wars into only one chapter was too ambitious, this chapter focuses on the Second World War. Even within this less ambitious framework, the absence of coherent data and other information, published or archival, constrains us to treat only one aspect of the subject – the Nigeria War Relief Fund, 1939-1945. The N.W.R.F. is singled out for attention here for two basic reasons. First, there is some coherent information in the archives on this subject; second, it was one of the most unsung strategies by which Britain squeezed out widows' mites from Nigerian citizens in aid of the imperial power's war efforts. What is more, it is not generally appreciated how heavy a burden the N.W.R.F. inflicted on its Nigerian contributors.

It remains to emphasise that the N.W.R.F. was just one out of many avenues by which Nigeria was exploited in the interest of the war campaigns of Britain and the Allies. In two other major areas Nigeria made enormous contributions towards the eventual victory of the Allies: the supply of men and material, specifically tropical agricultural produce which was in very acute demand by Britain. To this we shall return later for a brief comment.

On 3 September 1939, Britain and France declared war on Germany. The second European war within a generation had begun. It soon developed into a world war. Less than a fortnight after the declaration of war, 16 September,

70 very powerful and influential figures in Nigeria held a meeting in Lagos. The setting was Government House; the Chairman of the occasion was Sir Bernard Bourdillon, Governor of Nigeria, at whose instance the meeting had been summoned. The 70 personalities at the meeting were carefully selected to reflect a cross-section of various communities and organisations throughout the country.

With an air of urgency, Bourdillon intimated the invitees with the purpose of the meeting. This, he said, was to explore ways and means by which the civilian population of Nigeria would assist victims of the war in Britain and other Allied territories. There was total unanimity in the meeting on the desirability of and even urgency for such an assistance. That decision marked the genesis of the Nigerian War Relief Fund which remained operational until 28 January 1946.[3]

The war was fought as much in the battlefield by the combatant forces as by civilians on the home front, as much by the imperial powers in order to preserve their empires as by the colonised in support of their colonisers. Yet in the general literature which has been largely Eurocentric in its perception, European imperialism in Africa has been portrayed as a self-inflicted and somewhat unnecessary burden. The most overt of this line of thinking is to be seen in *Burden of Empire*. In actual fact, in the colonies, the civilian front had many sectors to it. In Nigeria, these included the fronts manned by farmers coerced to accelerate the production of export staples, propagandists who had to stir up sentiments of loyalty to Britain and the Allies, various forms of financial contributions in aid of the war, and so forth. The Nigerian War Relief Fund was also one of the many crosses Nigerians were compelled to bear in a war to which, strictly considered, they were not party, but in which they were unavoidably engaged, thanks to their being a colonised people.

Recently, however, a workshop was held in the School of Oriental and African Studies (London) in 1977 with the theme, 'Impact of World War I on Africa'. As it is usually the practice, the issue was seen from Eurocentric spectacles; hence the key word 'Impact'. At any event, as Richard Rathbone, himself a participant, confessed, the participants 'learnt little about the economic history of Africa between 1914 and 1918'.[4] This same can be said of the period 1939-1945.

It is not that this chapter is conceived as an epic on the Nigerian factor in that war. One simply hopes that, by shedding some light on the matter of the Fund, we would be in a better position than hitherto to appreciate an aspect of those sacrifices the Nigerian civilian population was called upon to make for the 'mother country'.

Affirmation of Loyalty

The meeting of the 70 held in Lagos in 1939 ended with three resolutions:
a) that a fund to be known as the Nigerian War Relief Fund be set up for the

purpose of relief of suffering caused by the war; b) that the Fund be administered by a central Committee selected by and under the Chairmanship of His Excellency, the Governor; and c) that contributions be made from the Fund to such organisations and of such amounts as the Committee may from time to time decide.

Three riders were, however, tagged on to the resolutions. First, the object of the receiving organisation must be either the relief of suffering caused by the war to the combatant forces or civilian populations of Britain or her Allies or for the provision of comfort for such combatants. Second, the Committee must publish the names of organisations to which contributions would be made with a description of their aims. Finally, subscribers to the Fund may, if they so wished, indicate the approved organisations to which their subscriptions should be devoted.[5]

In line with the resolutions, a Central Committee of eleven was appointed to set these resolutions in motion. It was composed of Sir Bernard Bourdillon, Chairman; two joint secretaries – F. Humphreys and G.H. Payton; and eight others: Honourables E.G. Morris (O.B.E.), A. Alakija (C.B.E.), D.D. Gibbs, H.J.A. Thomas, Lady Bourdillon, Mrs Abayomi and I.W.E. Dods.[6] The Committee at its inaugural meeting approved one organisation for the purpose of contribution from the Fund: the Joint Fund of the British Red Cross and the Society of St John of Jerusalem.

Local committees were to be set up at the various levels of the administrative ladder – the provinces, the divisions and the clans. The Residents were to oversee the provincial committees while the Divisional Officers (DOs) were to supervise the divisional and clan council committees. Lagos and the Colony Districts were to be under the charge of the Commissioner of the Colony. Subscriptions were to be sent to approved authorities and agencies. These included the Residents, the Commissioner of the Colony in the case of Lagos and the Districts, or such persons they may appoint, Local Government Treasuries and the British Bank of West Africa. The local committees had, of course, to liaise with the Central Committee which was the clearing house for the entire organisation.

It was urgent that the proposal take off as soon as practicable. The Central Committee accordingly set about its assignment with the immediacy the situation demanded. General guidelines of action were very quickly worked out and distributed to the DOs and Residents. Within a few weeks of the inaugural meeting of the Central Committee, the local ones had emerged in the districts.

The widest publicity was given to the Fund, as all available news and propaganda media were exploited to the full by the organisers. Posters were printed by both the Central Committee and the local ones and posted at strategic spots and popular resorts all over the country. The Governor and other influential Nigerian personalities such as Herbert Macauley occasionally made radio broadcasts on the matter to all Nigerians, inviting them to donate even their widows' mites to the Fund. The first such broadcast was made by the Governor on Wednesday, 20 September 1939, that is four days after the

inauguration of the Fund.[7] Boy Scouts and Girl Guides were also utilised to
preach the new gospel. At school, pupils were indoctrinated on the need for a
generous subscription to the Fund. They, too, were to carry the message home
to their illiterate and ignorant parents and relatives. Schools began their
morning worship with homilies on the Fund. In churches and mosques,
the same message was preached. Native Courts began their sessions with
fervent appeals for donations.

Thanks to the high-powered and effective propaganda of the British
government in the West African colonies, public opinion in Nigeria came out
massively and vocally in support of the British cause, even months before the
declaration of belligerence. The support was boosted in part by some racist
pronouncements and actions of Germany on which Britain did not fail to
capitalise. The *Daily Times* donated to the Central Committee a half column
space daily to advertise and promote the Relief Fund. The *West African
Pilot*, in editorial after editorial, led the vanguard calling for loyalty to
Britain and support for the allies. A budding Nigerian politician in a book
published during the war – *British and Axis Aims in Africa* – insisted that
Hitler and his men spelt 'spiritual doom and physical agony' to all Africa.[8]

Dr Nnamdi Azikiwe and Herbert Macaulay, perhaps the most colourful
nationalists Nigeria had yet produced, had been the most vocal critics of
British colonial administration in Nigeria. But they decided to bury the
hatchet, and turned their charismatic personalities to the cause of Britain
and her Allies. The major instrument of Azikiwe was his chain of newspapers,
particularly the *West African Pilot*. Referring to the German threat, Azikiwe
had, as early as January 1939, been calling on all Nigerians to 'resist this
challenge by concrete action in collaboration with the "Mother Country" '.[9]
On his own part, Macaulay urged the inhabitants of Lagos to contribute
generously to the Fund. 'Lagos honour your cheque: and rally round the
Union Jack', he pleaded, reminding them that 'Victory, Democracy and the
Freedom of mankind' depended on their determination and loyalty.[10]

Hon. A. Alakija, a member of the Legislative Council, Lagos, as well as
of the Central Committee of the Fund, also campaigned vigorously both on
the floor of the Council and outside it. He probably spoke for the Council
when he intimated the Nigerian population and assured the British government of the Council's

> firm resolve to support the Imperial Government to prosecute to a
> successful end the war which has been forced upon the British nation.[11]

Dr K.A. Abayomi, another member of the Legislative Council, assured Britain
that though Nigeria was poor in comparison with some other parts of the
empire, her loyalty was as rich as that of any.

The euphoria was as contagious as it was infectious, and was not confined
to the educated elite. Traditional authorities put the weight of their revered
office in support of Britain's cause. The Oba of Benin, Omonoba Akenzua II,
called on all Nigerians, whatever their political, cultural and moral persuasions,
to 'bury all our differences and use our strength, our money and everything

in defence of our country and Britain'.[12] In similar flashes of enthusiasm, the Sultan of Sokoto, the Shehu of Borno, the emirs of northern Nigeria and the Olubadan of Ibadan made their protestations of loyalty and their subjects'. The Galadima of Gwoza in apparent reference to World War I, fumed with indignation that it was 'They who killed my father and my mother'.[13] The possibility of a repeat performance galled him.

Christian churches did not want to be left out in the outbursts of declarations of loyalty. Nor did they think the war was too mundane an issue to be their concern. Accordingly, a meeting of some church leaders ended with a release inviting all Christians to 'guide and inspire your loyalty by the greater loyalty to the Lord, Jesus Christ'.[14]

One of the most articulate and emotive of the propaganda stuff dished out to the Nigerian public was a pamphlet published under the pseudonym, *Civis Britannicus*, in August 1940 by a British national resident in Nigeria. He expressed alarm at the easy victory of Germany in Europe 'as states of confirmed power and maturity topple week by week into the devil's cauldron'.[15] He reminded Nigerians that,

> Even in this remote Nigeria, our lives are overcast with the shadow of the wings of fate . . . Today brings the supreme test not only of the man who goes into the battle, but also of the civilian as remote from physical danger as we are in this hour, in Nigeria. . . To fail is to make slaves of your children and mine.[16]

Then followed something of a note of apology and self-criticism, but one which was not bereft of deceit and falsehood:

> We [the British people] are inarticulate, lacking in self-analysis, over-conventional, bad mixers, and incontinentally addicted to golf and pensions. But we honestly mean well, and honestly intend to give all Africans an absolutely fair deal, as fellow human beings with rights equal to those of any white man.[17]

The truth is that the British were adamantly ethnocentric and put their own interests far above those of their colonies. It was the height of hypocrisy and illogicality to assert that they 'honestly mean well' by their derision and exploitation of Africans. Nor was the promise to give Nigerians a fair deal worth the paper on which it was made. We shall return to this matter later.

It is not that Britain had any justification to expect loyalty from her Nigerian 'subjects'. In neither her economic policy nor in the provision of social amenities did she have an enviable balance sheet. Nigeria's affirmation of loyalty to the British cause was in part sentimental and emotional. But fundamentally, it was dictated by the morbid fear of the unknown alternative. In a choice between evils, it was less dangerous to choose the devil one knew than that which was unknown. Germany was presented to the Nigerian population by British propaganda media as the alternative to Britain. She was at the same time caricatured as a monstrous harbinger of darkness. *Civis Britannicus* could not have painted a greater horror picture than when he called on the Nigerian civilian population to —

> Consider the alternatives. Look at Poland, and the brutal annihilation
> of a noble and ancient people. Look at Abyssinia, and the foul massacres
> and tortures perpetrated there by Fascism . . . Yours, like ours, is the
> choice between cleanness and filth, life and death, God and the
> devil.[18]

This was the picture Nigerians dreaded to contemplate.

Amidst the din of affirmation of loyalty, there was only one voice of
dissent. It came from the sect of the Jehovah's Witnesses. In a letter to the
Director of Manpower, Lagos, they applied for registration as 'Conscientious
Objectors' so that their members could be excluded from compulsory military
or para-military service. They claimed that they were loyal and law-abiding
citizens, obeying all the laws of state, in so far as those laws were consistent
with the laws of God. Quoting from the Bible (Acts 4:19 and 5:29), they
insisted that when any law of man was in conflict with the law of God,
preference should be given to the law of God. They asserted that they had
covenanted with God to serve Him, and in view of that, 'our participation
in any wordly war activities, whether civil or military, will result in our
complete destruction at the hands of God. . . .'[19] They ended in something
of a note of admonition: the present civil world was passing away to be
replaced by the kingdom of God with its ever-lasting peace. This was what
they were preparing themselves for, not for the 'wars, struggles and
contentions of this world', in which, they insisted, 'we are perfectly neutral'.[20]

Theirs turned out, amidst the shouts of loyalty, to be a voice in the
wilderness. Never had there been and there was never to be again such
unanimity of intent and purpose between the exploiters and the exploited.

From Words to Action

Meanwhile verbal affirmation of solidarity with Britain was beginning to be
translated into concrete actions as contributions from all nooks and corners
of the country began to flow into the Fund. Contributors included individuals,
the highly placed and the lowly, the affluent and the indigent. Social
organisations, ancient and modern, and improvement unions were also
involved.

Sir Bernard and Lady Bourdillon had opened the Fund on the day of its
inception with personal donations of £250 and £50, respectively. Their
examples were followed by C.C. Wolley, Secretary to Government, with a
donation of £25. These donations sounded like a big bang. But they were
almost immediately silenced by the personal donation of the Olubadan of
Ibadan to the tune of £500.[21] Ibadan chiefs followed suit by authorising
monthly deductions of £28 in aid of the Fund. The Oba of Benin, Omonoba
Akenzua II, offered monthly donations of £10 from his monthly emolument.[22]
This wave of donations swept north, where the traditional rulers, emirs, etc.

donated generously to the Fund. From Kano province alone the emir's donations had reached the £3,000 mark by 1945.

It was not only the big shots who swelled the Fund. The masses did, too. The first offer came from the African staff of the Lagos Colony Services. They authorised a total sum of £1 18s 0d to be deducted monthly from their salaries 'till further notice'.[23] From the Forestry Department, Aba, came monthly donations of one shilling, sixpence and sixpence respectively, from J.O. Fagbe (Assistant Ranger), R.O. Idika and M.N. Eze (forest guards).[24] The rank and file of a Police Training Depot in Northern Nigeria donated £4; a Roman Catholic School in the south donated £3 3s 0d; the Victoria African Club, Lagos, £4 4s 0d; the Nigerian Union of Teachers, £2 15s 11d; Kaduna Ladies, £10; Ngwa Contribution Club, £3; Women Fruit Sellers' Union of Lagos, £1; Niger Pastorate Mission, Mbawsi, £7 8s 3d; the West African Picture Company, £850; and Syrian and Lebanese community in Nigeria, £850. It is an endless list, and cannot be exhausted here.

All sorts of entertainment — dances, football matches, fun-fairs, raffle draws etc. — were organised by private groups as well as by the local communities to raise funds. For instance, on Saturday, 4 November 1939, the Onitsha Native Orchestra, Lagos Branch, staged what it termed an African 'musicale' at the Glover Memorial Hall. The Chairman of the occasion was the Governor himself. Later on, the orchestra undertook a tour of Abeokuta and some northern provinces; all to raise money in aid of the Fund.

Similarly, on 15 November, a large crowd of spectators watched a football match between Yoruba XI and Igbo XI at Zaria. To put this type of competition on a regular footing, a football league — the War Memorial League — was formed. This involved teams from different parts of the country playing against each other. The gate fees from the matches went into the fund.[25]

In Calabar, a boxing match between Calabar and Kano teams was staged on 14 December 1939. This had been preceded a few weeks earlier by a concert or magic show in one of the public houses. Posters were distributed round the city and posted at strategic locations announcing a thrilling magic display. The posters invited all and sundry to come and see the wonderful display of French magic by one 'Professor B.A. Quenum'. Among the items the posters claimed was billed for the performance were

> (1) opening of an alive person's stomach; (2) turning sand into coin; (3) turning water into wine; (4) cutting of tongue; (5) carrying table with tongue; (6) Vomiting of eggs and (7) command a woman to be pregnant and deliver a rabbit ...[26]

It is evident from the above that the search for funds had degenerated to mean veneration of superstition, and even deceit.

In 1941, an organisation that called itself Delta Do Organisation was formed in Warri Province. Its declared primary aim was to raise money from time to time in aid of the Relief Fund. At its inaugural meeting, £272 was raised. The next year it raised £472, followed in 1943 by a contribution of

£1,060. It crowned its effort later by donating two ambulances to the Fund.[27]

The results of the spontaneous responses were impressive indeed. Within twelve weeks of the start of the war, £12,000 had been collected. By the end of 1941, Oyo, Ondo, and Abeokuta provinces in western Nigeria had respectively contributed £8,000, £3,000, and £1,400 to the Fund. Kano province came out tops in 1942 with a total contribution of £10,270. Total contributions to the Relief Fund during the first three years were respectively £40,253 4s 5d, £24,476 12s 10d and £23,094 2s 9d. By the time the accounts of the fund were finally closed on January 28, 1946, £210,999 0s 9d had been contributed to it.[28]

Meanwhile a new scheme had been tagged to the Fund by the end of 1940: the Mobile Canteen Scheme. This addition would seem to have been the brainchild of the Secretary of State for the Colonies. The Secretary had asked if the Government of Nigeria would assign a part of its relief fund for the purchase of mobile canteens to serve hot foods and drinks to Londoners bombed out of their homes or compelled by German air raids to spend long hours in shelters. He further suggested that such canteens could bear the name of the donor colony or the specific locality in the colony from which the donation was made. The rationale was that such inscriptions on canteens would help to forge a close link between the donors and the recipients.

The central Committee of the Fund was very receptive to the idea, and quickly cabled £2,500 to London for that purpose. It added that as soon as the exact cost of a canteen was communicated to it, the Committee would remit whatever balance might be outstanding. Clubs and social organisations followed the example of the Committee. The Port Harcourt Club donated one mobile canteen for the relief of distress in Liverpool. It requested that the canteen be named after the Club. The Central Committee decided to christen it 'Nigeria – Port Harcourt Club'. From Nsukka and from chiefs in western Nigeria came a mobile canteen each. They were appropriately christened 'Nsukka' and 'Western Provinces Chiefs'. The Lebanese community in Nigeria put its money where its mind was when it donated a canteen for use in the Middle East.[29]

It was hard to expect, however, that the euphoria that greeted the appeals for donations would continue unabated. Accordingly, as the war wore on, the flush of enthusiasm which we have noted above began to sag, weighed down, as we shall see below, by the increasing burden of the war. As we have said earlier, some of the donors had contributed what approximated to their widows' mites to the Fund. From the yearly figures of the contributions indicated earlier, it can be seen that the first year was the best year for the Fund. Thereafter a decline set in, gradual though it was. By the time the war had gone half its course, it had become evident that steps had to be taken to keep the zeal burning. Several devices were attempted, the most successful being a War Relief Week organised throughout the country. The War Relief Week deserves some examination, and we shall focus mainly on Aba Division, Eastern Nigeria, about which we have a coherent data. The Relief Week in the Division lasted from 28 October to 4 November 1944.

The Resident had set a target of £700 for Aba Division. But the Division was bent on over-shooting its target. The Aba Community League (ACL) which had the responsibility to organise the Week in Aba township, swore that 'the target set for Aba division must be smashed by Aba township alone and even exceeded'.[30] The actual week was preceded by more than three hectic and intensive weeks of preparation. Activities planned included cultural and ballroom dances, school sports and concert shows, football matches, fun-fairs, bazaars, wrestling contests, canoe races and special collections in churches on the Sunday of that week. The DO emphasised the need for the widest publicity. Court clerks were instructed to see that the week was daily intimated in the courts. Church leaders were encouraged to urge their flocks to donate generously to the Week's fund. Teachers were to organise their pupils or students for maximum participation to ensure the success of the Week.

To ensure that it kept its vow to overshoot the official target assigned to it, the ACL imposed a compulsory levy on every clan, cultural and other organised group within its area of jurisdiction. The letters to this effect warned every group to make sure that its assessment was raised 'to the last farthing on or before the 21st instant and paid to the Treasurer of the Fund at the Local Treasury on Wednesday, the 25th instant'.[31] Failure to comply would attract a further imposition. Receipts were to be obtained for payments and were to be shown to the DO during the actual week. The contributions were to be followed by 'shop-to-shop, stall-to-stall, street-to-street and house-to-house' appeals or drives for more donations.

Government left no stone unturned to see that the Week proved a huge success, and encouraged its employees to participate effectively in the fund-raising activities. For instance, at Aba, a ball-room dance was scheduled for Friday night (29 September) and a fun-fare in the afternoon of Saturday, 30. Public servants complained that it would be too strenuous for them to attend the dance, report at their offices the next morning and then attend the fun-fair later in the afternoon at the close of work. In reaction to this complaint, the DO issued a circular declaring Saturday morning work-free for public servants in the division. This order was to apply only to those who would attend the dance. Those who enjoyed the holiday had to show proof that they attended the dance, by producing the official five-shilling ticket stump.[32]

Apart from the levies imposed on organisations, government employees had to make contributions to the Week's fund. This was quite apart from the voluntary monthly contributions some of them were already making to the Relief Fund, and irrespective of the fact that these employees were also members of their clan and town unions which had been levied for the same purpose. In effect, these public servants were made to contribute to the fund through several avenues.

What is more, donations were meant to be voluntary and each employee was expected to contribute to the Fund according to his means and free volition. In reality, this was not so. It was not only that donations became compulsory, but that even the amount to be donated was imposed upon the donors. Two instances may suffice to illustrate this point. The Ngwa Local Council, at a meeting summoned to consider the issue of the Relief Week, resolved, apparently with very little debate, that each of its employees must contribute 10% of his October salary to be deducted at source. This decision was an outright imposition since the affected employees were not consulted before the council reached that decision. On the contrary, there is reason to suggest that the decision was in direct conflict with the amount of money the employees would have been willing to donate freely. For instance, on patting the council at the back for its 'generous' resolution, the DO remarked, with satisfaction, that the resolution meant that instead of a clerk on £4 per month paying five shillings, he would be paying eight shillings while a labourer would be paying two shillings instead of three pence.[33]

Public servants in Ndoki and Asa local councils received their own dose of intimidation. Their Native Treasurer, W.D. Okpokiri, had sent in their free donations of £4 2s 3d and £1 14s 5d respectively. The DO received the donations with indignation; not with appreciation! In a furious response, the DO expressed his utter disappointment at the paltry sums, and castigated the Treasurer for not being ashamed to send them. He said he was 'at first inclined to refuse it with contempt'. He then proceeded to berate the treasurer and his staff. It was nothing to them, he fumed, that thousands of Nigerian soldiers were suffering hardship and danger of death 'so that Nigeria may live in peace'. He accused them of unbridled selfishness, adding that their lack of generosity would harm 'no one but the soldiers of your country' because, he insisted, 'not a single penny goes to any European soldier or European organisation'. This was one of the most outrageous falsehoods dished out by the colonial administration to their Nigerian 'subjects'. He then drew the attention of the treasurer to the decision of Ngwa Local council, and said he expected nothing less from Asa and Ndoki. He set 2 November as the deadline he would expect further contributions from the people.

This was an *ex cathedra* ultimatum. And coming from such an authority the poor fellows had no option but to comply, no matter the financial distress that implied. By 3 November, Mr Okpokiri had already sent in an additional contribution of £18 13s 1d. No one, except the victims themselves could say exactly how much more financial strain the imposition brought on them. What seems very probable is that the money was squeezed out of them at a considerable agony to the unwilling donors.

At the end of it all, the administration congratulated itself for a job well done. For all the divisions over-shot their alloted marks, as Table 10.1 indicates. The sum total from the Eastern Provinces amounted to £17,839 15s 11d, as shown in Table 10.2

Meanwhile, the Central Committee of the Fund had been meeting regularly to deliberate on the progress reports from the provinces and to disburse the incoming contributions. At its ninth meeting, the Treasurer reported that the flow of subscriptions had remained very satisfactory, averaging £2,000 a month. As the war rolled on, applications for aid from organisations in various

Table 10.1

Division	Alloted Target (£)	Contribution (£)
Aba	700	1,020 5s 3d
Ahoada	—	104 4s 0d
Bende	—	882 14s 4d
Brass	30	32 16s 0d
Degema	300	381 17s 0d
Okigwe	100	212 3s 0d
Orlu	100	1,000 5s 7d
Owerri	—	1,000 0s 0d
Port Harcourt	750	1,259 7s 1d

Source: N.A.E., Aba Div 1/26/707.

Table 10.2

Calabar Province	2,981 10s 0d
Cameroons Province	5,456 2s 1d
Ogoja Province	1,122 14s 8d
Onitsha Province	3,139 6s 1d
Owerri Province	5,140 3s 1d

Source: NAE ABADIST 1/26/707: resdt. ow. prov. to D.O., Aba (11.12.44)

parts of the Allied countries streamed continuously into the Central
Committee. And so, meeting after meeting, the number of beneficiaries had
to be increased. Within the first two years of the war, the beneficiaries had
included the Lord Mayor of London's Air Raid Fund, the Lord Mayor's
Red Cross, Royal Air Force Benevolence Fund, Merchant Navy Fund, The
Polish War Relief Fund, and King George's Fund for Sailors, among others.
By the end of the war, a total of sixty organisations had benefited from the
Fund.

Fruits of Sacrifice

It should be appropriate at this point to consider more closely how much
burden the contributions imposed on the contributors and the reward for
their sacrifice. It may well be in order also to sound some notes of caution
here. It is impossible to advance a precise, quantitative computation of such a
burden. It would also be naive to pretend that it fell with equal gravity on
all Nigerians. Certainly, some might have donated only the expendable portion
of their money; but this latter group was a very small minority. For the vast
majority, the story must have been different. Nor will a clear picture emerge
by looking merely at the 'raw' monetary figures. There is always the intangible
dimension in every human drama. The mathematical difference between a

penny and a shilling is very obvious. The same is not true of their worth or 'significance' to two individuals.

It is instructive also that the conflicts leading to the war were an entirely European affair: a clash of nationalisms and imperialisms. Nigeria, indeed Africa as a whole, had no hand in this clash. She was merely one of its resultant victims. Therefore, the cross of the war which Nigerians were compelled to bear derived from British colonialism and European imperialism. It is arguable, though, that even if Nigeria was not a colonised country, she would still not have escaped the agonies of the war. This contention is a very likely probability because no country in the world is known to have done so. But the difference would have been that independent Nigeria would at least have had a choice and some decisions to make as to when and in what manner she would participate in the war.

From what we have discussed earlier, Nigeria's massive response to Britain's appeal for aid is not a matter for doubt. But this transparent display of loyalty and support did not induce the British government and its officials to deal with their 'friend in need' with decency and honesty. Consider, for instance, the pronouncement of the DO, Aba, to the people of his division regarding the purpose of the Nigerian War Relief Fund:

> The money collected is spent in buying all kinds of things for your boys in the Army . . . therefore EVERY BIT OF MONEY contributed will help your own boys and is used FOR NO OTHER PURPOSE.[34] [Emphasis added]

It was the height of falsehood and deceit for the DO to claim that 'every bit' of the money was expended to cater for the welfare of Nigerian soldiers and 'for no other purpose'. The truth is that only a very small part of the money was spent on Nigerian soldiers and other para-military personnel. The bulk of it was spent on purposes other than for Nigerians. Table 10.3 lists the major beneficiaries from the Fund (that is those which received from a thousand pounds upward).[35]

Table 10.3

1.	Nigerian Ex-Servicemen's Benevolence Fund*	£34,306	3s	5d
2.	British Red Cross Society	£23,500	0s	0d
3.	King George's Fund for Sailors	£21,089	8s	11d
4.	Saint Dunstan's Fund for the Blind	£18,000	0s	0d
5.	Nigerian Forces Comfort Fund*	£14,599	13s	2d
6.	Lord Mayor of London's Air Raid Relief Fund	£13,000	0s	0d
7.	Shipwrecked Mariners' Benevolence Fund	£10,000	0s	0d
8.	Secretary of State Mobile Canteen Fund	£8,655	0s	0d
9.	Mrs Churchill's Red Cross Aid for Russia	£8,000	0s	0d
10.	Royal Air Force Benevolence Fund	£6,900	0s	0d
11.	African Troops' Welfare, Burma*	£6,900	0s	0d
12.	Red Cross Society (Nigeria Branch)*	£5,000	0s	0d
13.	Merchant Navy Fund	£5,000	0s	0d

14.	Polish Relief Fund	£4,700 0s 0d
15.	Greek War Relief Fund	£2,050 0s 0d
16.	Help Holland Council	£2,000 0s 0d
17.	Finnish Relief Fund	£2,000 0s 0d
18.	Wharf Inn, Apapa*	£1,800 0s 0d
19.	Nigerian Disabled Soldiers' Fund*	£1,800 0s 0d
20.	Windcheater Leather Jacket Fund	£1,700 0s 0d
21.	Yugoslavia Relief Fund	£1,500 0s 0d
22.	Lady Cripp's Relief for China Fund	£1,500 0s 0d
23.	Salvation Army Fund	£1,400 0s 0d
24.	Lord Mayor of London's Air Relief Fund for Malta	£1,100 0s 0d
25.	Silver Thimble Fund	£1,000 0s 0d
26.	Hospital for Sick Children, Great Ormond Street	£1,000 0s 0d

* Nigerian/African beneficiaries.

From the above figures it should become abundantly evident that though the Nigerian armed forces benefitted from the Fund, they were far from being the favoured group. Apologists may well contend that the DO's statement should be seen as part of the war propaganda which was 'inevitable' at the time. It could be countered that propaganda is no licence for falsehood and distortion of facts.

We have seen the trend of the contributions to the War Relief Fund. Some personal donations were very paltry indeed from the point of view of the actual amounts involved. The sum total of the contributions to the Fund — £210,999 0s 9d — could also be considered to be unspectacular vis-a-vis the entire adult population of Nigeria at the time. From this standpoint, one could contend that the contributions *per se* could not have imposed much or any burden at all on the populace.

However, a realistic appraisal of the matter must demand a consideration also of other prevailing factors. Nor, as has been stressed earlier, do the raw figures represent reliable indicators of the weight of the burden on the contributors. First, the Relief Fund was only one among other financial contributions Nigerians directly and indirectly had to make during the war. There was, just to mention one example, the Win the War Fund. Thus, for example, Kano province had, by 1945, contributed £31,400 to the War Relief Fund. Within the same period it had contributed £11,000 to the Win the War Fund. These excluded £5,000 it sent to the British government for the purchase of a spitfire plane which was named 'Kano'.[36] Interest-free loans were also made by the Nigerian government to the British government. Needless to say that the loans came from the taxpayer's money. Needless also to say that the loans might as well have been used to provide social amenities which Nigeria so badly lacked. In the same vein, schoolchildren spent many days at school not on their studies but in palm-kernel-cracking competitions in aid of the Win the War or Relief Fund.

The financial distress the contributions caused the average donors may best be considered from two features of the living condition in Nigeria during the war. These were, first, the high cost of living brought about by the war, and second, the rickety financial capability of the masses. It is only against this background that such 'paltry' donations as six pence or less can assume the significance they should.

Imports, even of basic commodities, into Nigeria were drastically curtailed by the conditions of war. This was the result of two basic factors — the concentration of European factories on munition manufacturing and the decline in shipping due mainly to war-time maritime hazards. Such basic necessities as salt, baft cloths, sugar, cement, etc., became very scarce indeed, and consequently too costly for the average consumer. Tne situation was not helped by black-marketing and the 'marking up' of prices to which expatriate firms resorted to make fortunes out of the situation. By 1943, salt scarcity had reached a crisis point. The prices spiralled correspondingly and the average consumer who could not afford it had to do without. Some rural communities resorted to the traditional method, abandoned many centuries back, of making salt from wood ash; a process as tedious as it was unrewarding.

While the prices of imports were rising fast by the day, those of exports were made to stagnate at very low levels, levels far below the pre-war's. For instance, on the eve of the war, a 4-gallon tin of palm kernel was sold for 3/- and a puncheon of palm oil for £30. By 1943, the prices had come down to 6d and £6 12s 0d, respectively.[37] Tne British Ministry of Food had, at tne commencement of the war, taken complete monopoly of the purchase of the major staple exports from her West African colonies. It fixed the prices at which the exports were to be bought by appointed agents.

The implications of the sharp contrast between prices of imports and exports should be starkly clear. The Nigerian producer depended on the sale of his produce to purchase his imported and internally produced needs. Therefore, his standard of living was directly linked to the prices of his produce and of imports. As the former was rising in price while the latter was not, the situation inevitably spelt severe hardship to him, especially as it was confounded by scarcity of imports, and black-marketing.

It was not the prices of imports only that were soaring high. Those of domestic foodstuffs were affected in almost equal measure. The closure of the Mediterranean Sea route to the Allies and the seizure of the Far East by Japan from them in 1942 converted Nigeria into a strategic highway for the Allies' bombing missions in the Middle and Far East. Construction of military facilities was undertaken in Nigeria with great urgency. This drew a vast labour force away from the rural areas to the urban centres where the construc- tion was going on. The exodus was further stimulated by the large numbers of able-bodied men who left the farm to join the army. The result was that fewer hands were available in the farm than had been the case prior to the war. The demand for farm produce understandably easily outstripped the supply.

The position was worsened by the sustained effort of government to accelerate export production, even to the detriment of domestic food production. Supply of tropical produce to Britain from her Far Eastern colonies had been cut off by her enemies. To make up for the shortfall, the Nigerian government tried to coerce the farmers to concentrate their efforts on export production. This the government attempted not by offering attractive prices to the farmers but by applying the big stick. Under the Nigeria Defence Regulations of 1939, (Food Controls Order, 1943), the government tried to restrict trade in domestic produce between districts as well as between provinces and even regions.

Restriction by government on domestic produce trade was a reaction to the increasing switch by the indigenous producers from export to domestic production. The latter was fetching more money to the producers than the former. By the Tyre and Inner Tubes Order of 1942, sale of tyres and tubes of both motor vehicles and bicycles was placed under the control of Transport Officers.[38] Only transporters involved in the export trade were favoured in the purchase of these scarce commodities. The intention was to frustrate domestic trade in produce in favour of export trade.

The attempt by government to restrict domestic trade in foodstuffs only helped to drive up their prices higher still. Government reacted by pegging down the prices of foodstuffs, but this proved abortive because the official prices reflected neither production nor handling costs. Besides, government could not control the source of supply. Prosecution of price defaulters only drove the foodstuffs out of the open market. As in the case of imports, domestic traders resorted to black-marketing. By 1943, there was a real danger of famine. In November-December, 1944, a hungry mob of over 5,000 took to the streets in the Ikot Ekpene district of Eastern Nigeria in search of *gari*.[39] *Gari* was and remains the commonest staple food among the people of Eastern Nigeria, and its scarcity could be seen as indicating the lowest depth of the deplorable condition of food supply in the region.[40]

Nigerian workers had been driven to a very tight corner by the high prices of imports and domestic staples. The situation was further made impossible for the urban dwellers by the cost of rented accommodation which, like the prices of other consumer goods, had gone up several times over. Lagos was the worst hit. Here the monthly rent for an average-size room had moved up from its 1939 level of between 5/- and 7/6d to between £1 5s 0d and £1 10s 0d by 1943 – for employees on £4 per month and some much less. Add to these the contributions those poor fellows were coerced to cough out into the Nigerian War Relief Fund, it should be obvious that the Nigerian civilian population was in a withering, multiple squeeze.

Nor was the government willing to adjust the salaries of workers to take account of the high cost of living in the country. In 1942, a Cost of Living Committee of the Legislative Council, Lagos, taking cognisance of the deplorable condition of Nigerian workers, recommended to the government and other employers of labour a minimum wage of 2/- a day for labourers.[41] This recommendation was followed by a full-fledged commission on wages of employees in Nigeria headed by a British barrister, Tudor Davies. The Davies Commission recommended a minimum of 50% salary increase for all categories of workers.[42] In neither of these recommendations did govern-

ment show enthusiasm in its implementation beyond giving token bonuses
to workers.

Government's ground was that too generous a salary increase would only
further stimulate war-time inflation. The workers, however, were not asking
for too generous a salary increase, but a fair increase. But government gestures
only scratched the veneer of the problem, and by 1945, the cross had
become unbearable to the workers. Their desperation found vent in the
famous General Strike of 1945.[43] It is against all this background that the
donors' seemingly paltry subscriptions to the Fund must be viewed. It is also
against all this background that the burden of the donations must be
considered.

One may want to know what Britain had to show by way of appreciation
or reciprocity to Nigeria for all her sacrifices. Sadly enough, British government attitude to and policy on Nigeria remained inscrutably rigid, based,
as it was, on the doctrine of centre-periphery. By this, the interests of Britain
and the British were maintained as the central determining factor in the
consideration of any issue in which her interests and her colony's were
involved. For instance, in the matter of salaries, a Nigerian with the same
educational qualifications as, or even better than, a European, received much
lower salary than the European in the same service.

The government advanced three main arguments in support of this anomaly,
all three as racist as they were naive.[44] First, the government contended, to
pay the Nigerian employee a high salary, like his European counterpart, was
to detribalise him. This was seen as bound to destroy the merits of African
social cohesion. Second, it was asserted that even where a Nigerian had
equivalent academic qualifications to a European's or even higher qualifications, he lacked, so the argument went, the moral discipline to hold a very
responsible post. Finally, the European had been used to a high standard of
living and it was imperative that that had to be maintained.

It is too obvious that these arguments were based entirely on a very
slippery and racist ground for us to go into their rebuttal here. It is significant
though, that the critical issue of productivity was clearly side-tracked by
government. Nor was there proof of the allegation that educated Nigerians
were incapable of holding positions in government commensurate with
their educational qualifications.

Nigerians were also discriminated against in the provision of such social
amenities as medical facilities, water and electricity supply. In the same way,
in spite of their zeal, Nigerians were hardly admitted into the Nigerian Air
Force Squadron. Blacks were generally discriminated against in the Empire
Training Scheme as well as in admission into the Royal Air Force on the
specious ground that they had malaria parasites in their blood.[45]

Nigerian businessmen suffered the same discrimination. As Rathbone had
indicated, as in the 1914–18 war, so also in the 1939–45 war, shortage of
shipping space created bottlenecks which very adversely affected African
business to the gain of European business concerns through their close
connection with government. In West Africa, the West African Shipping

Conference, a creation of British business interests, kept non-British concerns out of the export-import trade of British West Africa by virtue of its virtual monopoly of sea freight. It blocked Nigerians' access to shipping, and this was at a time when some commercial-minded Nigerians were aware that considerable profits could easily be made in the export-import trade.[46] All the lamentations of Nigerian business concerns to the colonial government of Nigeria to compel the British firms to abandon their monopolistic practices came to nought. Yet, these Nigerian businessmen were compelled to contribute to the war effort.

The monies which were regularly sent to Britain from the Fund often received nothing better than a passing mention by the British Broadcasting Corporation, and usually belatedly, too. The neglect was such that even Governor Bourdillon was agitated by it. And at its twelfth meeting, the Central Committee of the Fund decided to protest to the BBC, for lack of publicity of Nigeria's War Relief effort.[47] In the end, the Committee had to content itself with telegrams of appreciation from the patrons or chairmen of the bodies to which it sent relief. Even the link which the Secretary of State for the Colonies had said the christening of the donated mobile canteens after their donors would forge between Nigeria and the receiving populations of London, Liverpool and other British cities turned out to be a mere mirage. No evidence is available that the populations of those cities during the war or after made any effort to forge such a link. This is notwithstanding all the glowing tributes which Viscount Swinton, the British Resident Minister in West Africa, paid to Nigeria for her contributions in men and material during that war.[48]

In consideration of the burden which Nigerians had to bear in support of Britain's war efforts, Nigerian political leaders were confident that the British government would develop a soft spot for Nigeria. This confidence was strengthened by the pronouncements of British propagandists who promised a 'New Deal' for Nigeria. Then came the declaration of the Atlantic Charter to boot. But all the promises turned out to be the empty sounds of cymbals.

When some members of the Nigerian political elite asked Sir Bernard Bourdillon what the British War policy was in reference to Nigeria, he gave them a curt answer which ran directly counter to their expectation. The British government, he said, did not anticipate any change in her policy towards Nigeria. He insisted that the war conditions did not provide opportunities for the acceleration of greater participation in the administration of the country by Nigerians. There was one gift, he said, Britain would make to Nigeria, as to her Empire in general: survival. To rub in the injury, the Governor asked the inquirers if a man should expect a reward for failure to cut his own throat.[49] The truth of Britain's stand on the matter was later brought home to the Nigerian nationalists when the most important voice in Britain, Sir Winston Churchill, insisted that the principle of national self-determination embodied in the declarations of the Atlantic Charter did not apply to African colonies.

That pronouncement broke the camel's back. Nigerian nationalists, we have seen earlier on, had come out vocally and demonstrably in support of Britain. Within two years of the start of the war their solid loyalty had begun to be cracked by British imperious and unrepentant attitude. Nnamdi Azikiwe had been in the forefront of the champions of the British cause. By the end of 1941, he was showing his disappointment at the trend of these developments. His evident dispair may be said to mirror the general loss of faith by the elite on Britain's sincerity to her colonies:

> Day by day as I taste the bitter pills of being a member of a subject race, I become sceptical and laugh at the effusions of those who proclaim to the world how paradisical is the lot of the colonial peoples in the present scheme of things.[50]

This was the same man who in 1939 had fervently called on his country men and women to make the supreme sacrifice for the sake of the 'Mother Country'.

Men and Agricultural Export Supplies

Before concluding, it is appropriate to return, for a brief comment, to Nigeria's contributions in men and agricultural export products about which mention was made in the introductory part of this chapter. For reasons stated earlier, these issues are not for detailed discussion here, but they are worthy at least of a passing comment in order, *inter alia*, to stimulate the interest of other scholars in the issues.

At the commencement of war, Britain's demand on Nigeria for military manpower was relatively small. But as the horizon of the conflict widened in a geographical sense to embrace regions of the world with differing climates and physical geography such as Abyssinia, Eritrea, Sudan, India and Burma, Britain intensified recruitment of Nigerians into her fighting forces. British soldiers were considered ill-equipped to fight effectively in these areas. Africans were considered the best materials to fight 'jungle' warfare including in areas with very harsh terrains and climate. It was an identical situation which led to the importation of Africans some five centuries or so earlier into the Americas for the working of the gold and silver mines there.

In discharging the roles which their imperial 'Masters' imposed on them, the Nigerian soldiers never let their colonisers down. Whether in India, Burma, Sudan, Abyssinia or Eritrea, Nigerian soldiers became indispensable to the British fighting machinery. This was particularly so in the jungle warfare of Burma where European soldiers found themselves almost entirely useless. Not only did the Nigerian soldiers exhibit exceptional bravery in the face of intimidating odds, they also showed unusual calmness and power of endurance even under very severe pressures. When it came to carrying heavy ammunition and supplies through jungles or over very hostile terrains, the Nigerian soldiers had few rivals.

In the para-military service, the Nigerian personnel played crucial roles. When Italy joined the war on the side of Germany the Suez route was cut off from the Allies. West Africa immediately assumed a new place of geo-military importance, especially for American air sorties to the Middle and Far East. Various construction works were immediately embarked upon by the Allies in Ghana and northern Nigeria. These included army barracks, air-strips and roads. With very little technical equipment available for doing these jobs, great reliance was placed on the brawn of the indigenous peoples. Indigenous technical know-how which has often been the subject of European ridicule was also called into service, and to very fruitful ends. Blacksmiths, those from Awka for instance, acquitted themselves creditably as technical hands in the railways and Public Works Department. They were said to have been 'experts', producing direly needed spare parts for various machines. Viscount Swinton, the British Resident Commissioner, the one-man-cabinet on the spot in British West Africa during the war, was all praises for Nigerian servicemen — direct combatants and the para-military.[51]

For all their incalculable services, these Nigerians received as their reward lamentably poor wages and uncertain future once the war was over. The average wages of Nigerian servicemen ranged between 9d and 3/6d per day.[52] When the war finally came to an end, the colonial government proceeded to demobilise the soldiers quickly without taking the trouble to provide them with alternative jobs. Within 18 months after the end of war, over 100,000 were due for demobilisation. As a British Administrative Officer remarked, against this number, only about 6,500 placings were available, adding that 'if only 10% of ex-servicemen get jobs, they will be lucky . . . the other 90% will go back to their farms'.[53]

With regard to the supply of agricultural exports to beleagured Britain, Nigeria also played an invaluable role. This subject has been discussed elsewhere by the present writer, and can only be mentioned briefly here.[54] After the supply of tropical agricultural produce from the Far East to Britain had been cut off by Japan, British West Africa became virtually her sole supplier. Of this, Nigeria was easily the giant. With the exception of cocoa, all the West African export crops such as palm oil and kernels, groundnuts, etc. were in very acute demand in Britain. It was basically to ensure a steady supply of these produce that Viscount Swinton was in the first place sent out to West Africa to take charge of the situation. One can only imagine how Britain in particular and the Allies in general would have fared in the war without Nigeria's supply of these products.

Notwithstanding all her contributions, and notwithstanding Swinton's testimony to that effect, not many British officials appeared appreciative of Nigeria's role in that war. On the contrary, they were wont to see Nigeria as the indolent benefactor from Britain's sufferings during that war. The DO, Ekot Ekpene District, put the British point of view bluntly:

> The debt Nigeria and all free world owe to Britain can be acknowledged, but can never be paid. In 1940 and 1941, Britain stood alone against the evil might of Germany and by so doing saved the cause of freedom for all the world.[55]

According to this simplistic and anglocentric perspective of the matter. Nigeria's efforts were merely 'taken as gratitude to the people of Britain for her unceasing effort and endurance'.[56] This school of thinking failed completely to appreciate the possibility that without those services Nigeria rendered to Britain during her direst hour of need the outcome of the war might as well have been different. Nor did it occur to them that, to begin with, the Nigerian people had no hand in bringing about the war either directly or indirectly.

Conventional notions such as the above have died hard, and unchallenged, But there are always two sides to every coin. And recent research works are increasingly insisting that the relations between the imperial powers and their colonies, whether in Nigeria or elsewhere in Africa, have never been in the fashion of an active and benevolent donor vis-a-vis an unrepentant indolent recipient.

The contributions which Nigeria made to the economic progress and even the survival of her colonisers were enormous. But this fact has either not been sufficiently appreciated by the imperial power or has been quietly and pretentiously ignored. Nor has it been generally appreciated, much less articulated, that it was the clash of the national jingoisms of European powers as well as their vaulting colonial ambitions which dragged Nigeria and Africa as a whole into the two World Wars fought within a generation. These were wars which, apart from Nigeria being a colonised country, need not have involved her, at least in the way and to the extent they did. This notwithstanding, Nigerians made their supreme sacrifices in defence of their colonisers.

Undue Eurocentric perception of Afro-European relations during the colonial era has merely helped to distort reality. But this reality can be achieved only by examining the two sides of the coin with even-handed justice.

References

1. Nigeria, *The Nigerian War Relief Fund: Its Aims and Achievements* (Lagos: Govt. Printer, 1943), p.1.

2. Exceptions include G.O. Olusanya, *The Second World War and Politics in Nigeria, 1939-1953* (London: Evans, 1973); L.O. Amadi, 'Political Integration in Nigeria, 1939–46' (unpublished M.A. Dissertation, University of Nigeria, Nsukka, 1981).

3. See W.D. Downes, *With the Nigerians in East Africa* (London, 1919).

4. R. Rathbone, 'World War I and Africa: Introduction', *Journal of African History*, 19, 1, 1978, pp.1-9, etc.

5. Nigerian Archives, Enugu NAE, ABADIST 1/26/707: Nigerian War Relief Fund; Resident, P.H. to D.O., Aba: 27 September 1939.

6. NAE, ABADIST 1/26/707: N.W.R.F.: 27 September 1939.

7. L.O. Amadi, op. cit., p.40.

8. K.O. Mbadiwe, *British and Axis Aims in Africa* (New York, 1942), p.20.

9. *West African Pilot*, 20 January 1939.

10. Quoted in M. Crowder, *West Africa Under Colonial Rule* (London: Hutchinson, 1968), p.491.

11. Nigerian Legislative Council Debate, 27 September 1939.

12. *West African Pilot*, 11 Sept. 1939.

13. Nigeria, *Annual Reports for Northern, Western and Eastern Provinces and the Colony of Lagos, 1939.*

14. G.O. Olusanya, op. cit., p.50.

15. NAE, ABADIST 1/26/792; Monthly Contributions towards the Win the War Fund, p.1.

16. NAE, ABADIST 1/26/792: Monthly Contributions, pp.1-2.

17. NAE, ABADIST 1/26/792: Monthly Contributions, p.3.

18. Ibid.

19. NAE, Calprof. 3/1/2741: N.O. Okoroji, et al to Director of Manpower: Application for Registration as Conscientious Objectors: 10 January 1943.

20. NAE, Calprof, 3/1/2741: Application . . . 10 January 1945.

21. Nigeria, *The Nigerian War Relief Fund: Its Aims and Achievements* (Lagos: Govt. Printer, 1943), SS/143/200, p.2.

22. Ibid.

23. Ibid.

24. NAE ABADIST 1/26/707: N.W.R.F.: Forestry Department to D.O., Aba, 7 November 1939.

25. Amadi, op. cit., p.40.

26. NAE, Calprof 3/1/2263 (Poster Advertisement) 'Magic and Dance'; 3 June 1939.

27. NAE, ABADIST 1/26/707, N.W.R.F.: Summary of Account, 1946.

28. NAE, ABADIST 1/26/707: N.W.R.F.: Summary of Receipts and Payments, 1946.

29. Nigeria, *The N.W.R F.*: Its Aims and Achievements, p.2.

30. NAE, ABADIST 1/26/707: Aba Community League, to Presidents of all 'Tribal' Unions; 14 October 1944.

31. Ibid.

32. NAE, ABADIST 1/26/707: D.O., Aba to Government Departments and Commercial Firms.

33. NAE ABADIST 1/26/707: D.O. Aba to Native Administration Treasurer, Ndoki and Asa; 28 October 1944.

34. Ibid.

35. NAE, ABADIST 1/26/707: D.O. to Native Court Scribes, Aba Division and Clan Councils; 23 September 1944.

36. NAE, ABADIST 1/26/707: Secretary's Office Eastern Provinces, Enugu, to Resident, Owerri Province, P.H.

37. Olusanya, op. cit., p.46.

38. NAE, Calprof. 7/1/95: Chief Umana to Senior Resident, Calabar; 29 December 1943.

39. NAE, CSE 1/85/8587: Control of Tyres and Inner Tubes Order, 1942.

40. NAE, ABADIST 1/26/707: S.E.P. Jan/Feb, 1942. National Archives, Ibadan CCI 1/1, File 4038/S.6: Restriction on Movement of Foodstuffs – Garri; 7 January 1943.

41. Olusanya, op. cit., p.87.

42. Nigeria, *Report of the Cost of Living Committee* (Lagos: Government Printer, 1942).

43. Gt. Britain, *Enquiry into the Cost of Living and the Control of the Cost of Living in the Colony and Protectorate of Nigeria,* (London: HMSO, 1946) p.11.

44. W. Oyemakinde, 'The Nigerian General Strike of 1945', *Journal of the Historical Society of Nigeria*, 7, 4 (1975), pp.693-710.

45. Olusanya, op. cit., pp.58-61.

46. Rathbone, op. cit., pp.1-9.

47. Olusanya, op. cit., pp.56-61.

48. Nigeria: *Nigeria War Relief Fund: Its Aims and Objectives*, p.2.

49. Lord Milverton, 'Nigeria', *African Affairs*, 47 (1948): pp.80-82.

50. *West African Pilot*, 4 January 1941.

51. Lord Milverton, op. cit., pp.80-82.

52. G.O. Olusanya, 'The Role of Ex-servicemen in Nigerian Politics', *Journal of Modern African Studies*, 6, 2 (1968), p.22.

53. NAE, ORLDIST, File OR/C/929. Home Chat No. 39; Oct. 1945.

54. O.N. Njoku, 'Export Production Drive in Nigeria During the 2nd World War', *Trans-African Journal of History*, 10, 1 (1981), pp.11-27.

55. NAE, ABADIST 1/26/857; File 1510: An appeal for yet more 'Unsinkable Cargo'.

56. Ibid.

11. Sharing Profits with Subjects: the Colonial Fiscal Policy

A. A. Lawal

In modern parlance, fiscal policy is geared towards observable aggregate effects of government expenditures and taxation on the general level of income, production and employment.[1] In the colonial period, however, such an impact of the colonial fiscal policy was not often taken into consideration. Instead, successive colonial fiscal policies favoured European businesses in Nigeria and overseas and negated the aspirations and yearnings of Nigerian civil servants. In other words, the Europeans and their families were the beneficiaries of fiscal policy on employment, wage differentials, perquisites attached to official status, and supply of amenities.

In practical terms, one could see the colonial government as playing the role of a state as a chief guardian of the socio-economic welfare and health of the society. And although on paper, the major fiscal objectives of the colonial government appeared laudable and presumably applied to all sectors of the economy, in theory the Nigerian populace was always the loser and Europeans the beneficiaries.

Colonial fiscal policies were carefully tailored to certain ends and from the Nigerian point of view, these ends were inefficient, uncertain and lacking in foresight.

There is no doubt that those relative social benefits enjoyed by Nigerians from expenditure activities were incomparable to what Europeans enjoyed. Indeed, Europeans would think otherwise when attempting an imputation of social valuation to the benefits which they enjoyed while in the Nigerian colonial service. Naturally therefore, they would conclude that expenditure endeavours were worthwhile. But on the contrary, Nigerians had often condemned social and economic injustice in the field of income and wealth distribution up to the attainment of independence in 1960.

However, throughout the colonial period, it must be observed that the rudiments of the theory of public finance were strictly adhered to, but in accordance with the objectives of economic imperialism. For example, in a typical annual budget one could find the division of a given amount of public expenditure into different items. In other words, economic resources were allocated between providing public goods and private goods.

Nowadays, one would expect that a responsible government should pay attention to the expenditure of a larger proportion of the annual revenue to achieve a maximum social advantage. In theory, this is glib talk   based on an assumption that certain available tools would be used for cost-benefit analysis of a number of social goods provided through expenditure activities. There was nothing of this sort in the colonial period simply because the Colonial Office in London superintended all expenses, sanctioned expenditure proposals and ordered periodical audits of colonial accounts.

Colonial expenditure can be functionally classified into departmental, economic, social and accounting heads. At the departmental level, auditing became easier and malversation could be instantly punished. However, one will always be in a quandary while attempting to identify certain economic effects of expenditure on the economy, or whether departmental expenditures were productive or not. For further elaboration, productive expenditure assumes the nature of investment that helps the economy to improve its productive capacity. Certain proportions of colonial revenue went into social overheads and their maintenance, investment in railways, harbours, roads and plantation farms. Thus, addition to capital assets and production of tangible goods were income-yielding, although their management could be open to searching questions. For example, the principal beneficiaries of social and commercial services were Europeans who were not made to pay fully for their enjoyment of them. In particular, the railway, though an income-yielding investment, was not made self-liquidating because of the conservative administrative policy of the colonial government.

Expenditures on administration, defence, justice, law and order, etc. were unproductive but were meant for the consumption of the departments concerned. As these departments expanded, so their recurrent expenditures assumed alarming proportions too. In the same vein, transfer expenditures such as payment of annual interests on debts or payment of pensions steadily eroded the financial capacity of the colonial government because the beneficiaries of such payments were resident abroad where they reinvested their receipts to develop their economy.

The colonial government, under the surveillance of the Colonial Office, the British Treasury and the Crown Agents, strictly adhered to the canons of expenditure, sanction, surplus and balanced budgets. In all departments, wasteful spending of public funds was prohibited while strict economy was observed. On no account could allocation to a certain end be diverted to another project and all proposed expenditures were sanctioned by the Colonial Office to avoid financial wastage.

Ironically, however, wastage became unavoidable because of the long and wearisome delay in formulating the plans of public expenditure especially in drawing the budgets and seeking statutory approval from the Colonial Office before their execution. Such recurring delays often resulted in loss of benefits of low current prices of goods and services which the government could enjoy at the right time. Indeed, colonial authorities had to pay more for capital goods when their prices must have soared. Thus, wrong timing of projects and long delays in raising loans often involved the colonial government in wasteful expenditures.

The canon of surplus spending also meant that the colonial government should be prudent and aim at meeting current expenditure needs out of current revenue. Rather than run into a debt through overspending, it was better to attain a moderate surplus. In other words, deficit spending was absolutely ruled out. At this juncture however, we must recall that this colonial practice was a spill-over of laissez-faire philosophy which had adverse effects on the colonial economy.

For conservative adherence to the policy of balanced budget discouraged the continuous financing of long-term projects without any interruption. Regardless of the intent of the colonial government to foster the tradition of financial discipline and efficient management of financial affairs in Nigeria, its balanced budgets also resulted in wasteful spending because on many occasions certain projects under execution had to be suspended on the pretext that the limit of approved expenditure for them must not be exceeded within the budgetary period. By the time work commenced on them, the cost of materials would have increased and these materials already purchased must have deteriorated. The Nigerian tax-payers had to pay more for several years in this manner before the projects were completed. But in the end, the British manufacturers and their construction firms consistently benefited from such wasteful expenditures by the colonial authorities.

Colonial fiscal policy had no means of measuring economic growth whatsoever in a budgetary period. One often reads about the all-pervading optimism of the colonial authorities on what the budget would achieve. In fact, such a descriptive literature can be so arresting as to form an overwhelming impression of how certain proposed expenditures would affect the working of the economy and the social welfare of the people in general. We should bear in mind that the British colonial administrators in Nigeria employed this medium to impress the imperial authority that they were doing well in compliance with colonial orders to attract annual promotions.

British fiscal policy rested on the stipulation that Nigeria should be self-sufficient and on no account should it be assisted financially by the British Imperial Treasury. By implication therefore, colonial administrators were expected to keep revenue and expenditure figures in equilibrium at the very best. If surpluses, rather than deficits, were recorded, the colonial administration was given the credit by the Colonial Office for good financial management.

But the practical reality of the colonial economic situation was at variance with this seemingly rigid policy because right from the beginning the colonial governors complained bitterly against financial restrictions which hindered ample expenditure of local funds to develop the colonial economy by establishing the necessary infrastructure and providing social services. Any proposals for capital developments from Nigeria had to be sent to London to be screened and vetted by the Colonial Office and only those items of expenditure sanctioned could be financed locally. The office of the Crown Agent was the custodian of Nigerian reserves in London. The office did overseas shopping on behalf of Nigeria, purchased its stores, recruited its

European staff, raised its loans and invested its surpluses in the stocks of other dominions and colonies.

In a number of ways, the British administrators effected a regular transfer of Nigerian revenue to Britain in form of annual reserves, profits on foreign investments, fixed deposits in the British banks, pensions, payment of annual sinking funds and the instalmental repayment of foreign loans. Again, the office of the Crown Agents superintended all these transfers from Nigeria to Britain. Similarly, the Colonial Office often ensured that provisions were made for all the above-mentioned items in the annual budgets, copies of which were despatched from Nigeria.

There is abundant evidence of financial exploitation of Nigeria in the various colonial records. The methods employed often varied in accordance with the prevailing economic circumstances such as during the world wars, the depression years and the trade booms. Indeed, fiscal policies were constantly adjusted in consonance with the performance of the local economy and the world market. It must also be noted that Nigeria received grants-in-aid from Britain on various occasions only to be robbed of its surpluses later by the same imperial benefactor!

By 1913, total British grants-in-aid to Northern Nigeria since 1899 amounted to £4½ million,[2] but Britain had an opportunity of recouping this from Nigeria indirectly during and after the First World War. When the war broke out, all the capital development projects already undertaken were suspended as all efforts were geared towards winning the war. Through the British war propaganda machinery and appeal for financial contributions, the Nigerian masses rallied round Britain in her war against the Germans in the Cameroons. The Northern emirs were persuaded vigorously by Lord Lugard to make available a large proportion of their emirates' revenue to Britain to win the war. In 1917 about twelve emirates contributed a total of £51,530 to the War Fund[3] in spite of their impoverished conditions. At Lord Lugard's instigation, all the Northern Native Administrations agreed to pay about £50,000 annually to the Imperial Government for 30 years or more.[4] But the Secretary of State for the Colonies rejected Lugard's proposal as unwise and indefensible and the arrangement was waived. By 1916, the total contributions by the North stood at £98,351 and yet under pressure from Lord Lugard, the emirs of Kano and Katsina paid £10,000 and £7,000 respectively[5] out of their personal money to the War Fund. The Secretary of State rejected their offers because it beat his imagination that the Nigerian central government personified by Lugard should make such a demand.

Several organisations throughout the country sponsored fund-raising activities and submitted the proceeds to the central government.[6] But owing to Lugard's proverbial hatred for the south, the southern native administrations did not make any contributions like their northern counterparts. Yet, Lugard continued to manipulate colonial fiscal policies to make Nigeria finance the Cameroons War single-handedly. Indeed, Nigeria's budget for the 1914–1918 War was as follows: 1914 – £8,500; 1915 – £493,791; 1916 – £319,290;[7] 1917 – £358,702. All the war expenses were financed from the central purse.

Allocation for 1918 was deliberately deleted from the year's budget in accordance with official directives from the Colonial Office simply because the Secretary of State scorned Nigeria's enormous financial commitment to the war. Eventually at the conclusion of the war in 1918, the colonial government had appropriated a total sum of £1,495,000.[8]

Notwithstanding all these financial sacrifices, Lord Lugard still committed Nigeria to payment of £6 million as its share of British war debt estimated at £2,000 million.[9] He argued that Nigeria should lead other colonies in rendering such financial assistance to Britain. By implication therefore, Nigeria should lead others in transferring abroad her means of capital formation. Lugard reassured the Nigerian Council about Nigeria's financial buoyancy to pay £6 million. His eloquence discouraged any undue attachment of importance to the figure but secured the unanimous approval of his decision that Nigeria should pay the first instalment of £3 million six months after the war, and the rest two years later.

The post-war reconstruction and restoration of normal trade relations among the belligerents stimulated increased demand for Nigeria's exports thereby enhancing local economic activities. As increased prices were offered for exports, so the colonial administration adjusted its fiscal policies and harnessed all the sources of revenue especially customs duties. The post-war reconstruction climaxed in the trade boom of 1920 which enabled Nigeria to realise a surplus of assets over liabilities amounting to £3,297,000. Its investments in the stocks and bonds of other colonies amounted to a market value of £1,649,244 while its debt obligation stood at £10,245,593. Hitherto, Lugard and his immediate successor, Hugh Clifford, had not dreamt of any plan of gradual industrialisation of Nigeria. They were content with the remission of local reserves abroad for investments to boost British businesses.

In fact, it is not an overstatement to submit that constant remission of the reserves of the Native Administrations and those of the central government was nothing short of a chronic addiction by the colonial officials. And this was a popular method employed to exploit and underdevelop Nigeria. According to official directives from the Colonial Office, all authorities whether native, provincial or central were to record annual surpluses which the Crown Agent Office invested abroad, rather than in Nigeria for economic development. This fiscal policy which was consistently enforced in Northern Nigeria, accounted for its pronounced economic backwardness from the 1920s to the 1930s as indicated in Table 11.1.

Thus in 1927–28 alone, nearly 40% of the total surplus of the NAs of Northern Nigeria was invested abroad while over 40% of the same sum was on fixed deposit with the British banks in Nigeria. Of course, this revelation of the financial management in Northern Nigeria should not be misconstrued as meaning that such a phenomenon was unknown in the south. Indeed, similar reckless inroads were made into the revenue of all the southern Native Administrations to ensure that surpluses were recorded and invested abroad. So, financing of development projects was also sacrificed for the promotion of British businesses abroad, as Obaro Ikime[10] has rightly observed. In the

Table 11.1

Year	Total Surplus of NAs of Northern Nigeria	Total Invested Abroad	Total Fixed Deposit
1927–28	£1,329,354	£509,583	£525,484
1930–31	£1,346,380	£606,873	£389,709
1931–32	£1,365,222	£622,341	£431,925
1932–33	£1,458,913	£636,921	£393,579
1933–34	£1,418,700	£642,217	£472,839

Source: Obaro Ikime 'The British and Native Administration Finance in Northern Nigeria, 1900-1934', *Journal of the Historical Society of Nigeria*, VII, 4 June 1975, p.680. Here round figures are used.

year 1933-34, when depression was biting hard on the Nigerian economy, the prevailing fiscal policy also demanded that £44,470 out of the total surplus of the NAs of the Southern Provinces (including the British Cameroons) which was £390,886, be invested abroad while £248,770 was on fixed deposit.[11] This trend persisted throughout the colonial period as an effective means of exploitation and underdevelopment of Nigeria.

Even the central administration was restricted to the minimum approved projects in spite of the post-war trade boom and improved finances. Instead of embarking on large-scale public works, as proposed by Hugh Clifford, Nigeria was compelled by the Colonial Office to remit large sums out of its accumulated reserves to the Crown Agents for investment in British bonds and the bonds of other colonies at some moderate interest. In 1924-25, Nigeria's investments overseas yielded an overall interest of £20,980, thus augmenting the colonial reserves. The remittance of £3,247,000 made in 1924-25 was the largest ever made since 1919 as indicated thus:[12]

1919	1920	1921-22	1922-23	1923-24	1924-25
£2,149,000	£378,000	£899,000	£1,674,000	£2,245,000	£3,347,000

The fact that accumulated interest from the various overseas investments augmented Nigerian reserves abroad could be seen as wise financial management, but the realisation that the reserves were not made available to Nigeria when necessary for development purposes makes the whole exercise indefensible and objectionable.

Another aspect of British fiscal policy which ill-affected individual Nigerian civil servants featured prominently during Clifford's salary review exercise in 1919 in response to the demands of all civil servants whether European or African. Nigerian civil servants, in particular, petitioned the colonial government on two occasions to erect model houses for the improvement of their health and efficiency at work. The war disturbed further progress on the plan of proposed houses to be built at Ikoyi. So the issue was reopened in 1919 when the government was financially viable to execute the plan.[13] Their demand, which centred on quarters both in the city of Lagos and at outstations just like those enjoyed by their white counterparts, was moderate. They also wanted free passages to be extended to them while on leave, sick leave to relieve them when overworked and travelling allowance. A special appeal was even made to the Governor to provide them with railway accommodation, especially second class apartments, while travelling on passenger trains.

The call for a salary review was justifiable because of the post-war boom that caused spiralling inflation especially in Lagos where a new port had just been opened. The influx of strangers and European businessmen into Lagos stimulated a whirl of commercial activities and complicated social problems, especially the difficulty of getting suitable accommodation. The commercial firms offered tempting and fabulous prices to the landlords to acquire houses and lands in Lagos for trade purposes. In the process, rents went up by 50 per cent and one could hardly get a decent house for £2 10s per month.[14] The current salary of workers could not help them sustain the biting inflation and the rising cost of living, hence the call for salary revision.

Hitherto, the retrogressive policy of the government of restricting appointments had precluded Nigerian staff from rising above the rank of clerkship whatever their qualifications and capabilities. On their part, Europeans regarded the higher posts as their exclusive domain and even continued to create new appointments for their rank and file. Yet by the 1920s Nigerians were still restricted to the original scale of salary fixed on amalgamation in 1906.

Moreover, educated Nigerians decried racial discrimination and European segregation especially in Lagos, Jos, Ibadan, Enugu, Port Harcourt, Kano and Kaduna. In these towns, fabulous sums out of Nigerian revenue were spent on expensive European quarters. Indeed, Nigerians were often humiliated when passing by these quarters because they were compelled to doff their hats and close their umbrellas.

In its report which was submitted to Clifford in 1921, the salary committee remarked that the grievances of the Nigerian staff were genuine indeed and thereby gave them favourable recommendations. Alas! the sum of £425,000 involved embittered Clifford to the extent of blushing at the thought of elevating the black man from his low standard.[15] His argument was that the financial position of Nigeria would not enable the government to give practical effect to the recommendations, whereas, on the spur of the moment a plan had been approved by him for more European Reservations at Kano, Kaduna, Yola and Lagos to be financed out of Nigerian revenue. In 1921-22 financial year, a surplus of £899,000 was remitted to London for safe-keeping!

Clifford boldly denounced the appointment of Africans to any posts normally held by Europeans and submitted that even if Africans were appointed into such posts their emoluments should not remain the same because, according to him, Europeans were required to live and work in a tropical environment very inimical to their health. He added that

the African who is appointed to a similar post in Nigeria is not called upon to make similar sacrifices or to expose his health to any unaccustomed risks, and he cannot justly claim the special emoluments that are given to an European on account of these things.[16]

According to the old rate of pay, a Nigerian who was appointed as a probationer in government service with £36 per annum would not receive a salary of £300 per annum until 30 years when he attained the status of a chief clerk. The salary committee increased the bar to £460 but another committee appointed by the governor sliced the bar down to £400, yet the bar for second class European officers was increased from £400 to £600. The points of entry for European technicians and professionals as well as administrative officers increased from £450 to £500; as their annual increments varied from £30 to £40, so their bars ranged from £720 and £800 to £920 according to seniority of appointments. Each of them was also entitled to an increment of £72 duty allowance.[17]

The revised scales of the senior political officers like the treasurer, secretary, resident, attorney-general and lieutenant governor, etc., reflected alarming salary increments and duty pay which demonstrated beyond any doubts the detestable chronic hypocrisy and selfishness which coloured British financial administration in Nigeria.

The intervening period between the World War and depression was one of financial buoyancy for Nigeria as shown in Table 11.2. Accumulated true surplus is the colonial term for true reserves out of which Nigeria remitted large sums to the Crown Agents for investment in the bonds of other colonies at moderate interest. Furthermore, the depletion in the figures within the column depended on the frequency and degree of inroads made into the reserves to rectify yearly deficits or to finance certain construction works out of the general revenue, pending the completion of arrangements by the Crown Agents for raising loans for such works. When eventually such loans were raised, any sums drawn out of the general revenue would be made good from the loans accounts to the revenue/expenditure accounts; these additions swelled the figures in this column.

The case for 1921/22: Since the 1914 amalgamation, the calendar year was adopted as the financial year till 1920. From 1921 onward the financial year was changed to begin on 1 April and end on 31 March the following year. This change affected accounting routine on revenue/expenditure figures recorded from 1921 to 1923.

Thus the surplus of £3,296,788 recorded in 1921 was employed to meet parts of the deficits recorded in 1922/23. When the new fiscal year began in 1921/22, revenue was £4,876,246 as against a total expenditure of £7,171,997, consequently, a total deficit of £2,295,751 was recorded, and in 1922/23 yet another deficit, of £903,079, was recorded. This trend continued owing to the inability of the spending departments to adjust to the new fiscal year.

The case for 1926/27 cumulative sum of £6,074,338: As a result of the boom

Table 11.2

Selected Years	True Revenue (£'s)	True Expenditure (£'s)	Accumulated True Surplus (£'s)	Deficits (£'s)
Jan.-Dec. 1920	6,738,042	6,080,990	3,758,390	–
Jan.-March 1921	1,566,748	1,431,271	3,296,788	–
1921/22	4,869,220	6,553,553	2,209,534	–
1923/24	6,260,561	5,501,242	3,063,335	–
1926/27	7,734,429	7,584,692	6,074,338	–
1928/29	5,894,658	6,861,099	4,688,818	966,441
1930/31	5,622,200	6,329,668	3,736,808	707,468

Note: Figures *included* expenses on construction works from loan funds.

Source: Nigeria Annual Report 1926; CO. 583/195/21036 Desp. 877, 5th Oct. 1934. Governor Cameron to S of S on Financial Position. P.R.O. London.

of 1926/27, increased duties on exports-imports and revised assessment of tax yielded a total revenue of £7,734,429 as against an expenditure of £7,584,692. Excess revenue was £149,739. A further excess revenue, totalling £4,238,840, recorded on 1 April 1925 was added to an excess of revenue over expenditure of £1,020,579 on 1 April 1926. By a previous arrangement another sum spent out of the general revenue on development projects was paid back to the revenue account in 1927 when a loan of £4,173,404 was raised.

On another occasion, a sum of £4,251,662 was recovered from Loan Funds in respect of Eastern Railway Construction and credited direct to surplus and deficit account instead of to revenue, thus swelling the reserves.

The case for 1928/29 true surplus: Actual revenue realised as at 31 March 1929 was £5,894,658 as against an estimate of £5,774,961. As a result of strict economy an estimated gross expenditure of £7,435,271 was reduced to £6,861,099, leaving an overall deficit of £966,441. This deficit was paid out of surplus revenue which was thus reduced from £6,074,338 in 1926 to £4,688,818 in 1929.

From 1927/28 financial year, the Railway Accounts were separated from the general revenue accounts, but the net profit of the railway department was still included in the general revenue, hence the increasing surpluses. The department contributed part of its earnings to the general revenue and paid part of the annual interests on various loans raised for construction work.

By 1927, much concern was expressed by many observers over financial mismanagement in Nigeria, especially the commercial community which openly attacked the colonial administration through the newspapers. *The Morning Post*[18] in particular, called for a commission to inquire into some unremunerative expenses in the form of the increasing cost of an expanding establishment made up of official European employees. Between 1925 and 1927, they had increased from 1,671 to 2,664 with the implication of unrestrained increases in pensions, gratuities, personal and travelling allowances, etc. As European employees continued to stream into Nigeria so the colonial government made unrestrained inroads into Nigerian reserves to build expensive European quarters costing about £700,000.[19]

It was quite disturbing to discover that the colonial government could not explain why recurrent expenditures increased annually when it was obvious to the critics that European employees were the only cause. For example, total salaries and duty pay in 1927-28 was £2,029,488 as against £2,449,638 in 1929-30. This very year, extravagant recurrent expenditure also reduced a credit margin of £1,700,000 realised in 1927-28 to £554,000.[20]

By 1929-30 again, from an increase of £803,431 in the same item, a sum of £322,324 was allocated for ocean and rail passages, travelling allowances, including assisted passages for the officials' wives, pensions and gratuities. Since the inception of colonial administration, it had been difficult to produce a reliable estimate of recurrent expenditure. Indeed, actual recurrent expenditure had increased from 12 per cent in 1925-26 to 24 per cent[21] in 1927-28 above government estimates. Similarly, annual pensionable liability was also not known in order to assess Nigeria's commitment to Europeans who had retired from colonial service: hence the public outcry for a probe into financial administration.

The Colonial Office, having been incensed by the sensational newspaper report in Nigeria, tried to justify the colonial government's policy on European housing projects by saying that economic and social progress in Nigeria depended solely on the importation of European officials, and therefore there was no need for a probe. The office insisted that accumulated reserves would be spent when necessary without any fear, since Nigeria's economy possessed strong and dependable recuperative powers.

But under official cover, the colonial governor was seriously querried for recording excess expenditure of £2,332,000[22] in 1928-29 on personal emoluments owing to the increase in staff and salary increments. Even in 1933-34, the Secretary of State had to reprimand him again for extravagances that could provoke press attacks from the mercantile community.

Thus far, Nigeria's finances were administered mostly for the benefit of Europeans until the depression years when the government faced hard times. From 1930 to 1934, deficits were recorded in spite of repeated readjustments of annual estimates according to directives from London. The trade slump became so severe that Nigeria had to suspend all development projects and retrench both African and European staff who were either redundant or whose appointments were not yet confirmed. The majority of those adversely affected were Nigerians. At one stage, Native Administrations had to render financial assistance to the central government and even voluntarily took over some social services.

As Nigeria smarted under the strain of economic depression, Britain, in the same plight, ironically advised the colonial governor to exercise great economy but to aid her positively by making financial contributions towards the costs of her naval forces operating in Nigerian waters.[23] Governor Cameron's negative reply infuriated the Colonial Office which later turned around to compel a readjustment of Nigeria's customs tariffs to give effective preference to British goods. This fiscal policy was given a warm welcome by the Legislative Council and was enforced forthwith. But as a result of much pressure from London, Cameron refunded £203.000,[24] which by 1931, Nigeria had received from the Colonial Development Fund, into the Exchequer.

Nigeria's deplorable financial position was the focus of an article by a correspondent in *West Africa*[25] in 1934. He recommended a number of wise measures to improve local finances, now that the lavish expenditure induced by the euphoria prior to 1929 had boomeranged on the British administrators, resulting in deficits and retrenchment. His emphasis was on the pensions paid to retired officers who were domiciled in Europe. He estimated that the aggregate total so transferred must be large in relation to Nigeria's liquid wealth. He wondered why the governor failed to suspend such remittances to balance annual budgets and improve the financial position. Indeed, the annual budget was not balanced until 31 March 1935 when a surplus of £185,589 was recorded.

Thus, a gradual improvement of trade and steady rise in prices stimulated increased production of export produce and necessary fiscal adjustments. Customs duties fetched about 48.6% of the total revenue in 1935 as against 41.7% in 1934, just as export figures rose by 30.7%.[26] All these developments culminated in the boom of 1936–37 which induced the passing of the Non-Native Income Tax (Protectorate) Legislation and Income Tax (Colony)[27] legislation to curb tax evasion throughout Nigeria. By 1937, all adult males henceforth started to pay uniform taxes. Until 1938, the customs tariff was revised upward to tax a variety of imports hitherto exempt from duty, to realise more revenue. All told, Nigeria was able to record a favourable trade balance of £4,300,000 and a revenue of £3,485,000[28] from duties in 1936, the highest figure ever recorded!

As improved finances enabled Nigeria to rehabilitate those retrenched during the depression, so it expanded a good number of establishments that encouraged the influx of Europeans again. Great care was however taken to watch recurrent expenditures and debt obligations as usual. But Britain thought it wise during the boom to drain Nigeria of its surplus funds again. This time, Nigeria was called upon to refund £865,000 the sum paid by Britain to the Royal Niger Company for the acquisition of its territory in 1899 prior to the establishment of Northern Nigeria Protectorate. It was not until 1935 that the Public Accounts Committee of the House of Commons accidentally discovered a file containing the relevant statute book.[29] The British Treasury proposed in 1936 that Nigeria should be made to pay either £220,000 in ten years or £200,000 in twenty years. The colonial governor implored the Colonial Office to influence the Treasury to effect a waiver of such a financial imposition. He called the office's attention to what financial contributions Nigeria made to the war and how it bore a proportion of British war debt. This plea made the Treasury indicate another option of a voluntary contribution of £75,000 either in lump sum or by instalments in aid of British defence.[30] Once this was done, it would be assumed that Nigeria's liability had been extinguished by 1937.

Shortly after the payment of this sum, the British Government passed the Remission Act which eventually compelled Nigeria to remit any sums which became payable to the Exchequer in respect of the Royal Niger Company territory, now part of Nigeria. Nigeria paid another £50,000 to secure another promise to write off this annuity but meanwhile Nigeria's revenue had been under consistent exploitation by the United African Company (successor to Royal Niger Company) that was entitled to a share of the mining royalties every year.

In 1943, the Colonial Office, in an attempt to strengthen Nigeria's financial position, called upon the Company to surrender its mining royalties to Nigeria. It would be recalled that at the revocation of the Royal Niger Company's charter in 1899, the company was granted a statutory right to half of the annual receipts from the royalties for a period of 99 years. The United Africa Company inherited this right later and received not less than £2,300,000 from tin-mining industry from 1906 to 1943.[31]

For the surrender of the mining rights, mining leases and prospecting licenses, Nigeria was formerly asked to pay £2 million, which was turned down. Yet the company insisted on an amount commensurable to its current capital value. The Colonial Office took the matter up in London and strongly defended Nigeria. The ongoing World War delayed any positive step in stemming the financial exploitation of Nigeria. However, the post-war revival of the tin trade and the attractive price per ton in the world market provoked virulent criticisms among the Nigerian members of the Legislative Council, of the government's policy on mining. By December 1949, a motion was moved for the nationalisation of the mines and minerals and the government paid one million pounds[32] for the purchase of UAC's mining royalties. Thus, Nigeria was henceforth entitled to all the royalties on tin: it realised £1,200,000 in 1952–53 from tin industry.[33]

The foregoing has demonstrated the various methods by which Nigeria's financial exploitation was effected without any qualms. Throughout the 1940s and 1950s, Nigeria's revenues continued to increase and reserves as well as surpluses were invested abroad. At no time was an industrial project mentioned or proposed by the central administration. A private concern that attempted such a venture by 1927 was frustrated. It was not allowed to establish a cement factory at Nkalagu because local production would compete with the Portland Cement from Britain that had been enjoying the monopoly of the Nigerian market!

The aftermath of the Second World War highlighted the political orienta-tion of the educated Nigerians as a result of their awareness of political developments in other colonies. Thus in Nigeria, sporadic intensification of nationalist agitation for a number of concessions from Britain in fulfilment of its promise to the colonies during the war, culminated in the drawing up of federal constitutions by which Nigeria was well groomed for independence in 1960. In 1945, Britain had introduced a ten-year development plan with emphasis on a large-scale construction of telecommunication and transport infrastructure. Thenceforward, Nigeria really began to appropriate a greater proportion of its revenue to train more staff to man the expanding establishments.

Since the early 1950s too, virulent attacks on European officials and intensified agitation for an immediate Nigerianisation of all departmental posts led to the cessation of restrictive appointment of Nigerians. By 1960, many qualified Nigerians manned various posts abdicated by their European predecessors and up till now, all the prerequisites attaching to such posts are still retained. Most senior officers are now entitled to live in reserved areas and enjoy allowances. Thus, one could say that if Nigerians were cheated for years in sharing profits with the British, then Nigerians are now cheating each other in sharing their profits since the demise of colonial rule. The bureaucratic status quo which we inherited from the colonial masters is still the order of the day, hence the proverbial colonial mentality which has hitherto hindered an introduction of a more dynamic and progressive bureaucracy in Nigeria.

References

1. H.L. Shatia, *Public Finance* (5th Revised Edition), (New Delhi: Vikas Publishing House, PVT Ltd., 1976), pp.284-287.

2. CO 583/5 Conf. 8 Sept., 1913, Lugard to S. of S. on Amalgamation Scheme, PRO London; W.N.M. Geary, *Nigeria Under British Rule* (London: Frank Cass, 1965 reprint), p.236.

3. CO 583/55 Desp. 49, 25 Jan. 1917, Lugard to S. of S. PRO London.

4. CO 583/55 Desp. 325, 19 March, 1917, S. of S. to Lugard, PRO London.

5. The emirs of Kano and Katsina were respectively on an annual income of £4,800 and £3,500.

6. By 1917, total voluntary subscriptions from various sources had increased to £84,000. These excluded public funds whether from the central government or Native Administrations.

7. CO 657/1 Nigerian Council Proceedings. Lugard's 2nd address, Dec. 31, 1915; CO 583/55 Desp. 7, 6 Jan. 1917. Report on the Blue Book, PRO London.

8. *The Red Book of West Africa* (London, 1968), p.46.

9. CO 657/11, Lugard's Address to the Nigerian Council, 31 Dec. 1915. PRO London.

10. Obaro Ikime, 'The British and Native Administration Finance in Northern Nigeria, 1900–1934', *Journal of the Historical Society of Nigeria*, VII, 4, June 1975, p.68.

11. Ibid., p.680 ff.3.

12. Annual Report, 1924–25.

13. CO 583/85, Conf. 30 March, 1920; African Staff Condition of Service:

Petition, PRO London.

14. CO 583/85 Appendix B, Petition to Governor Clifford, 21 Aug. 1919.

15. CO 583/99, Conf. 21 Feb., 1921. Clifford to S. of S. African Staff Revision of Salaries and grading — Report.

16. Ibid., p.21, para. 56 of the reports and comments to Churchill, the Secretary of State.

17. CO 583/84, Conf. 3 March, 1920 Clifford to S. of S. PRO London.

18. *The Morning Post*, 8 April, 1929, PRO London.

19. *West Africa*, 4 May, 1929.

20. CO 583/164/500 Ordinance No. 5 of 1929. Estimates 1929–30, PRO London.

21. CO 583/165/533, Colonial Office to Gwynne, PRO London.

22. CO 583/158/153, Governor Thomson to S. of S. X153/28/Nig. 14 June, 1928, PRO London.

23. CO 583/181/1310 No. 1349, 12 Dec. 1931. S. of S. to Cameron and Circular Desp. of 19 Sept., 1931. PRO London.

24. CO 583/181/1310. Desp. 647, 18 April, 1932. S. of S. to Cameron. PRO London.

25. *West Africa*, 24 March 1934, pp.299-300 in CO. 583/197/21088, 1934, PRO London.

26. CO 583/207/30037, Bourdillon's Address to the Legislative Council, 1936/37 Estimates, PRO London.

27. CO 583/213/30233, 1936. Non-Natives Income Tax (Protectorate) Legislation; CO 583/213/30231, Desp. 491, 6 June 1936, Income Tax (Colony) Legislation. Bourdillon to S. of S., PRO London.

28. CO 583/215/30037 Bourdillon's Second Annual Address to the Legislative Council, 22 March 1937. PRO London.

29. CO 583/221/30217, 20 July, 1937. Comment by the Secretary of State, on the (Remission of Payment) Act, 1937, Nigeria Company Purchase Annuity, PRO London.

30. CO 583/213/30217, 26 Nov. 1936. Colonial Office to Bourdillon, PRO London.

31. CO 583/263/30568, Mining Royalties, in Nigeria, 1943, PRO London.

32. National Archives Ibadan (NAI) Comcol I 250/s.13 Vol. VII Governor's Address to the Legislative Council, March 1951, p.11.

33. By March 1953 the price of tin per ton had soared to £956.

12. The Illusion of Economic Development

J. Ihonvbere and Toyin Falola

Introduction

The current debates within and between social science and social scientists in Nigeria, while symptomatic of the crisis of the political economy and the crystallisation of class forces as well as the heightening of contradictions, have their roots in the pre-colonial and colonial periods. The emergence of a largely complacent and orthodox school of thought which came to dominate postcolonial social science in the country has had a far-reaching impact not only on the ability to develop alternative approaches but also on the capacity to make prescriptions and projections on the future of the economy. The traditional denial of social contradictions, social classes and class struggles was the product of the adherence to bourgeois and superficial research methodologies and concepts. In addition, the domination of the educational institutions, planning offices and decision-making and implementation centres by formulators of these bourgeois and neocolonial concepts or those steeply indoctrinated in them have largely contributed to the stagnation of Nigerian social science and the reproduction of contradictions and underdevelopment in the social formation.[1]

To comprehend and expose the roots of contemporary underdevelopment and crises in Nigeria therefore, it is paramount that an intellectual trip be made to the colonial period. Such a trip would provide us with an ability to conceptualise the institutions, structures and mechanisms with which Western imperialism subjugated precolonial structures and power elites and laid the foundations for the contemporary peripheral location and role of the Nigerian formation in the international division of labour. In addition, to understand contemporary institutions, the nature of factions and fractions of the bourgeoisie, the roots of ethnic and religious chauvinism in Nigerian politics, the power of foreign capital, the peripheral state and class organisation and struggles, we have to understand the power, organisation and policies of the colonial state.[2] In pursuing this line of investigation, two important points have to be made. First, the reason for such a quest is not to find an excuse for the bankruptcy, inefficiency and decay of contemporary socio-economic and political systems and institutions. The primacy of any serious political economy analysis must necessarily be the mode of production and the content and dynamics of class contradiction and struggles. Thus, the aim is to provide a historical understanding to contemporary problems in order to bypass superficial or cosmetic solutions and projections often advanced by establishmentarian and orthodox scholars. The second point relates to the question of theory and relevance. The aim of theory is to build a formidable foundation for social praxis and social reconstruction.

This chapter concerns itself with the question of economic development and the basis of underdevelopment in the colonial period. To discuss these effectively we shall examine relevant aspects of the development controversy. It is on the basis of our discussion here that we shall seek to evaluate the contributions of the colonial state to the development of Nigeria.

The Development Controversy

Since this chapter is essentially concerned with development in the colonial period, it becomes essential to review briefly the development controversy. Unfortunately, the debate over development strategies in developing countries has been so intense as to lead to a complete lack of clarity on the fundamental issues involved. While the theories of the orthodox economists continue to meet with challenges from the emerging radical schools, the dependency perspective as a fraction of the latter has done no more than sensitise us to the general issues involved in the debate without actually addressing in concrete terms the internal dynamics of class formation, capital accumulation, the state and class struggles. More often than not, the debate has not specified the 'development' being discussed — capitalist or socialist. Lynn Mytelka and Steven Langdon provide an insight into this direction thus:

> *Development* . . . can be thought of as a process of structural change and capital accumulation that moves a society closer to conditions in which the basic needs of people (for shelter, food, clothing etc) are met, full employment prevails, and social-economic equality is increasing.
> *Underdevelopment*, in turn can be thought of as a process of structural change and capital accumulation that moves a society in a direction that makes it more difficult to achieve these conditions. Underdevelopment in this sense can involve significant increases in per-capita incomes, but in a form that concentrates gains among a well off minority and imposes social costs on a poor majority. Underdevelopment is, thus, different from stagnation.[3]

This comprehensive definition lays to rest the arguments of orthodox scholars who identify increases in the number of schools, hospitals, employment, growth in per-capita income and so on as indicators of development without paying adequate attention to issues of ownership and control of productive factors, relations of production and accumulation, the nature of and use of state power, class formation and struggles. These factors significantly affect the arrangement of societal priorities, the allocation of resources and the content and context of overall development. Even if Mytelka and Langdon's definition of development and underdevelopment is taken broadly to capture the essence of socialist development, in the case of Nigeria and other formations that came in contact with imperialist powers, it would be difficult to find *capitalist development* as having been the precipitate of such a contact. By capitalist (as against peripheral) development, we mean a situation of structural change and capital accumulation, where pre-capitalist mode(s) of production have been destroyed or extensively incorporated into the dominant capitalist mode of production and accumulation, where a national bourgeoisie exists and this bourgeoisie, through its productive (as against distributive) and accumulative activities, promotes the creation of a proletariat proper with very limited 'exit options'; the sectors of the economy are integrated in order to promote self-sustained production and accumulation; and a 'stable' state exists which promotes class reproduction. On the basis of this definition, it is quite possible to evaluate Nigeria's experiences between 1900 and 1960 when it achieved *relative political* independence.

It is clear, therefore, that we completely reject the emerging line of thought in the discussion of class, state and development in Nigeria which emphasises the 'activity' of the bourgeoisie but not its *nature*. In other words, it is argued that pre-occupation with the existence or otherwise of a *national bourgeoisie* (even if represented by a nationalist and stable capitalist state) is essentially irrelevant.[4] To us, the importance of such a class lies in its ability to capitalise on its power and location in the production and accumulation processes to reproduce itself consistently and protect and expand its interests at the expense of other forces, particularly foreign capital. A social formation where the peripheral state is inherently unstable, where the bourgeois forces are concentrated in the exchange and commercial sectors of the economy and this bourgeoisie largely plays an auxiliary role to metropolitan capital, cannot be expected to experience *capitalist* development. The unproductive and mortgaged accumulative base of the bourgeoisie will constantly reproduce sectoral disarticulation, political instability, social alienation and underdevelopment.

The neo-classical growth paradigm or the 'centre-down' paradigm which has its roots in the balanced versus unbalanced growth debate of the 1950s was first popularised by Gunner Myrdal.[5] He argued that the initial advantage of some regions in the development process introduces regional inequalities into any society. However, the play of market forces tends to increase rather than decrease such inequalities. These inequalities, according to Myrdal, are attributable to circular and cumulative mechanisms (because some areas are more attractive to investors than others) and to the operation of 'backwash' effects which could be partially offset by 'spread effects'. Albert Hirschman[6] has argued that 'polarization effects' of economic development are inevitable. In view of this inevitability, Hirschman argued that development strategies should concentrate on a few selected sectors, determined by measuring backward and forward linkage effects in terms of input-output maxima. This 'growth pole' strategy was supposed to first concentrate wealth in the favoured sectors and at a certain stage a 'trickle down' to the neglected sectors would follow. John Friedman,[7] popular for the 'core-periphery' model, maintained in his own contribution that for an effective regional development policy, a country must plan according to a 'core region policy', upward and downward transition areas, resource frontiers and special problem areas. The cumulative process of innovation and development in the core areas when diffused to the peripheral areas will lead to development.

These theories taken together do not address the concrete problems of underdeveloped formations. If extended to include nations, the implied projections would be that wealth should first be concentrated in the powerful, wealthy and developed countries, then at a stage to be determined by the already powerful and wealthy, the poor underdeveloped countries can hope for a 'trickle down'. Writing with the imperialistic and exploitative experiences of the metropolis in mind, these theorists were incapable of seeing issues of equity and development as social issues and that planning itself is not a technical or mechanical affair but a social one which cannot be divorced from internal and external class relations and alliances. Just as the colonial powers had to be compelled through the militancy of nationalist and liberation movements to give up their 'poor' colonies, it is impossible to expect the 'growth' regions and the dominant forces benefitting from such a 'growth' or development to allow voluntarily a 'trickle down', unless such a 'trickle down' would aid the reproduction of their dominant class position. Neglecting issues of class domination of planning and decision-making institutions, the state, class contradictions and struggles, neo-classical theories of development are unable to provide us with adequate approaches or methodologies with which to evaluate planning and development in peripheral regions, particularly in the period under study.

The prescription of neo-classical theorists included emphasis on the use of foreign 'experts', technology, aid and ideas. Little attention was paid to the need to mobilise and utilise internal resources as well as the elimination of internal social contradictions. Their industrialisation strategies and prescriptions emphasise import substitution, the provision of numerous resource-draining benefits to foreign investors and not sectoral linkages and the need to raise the purchasing power of the local market. Nationalisation was decried and regional integration discouraged as a human interference in the 'natural' play of market forces. In the agricultural sector, there was a bias for so-called 'cash crops', and efforts were not made to encourage linkages between agriculture and industry even if only to promote local processing of raw materials. Robert McNamara has rightly observed that, in relation to the social prescriptions of neo-classical approaches, 'the trickle down theory of growth is an insufficient basis on which to expect human needs to be met in a reasonable period of time'.[8] The application of neo-classical strategies of development planning all over the developing world required heavy dose of foreign aid. These increased inequalities, facilitated foreign domination and exploitation and furthered the peripheralisation and incorporation of such formations into the world capitalist system.[9]

Dependency and underdevelopment analysts attempted to go beyond the neo-classical paradigms by focusing on structures, institutions and processes particularly at the international level which have continued to reproduce underdevelopment in the periphery.[10] The unequal exchange relationship, the manipulation of terms of trade against developing countries, the debt trap, the export of outmoded technology and equipment and the formation of exploitative transnational linkages were identified as some of the mechanisms which have led to the 'development of underdevelopment' in the periphery. While in the works of Osvaldo Sunkel, Gunder Frank, T. Dos Santos and Samir Amin, we see very erudite discussions of these forces and mechanisms, limited attention has been paid to the sub-structure – the local relations and forces of production and exchange, the dynamics of class reproduction, class struggles and the power of the state. Thus, the super-structural focus of the dependency school has made only a limited contribution to our understanding of internal forces and factors which impede development.

In the efforts to provide an alternative to the 'centre-down' approach to planning and development, D.R.F. Taylor, Walter B. Stohr, Dennis Rondelli and Kenneth Ruddle have come up with the 'bottom-up' approach to planning and development. Though it is an outcome of the dependency debate, this approach emphasises the need to create an articulated network of growth centres and linkages in order to promote commercialisation of agriculture, savings and investment in productive activities. In this process, the starting point must be the rural areas:

> a more balanced spatial system can be achieved in most developing countries by building from the 'bottom up', by stimulating increased production, employment and demand in rural areas and by extending to smaller settlements the services and facilities that will encourage increased productivity and the consolidation of rural population into larger economic centres.[11]

In the same vein, the basic values of 'development from below' are explained thus:

> It is a development determined from within by the people of that society themselves, based on their own resources – human, physical and institutional. Each strategy is therefore unique to the society in which it evolves. Secondly, it is egalitarian and self-reliant in nature, emphasising the meeting of basic needs of all members of society. It is therefore communalist . . . in nature. The ultimate aim of such a strategy is an improvement of both the quantitative and qualitative type in the life style of all members of society . . . It involves selective growth, distribution, self-reliance, employment creation and above all respects human dignity. It is at one and the same time a new develop-ment strategy and a new development ideology.[12]

For the 'bottom up' strategy to be effective, it must integrate its objectives with provisions for mass mobilisation and education. More importantly, it must be capable of withstanding the resistance of social forces which benefit from the unequal spatial system and relations of production. Thus, such a strategy cannot be piecemeal, it must at one and the same time, recognise the specificities and contradictions of society and be prepared to confront internal and external opposition forces.[13]

In the Nigerian situation, can it be argued that the colonial experience, in any way, laid a foundation for meeting the basic needs of the majority? Did colonialism have such a capacity to lay a broad based and viable foundation? If it did not, what factors were responsible for this?

Early Foundations of Neo-Colonial Capitalist Underdevelopment

By 1900, the subjugation of the precolonial power-elites, and the incorporation of the Nigerian formation into the world capitalist system was complete. The wars of conquest which followed the exploitative period of 'informal empire' had not only destroyed some formations, institutions and development initiatives but also imposed new leaders and institutions which were to contribute to the reproduction of the colonial formation. By 1914, the Southern and Northern wings of the colonial entity were amalgamated to form Nigeria. From 1914 the British initiated several policies and programmes which were directly aimed at incorporation, and exploitation:

1. A colonial civil service was introduced to facilitate the control of colonial people and the extraction of surplus. This civil service lacked a base in the objective dynamics of development and thus existed at a superficial super-structural level. The exploitative, insensitive and discriminatory nature of this service created the 'we' versus 'they' mentality — a situation where the masses of the people saw the bureaucracy as 'they', an enemy that was to be avoided. Invariably, if it was this bureaucracy in which the masses of the people had no confidence that was to be charged with the initiation and implementation of planning efforts, it can be easily seen that such would be an effort in futility.

2. The colonial state, in order to ensure its own reproduction and hegemony as well as to support the activities of metropolitan bourgeoisies while at the same time executing with efficiency its mission of surplus extraction, established the colonial army and police. These agencies worked closely with the court messengers, tax collectors, labour conscriptors and the colonial courts. The brutal activities of these agencies on behalf of the colonial state contributed not only to the way the armed forces came to be perceived in postcolonial Nigeria but also to the nature of these agencies in the contemporary periods. Cases of rape, extortion, indiscipline and oppression were rampant within the ranks of the armed forces in colonial Nigeria.

3. A rudimentary educational system was introduced to service the colonial machinery. Initially this effort was abandoned to the Christian missionary

groups who were effectively barred from the Northern Protectorate. By the time the ban was removed, very limited efforts were made to bridge the gap. But the fault of the system was in its denial of the history of Nigerian peoples, its contribution to diseducation and miseducation, the emphasis on the humanities at the expense of the sciences and concentration on the production of interpreters, messengers, office clerks, cooks and later on low level executives. The University College, Ibadan, the country's premier University, was not established until 1948 as an affiliate to the University of London as part of the politics of decolonisation. Even then, with a very restricted curriculum, its goal was the production of local petty-bourgeois elements who could be relied upon to protect metropolitan interests in the postcolonial period.

4. The proletarianisation of the peasants and independent rural artisans was undertaken through the provision of wage employment, forced de-peasantisation, introduction of taxes which had to be paid in the new currency which was available only through the sale of cash crops or through wage employment in the bureaucracy, armed forces or merchant firms. The state, however, ensured that it passed several punitive labour regulations and laws in order to domesticate the emerging proletariat. More important than that, the state ensured that the response of its security agencies to acts of protest and resistance by workers was always very swift and violent.

5. Because one of the objectives of the colonial system was the extraction of agricultural surpluses, the colonial state, after the Second World War, introduced institutions such as the Marketing Boards which monopolised the purchase of cash crops through middlemen and constantly short paid the producers. The deliberate emphasis on cash crop production led to the relative neglect of food production and laid the basis for an outward oriented and food-dependent economy. Even in terms of resource allocation to research centres, efforts were not made to provide enough funds for research into tropical cash crops.

6. Industrialisation was practically discouraged by the British in colonial Nigeria, at least until after the World War I. Not only did industrialisation policy after this period emphasise import substitution which in any case did not conserve foreign exchange or encourage the transfer of skills and technology, but very limited efforts were made to generate inter-sectoral linkages particularly between agriculture and industry. The limited processing that took place was exclusively aimed at reducing the bulk of the commodities to be transferred to the industries in the metropolis.

7. The colonial state, through a discriminatory policy of granting licences, leases and location sites, laid the basis for the underdevelopment of Nigerian entrepreneurship. It deliberately refused to encourage indigenous efforts or grant loans to the emerging bourgeois elements and discriminated in terms of protection and taxes against local investors. The net result was that the influence and power of foreign capital was heavily entrenched in this period — they came to dominate the commanding heights of the colonial economy and with the support of the colonial state they won very huge and generous

leases as in the oil industry, sole rights to import and distribute consumer products, had very generous tax breaks and paid almost no royalties. They also benefitted from state subsidies and political support in their efforts to domesticate their work force. Local bankers were discouraged or discriminated against and the educational system contributed to the production of local elements who were prepared to occupy the lucrative but inherently unproductive position of compradors.

It is with these developments and many more that the colonial state claimed (to the satisfaction of the emerging elite) that it was contributing to the elimination of inter- and intra-ethnic conflicts in Nigeria as part of its programme to develop the undeveloped formation. However, and in spite of such pretensions, it was obvious that economic, political and social development of the colony was far from the goal of the British government. Its ideological and in fact, direct political role and goal was to extend and consolidate British capitalist hegemony and power, exploit the colony and ensure the peripheralisation and incorporation of the formation into its sphere of world capitalist domination. This fact was betrayed in a statement by Ian Macleod, a one time Colonial Secretary:

> The Prime Minister has recently in a striking phrase spoken of turning the empire into a family. We did not go abroad to govern, we went abroad to trade . . . so, if we are wise, we can stay in countries that we once ruled . . . as traders, farmers, planters, shippers, businessmen, engineers.[14]

Macleod's statement did not contradict that of the Prime Minister. While the former was describing the situation in the colonial period and probably confusing it with the possible policies in the postcolonial, the Prime Minister was thinking of ways in which the colonies would be sufficiently under-developed and incorporated as 'children' of the so-called family. Lord Lugard, who himself supervised the subjugation and incorporation of the formation into the British capitalist system, also exposed the fact that the British were in no way interested in the development of Nigeria or any other colony for that matter. On the contrary, Britain was only governing and exploiting such colonies on behalf of the peoples of Europe:

> The nations in control are 'trustees for civilization' a phrase which, repeated in the covenant of the League of Nations, has become a house-hold word throughout the world. In carrying out this trust they exercise a dual mandate . . . as trustees on the one hand, for the development of the resources of these lands, *on behalf of the congested populations (of Europe) whose lives and industries depend on a share of the bounties with which nature has so abundantly endowed the tropics.* On the other hand, they exercise a sacred trust on behalf of the peoples who inhabit the tropics and who are so pathetically dependent on their guidance.[15]

This statement removes any doubt about British colonialism having been a mission undertaken for the development of Nigeria. The underdevelopment wrought by the contact with Britain was executed on behalf of the 'congested populations' of Europe, particularly Britain. Thus, Lord Lugard and his men in the Colonial Office, gradually but effectively, discouraged the development of indigenous technology, distorted the Nigerian formation spatially, economically and socially, emphasised cash at the expense of food crops, initiated policies that promoted rural-urban migration thus providing surplus unregulated labour for the foreign-dominated industrial and service sectors, discriminated against local investors so as to guarantee the domineering position of the metropolitan bourgeoisie, ensured that local resources were divorced from the productive sectors which were dominated by foreign capitalists and initiated broad and specific policies to orientate the economy generally outwards towards dependence on the Western capitalist world particularly the United Kingdom.

In support of these assertions, R.O. Ekundare has argued that, though it is possible to present statistics on the number of schools built, roads constructed, hospitals established and so on, for 'the greater part of the period before 1900, the British government did not contribute significantly towards financing social and economic development projects in Nigeria'.[16] The policy of granting direct financial aid to the colonies was introduced by Joseph Chamberlain in 1895 as part of his grand but dangerous programme of 'constructive imperialism'. After 1900, this policy of constructive imperialism was intensified to protect the Nigerian market exclusively for British exploitation, and as a source of raw materials for the exclusive use of British industries.

It is, however, possible to identify three major phases in the relationship between the British colonisers and Nigeria: a) the period up to 1945, when the British were concerned with the subjugation and incorporation of the totality of the Nigerian formation to serve their own colonial needs; b) the period following 1945, when, largely as a precipitate of the crises of capitalism, the emerging nationalist upsurge and other consequences of colonial exploitation and the World Wars, the British introduced what it called 'Planning for Development and Welfare'. This was introduced primarily as one of the strategies for influencing and directing the politics of decolonisation in the interest of the metropole; and c) the period following 1955, when as a precipitate of the granting of limited autonomy to the three regions (East, West and North), the regions as well as the centre introduced so-called Development Plans.

The Consolidation of British Hegemony and Institutions, 1900–1945

As far as planning was concerned, it was totally alien to the British colonisers in this period. The primary interest of Britain was not only to win absolute control over the totality of socio-economic and political activities in its colony, but also to expand the trade in primary products. The introduction of ordinances, railways, taxes, etc., though uncoordinated and conflicting, were specifically geared to the increased production of groundnuts, cocoa, rubber, millet, and other agricultural products. To this end, policies and programmes were initiated to either compel or attract the indigenous people to produce more cash crops. In the Oyo province of south-western Nigeria, direct taxation was introduced in 1918 under the Native Revenue Ordinance No. 29. Though the Ordinance called it an income tax, it was implemented and collected as a poll tax. Between 1900 and 1912 when the railway of Northern Nigeria was amalgamated with the Southern Nigeria railway, a network of roads, railway lines and other means of transportation was introduced. Like the taxes which were aimed at raising revenues for the administration of the colony without placing burdens on the average British taxpayer, the roads distorted the spatial system of Nigeria. Virtually all the communication networks were directed to major agricultural centres or the sea ports to facilitate the collection and exportation of raw materials.[17] Though Nigerian producers responded to price incentives, mainly during the World Wars, the colonial government did little to provide direct encouragement. While land alienation was not as common in Nigeria as say in Tanzania or Kenya, this was largely as a result of the relative success of the policy of extracting surpluses from peasants. Ekundare notes on colonial agricultural policy:

> A notable and serious defect of the agricultural system in Nigeria was the absence of any provision for financing the farmer's work, apart from the locally organised community help and the few agricultural associations and co-operative societies which developed in some areas (particularly in the South) in the twenties and the early thirties. In the event of a serious epidemic of disease in the major crops . . . there were no established procedures for providing immediate relief to the farmers and for financing new enterprises.[18]

This was in spite of research centres and plantations, established as show-cases, and institutions for research into tropical crops, not with a view to encouraging local research and production but generally to the advantage of the European bourgeoisie and consumer. Between 1912 and 1916, the colonial state developed the Moor Plantation at Ibadan. Experimental agricultural stations were also established at Benin, Zaria and Umuahia.

Industrial policies in this period were essentially aimed at the discouragement and sometimes destruction of local initiatives that were likely to compete with European goods. As pointed out earlier, the colonial state discriminated against indigenous entrepreneurs except where their activities would do no more than service those of foreign investors. Local craft was looked down upon and Lugard was obviously pleased with the decline in local industrial undertakings:

> I forsee with great regret the decline of Kano as a commercial centre when European goods supersede her manufactures, and the exports of other provinces are diverted by more direct routes to the factories of British merchants, instead of passing through the hands of her middle-men and brokers. The cotton of Zaria will then cease to come to the looms of Kano or the skins and hides to her tanneries.[19]

With formal colonialism came the invasion of British and other European companies and business interests. Even the Royal Niger Company began tin-mining in 1906 and by 1918 there were 82 tin-mining companies in Nigeria. Oil companies were granted large leases, such as the 1921 oil exploration licence issued to D'Arcy Exploration Company and to Shell-BP Petroleum Development Company; and by 1924, Lever Brothers had established its control over a large part of Nigeria's market. Cigarettes were produced at Osogbo by the British American Tobacco Company in 1933; this moved to Ibadan in 1936.

The crucial point to note in these developments is that the colonial state made little or no effort to involve indigenes in these enterprises and initiatives. The only sector of the economy that was protected against foreign investors was agricultural production through the Land and Native Rights Ordinances of 1910 and 1917. Even then, these rights were limited to the production of cash crops, while the marketing of such products was reserved for foreign merchants. In order to meet the specific requirements of British industries, not only did the colonial state express displeasure at the presence of some minor German products in the Nigerian market in 1910, but by 1919, the Parliamentary under-secretary of state for the colonies made moves to ensure that exports from the colonial (including Nigeria) markets did not go outside the British Empire.

By 1945 major British companies had established their control over one or more sectors of the economy, the local entrepreneurs had been peripheralised and reduced to agents and distributors, and policies after that period were only aimed at rationalising this unequal arrangement. A major point often overlooked in the discussion of this period in the available literature is that the colonial state and bourgeoisie had the full support of the metropolitan state (and army), bourgeoisie and financial power. It was the removal of this support from the underdeveloped institutions and indigenous bourgeois elements after 1960, that was to lead to the inability to impose a viable hegemony, maintain stability, promote accumulation and rationalise (or control) exploitation. This culminated in the breakdown of law and order. Companies like John Holt, Elder Dempster, Shell-BP, Witt and Busch and so on which still dominate major sectors of the Nigerian economy today, laid the foundation for such a domination in this period. In relation to overall development or popular planning, the British achieved very little:

> The free enterprise philosophy affected the colonial government's policy towards economic development. There was no deliberate government planning for the social and economic development of the country. The bulk of the government's revenue — derived mainly from customs duties — was devoted to financing the civil establishment, leaving very little if any, for social and economic projects.[20]

Though the observation above clearly explains the British approach to planning and development in this period, it is important to note that there was nothing 'free' about colonial policies. If we note the expensive and luxurious life styles of colonial officials, the heavy extraction of surplus, the social discrimination against indigenes and the numerous policies initiated to favour and protect foreign investors against indigenous entrepreneurs, then it is difficult to take the British seriously on the so-called 'free enterprise philosophy'.

The Rationalisation of British Exploitation of Nigeria, 1945–1956

The hallmark of this period was the effort by the British government, through the colonial state and later in alliance with international capitalist institutions to initiate what it called 'planning' in Nigeria. An immediate question that comes to mind is: why was it necessary to plan for development and welfare in this period? Several internal and external factors forced the hands of the colonial government to adopt a new approach to its exploitation and incorporation of Nigeria.

Segun Osoba provides a very important explanation in this regard when he argues that the

> alleged planning initiative by the British was clearly motivated by the realisation that the political forces of socialism and national liberation unleashed world wide by the Second World War made the operation of colonial domination on the old basis of crude coercion and the hollow-ringing rhetoric about 'tutelage', 'dual mandate' and 'trusteeship' unviable.[21]

In addition to this development and at the internal level, the increasing restlessness and militancy among workers evidenced in lock-outs, work-to-rule actions, demonstrations and strikes against racial discrimination, bad management, low pay and poor working conditions demonstrated clearly the yearning of the working class, not just to have a say in the administration of the country but its willingness to contribute to national liberation.[22] The few educated elements who qualified at home and abroad as lawyers, teachers, engineers and so on were put below less qualified expatriates or given lower salaries. Their political activities and struggles against colonial exploitation and domination were also significant. Other factors included increasing capital accumulation by certain elements of the emerging local bourgeois class and their desire to expand or secure their spheres of accumulation sometimes at the expense of expatriate interests, and the glaring inequities of the colonial system which offended the sensibilities of the colonised – urban bias in resource allocation and the provision of social amenities, the lack of sufficient schools and the brutality of colonial security forces, all forced the people affected to put pressure on the colonial state.

There were also political developments which forced changes in the operation of colonial rule through coercion. Though the country had not been divided into regions, the 1946 Richards constitution established three regional councils; in 1951, as a first step towards political independence, the country was divided into three regions with little rationality, justification and foresight (North, East and West) and in 1954, a Federal constitution which was vague in several respects was introduced. Essentially, these developments demanded some level of local participation though the British ensured that control was retained by the colonial state. However, they all were initiated and executed as part of the British policy of decolonisation along lines that would not jeopardise British interests and would ensure continued British control.

The 1945 Colonial Development and Welfare Act included a scheme for Nigeria which culminated in the introduction of the first colonial Development Plan — A Ten-Year Plan of Development and Welfare for Nigeria — in 1946. The Plan was to have a total capital expenditure of N106 million of which between N30 and N32 million was to be raised from Nigerian sources and the balance contributed by Britain and other external sources. In the same year, 1946, the Development Loan Ordinance No. 3 and the Nigeria (Ten-Year Plan) Local Loan Ordinance No. 10 were passed. The former empowered the Governor of Nigeria to raise a loan of £8 million in England while the latter empowered him to raise £1 million in Nigeria.

The general unseriousness of this 1946 plan is immediately evidenced in its time-span — 10 years; especially as this was an initial effort by a country which hardly had a development plan. In addition, the emphasis was on transportation which received the largest share in order to facilitate the extraction and export of agricultural products as well as promote the systematic penetration of the hinterland by British merchant firms and other business interests. Even though the majority of Nigerians lived in the rural areas in 1946, the 'plan' allocated more money to the urban centres in terms of water supply (see Table 12.1). Dupe Olatunbosun, commenting on the motive force behind the introduction of the plan, has argued that:

> After the Second World War the colonial government realised that only by interfering in the organisation of primary and other activities could it remedy the acute shortage of export crops badly needed by its home markets. Besides, all of Western Europe needed planning.[23]

Commenting specifically on the 10-Year Plan, Olatunbosun notes that it

> was actually not a plan but a collection of projects which the colonial government felt would help it achieve its twin objectives in Nigeria, mainly to provide markets and raw materials for industries in the 'mother country'. The colonial administrators did not increase investment funds for the rural sector because the export demand requirements were being met. All they had to do was to set up extension services for commodities with special problems.[24]

Thus, the plan was hardly aimed at developing Nigeria either economically or otherwise. It did not show any intention of establishing popular and democratic institutions or a preparedness to involve the majority of the people in the planning of their lives and society. Its conceptualisation and implementation were highly static, elitist, discriminatory and undisciplined. The projects had no linkages with one another and rather than improve the living standards of the people, the Plan had an opposite effect. In fact, a select Committee of the British House of Commons also expressed its reservations on the Ten-Year plan in 1948:

> This is not to say that these various kinds of proposed expenditure are unnecessary, all of them are desirable, and most of them are urgent. The point of criticism is that if the Ten-Year Plan were carried out overnight the improvement in the condition of the mass of Nigerians would be barely perceptible.[25]

A very major negative impact of the 10-Year Plan was the introduction of the idea which has continued to characterise post-independence plans, that planning involved a search for huge external loans and other forms of assistance. The Ten-Year plan not only attempted to establish financial dependence on Britain but also encouraged the colonial Governor to raise huge internal and external loans. Osoba has also criticised the idea introduced into decision-making circles from 1946 onwards that planning is 'an exercise in spending large sums of money on a number of separate and unrelated projects'.[26] In spite of the hitherto demonstrated efficiency of the colonial state at the subjugation of local peoples, the destruction of traditional opposition movements, the forceful collection of taxes and recruitment of forced labour and the extraction of other surpluses, it was unable to manage the plan successfully:

> Colonial planning was highly undisciplined, unco-ordinated and largely irrelevant to the priority requirements of the country. Though designed for strict accountability, some planned expenditures were not incurred, some development expenditures were not planned, while some expenditures were neither developmental nor planned.[27]

In 1947, the colonial state set up commodity Marketing Boards for cocoa, and in 1949 for groundnuts, palm products and cotton, which broke the monopoly of British merchants and enterprises over the purchase and distribution of raw materials. This was not done in the interest of Nigeria or local entrepreneurs. British enterprises were already developing several affilliates outside the UK, Nigerians were beginning to try alternative West African markets and there was the need to promote medium-level capital accumulation among local elites in order to create a class that would not only have benefited from the colonial system but would be committed to its preservation. Not only were the marketing boards forbidden by law to improve the non-export crop sector of the economy, they were supposed to buy their products from licenced agents who served as a second layer of exploitation.[28] Commenting on the role of the marketing boards, Gavin Williams has argued that they

> have never been used to protect farmers, who have had to bear the full brunt of fluctuations in world prices and the additional costs of government marketing and deductions, usually between 25 and 70% of the price realised on the world market.[29]

Olatunbosun also reveals that

> The marketing boards became an effective mechanism for taxing the
> rural sector to finance 'development' in order to increase capital
> formation. For instance, in Nigeria in 1946, the boards paid only
> N33.5 for a ton of palm oil and sold it for N190 at a gross profit of
> 488 per cent. Groundnuts, which received only N30 per ton when
> bought by the boards, were later sold in Britain at N220 per ton at a
> gross profit of about 633%. Over 70 per cent of the surplus
> accumulated was reinvested in urban centres while little attention
> was given to the rural sector. Rather than stabilize the prices, the
> boards de-stabilized the prices and deviated completely from the
> declared purpose of their existence. Furthermore, export duties and
> produce sales tax were levied on the boards' sales by the colonial
> administrators.[30]

Though the colonial state technically restricted its role to the provision of
physical and social infrastructure, given the contradictions that followed the
first ten years of planning activity, it became necessary to deepen capitalist
penetration of Nigeria. It was at this point that the International Bank for
Reconstruction and Development, alias the World Bank, was invited to send a
mission to Nigeria and to, among other things,

> assess the resources available for future development, to study the
> possibilities for development of the major sectors of the economy and
> make written recommendations for practical steps to be taken, including
> the timing and co-ordination of departmental activities.[31]

Prior to this invitation, a limited transfer of political power to the emerging
dependent bourgeoisie had taken place in 1952, and this was formalised in
1955.

The colonial state, through this single political initiative, laid the
foundation for Nigeria's political underdevelopment and instability. It
confined and encouraged the foster-elite to remain in their respective regions,
thus depriving the centre of men and material resources. The plans which the
regions were to draw up, based on the World Bank's advice, incorporated all
the confused and unrealistic projections of the Bank and the policies contained
in the colonial Ten-Year plan. The Bank itself argued, after a 'comprehensive
study', that 'without foreign investment, neither public nor private endeavour
can achieve the rate of growth the Nigerian people desire'.[32] This philosophy
of 'the indispensability of foreign private investment' only complemented
and tried to give rationalisation to the colonial policies which had favoured
foreign investors and underdeveloped indigenous entrepreneurs.[33] The task
of the Bank and the colonial government at that point in time was to sell the
rationality and correctness of this status quo of foreign domination to the
emerging power elite that was soon to capture political (but not economic)
power. As a sign of the conspiracy between the British exploiters and the
Bank, the report advised that for foreign investment capital to 'be sure of its
welcome, there should be a reasonably good prospect of attracting it,

primarily from the United Kingdom but also from other countries'.[34] This recommendation was an indirect warning that the numerous tax relief policies, soft loans, restrictions on local investors, subsidies and state supply of overhead capital were not only to be retained but probably increased to accommodate capitalist interests from outside the United Kingdom. The 'assurance of free transferability of profits and repatriation of capital' and the total prohibition of government direct participation in industrial development were also strongly recommended by the World Bank.

The recommendations of the Bank and the enthusiasm with which the colonial state not only sold them to its foster bourgeoisie but implemented most of them, significantly contributed to the internal underdevelopment and peripheralisation of Nigeria in the international division of labour. Ekundare notes that the 'findings and recommendations of the mission played a considerable part in the framing of Nigeria's future plans for development'.[35] hence, it is quite easy to see the root of contemporary poverty, alienation, instability, exploitation and foreign domination in Nigeria.

Regional 'Development' Plans, 1956–1960

Though regional planning was supposed to have been initiated in 1955, the British government had announced in 1955 that the colonial development and welfare scheme was being extended to 31 March 1960. Thus, the regional plans were to operate under the guidance and influence of the colonial plan. The sort of guidance and influence provided by the colonial plan is explained thus:

> The policies of colonial planners were dominated by financial conservatism, under-utilisation of resources, discouragement of industrialisation, and characteristic lack of urgency. Fiscal orthodoxy was applied to reduce the growth rate and to plan projects in order to service a budget surplus for British capital accumulation. Open unemployment, under-employment, low level of planned expenditure, and a general failure to mobilise the people implied 'hidden' reserves of the country were not tapped for development. The loan on industrialisation also meant that available resources of raw materials, entrepreneurship, labour etc could not be utilized for raising value-added in manufacturing . . . In terms of technical style, the colonial plans were experiments in what has been dubbed 'GDP planning'. This underlined the technical and bureaucratic character of the plans.[36]

Thus, though the Federal Loans Board was set up after the World Bank's report (which was published in September 1955) along with the Western Region Finance Corporation and other development corporations in the three regions, these did not mediate the contradictions between social classes or stimulate rapid development. The establishment of the National Economic Council (NEC) on the recommendation of the World Bank, in 1955, to serve as a consultative body and promote Federal-regional cooperation was largely an attempt to set up a broad institution to mediate contradictions within the ranks of the dominant classes under Federal supervision. The NEC still plays this role to this day. The establishment of a Joint Planning Committee in September 1958 to operate in an advisory capacity to the NEC with powers to co-opt experts from all sectors of society and to promote co-ordination in development planning only intensified contradictions between the centre and the regions. As Onimode notes,

> some of these improvements . . . were offset by the unsettling effects of administrative reshuffling involved in regional reorganisation, the damaging effects of regionalization on integrated planning as well as difficulties of co-ordination.[37]

However, regional planning opened up hitherto closed opportunities to the Nigerian bourgeoisie who unfortunately did not attempt to capitalise on the available openings to expand their accumulative bases at the expense of foreign capital. On the contrary, the bourgeoisie struggled to win comfortable but very unproductive locations within the distorted and foreign dominated economy as partners, shareholders, agents, legal advisers and so on. This bourgeoisie also initiated a grand programme for identifying and carving out spheres of interest. In the intra-class struggles which followed, some amenities were spuriously extended to the people as bribes. But in most cases the struggles were rationalised in chauvinistic terms – region, ethnicity and religion. These were to have long-term political implications for the unity and stability of the country. Since the colonial state encouraged regionalism, it turned out that the regions became more powerful (and in some cases richer) than the centre. The contradictions involved in this development were not to be resolved until 1970 with the end of the Civil War and Creation of States.

If we take a closer look at the development plans of the regions, they resemble those of the colonial state. A total capital expenditure of N456.78 million was planned. Of this total primary production received only N54.6 million and as in the colonial plan, transportation and communication received the largest amount N125.976 million or 27.70 % (see Table 12.2). The efforts of the regions, especially the East and West, a year before political independence, to go into direct agricultural production ended in complete failure because not only did they fail to consider the socio-economic consequences of such efforts on rural producers, but they were technical in conception and implementation and half-heartedly pursued.[38] The bias against the rural majority, the exploitation of urban workers, the non-involvement of the majority in the initiation and implementation of development plans continued as in the early colonial period. Commenting on the impact of regional and colonial planning efforts on the rural majority, Olatunbosun notes:

> there can be little question that the colonial government, which might have constituted an important source of initiative and a dynamic element in promoting rural development in Nigeria, restricted its role to mainly that of trading and developing the agricultural exports to ensure adequate and cheap supply of raw materials for the industries in the metropolis. The rural areas were particularly denied social

services that are essential for rural development.[39]

Conclusion

In view of our discussion it becomes obvious that any claim that the British colonial government developed Nigeria either in terms of laying the foundation or of achieving concrete development on behalf of the people must be illusory. The effects of one and a half decades of colonial planning on the Nigerian economy 'can be dialectically approximated to the state of productive forces and social relations of production which together constitute the mode of production'.[40] If we carry out this approximation, it becomes very clear that the peripheral role and location of the Nigerian formation today in the international division of labour, the existence of a weak and largely unproductive bourgeoisie, the co-existence of modes of production (the pre- and capitalist modes), the existence of an unstable state and the generally low standards of living were the direct consequences of the colonial planning and policies which are being re-produced in the contemporary period. The outward orientation of the Nigerian economy, the absence of a technological base, the neo-colonial content of the educational system, the viciousness and unproductivity of the armed and security forces and the existence of inefficient and ineffective institutions are also products of colonial rule which deliberately emphasised the interests of the metropolis at the expense of Nigeria and Nigerians.

Finally, it is difficult, given available evidence to even contemplate the fact that colonialism could have developed or laid the foundation for development. By the end of formal colonial rule on 1 October 1960, the new power elite had accepted and absorbed a number of mythical notions about development and planning which were to influence thinking in post-colonial Nigeria: (1) planning had to be elitist in initiation and implementation — there was no need to involve the masses whose lives and future were being planned; (2) planning had to be heavily centralised and kept secret from the people, because the decentralisation of decision-making and -executing institutions demands a level of political and power decentralisation; (3) for a plan to be successful, it must involve huge expenditure on all sorts of projects, whether co-ordinated or not was a secondary matter; and (4) planners must rely on foreign aid — capital, technology and manpower. These are just a few of the myths implanted in the colonial period which have continued to persist.[41]

Table 12.1
A Ten-Year Plan of Development and Welfare for Nigeria, 1946–1956

Projects	Funds Allocated *(N Million)*	Per cent *Allocation*
Primary Production	6.976	6.5
Water Supply		
(a) rural	8.004	7.5
(b) urban	9.120	7.6
Transport and Communication	22.788	21.4
Electricity	3.088	2.9
Health	13.276	12.4
Education	10.654	10.0
Commerce and industry	522	0.5
Building Programs for Development	18.068	17.0
Social Welfare including village		
Reconstruction	1.432	1.3
Local Development Schemes	4.000	3.8
Others	9.726	9.1
	106.654	100.0

Source: Dupe Olatunbosun, *Nigeria's Neglected Rural Majority* (Ibadan: Oxford University Press, 1975), p.51.

Table 12.2
A Development Plan for the Federation of Nigeria, 1955–60 (N Million)

Items	Federal	North	West	East	Total	Percent Allocation
Banking	0.700	–	–	1.242	1.942	0.4
Building Society	1.000	–	–	–	1.000	0.2
Cameroon Dev. Corp.	2.000	–	–	–	2.000	0.4
Co-Operatives	–	3.310	0.160	0.152	3.622	0.8
Electricity	14.340	9.160	2.000	–	25.500	5.6
Miscellaneous	3.908	13.160	14.498	0.040	31.616	6.9
Primary Production	2.088	30.012	1.844	20.610	54.554	11.9
Trade and Industry	3.710	3.562	0.064	0.400	7.736	1.7
Transport and Communication	102.244	9.722	8.00	66.010	125.976	27.6
Water						
(a) Rural	–	7.112	1.00	5.908	14.020	3.1
(b) Urban	–	10.224	9.120	1.636	20.980	4.6
Education	6.416	43.968	15.242	2.000	67.626	14.8
Health	1.511	23.984	4.338	6.528	39.966	8.8
Information	1.500	–	0.436	–	1.926	0.4
Social Welfare	0.104	0.732	0.256	–	1.092	0.3
Town and Country Planning	19.924	3.312	1.468	3.000	27.704	6.1
Other Administrative Ex.	0.080	–	8.738	–	8.818	1.9
Others (Mongining for Increased Cost)	12.410	–	–	–	12.410	2.7
Security	8.282	–	–	–	8.828	1.8
Total	*183.822*	*158.268*	*67.164*	*47.526*	*456.780*	*100.0*

Source: 'Dupe Olatunbosun, *Nigeria's Neglected Rural Majority* (Ibadan: Oxford University Press, 1975), p.55.

References

1. Examples of orthodox works on the Nigerian political economy include Sunday M. Essang, 'The Distribution of Earnings in the Cocoa Economy of Western Nigeria: Implications for Development', (Ph.D. Thesis, East Lansing: Michigan State University, 1970); Peter Kilby, *Industrialisation in an Open Economy: Nigeria, 1945–1966* (Cambridge: Cambridge University Press, 1969); R. Olufemi Ekundare, *An Economic History of Nigeria 1860–1960* (London: Methuen and Co., 1973) and Gerald K. Helleiner, *Peasant Agriculture, Government and Economic Growth in Nigeria*, (Homewood: Richard D. Irwin, 1966). Radical contributors include Okwudiba Nnoli (ed), *Path to Nigerian Development* (Dakar: Codesria, 1981); S.O. Osoba, 'The Nigerian Power Elite, 1952–65' in P.C.W. Gutkind and P. Waterman (eds), *African Social Studies – A Radical Reader* (New York: Monthly Review Press, 1977); Ola Oni and Bade Onimode, *Economic Development of Nigeria: A Socialist Alternative* (Ibadan: The Nigerian Academy of Arts, Sciences and Technology, 1975); Julius O. Ihonvbere and Timothy M. Shaw, *Towards a Political Economy of Nigeria* (Forthcoming) and Toyin Falola and Abiodun Goke Pariola (eds), *Politics and Economy in Contemporary Nigeria: Selected Works of Segun Osoba* (Forthcoming).

2. See for instance, A.G. Hopkins, *An Economic History of West Africa* (New York: Columbia University Press, 1973); Walter Rodney, *How Europe Underdeveloped Africa* (London: Bogle l'Overture Publications, 1972); E.A. Brett, *Colonialism and Underdevelopment in East Africa: The Politics of Economic Change* (London: Heinemann Press, 1974); and G. Kay, *The Political Economy of Colonialism in Ghana* (Cambridge: CUP, 1972).

3. Steven Langdon and Lynn Mytelka, 'Africa in the Changing World Economy' in Colin Legum et al., *Africa in the 1980s – A Continent in Crisis* (McGraw Hill Book Company, 1979), p.124.

4. See for example the works of Bjorn Beckman, 'Whose state: State and Capitalist Development in Nigeria', *Review of African Political Economy*, 23 (Jan-April 1982) and 'Imperialism and the National Bourgeoisie', *Review of African Political Economy*, 22 (October-December 1981).

5. See Gunner Myrdal, *Rich Lands and Poor* (New York: Harper and Brothers, 1957).

6. Albert O. Hirschman, *The Strategy of Economic Development* (Glencoe: The Free Press, 1958). For a Critique of the 'trickle down' approach see Mahub Ul Haq, *The Third World and the International Economic Order*, O.E.C.D. Paper 22 (n.d.).

7. See John Friedman, 'Agropolitan Development – Towards a New Strategy for Rural Regional Planning in Asia' in *Growth Pole Strategy and Regional Development in Asia* (Tokyo: UNCRD, 1977).

8. Robert McNamara in *New York Times*, 2 April 1978.

9. See Frances Moore Lappe et al., *Aid as Obstacle – Twenty Questions about Our Foreign Aid and the Hungry* (San Francisco: Institute for Food and Development, 1981).

10. See Andre G. Frank, *Colonialism and Underdevelopment in Latin America* (London: Monthly Review Press, 1969); Colin Leys, *Underdevelopment in Kenya* (Ibadan: Heinemann, 1976) and the works of Samir Amin, Immanuel Wallerstein, Celso Futado, Henrique Cardoso and Enzo Falleto.

11. Dennis Rondelli and Kenneth Ruddle, *Urbanization and Rural Development: A Spatial Policy of Equitable Growth* (New York: Praeger, 1978), p.77.

12. Walter B. Stohr and D.R.F. Taylor, 'Development from Above or Below? Some Conclusions' in *Development from Above or Below* (London: John Wiley and Sons, 1981) p.454.

13. For a critique of 'development from below', see Julius O. Ihonvbere, 'Oil Revenues and Rural-Urban Inequities in Nigeria'. Paper read at the 12th International Conference of the Institute of International Cooperation and Development, University of Ottawa, Ottawa, Canada, 29-31 October 1981.

14. Ian Macleod in *West Africa*, 2 April 1960, p.390.

15. Lord Lugard, 'The White Man's Task in Tropical Africa' in *Foreign Affairs Reader* (New York, 1964), p.6.

16. R.O. Ekundare, op. cit., p.69, fn.1.

17. For details, see ibid., pp.127-155.

18. Ibid., pp.157-158.

19. Lord Lugard in *Colonial Annual Reports*, No. 476, Northern Nigeria, 1904, pp.88-89.

20. Ekundare, op. cit., p.97.

21. Segun Osoba, 'Considerations on Some Conceptual and Ideological Aspects of Nigerian Underdevelopment in Historical Perspective', University of Ife, Department of History Seminar Series, 1979/80, January, 1980, p.17.

22. Nigerian workers have historically demonstrated a high level of class/ trade-union consciousness, in spite of the numerous factors inhibiting unity, organisation and the development of revolutionary consciousness. For instance, there was a major strike action in Lagos as far back as 1897; in 1929 the coal miners at Udi called a successful strike; in 1948 20 industrial disputes in the country resulted in strike actions; in 1948 70 industrial disputes were declared, resulting in 36 strikes involving 46,698 workers and the loss of 500,000 man-days. The Railway Station Staff Union called a nation-wide general strike in July 1949 which was successful. In 1950 82 industrial disputes were declared resulting in 26 strikes involving 26,876 workers. These strike actions are important landmarks in the history of working class contribution to challenging the exploitative colonial status quo especially in the context of stiff colonial anti-labour regulations.

23. 'Dupe Olatunbosun, op. cit., p.50.

24. Ibid.

25. Cited in W.F. Stopler, *Planning Without Facts: Lessons in Resource Allocation from Nigeria's Development* (Cambridge, Mass: Harvard University Press, 1966), p.37.

26. Segun Osoba, op. cit., p.18.

27. Bade Onimode, 'Planning for Underdevelopment in Nigeria' in Okwudiba Nnoli (ed), op. cit., p.139.

28. For details see Olatunbosun, op. cit., and 'Commodity Marketing Boards and Agricultural Development' in *Proceedings of a National Agricultural Seminar* (Ibadan: Ibadan University Press, 1975), and with S.O. Olayide 'Effect of Marketing Boards on Income and Output of Primary Producers', in D. Olatunbosun and H.M.A. Onitiri (eds), *The Marketing Board System: Proceedings of an International Conference* (Ibadan: Ibadan University Press, 1973).

29. Gavin Williams, 'Taking the Part of Peasants: Rural Development in Nigeria and Tanzania' in P.C.W. Gutkind and Immanuel Wallerstein (eds), op. cit., p.133.

30. 'Dupe Olatunbosun, op. cit., p.53.

31 For details on terms of reference, findings and recommendations see *The Economic Development of Nigeria*. Report of a Mission Organised by the International Bank for Reconstruction and Development (Baltimore: Johns Hopkins University Press, 1955).

32. Ibid., p.28.

33. For details on how the colonial state systematically underdeveloped indigenous entrepreneurship and blocked Nigeria's scientific and industrial take-off see the collections in Okwudiba Nnoli (ed), op. cit., and Gavin Williams (ed) *Nigeria Economy and Society* (London: Rex Collings, 1976). See also Akeredolu Ale, *The Underdevelopment of Indigenous Entrepreneurship in Nigeria* (Ibadan: Ibadan University Press, 1975).

34. See *The Economic Development of Nigeria*, op. cit., p.28, pp.28-30, and 352-354.

35. Ekundare, op. cit., p.233.

36. Bade Onimode, op. cit., p.139.

37. Ibid., p.140.

38. See 'Dupe Olatunbosun, and R.O. Ekundare, op. cit.

39. 'Dupe Olatunbosun, op. cit., p.57.

40. Onimode, op. cit., p.140.

41. See Julius O. Ihonvbere and Timothy M. Shaw, *Towards a Political Economy of Nigeria* (Forthcoming); Claude Ake, 'Explanatory Notes on the Political Economy of Africa', *Journal of Modern African Studies* 14, 1 (1976); and Toyin Falola and Abiodun Goke Pariola (eds), op. cit.

13. The Transition to Neo-Colonialism

S. O. Osoba

A most significant outcome of British colonial rule in Nigeria was the creation of an economy that was foreign-dependent and export-oriented, and of an elité which, conditioned by the colonial educational system and persuaded by the substantial political and economic advantages that would accrue to it from power-sharing with the colonial authorities, was broadly committed to protecting this colonial economic bequest.[1] This, in a way then, means that with this notion of community of interests between the colony and the metropolis carefully nurtured by the departing colonial authorities in the Nigerian foster elite, the British could look forward to Nigeria's independence without any fears for the safety and security of British investments and other economic interests in Nigeria.

It is true that the British colonial authorities attached great importance to their achievements in bringing up a Nigerian elite that was broadly in sympathy with Britain's dominant position in Nigeria's economy and aspired only to enhancing the participation of its members alongside British financial and commercial interests. In this way, the British hoped that they could dismantle their formal colonial empire while at the same time they would be strengthening their informal colonial powers, variously characterised by critical former colonials as 'economic imperialism', 'neo-colonialism' and 'neo-imperialism'. This included the cultivation of friendly relations and a community of interests between the departing colonisers and the colonial foster elites, but it was not narrowly and passively conceived. Available evidence seems to indicate that the British colonial authorities in Nigeria were not persuaded that the much-vaunted cordial relations existing between them and the top Nigerian leaders from 1952 on were alone sufficient to protect Britain's economic interests in an independent Nigeria, and to ensure that Nigeria would remain in its desired orbit as an economic and political satellite of Britain. Consequently, they felt constrained to bend their energies to hammering out in the period of 'decolonisation', significantly between 1952 and 1960, more concrete legislative and executive measures as additional protection for Britain's dominant position in the neocolonial economy and political system of an independent Nigeria. These measures of neocolonial control formulated with the active collaboration of the Nigerian majority in the Federal government, can be divided into three broad categories for the purposes of this analysis: economic and fiscal measures; political measures; and measures taken to prepare a Nigerian diplomatic corps.

Economic and Fiscal Measures

These measures were of a ramified and comprehensive nature, ranging from tax laws, spurious bilateral contractual agreements between Britain and Nigeria to the inauguration of an orientation to 'economic development and welfare' planning, calculated to reinforce Britain's domination of the Nigerian economy and thereby cheat a politically independent Nigeria out of her economic independence. In short, they were designed to perpetuate, in a situation of formal-legal independence, the client-patron relationship subsisting between Nigeria and Britain under formal colonial rule.

A significant way in which the British colonial administration provided for the continued economic exploitation of Nigeria by British business enterprises was by arranging unjust and blatantly dishonest 'bilateral' economic and financial agreements between Nigeria on the one hand and the British government or British business concerns on the other. The aim of such agreements was clearly to guarantee extremely profitable conditions for British monopoly capital operating in Nigeria, with the equally clear implication of ensuring the long-term dependence of the Nigerian economy on British capital and British technical and managerial expertise. A classic example of such crooked deals came to light in the Federal House of Representatives on 15 March 1957, when Jaja Wachuku (NCNC member for Aba, who was to become the disastrous Foreign Affairs Minister from July 1961 to December 1964) raised the issue of what he regarded as the tax evasion manoeuvres of some foreign companies operating in Nigeria. Jaja Wachuku asked the Financial Secretary whether he was aware of the fact that a number of foreign firms operating in Nigeria were beginning to convert themselves into 'Nigerian companies in the form of agencies'. Citing the example of the Elder Dempster Lines Agencies Ltd., a British and the largest shipping enterprise in Nigeria, he claimed that even though such 'puppet agencies' made millions of pounds sterling profit on their operations in Nigeria, the Nigerian government could only tax these agencies on profits they declared from agency fees paid them by their metropolitan principals. Jaja Wachuku wanted to know if this kind of arrangement was 'not a very serious depletion of the income tax profits' that should accrue to Nigeria and what the Financial Secretary was doing 'to prevent that depletion'.[2]

The Financial Secretary, without denying Jaja Wachuku's charge of sharp business practice by some foreign companies, proceeded to make a more startling admission implicating the British government in an even more serious case of dishonesty. The crux of his reply was as follows:

> There is a provision in Section 9 of the existing Income Tax Ordinance which states that the gains or profits from the business of operating ships or aircraft carried on by persons not resident in Nigeria shall be

exempt from tax provided that a reciprocal exemption from tax is granted by the country in which such person is resident. So that exemption is already granted in our law and also in the double taxation arrangement with the U.K. There is already in the statute legal exemption for profits earned by overseas transport companies. Therefore, if one such company creates an agency in Nigeria, it does not alter the income tax position.[3]

Now, one does not need any economic expertise to grasp the essentially roguish intent of this so-called mutual and reciprocal agreement on tax exemption existing in law between Nigeria and Britain. In so far as only British companies could benefit from it, because there were no indigenous Nigerian transport companies operating on any appreciable scale in Britain, the contractual agreement was simply a device for syphoning from Nigeria to Britain financial resources critically needed for social and economic development in the country and for consolidating its impending fragile independence. Another crucial point ignored by the Financial Secretary (and I suggest, deliberately) is that these metropolitan companies, referred to by Wachuku, were only too well aware that, with Nigerian independence around the corner, this type of fraudulent tax holiday they were enjoying might not last for ever. Therefore, in creating these ghost agencies, they were already looking far ahead and evolving their own tactics and strategy for defeating the aims of any remedial measures that might be taken in future by a politically more conscious and radical Nigerian government.

An indication of the size of British profit and Nigeria's loss from this scandalous Anglo-Nigerian agreement on mutual tax exemption is given by a revelation concerning the level of profit being made by the British-dominated shipping monopoly, the West African Conference Lines Ltd., from the maritime carrying trade of the British territories in West Africa. In an editorial published by the *West African Pilot* of 16 February 1957 under the caption 'End this Monopoly', the newspaper called for the abolition of the strangulating monopoly of the West African Conference Lines Limited, which 'bagged over £46 million (N92 million) profit in 1953 without paying a penny as tax to the Nigerian government'.[4]

It was therefore, not surprising that on 20 March 1957 (five days after Jaja Wachuku made the Financial Secretary confess to the reciprocal tax deal), the Nigerian Minister of Trade and Industry, R.A. Njoku, was being queried about the monopoly control which the West African Conference Lines Limited was exercising on the shipment of export and import goods from and to Nigeria. While the Minister did not bother to deny that the Conference Lines held a monopoly on Nigeria's shipping business, he, however, betrayed in his reply a tendency which was all-pervading among the Nigerian Federal Ministers during the twilight days of Britain's formal colonial rule in Nigeria — the tendency of being enthusiastic defenders of British economic interests against those of the country they claimed to be representing. In the Minister's own words, marked by extreme naiveté or insincerity or both:

> What I want to emphasise is this. The Conference Lines are in
> agreement with the Marketing Company in London for the
> evacuation of the produce handled by the Marketing Boards . . . The
> Marketing Company naturally has to obtain for the producers of this
> country the best terms and therefore any shipping company or group
> of shipping companies which gives it the best terms will be accepted
> by agreement and these agreements are subject to review from time
> to time.[5]

Minister R.A. Njoku, while vigorously defending the legitimacy of the
contract between the Conference Lines and the Nigerian Produce Marketing
Company based in London, failed to confess to his parliamentary audience
that, since even he as Minister of Trade had no say in determining this
contract, he was merely playing the role of 'his master's voice'. He also
failed to recognise that, since both partners to this deal on behalf of Nigeria
were under the control of British officials and business concerns (for example,
big monopoly firms like the UAC and John Holt had their feet firmly planted
in both camps), his rhetoric concerning 'the best terms' for Nigeria in such
circumstances amounted to no more than idle prattle.

Subsequent developments in the area of managing the country's overseas
transportation links revealed that the Federal government was determined
not only to maintain its dependence on British transport companies, but
also to enlarge it. For example, in November 1958 C.O. Komolafe (NCNC
member for Ilesa) charged in the Federal House of Representatives that
some big foreign companies had been making underground moves to get the
government to set up a puppet shipping line and he expressed the fear that
'the Shipping Line will, as in the case of the Nigerian Airlines, be controlled
by the same monopolists headed and manned by their brothers'.[6] Although
R.A. Njoku, by this time Her Majesty's loyal Minister of Transport, denied
in his reply to Komolafe that shipping monopolists suggested the formation
of a shipping line to the government, he nevertheless argued enthusiastically
in favour of collaboration with 'an experienced line operator'. 'We must
start,' insisted Minister Njoku,

> in such a way as to make it succeed, we must start in partnership with
> an experienced line operator in whom we have implicit trust. It is only
> after some years of very close cooperation with such experienced people
> that we can take over the management ourselves.[7]

What came out in these parliamentary exchanges about the agreements
entered into by the government over the two national transport companies
was this: the government had a slim majority shareholding of 51 per cent in
the companies, while the British Overseas Airways Corporation (a British
government-owned giant) held the remaining 49 per cent in the Nigerian
Airline and was responsible for the technical and managerial aspects of the
business. In the case of the Nigerian National Shipping Line, the technical
partners were the Elder Dempster Agencies and the UAC (both British
shipping giants in West Africa and leading members of the shipping monopoly,

the West African Conference Lines Limited) which, between them, held the remaining 49 per cent.

About three months later, on 7 February 1959, Jaja Wachuku, reflecting the suspicion among a section of the House of Representatives about these agreements, called on the government to make public the details of the agreement signed with the foreign companies participating in these two ventures. This, he argued, was important in view of a broadcast over Radio Nigeria that morning in which one of the expatriate directors of the National Shipping Line asserted that the company was not going to enter the passenger transport business immediately.[8] Even though the government did not respond to his call, he raised the issue again after one week and this time armed with some figures. He pointed out that out of the £800,000 which the federal government alone was going to spend on overseas passages in the 1950-60 financial year about £600,000 would go to Elder Dempster Lines as cost of transporting government officials and public figures overseas. Clearly implying some dubious business in the matter, Jaja Wachuku concluded with a touch of sarcasm: 'If our Shipping Line goes into passenger traffic, we get all that money. That is why we are not going into passenger traffic; that is where the ready money goes'.[9]

In his reply, Minister R.A. Njoku, far from allaying the fears of the House about the continued foreign monopoly domination over Nigeria's shipping, confirmed them and, for good measure, contradicted his position of three months before concerning the legitimacy of the Nigerian Marketing Company's shipping contract with the Conference Lines and of the huge profits accruing therefrom. After suggesting unconvincingly that 'it is not passenger traffic that pays in the Ocean Line business', he proceeded to betray the half-hearted and symbolic gesture of his government on the issue when he declared:

> If this House will remember, the complaint has been that a lot of produce is exported from this country on which millions of pounds by way of freight are paid, and it is an attempt to repatriate some of this that the Shipping Line has been formed.[10]

However, the sheer ineffectiveness of the Nigerian government's action in entering the shipping business is clearly revealed by the fact that the Nigerian National Shipping Line soon became a member of the West African Conference Lines Limited, whose monopoly some Members of Parliament wanted the government to liquidate. The Conference Lines, on their part, had no difficulty in domesticating the Nigerian national company, to the extent that by 1963, five years after it was launched, it succeeded in begging off the Conference Lines only 4 per cent of Nigeria's maritime carrying trade.[11]

The British colonial administration also made sure before it handed political power over to an indigenous Nigerian government in October 1960 that it committed the exploitation of Nigeria's vast petroleum reserves in the Niger Delta area to the safe hands of two foreign monopoly concerns,

British Petroleum and the Royal Dutch Shell Company (the former 100 per cent British-owned enterprise and the latter a joint Anglo-Dutch concern). The agreement under which these two companies had a virtual monopoly of Nigeria's petroleum resources was based on the notorious 'fifty-fifty' formula for sharing petroleum proceeds between the prospecting company and the host country. It was this formula, designed to make cheap petroleum available to the industrial societies of Europe and America while keeping the petroleum-producing countries in a state of relative poverty and underdevelopment, that caused so much friction between the foreign mono-polists and Middle-Eastern countries (especially Iraq and Iran) in the immediate post-World War II period. The Arab producing countries had long rejected this formula, formed themselves into an Arab Organisation of Oil Exporting Countries (AOPEC), subsequently enlarged into the Organisation of Oil Exporting Countries (OPEC) as a body for conducting collective bargaining with oil-consuming nations for better prices and conditions of operation.

Under the colonially imposed terms of agreement, the Nigerian government was to take 50% of the companies' profits (to be made up of import duties on equipment brought into the country by the companies, the statutory mining royalties and income tax on overall profits). The implication was that the net operational profit of the companies would not be subject to company tax in Nigeria if it did not exceed the total of import tax and royalties paid by the company to the government in any given year. The Nigerian government's share of the profits from the petroleum industry was further reduced by the companies' right to deduct from their taxable gross profit allowances on their capital outlay under the government programme of incentives to investors in industry.[12]

In spite of the great disquiet among many members of the House over the deal with Shell-BP, and of the fact that, given the chance, some petroleum companies from other parts of the world were ready to make much fairer deals with the Nigerian government (the AGIP-Mineraria deal of 1962 is a shining example), the government of the First Republic felt unable to review the crooked 30-year agreement which the departing colonial authorities had signed with Shell-BP. The agreement between Nigeria and AGIP-Mineraria, an Italian petroleum company and a subsidiary of the state-owned ENI Group, for AGIP to prospect for oil in Nigeria was announced by the Federal Minister of Mines and Power, Maitama Sule, to Parliament on 3 April, 1962. The AGIP offer, as outlined by the Minister, was unusually favourable for two main reasons. First, apart from the fifty-fifty formula by which profit was to be shared with British and American firms, Nigeria also had an option to buy 30% of the AGIP shares after oil had been struck in commercial quantities, which would yield Nigeria another 15% of the profits, thus bringing her total share of profits to 65%. Second, taking into consideration Nigeria's critical shortage of capital at that time, AGIP agreed that the 30% share-holding could be paid for in instalments over a reasonable period to be determined by the two contracting partners.[13]

It is symptomatic of the federal government's pathetic dependence on British economic and political control that, even though Minister Maitama Sule recognised the AGIP offer as being far more conducive to Nigeria's economic interest, he and his government were unable to use it in challenging Shell-BP's extortionate privileges. In a flight of rhetoric, Maitama Sule characterised the AGIP offer as 'unique in the history of the oil industry. An offer which positively takes into consideration the interests, progress and development of producing countries'. Yet in concluding his speech in Parliament, the minister felt the need to give a firm assurance to the other oil companies wheeling and dealing in Nigeria to the effect that:

> Government's participation with AGIP-Mineraria will in no way jeopardise their legitimate activities in this country. They will continue to enjoy the fair and just treatment that the government has always given them.[14]

Clearly, one of the ways in which the government kept its promise not to 'jeopardise' the so-called legitimate activities of Shell-BP and their allies was by refusing to join the militant OPEC until 1970 and, therefore, for ten years after independence allowing these international sharks to defraud the Nigerian nation of the difference between what the oil companies paid for OPEC petroleum and Nigerian petroleum − a fraud amounting to hundreds of millions of naira.[15]

Furthermore, the worth of the fifty-fifty deal to Shell-BP could best be appreciated if one considered the fact that, until it was finally clinched with the colonial government just before independence, the two foreign partners were very reticent on the size of Nigeria's petroleum reserves that they had discovered.[16] However, once they got the dishonest agreement tied up, the petroleum which they were not sure existed in commercial quantities in 1959 started gushing out in a flood. Nigeria's crude oil production then dramatically shot up from 245,000 tons in 1958 to 2,219,000 tons in 1961, 3,301,000 tons in 1962, 5,853,000 tons in 1964 and 12,101,000 tons in 1965.[17] Moreover, even though by 1965 petroleum had displaced cocoa and groundnuts as Nigeria's principal foreign exchange earner, officials of Shell-BP in Nigeria (according to a *Times* of London correspondent in the 3 May 1966 issue of the paper) 'are agreed that what they have done so far is small beer compared with progress they expect in the next few years'.[18] That this optimistic projection by Shell-BP officials of the rich harvest they would reap in the immediate future did not materialise until the Nigerian oil boom in the 1970s was no reflection on their understanding of Nigeria's oil potential and their own powers of controlling it. They were rather frustrated in their hopes by the unpredictable circumstances of two military coups and a civil war that put most of Nigeria's oilfields out of action for some four years.

In pursuing their plans for the neocolonial exploitation of Nigeria after independence, the British colonial administrators took care to leave behind in Nigeria a complex network of tax laws (embracing tax reliefs and tariffs), company and banking laws which would make it possible for foreign businesses in Nigeria to continue to operate on exceptionally advantageous terms. The Income Tax (Amendment) Ordinance of 1952, further amended in 1957 and 1961, gave foreign capital investors massive fiscal concessions which had the effect of whittling down the Nigerian government's share of the profits made by foreign companies. This ordinance, according to an official publication

> gives generous 'initial allowances' as well as 'annual allowances' so allowing companies, both public and private, to write off from profits for the purpose of computing taxable income a large amount of their capital investment in fixed assets during the early years of trading.[19]

The Companies Income Tax Act (No. 22 of 1961) confirmed this principle, and another government publication in 1964 spelled out the scope of these allowances thus:

> Initial allowances vary from 20 per cent in the case of buildings to 40 per cent in the case of machinery and plant. Annual allowances vary from 10 per cent to 33½ per cent, depending upon the type of assets and the amount of wear and use involved in each case. It is possible, therefore, for a company to claim and be granted up to 73½ per cent of the original cost of a commercial vehicle in the first year that the asset is brought into use, and, in the case of plant and machinery working on one shift, up to 50 per cent.[20]

Government extended further tax reliefs to companies operating in Nigeria under the following laws. The Aid to Pioneer Industries Ordinance of 1952, modified by the Industrial Development (Income Tax Relief) Act of 1958, provided a tax holiday of up to five years to pioneer companies according to capital invested in fixed assets, and allowed for an extension of the holiday to compensate for the period in which a loss was sustained.[21] The Industrial Development (Import Duty Relief) Act of 1957, amended by subsequent Acts, gave exemption, wholly or in part, of custom duties on materials or components imported for use by industrial concerns operating in Nigeria provided that such companies had up to 45% Nigerian components in their products; and this had nothing to do with whether such companies had Nigerian components in their shareholding or not.[22] Government even went further to declare specifically in 1964 that concessions under both of these laws were not mutually exclusive. In the government's own words, 'companies are free to apply for both on an appropriate documented basis'.[23]

The official definition of a 'pioneer industry' in a 1964 government publication clearly revealed the commitment of Nigeria's political decision-makers to the defence of the dominant position of foreign business concerns and their bumper profits provided they were willing to extend to members of the Nigerian business elite profitable minor partnerships. A pioneer industry, according to this definition, was

230

one which is either not being carried on in Nigeria at present, or one which is not being conducted on a commercial scale suitable to the economic requirements or the development of Nigeria. [It must also] be incorporated in Nigeria and be a public company with at least 10 per cent of Nigerian share in the equity capital and up to 45 per cent Nigerian components.[24]

In addition to all these overgenerous tax reliefs enjoyed by private business enterprises in Nigeria, company tax in Nigeria stood at 40% under the Company Tax Act of 1961. Furthermore, government felt obliged to give an undertaking in 1956, reaffirmed in 1964, to the effect that 'profits and dividends arising from sterling and non-sterling capital in approved projects may be freely transferred to the country of origin and that such capital may be repatriated at will'.[25] In effect, therefore, foreign companies operating in Nigeria were free to repatriate up to 60% of their gross profits from the country, while in Ghana, under new fiscal measures introduced in October 1963, they could only repatriate 35%.[26] Against this background, the differential response of Western capitalist interests to the Nigerian and Ghananian governments under Balewa and Nkrumah respectively becomes at least partially intelligible. For Nigeria's leaders it was lavish praise and endorsement, while Nkrumah and his government became targets for vicious capitalist abuse, slander and plots.

The obvious corollary of the overgenerous tax policy operating in Nigeria in favour of foreign business concerns was the almost total lack of control by the government on the activities of these companies. This left foreign monopoly capital and its agents free to invest their resources in Nigeria with the sole purpose of maximising their profits and generally without any consideration for the real interests and development needs of the country.[27] For example, the government had no reliable or usable information on foreign businesses operating in Nigeria, nor did it bother to distinguish between foreign and indigenous industrial enterprises – an unbelievable state of affairs in a country where business ambitions and the profit motive were so widespread among different sections of the elite. Asked in the House of Representatives in 1957 for details about the nature of industries set up in Lagos since 1945 and their distribution among foreign and indigenous capitalists (Question W257 by T.O.S. Benson), the Minister of Trade and Industries regretted that he could not furnish the information required because

> ... people who set up industrial concerns, unless for instance they are obliged to register business names, need not inform the authorities of what they are doing.[28]

When similar questions were asked on 15 August 1960 (Questions O.419 and O.420 by Zakari Isa), the official reply to it was:

> There is no system of industrial licensing in force in Nigeria, nor is it necessary for a company wishing to start an industry to apply for permission to do so; there is therefore no complete record of industrial

firms operating in the Federation . . . It is not possible to distinguish between foreign-owned and Nigerian-owned firms.[29]

As a result of the colonial bequest of official laissez-faire in relation to private industrial and commercial enterprises, industrial growth in the post-independence period was distinguished by an intensification of speculative activities by foreign concerns and of the foreign-dependence syndrome that had been built into Nigeria's colonial economy. This colonial bequest of industrial and general economic clientage became so firmly established in the post-independence era that the authors of the Second National Development Plan, 1970–74, after reviewing all the facts, had to admit that:

> Most industrial activities in the country are still not manufacturing in the true sense of the term, but mere assembly industries. Very often, all the components used are imported and are merely put together behind the tariff wall. Whether one is considering the manufacture of shoes or cosmetics, beer or soft drinks, the story is broadly the same . . . All that happens at most of the breweries is that all the imported inputs are mixed and sealed in imported bottles.[30]

Apart from all these dubious legal measures and contractual arrangements worked out by the departing colonial authorities to domesticate the economy of an independent Nigeria and subject it to their own interests, perhaps the most effective weapon in their struggle for the continued domination and control of Nigeria was the ideology of planning for 'development and welfare' which they inaugurated in Nigeria and carefully nurtured behind the smoke-screen of decolonisation. It was through the formulation and constant elaboration of this spurious ideology that they succeeded in brainwashing the Nigerian foster elite to come to appropriate to themselves, even enlarge upon most of the anti-Nigerian measures outlined above. The history of this ideology had its humble beginnings in the symbolic gesture made by the colonial authorities in their first attempt at knocking a development plan together for Nigeria, A Ten Year Plan of Development and Welfare for Nigeria, 1946. The document envisaged the spending of a total of £53,327,249 over the ten-year period, 1946–47 – 1955–56. To reinforce the myth of British 'philanthropic imperialism' in Nigeria, the authors of the plan patronisingly stated that:

> Of this total there will be some £15,800,000 of expenditure suitable for financing from loans to be raised by the Nigerian Government. Towards the remaining £38,000,000 odd, there will be the *generous contribution of $23,000,000 allotted to Nigeria under the Colonial Development and Welfare Act* leaving between £15,000,000 and £16,000,000 to be found from Nigerian revenue. [Emphasis is mine][31]

The conclusion that the British colonial authorities wanted Nigerians to draw from the stated 'financial implications of the ten-year plan', was that the development of Nigeria was bound to depend in the main, not on indigenous Nigerian enterprise or resources, but on the initiative and beneficence of the

British and other foreign philanthropists. If Nigerians and their leaders could be persuaded that the ten-year plan was a genuine programme designed for their development, but that only £15 to £16 million out of its total cost of £53 million (between 28.30 and 30.18%) could be raised from local Nigerian revenue, the rest coming from outside, then a good beginning would have been made in reinforcing among leading Nigerians a dependence mentality, which was crucial for maintaining in perpetuity a client-patron, colony-metropolis relationship not only in economic, but also in political and cultural matters. However, this line of propaganda was not as yet being overtly pushed; it was just being hinted at, and was judiciously hidden in hard statistical facts which should be able to speak for themselves.

The most significant thing, however, about the ten-year plan of 'development' is that it was neither a plan nor was it concerned with development. It did not envisage an integrated strategy of development. On the contrary, it merely proposed that money be spent over a ten-year period on a number of separate unrelated projects. It was informed by a naive kind of optimism that this spending spree would generate growth in these various sectors of the Nigerian society so as 'to elevate the conditions of life of its people so that their output might be greater and their economy correspondingly improved'.[32] It is, therefore, with full justification that a Select Committee of the British House of Commons that reviewed it in 1948 pronounced that 'this is not planning'.[33]

In spite of the fact that this gloomy prediction was substantially proved right by the time the ten-year plan had run its ill-fated course, the plan itself, as a low-key ideological programme, helped to create in Nigeria a tradition whereby political decision-makers have tended to confuse development planning with merely spending increasingly huge sums of money (both locally raised and borrowed or begged from abroad) on big prestige projects which are neither conceptually nor functionally related and which, in spite of official platitudinous pronouncements, could not perceptibly alter the quality of life of the Nigerian masses. To this extent, the 1955-62, the 1962-68 and 1970-74 plans are only different from 1946-56 plan in scale rather than in kind. They were all informed by the same formalistic, piecemeal and seemingly value-free orientation to economic development planning, within which 'growth' and 'development', 'change' and 'progress' are synonymous and interchangeable terms.

When, in 1945, the ten-year plan was drafted, the British colonial administration felt no need to raise in the plan the issue of the position of foreign private enterprise and investment in the Nigerian economy. However, the rapid change, from 1952 onwards, in the political balance of power in Nigeria in favour of the Western-educated foster elite meant that the colonial authorities were confronted with a new challenge to safeguard the future of British investment and that of their allies in Nigeria by means other than those which were purely legalistic or openly coercive. Their new strategy from the 1950s for the domestication of Nigeria's development and its subordination to the all-important interests of British investment capital was the mounting of a powerful three-pronged propaganda offensive. This offensive was geared towards inducing the internalisation (among the up-and-coming indigenous Nigerian political decision-makers) of the following subversive and paralysing beliefs, concerning a) the crucial importance of private foreign investors to Nigeria's rapid economic development, and the prime necessity of attracting such investors by every conceivable means; b) the indispensability of 'foreign aid' – in the form of foreign government grants, loans, technical personnel, etc. – to Nigeria's very economic survival; and c) the danger to Nigeria's development of direct government participation in commerce and industry – thus envisaging the control of the nation's commerce and industry in perpetuity by a partnership between foreign entrepreneurs (as senior partners) and indigenous Nigerian businessmen (as junior partners).[34]

This propaganda offensive was formally inaugurated in the 1955 IBRD report on *The Economic Development of Nigeria*, which became, from 1955 through the 1960s, the blueprint for economic planning and development in Nigeria, and government leaders, embattled over the policies they upheld, often cited its arguments almost with the same awe and reverence with which devout Muslims or Christians refer to passages in the Koran and the Bible. In effect, it became the infallible authority on the basis of which the Federal government and its planning experts in the five years before independence and throughout the life of the First Republic, came to embrace the dangerous and suicidal notion that foreign aid and foreign private enterprise had a more decisive role to play in Nigeria's development effort than public and private indigenous enterprise put together. The IBRD report is categorical on this point when it claims that:

> Without foreign investment, neither public nor private endeavour can achieve the rate of growth that the Nigerian people desire.[35]

In another of its oracular pronouncements the IBRD report insists that for foreign capital to 'be sure of its welcome, there should be a reasonably good prospect of attracting it, primarily from the United Kingdom but also from other countries'. Among the conditions considered by the report to be crucial and congenial to the desirable inflow of foreign capital are 'an assurance of free transferability of profits and repatriation of capital', the enactment of generous tax laws, and the disengagement of the Nigerian governments from direct participation in industrial enterprises and, therefore, from competition with foreign investment capital.

Consequently, the half-hearted attempts at development planning in Nigeria centred on the wisdom of leaving the high points of the economy in the hands of private, preeminently foreign, investors. State ownership should not go beyond the existing public utilities like electricity, ports, railways, public water supply, postal and domestic telecommunication services. Nationalisation of existing private enterprises was considered a disaster of monumental proportions. Leading Nigerian political decision-makers often reacted with crude, abusive and violent effusions to any suggestion concerning the need to nationalise 'enterprises exercising a dominant influence over the people's livelihood' (as Mokwugo Okoye demanded in October 1960) or 'basic industries and commercial undertakings of vital importance to the economy of Nigeria' (as Awolowo proferred in November 1961). For example, representatives of all the four governments in Nigeria dissociated themselves from Mokwugo Okoye's call with varying degrees of crudity, but M.I. Okpara, the Premier of the Eastern Region and National President of the NCNC, excelled everybody else when, in a tantrum, he declared that:

> Those who are advocating nationalization are communists and they should have the moral courage to say so . . . Every member of the NCNC should stop saying or doing anything contrary to our policy of working in association and partnership with foreign capital.[36]

Federal Minister of Finance Festus Okotie-Eboh's denunciation of Awolowo's nationalisation call in November 1961 was grounded on impeccable IBRD arguments. He insisted that 'irresponsible statements' about nationalisation would scare away foreign investors, whose capital and technical know-how would be vital to the success of the 1962-68 Development Plan, and that 'friendly governments might question the desirability of imposing additional burdens upon their tax-payers to assist Nigeria in those circumstances'.[37]

By capitulating totally to this British-inspired propaganda concerning the crucial importance of foreign aid and investments to the survival and development of the Nigerian economy, the Nigerian political leaders, supposed custodians of their nation's economic and other interests, became completely dissociated from the real needs of their country and the realities of international economic relations. For instance, at the time that Festus Okotie-Eboh and a myriad of other federal and regional government leaders were invading, cap in hand, the major capitals in Europe and America, abjectly begging for loans and investments which were either not there or were available at exhorbitant rates of interest, Nigeria's investment in the UK in the form of sterling assets and the gilt-edged securities was well over £200 million and earning what Okotie-Eboh evasively termed to be in excess of 5% interest.[38] When it is recognised that the British authorities made it near impossible for Nigeria to repatriate her own capital investment in the UK for critically needed development at home, then the issue of who was aiding whom gets into proper focus.

Political Measures

Protection against 'communism'
The concrete political measures taken by the British administration in Nigeria during the period of decolonisation were designed to ensure that Nigerian society after independence would not be exposed to certain forms

of external relations which might generate pressures on the Nigerian political decision-makers to terminate or drastically reduce the especially close and intimate relationship that the British would want to subsist between them and their former colony. The British colonial authorities correctly identified the two major problem areas in future Anglo-Nigerian relations as a) the possible development of links, formal and informal, with socialist countries and b) involvement in the anti-colonialist and anti-racialist struggles that were brewing and were likely to intensify in southern, eastern and central Africa.

Britain, or at least her agents of decolonisation in Nigeria, believed that she had vital economic, political and strategic interests in Africa which might be in great jeopardy were Nigeria to be taken over by 'atheistic communism' or become an ally of the 'insurgents' and 'terrorists' who were already threatening to embattle or were embattling Britain in her colonies of Kenya and the Central African Federation and her allies in apartheid South Africa, Portuguese Angola, Mozambique and Guinea-Bissau. This belief was elevated into something akin to a religious orthodoxy, especially in view of Nigeria's undeniably vast potential in terms of the size of her population (at independence every fifth African was a Nigerian) and the rich variety of natural resources at her disposal that Britain wanted to 'help' tap with appropriate rewards to herself. The British might also have calculated that, since they experienced in their colonial administration of Nigeria virtually no difficulty with extreme radical or revolutionary nationalist movements, and since they had succeeded in creating an elite cadre of moderate and 'responsible' leaders that would succeed them, it would be a feasible, even necessary, thing to leave Nigeria as the 'bulwark of democracy' in Africa.

Now, what the British and their ideologies would expect from such a bulwark or bastion of democracy would be not only that it should insulate its people from the virus of communism — reckless egalitarianism that does not mix with business — and from disruptive anti-colonialist and anti-racialist wars in other areas of Africa, but also that it should become an active partner with Britain and her allies in containing these 'evils'. However, in dealing with these two problems the British colonial authorities accorded pride of place to the outlawing of communism from Nigeria, apparently because, while 'insurgency' in the remaining bastions of European colonialism and racist-minority rule in Africa remained essentially a potential threat, Britain and her Western allies were already engaged with communism in a dangerous cold war and its balance of nuclear terror in Europe, the Americas and Asia, and they were anxious to preserve Africa as their exclusive sphere of influence and as a counterweight to the massive communist influence in Asia and Eastern Europe.

The British colonial policy of containing communism in Nigeria was a permanent feature of colonial rule in Nigeria. In the period of unmitigated colonial rule, when the colonial administrators monopolised all the power of political decision-making and of coercion, it was a relatively easy task to make Nigeria safe from communism, since they could then ensure that no known communist was allowed into Nigeria to contaminate the 'natives' and no Nigerian was allowed a passport to travel to any communist country on any business whatsoever. However, it soon became clear that the *cordon sanitaire* thrown around Nigeria against communism was not totally foolproof or unbreachable, especially as Nigerian students were allowed to go to Britain where if they wanted, they could liase with the British Communist Party and other Marxist groups and from where some of them actually travelled to socialist countries either to study or on visits. By the early 1950s some of these Nigerians 'tainted with communism' were already returning to Nigeria, and this development naturally excited all the protective instincts of the colonial government almost to the point of hysteria.

Consequently, the British colonial government proceeded to sharpen its anti-communist defences and succeeded in launching what in effect amounted to mildly orchestrated communist witch-hunting. In pursuing this task it found a ready ally in the top leaders of the Nigerian foster elite from all the major political parties because of their vested political and economic interest in a Westminster-style political system and in the capitalist free-enterprise economy that were being planted in Nigeria. For instance, an Executive Council order was issued in Lagos on 28 June 1955 under the signature of one A.M. Muir (Acting Deputy Secretary to the Council of Ministers) banning a total of 33 books and publications feared to carry communist propaganda materials which might be injurious to the people of Nigeria.[39]

This was part of a general government policy aimed at excluding 'active communists' from the public services and public corporations in Nigeria. By July 1957 the last British Chief Secretary to the Nigerian government could claim with pride that:

> It is the policy of the Government, endorsed by this House, to exclude active communists from the Public Service, and from the service of the Public Corporations, and this policy has been followed voluntarily by a number of commercial organisations (Interruptions!). But I understand, Sir, that this is the policy not only of the Government, but of the whole of this House, and in pursuance of it, it has been necessary, from time to time, for the Governor-General, acting in his discretion to withhold passports or travel documents from people who wish to travel, without apparent reason, to countries behind the Iron Curtain.[40]

Even though the Chief Secretary, responding to the hostile reaction from a section of the House, pleaded that there was no 'suggestion of witch-hunting in this respect', the whole business actually turned out to be the Nigerian, relatively low-key, version of its contemporary, the McCarthyite anti-communist campaign in the USA. This anti-communist programme of the colonial government was enthusiastically carried out by the various Nigerian governments and, as Mokwugo Okoye has pointed out, neither Nnamdi Azikiwe nor the NCNC government of the Eastern Region which he was heading was to be left out of this fiesta of communist persecution. What gives the Azikiwe scenario added significance and an ironic twist is, as Okoye revealed, that in the not too distant past specifically in 1949, he had declared in a speech made on the platform of the British Communist Party in London that the communist anti-imperialist policy was 'not one whit different from the NCNC programme', adding that 'we speak one language with regard to imperialism as a crime against humanity which must be destroyed'. Yet, his NCNC government in the Eastern Region, under the watchful eye of the British colonial Governor, gave the anti-communist law a much wider interpretation than the colonial government had overtly directed. Azikiwe's government is reported to have threatened to withdraw grants-in-aid to various schools if branded communists were not dismissed from their teaching staffs.[41]

It would appear that Azikiwe and his henchmen among the NCNC's top leadership even carried their anti-communist crusade into their party and showed remarkable vigour in their attempt to root out communists and their fellow-travellers from the party. This action was triggered off by the restiveness of the remnants of the Zikist Movement within the NCNC in 1955. These heroes of the only thing that approximated to a militant anti-imperialist movement in Nigeria were becoming increasingly frustrated with the growing strength of the bourgeois elite in the NCNC leadership and with the party's progressive back-sliding from the ideals of a 'socialist commonwealth' which, the youths believed, had earlier inspired it. So, they began to speak out against what they saw as the 'bourgeois revisionism' of their leaders. Nduka Eze and Adesanya Idowu were the first Zikists to be dismissed from the party for 'disloyalty' on 3 May, 1955 in this anti-communist offensive. When Mokwugo Okoye and Osita Agwuna (the Secretary and President of the Zikist Movement respectively in 1951 at the time the colonial government banned it and jailed a number of its members including these two) wrote a petition on their behalf to the 6th NCNC Convention held at Ibadan a few days later, they too were expelled by the Convention for having exposed the party to 'public obloquy' (a favourite phrase of Azikiwe, the political polemicist). The Zikists clearly saw their summary dismissal from a party they had served with unequalled dedication as explicable mainly in terms of the growing anti-progressive stance of the leadership, and they underscored this point in their petition to the Ibadan Convention thus:

> When the young men make any attempt to defend and sustain the ideals and policy of the party they are branded as rebels, bevanites, communists, irresponsibles and anything that suits the dominant leadership.[42]

The British colonial government, on its part, used these anti-communist laws against various public figures with progressive political ideas, even though there was no shred of evidence to support the charge that they were communists. For example, a radical trade unionist, Gogo Chu Nzeribe, one of those who opposed the affiliation of the Nigerian central labour organisation (the All Nigeria Trade Union Federation – ANTUF) to the capitalist and American controlled International Confederation of Free Trade Unions (ICFTU) or to any other international trade union organisation for that matter, was promptly labelled a communist by his rivals in the ANTUF of which he was Secretary General. This baseless and unsubstantiated accusation was, however, enough to make the colonial government impound his passport.

About the same time another notable case of official communist witch-hunting came to light. The government seized the passport of Mrs Funmilayo Ransome-Kuti, a pioneer in organising Nigerian women for social and political action and at that time the President of the Nigerian Women's Union. A few months after Mrs Kuti's passport had been seized, her matter was raised in the Federal House of Representatives by some members on 3 March 1958. In his reply to members' queries, the Prime Minister, Abubakar Tafawa Balewa explained that Mrs Kuti's passport was withdrawn because, against government advice, she had attended communist-inspired meetings of Women's organisations in Europe and China and had contacts with communist front organisations. More significantly, the Prime Minister seized the occasion to restate, and even enlarge upon, the official government policy:

> Hon. Members are already aware, [Balewa claimed] of the policy laid down by the Federal and Regional Governments of excluding Communists from branches of the Public Service, and in connection with this policy the Council of Ministers has for a number of years taken the view that to allow unrestricted access into communist countries is not in the best interest of Nigeria.

Commenting specifically on Mrs Kuti, the Prime Minister asserted:

> It can now be assumed that it is her intention to influence the various Nigerian women's organisations, with which she is connected, with communist ideas and policies. It is in this respect that the danger from Mrs Ransome-Kuti's contacts with, and belief in, Communism lies.

Prime Minister Balewa ended his reply on a very aggressive and uncompromising note:

> Finally, I should like to state here, as I have already said in a letter to Mrs Ransome-Kuti, that I and my colleagues are determined that, while we are responsible for the government of the Federation of Nigeria and for the welfare of its people, we shall use every means in our power to prevent the infiltration of Communism or communistic ideas into Nigeria. I feel sure that the whole House will endorse this policy.[43]

The Prime Minister not only got the support for his government's anti-communist policy which he expected, at least for the meantime, but the Immigration Department became more active in excluding suspected communists from Nigeria. Immigration officials were reported to have turned back at Ikeja international airport a group of Czech students who had come to attend an international students conference held at the University College Ibadan in September 1957. The Czech students were representing the International Union of Students (IUS) which was regarded by the Nigerian government and its Western allies as a communist-front organisation.[44]

In view of this massive campaign against communism and the socialist system in Nigeria, it so happened that the few Nigerians with Marxist leanings, not feeling able to confront official persecution and obscurantism, chose one of two options. Some of them relapsed into isolationism and political inaction, while others, after a disastrous attempt to create the nucleus of a socialist movement, chose to join one or the other of the two major southern-based political parties – the AG and NCNC. An example of the latter in R.L. Sklar's account, was a group of Marxist intellectuals who formed the United Working People's Party (UWPP) in Abeokuta in 1952. However, by March 1953 officialdom had caught up with them: the homes of the UWPP members were raided by the Nigeria Police, and a few of their leaders were tried for sedition and fined. Taking discretion to be the better part of valour, most of the members of the UWPP decided to dissolve the party and seek or reactivate their membership of one of the two major southern parties, some of them being quickly acculturated into the bourgeois ethos that was bourgeoning in the 1950s onwards in these parties.[45] It was for the same reason that the so-called 'Communist Party of Nigeria', according to its self-styled 'First Secretary', one Chukwudolue Orhakamadu, remained in hibernation for nine years from 1954 to 1963. Although Orhakamadu claimed at the latter date that the party was 'coming out from a period of hibernation' to take an active part in national politics, nothing has been heard or felt concerning its activity since then.[46]

Distancing Nigeria from Southern Africa

The other political problem area that the departing colonial authorities attempted to eliminate by appropriate legal measures before independence was Nigeria's possible involvement in the anti-colonialist and anti-racist upheavals that were already brewing in southern, central and eastern Africa. With the scary Mau-Mau rebellion in Kenya in the early 1950s as an indication of what might happen in South Africa, the Rhodesias, Nyasaland, Mozambique and Angola, in all of which Britain had vital interests, the British policy of decolonisation in Nigeria envisaged preventing independent Nigeria from giving any active support to the African nationalist forces that Britain and her allies seemed destined to engage in a fierce war of liberation. It would appear, for instance, that the controversial Anglo-Nigerian Defence Pact proposed by Britain and accepted by the four main Nigerian leaders (the Sardauna, Balewa, Azikiwe and Awolowo) at the London Constitutional Conference of 1958 was conceived by its British authors as the ultimate guarantee (with the British military presence in Nigeria written into it) of the success of their policy of insulating Nigeria from pressures and influences that might be exerted on her by communist countries and the embattled African freedom fighters in the white redoubt south of the Zambesi. Even the elaborate rationalisation of the pact presented to the Nigerian leaders by the British Secretary of States for the Colonies at the London Conference would seem to reinforce this interpretation:

Throughout the talks [the Colonial Secretary claimed] the Conference had been conscious of all the dangers confronting the free world today and it recognised that an independent Nigeria would be subject to new and heavy pressures. In this connection, I am glad to tell the Conference that the Federal Prime Minister and the Premiers were at one with Her Majesty's Government in believing that there would be mutual advantage to Britain and Nigeria in cooperating in the field of defence and that they had exchanged views and reached unanimous agreement on the facilities and help which each country would render to the other after independence.[47]

Later in the year, the British authorities inspired further legislative action in Nigeria in a badly camouflaged attempt to so circumscribe Nigeria's political initiative that the oppressed peoples of Africa struggling for their freedom would not be able to obtain from her material and moral support. On 21 November 1958 the Federal House of Representatives passed into law an Immigration (Amendment) Bill that had far-reaching implications for Nigeria's future policy on African affairs. Under the old immigration law that was being amended, a 'native foreigner' was defined as a man or woman from any 'tribe' indigenous to Africa irrespective of his country, and such a person could, under the law, enter Nigeria without let or hindrance. However, according to the crucial provision in this amendment to the law, the term 'native foreigner' became applicable only to 'a person whose parents were members of a tribe or tribes indigenous to Ghana, Sierra Leone, Gambia, the Sudan and the Republic of Guinea'.

The brief, almost perfunctory, debate on this crucial Bill and the ease with which it was passed into law was symptomatic of the willingness with which the majority of the Nigerian ruling elite represented in Parliament would collaborate with their colonial mentors in committing Nigeria to a reactionary foreign policy even ahead of independence. The only substantive reason given by Prime Minister Balewa to justify such reactionary legislation, at a time when there were very strong feelings after African unity and total liberation from all forms of oppression all over the continent, was that 'under the new conditions in Africa, it would be wrong if we opened our gates to all other African countries near or far from us'.[48] Prominent among those who spoke in support of the Bill was T.T. Solaru (AG member for Ijebu West) who produced a most palpably illogical and ignorant argument:

This does not mean that we are inhospitable. It only means that we want them to be accredited for by their own Governments first and then we accord them all the facilities at our disposal and vice-versa.[49]

How he thought freedom fighters from South Africa, Mozambique, Central African Federation, Angola and Namibia were going to get accreditation from their oppressive governments for the purposes of fleeing from the hangman's noose or long terms of imprisonment Solaru did not think was worth explaining.

The few MPs, like O.C. Agwuna and L.A. Lawal, both NCNC members, who expressed serious reservations about the law, were massively outnumbered by the Balewas and Solarus of this world. O.C. Agwuna's heart-rending plea fell on generally insensitive hearts:

> What can we give as our reason for preventing indigenous Africans from East Africa and the Union of South Africa from entering this country? People in these areas are looking forward to Nigeria as their saviour country, . . . to help them in overcoming some of their problems of race prejudice.[50]

Creating the Nucleus of a Nigerian Diplomatic Corps

As a result of the vociferous campaign conducted by the major Nigerian political parties (especially the NCNC and AG) the colonial administration had by 1954 accepted in principle the policy of accelerating the Nigerianisation of the top decision-making positions in the public services of the Federation, but when it came to executing this policy the colonial government tended to drag its feet and was constantly badgered by its critics in the legislatures and among the public to speed things up. However, it was probably in preparing cadres for manning Nigeria's foreign service and in transferring the control of the country's foreign policy to Nigerians themselves that the fabian strategy of the colonial administration was most noticeable. It was not until 1956 that the colonial government, in response to the relentless demands of some members of the Federal House of Representatives since 1954, agreed in principle to start recruiting and training Nigerians who would represent their country overseas after independence.[51] Before 1957 practically nothing was done to prepare the country to manage her external relations after independence apart from the acquisition of 'a 42-year lease-hold' on a house in London to serve as the 'new Nigeria House', and a proposal for 'a modest expansion of the Liason Office in Washington, which hitherto has existed to look after the interests of students from Nigeria who are in the United States'.[52] Sir Ralph Gray, the last colonial Chief Secretary of Nigeria, who gave this information in the House, clearly underscored the limited objective of his government in this matter by declaring that the 'modest expansion' to the Nigerian Liason Office in Washington must be such 'that can be integrated with the activities of the British Embassy'.[53]

On the crucial issue of training career dilpomats for the Nigerian foreign service the government could only announce by 3 March 1957 that the applications of the first batch of potential recruits were just being considered; and by 26 February 1959 the Prime Minister was at last able to tell the House that the first batch of 28 recruits had been selected for training.[54] When the Governor-General, in an address to the House earlier in the month, declared that 'it is confidently expected that in the course of this year the planned total of forty officers will be reached',[55] he merely buttressed the suspicion among some MPs concerning Britain's reluctance to give up the control of Nigeria's external relations. K.O. Mbadiwe seemed to be speaking for a significant

section of the House when he retorted thus: 'We are told only 40 people
are being trained for the Foreign Service. Very poor. In 1960 we will be faced
with a tremendous responsibility in our Foreign Service'.[56]

Apart from the paucity of Nigerians selected for training as career diplomats, the few selected were sent for training almost exclusively to Britain.
In reply to the concern expressed by Jaja Wachuku about the exclusion of
Asian Countries, especially India, from the list of countries to which trainee
diplomats were sent, the Prime Minister simply said:

> they have their training in the U.K. Foreign Office. Also they go to
> Oxford University and we attach them to British Embassies in other
> parts of the world . . . I do not say that the Indian Foreign Service is
> not efficient, but I think that from other countries that have been
> established for so long we will benefit more than from the newly
> established ones.[57]

Even more significantly, the colonial authorities made sure that right up
to independence and beyond, the home branch of the Nigerian foreign service
remained the exclusive preserve of British colonial officials. For instance
S.L. Akintola (AG, Ogbomoso), commenting in March 1957 on the budgetary
allocation for external affairs and specifically on the external branch of the
Chief Secretary's Office, observed that

> it is a closed door, and the men who are in charge of decoding messages
> there are all expatriate officers. No Africans are ever allowed to be in
> the decoding section of the Chief Secretary's Office.[58]

Furthermore until 1 October 1960 the Governor-General retained statutory
control over Nigeria's foreign policy which, since the constitutional changes
of July 1957, was formulated and executed for him by the Secretary to the
Prime Minister and the Cabinet. This crucial post was held by a British officer,
one Peter Stallard, until June 1961 when pressure of public opinion forced
the Prime Minister to replace him with a Nigerian, S.O. Wey. In essence,
therefore, the grudging acceptance of the colonial authorities, under pressure,
to train a skeleton staff of Nigerian diplomats did not mean that they intended
to create a genuinely Nigerian foreign service, but rather one in which Nigerians
would serve alongside British officials in more or less subordinate positions.

Special care was also taken right up to independence to ensure that Nigeria
had no diplomatic contacts with the outside world beyond the limit considered
safe for the role earmarked for her in the Western bloc — that of a satellite
state. Apart from a Nigerian Pilgrims' Office attached to the British Embassy
in Khartoum, and a Nigerian Liaison Office in Washington (managed by a
British official as part of the British Embassy), the only foreign missions which
Nigeria had before independence were in Britain and Ghana. The Nigerian
Commission in Accra (opened in 1957 after Ghana's independence) was under
the general supervision of the British High Commission there, and like the
other Nigerian foreign missions, was ultimately responsible to the Governor-
General until 1 October 1960.

As a corollary to this, the countries which were allowed to establish some rudimentary foreign missions in colonial Nigeria were carefully selected to exclude all socialist countries, and to include all the major Western allies of Britain and some 'safe' Asian and Middle-Eastern countries like Japan, India, Pakistan, Israel, Lebanon and Syria. While Nigeria was thus being screened away from 'communist influence', the United States Information Service and the British Council, the main overseas propaganda agencies of the USA and UK respectively, were given a free rein by the colonial administration to peddle all over the country ideas aimed at drawing Nigeria into the orbit of the Western capitalist powers and at creating in people's minds fear and suspicion of anything socialist or communist.

The susceptibility of the bulk of the Nigerian ruling elite to the clever manoeuvres of the British colonial authorities during this crucial period in the country's history, the period of decolonisation, resulted from a conjunction of circumstances. Firstly, the paternalistic isolationism with which Nigeria was shielded from the world at large and from the various currents of ideas running through it ensured that, even among some of the most politically sophisticated Nigerians, there was abysmal ignorance of the outside world. This, in turn, gave rise to the lazy and unenterprising idea that you should prefer 'the devil you know to the angel you do not know', a concept that worked in favour of maintaining uncritically the colonial ties to the virtual exclusion of all others. Secondly, there was also a widespread illusion among many members of the Nigerian Western-educated elite that, because they were literate in English, wore English clothes and subscribed to the bourgeois ethos and life-style of their counterparts in Britain, therefore they had a cultural affinity with Britain and the whole of the English-speaking world, which affinity constituted, in their view, a sufficient and necessary condition for forging international political alignments. In this illusory state of mind, they could not see that at least 80% of their compatriots (the rural and urban masses) on whose behalf they would strike such alignments could not conceivably share this affinity which was one of the main forces buttressing their exploitation by a domestic bourgeoisie in collusion with foreign interests.

It is important to emphasise that the subversive way in which Nigeria was prepared by the departing colonial authorities to manage her foreign affairs (with the active collaboration of Nigeria's top leadership) had an enfeebling impact on the structure and functioning of Nigeria's diplomatic missions abroad after independence, and enhanced Britain's capability to continue to exercise a remote control over (or, in Nkrumah's terminology, to 'teleguide') Nigeria's foreign policy after independence. For instance, at independence there were too few trained Nigerian diplomats to man effectively the home branch of the Foreign Service and the few foreign missions that were initially opened. The result was that graduates fresh from Universities and other less highly trained personnel, with a motley variety of qualifications, often unrelated to diplomatic work, were drafted into Nigeria's foreign service and sent to man foreign missions. Inevitably, these new Nigerian diplomats, with a few honourable exceptions, knew no other foreign language apart from English, and were often totally ignorant of the politics and internal situations of the countries to which they were posted until they arrived there. Consequently, they tended to rely on the 'expert' advice of their British and Commonwealth colleagues and, to this extent, the regular consultative meetings of Commonwealth Heads-of-Missions held in every diplomatic centre of the world were tantamount to a kind of remote control over the conduct of Nigeria's international relations.

Furthermore, right up to the end of the First Republic in January 1966, it was the policy of the Nigerian government to entrust British embassies, in countries where Nigeria had no diplomatic missions, with the responsibility of looking after Nigeria's interests in these places. It was in the implementation of this policy that, until 1962 when Nigeria opened an embassy in Moscow, Nigeria's interests in the USSR and other socialist countries of Eastern Europe were looked after by British diplomatic missions in this area. It would be naive in the extreme to imagine that British diplomats, acting as Nigeria's diplomatic agents in these countries, would work for the promotion and strengthening of friendly and mutually beneficial relations between Nigeria and the socialist countries. Anthony Enahoro, the AG Opposition spokesman on foreign affairs, commented sharply on this 'deplorable' state of affairs in a debate in Parliament in March 1962.[59]

The British-engineered domestication of the Nigerian diplomatic service created a staggering imbalance in the geopolitical distribution of Nigeria's foreign missions and in the distribution of personnel among these missions, in favour of the UK, USA and the Western bloc and against the socialist countries, the Afro-Asian, Latin American and Caribbean Countries. Even by April 1965, out of 213 Nigerian officers (excluding substantive Heads-of-Missions) serving in 33 overseas missions, 98 were accredited to 8 missions in 6 Western countries, 78 to 19 missions in African countries, 18 to 4 Asian and Middle-Eastern countries (Pakistan, India, Japan and Saudi Arabia), 14 to the United Nations in New York, 5 to the USSR, the only socialist country hosting a Nigerian mission, and none to Latin America and the Caribbean. Even more significantly, out of the 98 officials serving in the Western bloc countries 53 were located in Britain, 17 in two missions in the USA, 10 in Belgium, 9 in Western Germany, 7 in Italy and 2 in the Republic of Ireland.[60]

References

1. See, for instance, S.O. Osoba, 'Ideology and Planning for National Economic Development 1946–72' in Mahmud Tukur and Tunji Olagunju (eds) *Nigeria in Search of a Viable Polity* (Zaria: ABU Inst. of Admin., 1975), pp.90-116.

2. House of Representatives, Debates (HRD), 15 March 1957, 1957–58 Session, Vol. II, p.447.

3. Ibid., p.449.

4. *West African Pilot*, 16 February 1952.

5. HRD, 20 March 1957, 1957–58 Session, Vol. II, p.563.

6. HRD, 25 November 1958, 1957–58 Session, Vol. IV, pp.106-7.

7. Ibid., p.111.

8. HRD, 7 February 1959, 1950–60 Session, Vol. 1, p.48.

9. HRD, 14 February 1959, 1959–60 Session, Vol. 1, p.258.

10. HRD, 19 February 1959, 1950–60 Session, Vol. II, p.400.

11. S.G. Ikoku, *Nigeria for Nigerians: A Study of Contemporary Nigerian Politics from a Socialist Point of View*, (Lagos, 1963), p.28.

12. See Federal House of Representatives, *Sessional Papers*, No. 3 of 1958, p.3 and No. 6 of 1964 p.3, and *West Africa*, 7 May 1966, p.521.

13. HRD, 3 April 1962, 1962–63 Session, Vol. 1, col.752-754. It should be noted that the relatively generous terms offered by AGIP were not indicative of philanthropic disposition on the part of the company, but marked the keenness of AGIP to enter into a highly lucrative market tradition- ally regarded as an exclusive British sphere of influence.

14. Ibid., col.755.

15. See L.H. Schatzl, *Petroleum in Nigeria* (Ibadan: Oxford University Press, 1969), pp.84-93. At the time when Schatzl was writing he computed Nigeria's loss from such manoeuvres thus: out of an oil company's gross income of £1000 (N2000) an OPEC member state obtained roughly £415 (N830) as compared to £300 (N600) by Nigeria.

16. See Jaja Wachuku's comments in HRD, 7 February 1959, 1959–60 Session, Vol. 1, p.49.

17. Nigeria, Federal Office of Statistics, *Annual Abstract of Statistics*, (Lagos, 1964), p.88 and *West Africa*, 7 May 1966, p.521.

18. *West Africa*, 7 May 1966, p.521

19. Nigeria, Federal House of Representatives, *The Role of the Federal Government in Promoting Industrial Development in Nigeria* (House of Representatives Sessional Paper No. 3 of 1958), p.3.

20. Federal Republic of Nigeria, *Statement on Industrial Policy* (Fed. House of Rep. Sessional Paper, No. 6 of 1964), p.3.

21. Ibid., p.2 (See also Sessional Paper No. 3 of 1958, p.4).

22. Ibid., p.3 (See also Sessional Paper No. 3 of 1958, p.6).

23. Ibid., p.4.

24. Ibid., pp.2-3.

25. Sessional Paper No. 3 of 1958, op. cit., p.7; and Sessional Paper No. 6 of 1964, op. cit., p.2.

26. *Africa Diary*, Vol. III, No. 47, 16–22 November 1963, p.1450.

27. See S.A. Aluko, 'Patterns of Foreign Investment in Nigeria', *Daily Times*, 26 September 1961.

28. HRD, 1957–58, Vol. 1, p.20.

29. HRD, 15 August 1960, 1960–61 Session, Vol. IV, cols.2300-1.

30. Op. cit., p.285.

31. *Nigeria. A Ten-Year Plan of Development and Welfare for Nigeria, 1946* (Sessional Paper No. 24 of 1945 laid on the table of the Legislative Council on 13 December, 1945 as amended by the Select Committee of the Council and approved by the Legislative Council on 7 February, 1946) (Lagos: Govt. Printer, 1946), p.33.

32. Ibid., p.37.

33. Cited in W.F. Stolper, *Planning Without Facts: Lessons in Resource*

Allocation from Nigeria's Development (Cambridge, Mass: Harvard University Press, 1966), p.37.

34. The Economic Development of Nigeria: *Report of a Mission Organised by the International Bank for Reconstruction and Development* (Baltimore: Johns Hopkins University Press, 1955) *passim*, but especially pp.28-30 and 353-54.

35. Ibid., p.28.

36. For a detailed analysis of this incident see S.O. Osoba, 'Ideological Trends in the Nigerian National Liberation Movement and the Problems of National Identity, Solidarity and Motivation, 1934–65: A Preliminary Assessment', *IBADAN*, No. 27, Oct. 1969, p.37.

27. HRD, 29 November 1961, 1961–62 Session, Vol. IV, cols.3540-42. For a detailed discussion of the colonial ideology of development in Nigeria and the way in which it was incorporated into the ideologies of economic development and planning in the post-colonial period, see S.O. Osoba, 'Ideology and Planning for National Economic Development, 1946–72', op. cit.

38. HRD, 4 April 1960, 1960–61 Session, Vol. II, col.794. Okotie-Eboh volunteered this piece of information in an attempt to refute the charge of lack of patriotism implicitly made against the Federal government by Chike Obi (NCNC member for Onitsha) in the following part of his highly critical maiden speech in the House:

> Is it not exasperating to all sincere nationalists to know that Nigeria's investments overseas in so-called gilt-edged securities is £250 million, bearing interest at 2½ per cent per annum, and that our Minister of Finance as the spokesman of a feeble Government goes about borrowing £10 million this day; £12 million another day, and this at 8 to 10 per cent interest? Surely the common people will recoil at parliamentary democracy if, as it now appears, it gives immunity to highwaymen. [Ibid., col.614].

39. See *Laws of Nigeria*, 1955 (Lagos: Federal Govt. Printer), pp.B181-B182 for a full list of the banned literature.

40. HRD, 1957–58, Vol. II, 8 July 1957, pp.251-52. Note the Chief Secretary's reference to communist countries in a typical cold-war formulation 'behind the Iron Curtain'.

The case of Dr Bankole Akpata became a *cause celebre* in the implementation of this official policy of excluding communists from gainful employment. Dr Akpata initially went to the UK to study economics at the London School of Economics during which time he came in contact with some socialist group, and made the acquaintance of Dr Kwame Nkrumah. He then proceeded to Prague where he studied for a higher degree in economics returning home in 1954. For three years (1954–57) he was harried from one job to another, because he was a suspected communist, until the liberal-minded principal of Ibadan University College (Dr J.H. Parry), in spite of pressures from the colonial government, decided to give him a job, not as a teacher of economics, but as an Assistant Librarian.

41. Mokwugo Okoye, *Storms on the Niger* (Enugu, 1965), p.231.

42. Cited by R.L. Sklar, *Nigerian Political Parties: Power in an Emergent African Nation* (Princeton: Princeton University Press, 1963), pp.150-51.

43. Sam Epelle (ed), *Nigeria Speaks: Speeches of Alhaji Sir Abubakar*

Tafawa Balewa (Ikeja: Longman, 1964), pp.9-10.

44. *West African Pilot*, 23 September, 1957.

45. See R.L. Sklar, op. cit., p.270 for a more detailed discussion of the brief career of the UWPP.

46. *African Diary*, Vol. IV, No. 1, 28 Dec. 1963-3 January 1964, p.1250.

47. HRD, 12 April 1960, 1960–61, Vol. II, cols.1077-78. Cited by the Prime Minister, Balewa, from the official report of the 1958 Constitutional Conference in London.

48. HRD, 22 November 1958, 1958–59 Session, Vol. IV, p.29.

49. Ibid., p.31.

50. Ibid., p.30.

51. Federal House of Representatives, *Sessional Paper No. 11* of 1956.

52. HRD, 8 March 1957, 1957–58 Session, Vol. 1, pp.252-53.

53. Ibid.

54. HRD, 26 February 1959, 1959–60, Vol. II, p.746-7.

55. HRD, 5 February 1959, 1959–60, Vol. 1, p.8.

56. Ibid., p.45.

57. HRD, 3 March 1958, 1958–59, Vol. 1, pp.385-87.

58. HRD, 14 March 1957, 1957–58, Vol. 1, p.415.

59. HRD, 28 March 1962, 1962–63, Vol. 1, col.413.

60. Figures computed from Nigeria: Federal Ministry of External Affairs, *Office Directory* (mimeographed), Lagos, April 1965.

Index

Aba women 128
AGIP 226
agriculture: precolonial 4, 5; colonial 80-90; and peasants 81-2; for export 82-3; and World War 181-3
agricultural society 44
Ake, C. 90n4, 124
amalgamation 77
Angola 19, 44
Aro 40

banking 74-6
Bastard, R. 94
Benin 38
Benue 44-51
bourgeoisie 10, 11, 16, 20, 22, 23, 25
British: capital 1, 14; government 1
British Overseas Airways Corporation (BOAC) 224
Buxton, F. 52

capitalist: 9, 25; state 9, 11; hegemony 14; development 16-17
carriers 147-51
Ce'Saire, A. 2, 3, 4, 19, 21
class: 2, 3, 10, 14, 22, 24; formation 4
coal 68, 69, 96-8, 157
cocoa 84, 158
colonial: 1, 4; administration 76-8; armed forces 143-7; consolidation 208-11; economy 25, 221; expansion 8, 10, 48, 120; experience 3; capitalism 14-15; fiscal policy 186-99, 222-3; policy 19, 20; state 2, 5, 20
colonialism: 1, 2, 5, 6, 9, 10, 11, 12, 14, 25, 59; and underdevelopment 1, 23; evils of 2, 23; exploitation 1, 2, 7, 14, 19-24; impact 3, 4, 8, 10; motives 55-65, 124; perspectives on 1-4, 56-8; economic division 5, 16; and historic mission 8-18; and trade 135-6; foreign policy 238-48; and struggle against communism 233-8
companies: 44, 64, 135, 210, 222, 223; chartered 32, 34, 37, 38; Royal Niger 45, 61, 64, 84, 93, 95, 98, 127, 144, 145; Royal African 38; control of 99-101; Juga Mining and Water Power 94
Consuls 46
cotton 44, 85, 88
cowry 72, 73
crafts 3

decolonization: 221; British measures during 221-43
development see underdevelopment
Doherty, J.H. 133

education 21, 205-6, 221
Elder Dempster Lines Agencies Ltd 222-5
elite 221
exploitation: 2, 4, 11, 14, 16, 18, 20, 50, 66; and trade 52; of minerals 91-113, 142; rationalization of 211-15; of revenues 186-99; in World Wars 164-85; reactions to 50-52; modalities, in pre-colonial Nigeria 44-50; of labour 40-1, 101-8, 142-63; infrastructure of 66-79 see also colonialism

Falola, Toyin 1, 19, 30n50
Fanon, F. 22
farmers role in colonial trade 125-30
firms see merchants
Freund, B. 101, 108

Goldie, G.T. (Sir) 45, 46
groundnuts 84-5
Great Depression 128, 134, 137
Guinea Coast 38

Hawkins, J. 36, 38
Holt, John, and Co. 167, 224
Hobson, J.A. 56
Hopkins, A.G. 60, 137, 148

Indirect Rule 77-8
industries 25
Industrial Revolution 1
industrialization: 114-23; and colonial
    policy 114-16

Jaja of Opobo 48, 63
Jehovah's Witness 169

Kano 3
kernels 84
kidnapping 39
Komolafe, C.O. 224

labour: 7, 20, 25; organisation of 103,
    105-6; and strike 106-7; and wage
    135-6; forced 152-5; in construction
    151-5
Lagos Constabulary 143
land 6
Lenin, V.I. 5
Lugard, F. (Lord) 68, 70, 77, 124, 155

Macleod, I. 207
Macdonald, G. 94
Macmillan, A. 139
manufacture 25, 120
manillas 71-2
Marx, and colonialism 8-19
Marketing Board 83, 84, 119, 138, 224
merchants 6, 36, 43, 67 *see also* traders
mineworkers 1-108, 155-9
mining: 155, 156; in pre-colonial Nigeria
    91-2; capitalist take-over 92-3
minerals 96-9
missionaries 2, 5, 34, 48, 50, 52, 135

Nana Olomu 47-8
National Economic Council 120
neo-colonialism 23, 24; transition to
    221-46
Niger 44, 51
Niger delta 38, 72
Nigerian National Shipping Line 224, 225
Njoku, R.A. 223-5

Obisesan, J.A. 133
oil palm 83, 84
Okotie-Eboh, F. 233
Okoye, M. 235
Okwei, O. 133
OPEC 99, 226, 227

peasants 81, 82, 206
Pepple of Banny (King) 46-7
petroleum 98-9, 225, 226
producers 2, 7, 80
production: 5, 6, 10; Asiatic modes 8-11,
    20; and vent for surplus theory 5-8;
    goods 34; in mines 108-10

railways 32, 68, 70, 93, 151
roads 32, 70-71
Robinson, R. 58-9
Rodney, W. 23

Salisbury (Lord) 55, 56, 63
Schumpeter, J. 57-8
Shell, B.P. 226

tax: 20, 223, 226, 227; relief to British
    Company 227-9; laws 222
taxation 142, 209
timber 87-9
Tiv 50
trade: barter 70, 71; profits from 3, 25,
    36, 62, 226; trans-Saharan 3; inter-
    national 5, 6, 8; competition 63, 64;
    in slaves 25, 32, 34; in colonial Nigeria
    124-41; trans-Atlantic 32-54; tricks of
    32, 33; in the hinterland 32, 33, 34;
    legitimate 41-3
traders: European 32, 34; Portuguese
    33, 34, 35, 36, 59; British 33, 34, 36,
    51, 52, 60; Nigerian middlemen 130-35;
    Dutch 34
transport 66-71, 149, 224

UAC 127, 131, 132, 134, 135, 224
underdevelopment: 1, 2, 7, 20, 23, 25;
    and colonialism 19-24, 200-22; and
    capitalism 16, 17, 205-15; concept of
    201-5; and attempts at solution 215-17,
    230

Victorians 55

Wachuku, J. 222, 223, 225
Warrant chiefs 148-9
waterways 67-8
World Bank 215
West African Company 44
West African Conference Lines Ltd. 223,
    224
West African Frontier Force 145, 146
West African Pilot 223
World Wars: loyalty and contribution to
    169-74; burden of 174-81